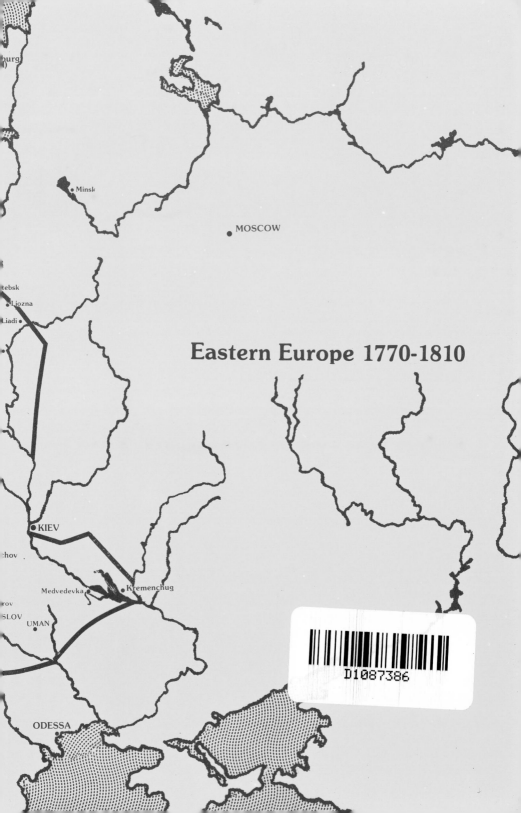

Eastern Europe 1770-1810

Minsk

MOSCOW

tebsk
Liozna
Liadi

KIEV

chov

Medvedevka   Kremenchug

rov
SLOV   UMAN

ODESSA

D1087386

UNTIL
THE
MASHIACH

UNTIL THE MASHIACH

Rabbi Nachman's Biography:
An Annotated Chronology

by

Rabbi Aryeh Kaplan

Edited by

Rabbi Dovid Shapiro

PUBLISHED BY
THE BRESLOV RESEARCH INSTITUTE

for further information:

Rabbi Chaim Kramer
Breslov Research Institute
POB 5370
Jerusalem, Israel   91053

or:

Breslov Research Institute
3100 Brighton 3rd Street
Brooklyn, New York   11235
U.S.A.

cover design: Ben Gasner

Photo-composition by:
HaNachal Press — דפוס הנחל
of the Breslov Research Institute

This work is dedicated
to the memory of

AHARON TZVI ben MEIR HaLevi
ז״ל

in recognition of the devoted efforts
of his son

YITZCHOK LEIB שיחי׳
(Trevor Bell)

on behalf of
the Breslov Research Institute

TABLE OF CONTENTS

Publisher's Preface

Rarely in the annals of Jewish History has any leader evoked as much emotion as Rabbi Nachman of Breslov — whether awe or respect, admiration or even the reverse. Very few have remained indifferent to Rabbi Nachman.

Born in 1772, Rabbi Nachman's life expressed in microcosm the aims and achievements of mankind in the dawning age. He struggled unremittingly towards freedom. His attainment was to rise above the shackles that held him back from his goals.

Rabbi Nachman has been the subject of numerous studies including several full-scale biographies. None of them, however, presents Rabbi Nachman as he really was. Speculative accounts based on a selective use of evidence and purporting to portray his inner life are at best futile and at worst misleading. Attempts to perceive him through a screen of contemporary psychological or literary concepts cannot succeed, especially when they ignore the Torah experience which made up the very fabric of his life. How can one attempt to perceive, analyze and explain Rabbi Nachman's thoughts and deeds from a present-day perspective without trying to empathize with the actual mental world in which he lived?

Until now, the English-speaking reader has been at a particular disadvantage in trying to understand Rabbi Nachman's life for himself. There has been no authoritative factual account of his life. And most of the original biographical material, ample though it is, has been scattered in a bewildering variety of sources.

The present work is the first attempt to provide a comprehensive, detailed and accurate chronolgy of Rabbi Nachman's life. The aim is to provide the factual basis that until now has been missing. Every event or episode that could be dated, even roughly, has been included. All the sources — including several as yet unpublished — have been researched, checked and verified. Where there are contradictions between them, the contradictory material has been presented so as to enable the reader to come to his own conclusions. Where facts are unconfirmed, this is indicated in the text.

In order to keep the work within manageable proportions, it was necessary to condense many of the detailed accounts of specific events as found in the sources. Inevitably, some of the force of the original descriptions has been lost in the process. Yet, great pains have been taken to ensure that the condensed versions presented in the text remain as faithful as possible to the general tenor of the originals.

Besides strictly biographical material, much additional information has been included in the introduction, text and appendices. This covers contemporary historical events and trends in both the Jewish and wider world, significant personages, relevant geographical and topographical data, etc. There is also a full bibliography.

The original manuscript of this work was prepared by the late Rabbi Aryeh Kaplan. It was a monumental task to collate information spread through so many sources. With much of it undated, Rabbi Kaplan had many occasions to draw on his extensive knowledge of the period and its literature and combine it with his acute eye for the finest details. The Breslov Research Institute wishes to record its appreciation to Rabbi Kaplan for his work.

At the time of his tragic death in 1983, the manuscript was left unedited. We extend our appreciation to Rabbi Dovid Shapiro for his painstaking work of editing. During the course of his research and thorough evaluation of all the material presented in this book, a wealth of additional facts came to light, and it is to Rabbi Shapiro that we owe their inclusion here. The work on Rabbi Nachman's genealogy was done by Rabbi Shapiro with the expert assistance of Shmuel Gorr.

Credit is also due to Avraham Greenbaum, who initiated

most of the research for the Introduction and Appendices, and to Moshe Mykoff both for his additional research and for the great patience with which he reviewed successive drafts of the text to ensure complete accuracy. Credit is also due to Rabbi Moshe Brienes for his assistance in the research and authentication of the source material, to Rabbi Nachman Burstyn, for his invaluable help clarifying much of the obscure material, and to Dovid Nakab for his work on the maps.

We are left with a full account of the outer details of Rabbi Nachman's life. Yet the inner man remains a mystery! This was true even for those who were closest to him. Rabbi Nathan, his closest student, writes that for most of the day, he was closed up and hidden from everybody. Only for brief periods would he emerge from his devotions to speak to his followers. And as Rabbi Nathan again and again reiterates, they felt they understood not more than "a drop of the ocean" of what he truly was.

Yet what was ultimately important for them — and for us — was not what Rabbi Nachman was in himself. It was the challenge he offered as a leader and teacher: to be free! It was the same challenge that Rabbi Nachman gave to generations to come when he exclaimed, "My fire will burn until the Mashiach will come...."

May it be the will of the Almighty that we see the fulfillment of the prophecy of Jacob our father: "The ruler shall not cease from Judah, nor the leader from among his descendants, *until the Mashiach* will come... (Genesis 49:10). May he come speedily in our time, Amen.

Chaim Kramer
Kislev 5745

Editor's Note

Rabbi Nachman teaches us (*Likutey Moharan* II, 52) that just as God is beyond our comprehension so are the ways of the Tzaddikim who simulate the ways of their Creator. Therefore, it would have been presumptuous to attempt to present in this work an interpretation of the Rebbe's life and works. Rather, we have attempted to give a detailed, factual, and authoritatively documented sourcebook. Generally, facts which are not explicit in the sources but derived by calculation, are included in footnotes (calculations based on distances of travel have remained in the text). We have tried to avoid surmise as much as possible but did not feel justified in deleting the results of the late Rabbi Aryeh Kaplan's extensive research even when his conclusions are speculative. In such cases the text indicates that a given statement is "probable" or "approximate" or the like.

But Rabbi Nachman also teaches us (*Sichos HaRan* #1) that the greatness of God is perceived by each person according to what he appreciates in his own heart. Hence the same must be true of the greatness of the Tzaddik. We have therefore left an opening for anyone who wants to probe into the depths of Rabbi Nachman's life by suggesting cross references (indicated by cf.) to what may be relevant verses and statements in Bible, Talmud, *Zohar*, writings of prominent Kabbalists, *Shulchan Arukh*, etc., and of course of Rabbi Nachman's (and his followers') own statements. We have also suggested relevency between Rabbi Nachman's teachings and events occuring at the time he gave each lesson. The reason we have summarized some of his lessons while others seem to have been ignored was with the intention to point out the relevancy to current events. Some of these connections are mentioned in traditional Breslover sources, but much was discovered in the course of this work as a result of chronologizing previously dispersed material. This should not be taken as an indication that those lessons are relevant only to Rabbi Nachman's contemporaries, but rather an illustration of how the Rebbe applied the Chassidic teaching (cf. *Likutey Moharan* #1) that one must look at every occurence as a call from on High, hinting at some relevant concept, for there is no coincidence.

It is an interesting phenomenon that there has been, especially of late, a deep interest in Rabbi Nachman's writings by academic circles who are very distant from any commitment to the strictly traditional Judaism of Rabbi Nachman. While reviewing the text, I couldn't help wondering if this might be related to some of the Rebbe's statements and activities in Uman during his last half year of life. Why was he so involved with the heretics there? What did he intend with such statements as, "If the Tzaddikim don't follow me I must appeal to the wicked. Perhaps I can make them into good Jews." "No generation is an orphan!" "We are at the boundary of Jewishness!" The heretics in Uman were importing the German *haskalah* to Russia and Poland, whence various heretical movements were to spread it to America and Israel and all corners of the globe. Was Rabbi Nachman planting seeds so that the ideological descendants of the heretics of Uman would find an affinity to his ideas? Perhaps we will better understand when we see a further materialization of the Rebbe's promise, "I have accomplished and I shall accomplish."

Dovid Shapiro
Menachem Av, 5744
Jerusalem

HISTORICAL OVERVIEW

Rabbi Nachman lived in a period which must count as one of the most significant turning points in history — the history of the world and that of the Jewish People.

Rabbi Nachman was born in 1772. In the two centuries since then human society has changed at a faster rate than it did for several thousands of years before. It was during Rabbi Nachman's lifetime that the Industrial Revolution was first beginning to gather momentum. The old techniques by which man until then had satisfied his physical needs have come to look primitive compared to contemporary technology, with its complexity and sophistication. In most parts of the world people's material life has been more or less completely transformed, and hitherto undreamed of possibilities — for good and evil — have now become a reality.

The American Declaration of Independence was made when Rabbi Nachman was a boy of four. He was seventeen when the French Revolution began, and by the end of his lifetime the Napoleonic Wars were approaching their climax. These events initiated waves of change, social and political, throughout the world. Since then the old regimes of kings and emperors, aristocrats and serfs, clerics, burghers and beggars have all been swept away. They have been superseded by often mammoth national states and supernational entities characterized by a scale and methods of social organization unthinkable in previous eras.

The profound changes in people's material lives have been accompanied by complex developments in the realm of knowledge and belief. Not only has there been an unparalleled explosion of knowledge, but the entire framework of beliefs and assumptions on which people base their lives has been radically changed. Historians are agreed that the watershed in the expansion of human thought came in the eighteenth century, when philosophers and thinkers first began to entertain fundamental doubts about received beliefs and sought to "understand" and "explain" the universe without reference to the divine.

Jewish History

As soon as we begin to think about the history of the Jewish People over the last few hundred years we are immediately confronted with the stark reality of the holocaust, which changed the face of world Jewry. The old European centers, which had for centuries constituted the most populous and flourishing communities, were almost totally shattered. Yet even the holocaust itself was only the most devastating of a murderous series of persecutions which have led to the greatest shift in the center of gravity of the Jewish world since the destruction of the Second Temple.

During Rabbi Nachman's lifetime almost the entire Jewish People, Ashkenazim and Sephardim alike, were concentrated in the old world. Rabbi Nachman's native Ukraine and the neighboring regions of Poland and Lithuania had for centuries been Ashkenazic Jewry's foremost center. It was during his lifetime that the successive partitions of Poland brought almost a million Jews under Russian sovereignty, and in his last years the framework was laid for the repressions which were to drive waves of emigrants away from the region in search of new homes. Since then there have been mass movements of Jews to entirely new locations: the Americas, South Africa, Australia, etc. Perhaps most significant of all has been the return of Jews to the Land of Israel.

As significant as the physical changes are those which have taken place in the spiritual life of the Jewish People since the time of Rabbi Nachman. Torah and prayer are the very foundations of Jewish existence. For thousands of years the very fabric of Jewish life was made up of devotion to Torah. The synagogue and study hall had been the centers of day-to-day Jewish life — nowhere more so than in Poland-Lithuania. Prior to Rabbi Nachman's time there had been several periods in Jewish history when significant numbers of Jews had become assimilated into the surrounding culture. Yet these movements had little lasting impact on the attachment of most Jews to Torah tradition. For most of the period of the exile the supreme authority of the Torah, written and oral, was undisputed by the overwhelming majority of Jews. But in the generations immediately prior to Rabbi Nachman's it became evident that assimilation was assuming more serious proportions. And during his lifetime the foundations were laid for what were to become the biggest onslaughts in Jewish history against devotion to Torah: attacks from within the Jewish people and attacks from without.

The Polish Center

Nowhere in the Diaspora had Torah life been more vibrant than among the communities of Poland and Lithuania. Jews had lived in Eastern Europe in the lands of the Slavonic peoples from very early times. But the major influx came in the thirteenth century, when severe persecutions especially in Germany led considerable numbers of Jews to migrate eastwards, spreading throughout the Polish territories. The culture of these German Jews attained pre-eminence in the Jewish communities of Poland, and the language they spoke became the language of all the Jews in the region — Yiddish.

The Jews were involved at every level of the Polish economy, albeit subject to the restrictions imposed by Christian society. In language, culture and customs, however, the Jews were a nation apart. They elected their own rabbis and judges, and through their *kahals* and *va'ads* — the community organizations and regional agencies — Jewish civil as well as religious life was governed in accordance with Torah law. The leadership of Polish Jewry was a Torah leadership, and the great luminaries of Torah scholarship in Poland, such as Rabbi Yaakov Follak (the *S'MA*) of Cracow (c.1460-1522), Rabbi Shalom Shachneh (the *RaShaSh*) of Lublin (c.1510-1558), his son-in-law Rabbi Moshe Isserles (the *ReMA*) of Cracow (c.1525-1572) and Rabbi Shlomo Luria (the *MaHaRSHaL*, c.1510-1574) were actively involved in the life of the community.

By the sixteenth century the overwhelming mass of Ashkenazic Jewry, including the remnants of the exiled communities of medieval England, France and Germany, were all concentrated in Poland. With the collapse of the Jewish centers in Spain (1492) and Portugal (1497) the leading community in the Diaspora was that of Poland, an outstanding center of Torah learning and Torah living.

Disaster

It was widely expected that the year 1648 would be the time of the Messianic deliverance, and the *Zohar* (I:139) was thought to contain allusions to this. Yet not only did the hoped for deliverance not occur, the year was marked by a catastrophic disaster which threw its shadow over all aspects of Jewish life in Poland and indeed the entire Jewish world.

The Messianic deliverance will be a time of glory for the Jewish People, when the souls of the exiles will be gathered together in splendor. For the root of the souls of the Jewish People lies in God's glory (see *Likutey Moharan* I, 67), and it is to His glory, which will be revealed in the time of Mashiach, that they will be drawn. Rabbi Nathan explains (*Likutey Halachos, Choshen Mishpat, Hilchos Chovel be-Chavero* 3:7-8) that the year 1648 was indeed a time when glory was destined to come to the Jewish people. But the Jews were not yet prepared for the Messianic deliverance, and accordingly the destined revelation of God's glory had to come about differently: through the deaths of hundreds of thousands of martyrs who sanctified and glorified God's name rather than embracing an alien religion.

The Ukraine (literally "border" or "frontier") is the vast region around the southern basin of the Dnieper river, comprising the provinces of Kiev, Poltava and Chernigov and including parts of Podolia and Volhynia. In the seventeenth century the region was subject to the political power of the kings of Poland and consisted of enormous feudal estates owned by Polish Catholic aristocrats and worked by Russian Orthodox peasants. The Jews were the middlemen, leasing the estates from their owners and dealing with day-to-day management.

The peasants of the Ukraine looked to the bands of Cossacks (the word probably means "rider" or "adventurer") who roamed the region as a kind of liberation army which was to free them from what they saw as Polish and Jewish domination. After a number of preliminary outrages, in the spring of 1648 Bogdan Chmielnicki incited the Ukrainian Cossacks to armed resistance. His defeat of the Polish army signalled a general uprising throughout the region. Bands of peasants went from town to town and village to village slaughtering thousands of Jews, who preferred martyrdom rather than forced conversion to Greek Orthodoxy. In the decade of war and dislocation that followed some seven hundred Jewish communities suffered massacre and pillage, carnage and pogrom, with Jewish losses estimated at between two hundred thousand to five hundred thousand. Many were taken captive and sold as slaves in Turkey. Others fled to Lithuania, Central Poland and Western Europe. As far afield as Amsterdam and Istanbul fugitives told stories of women forced to marry Cossacks, children brought up as Christians, and every other form of barbaric atrocity. Families had been split up, lives disrupted, and the effects of the shock on the heart and the soul are incalculable.

Alienation

The decade of turbulence led to widespread impoverishment. Jewish communal life had been severely disrupted and the system of Torah education was left seriously weakened. Among the mass of the people there was a growing sense of alienation from the traditional community leadership, and this found expression in the repeated outbursts of sectarianism in the years that followed.

When Shabbetai Zvi declared himself Messiah in May 1665 the news spread like wildfire to all parts of the Jewish world. The first wave of excitement swept up not only the uneducated but even great scholars and rabbis. Coming so soon after the suffering in Poland the "revelation" seemed like the destined divine visitation. In Poland, Lithuania and especially the Ukraine the Shabbatean movement made a particularly deep impression. It took time for the opposition to Shabbetai Zvi to crystallize, partly because of slow communications. But with his arrest by the Turkish authorities and subsequent conversion to Islam (1666), the rabbis throughout the Jewish world declared his messianic claims to be false. It is indeed a sign of the enduring strength of the traditional leadership that their verdict was accepted by the greater part of the Jewish people.

Yet significant numbers were unwilling to fall into line. Shabbatean cells persisted in a number of places, especially Turkey, whose proximity to Podolia gave added strength to sectarian activities there. Many of the rituals went beyond the bounds of Torah law, and the rabbinate intervened with a series of *cherems*. Sectarianism persisted, however, taking a sinister turn in the mid-eighteenth century under the leadership of Jacob Frank (1726-92). Claiming to be the reincarnation of Shabbetai Zvi, he encouraged his followers to indulge in acts of gross immorality. Defying a *cherem* by the Polish rabbinate (1756) he turned to the Church authorities for support against his opponents, giving them to understand that his teachings bore affinities to Christian doctrines. Unleashing a fresh wave of anti-Jewish persecutions, Frank and some five hundred followers were baptized in Lemberg in 1759.

Chassidism

The various expressions of religious and pseudo-religious fervor testified to something greater than mere devotion to false messiahs. There was a profound yearning for deepened religious consciousness among scholars and simple folk alike. While the existing rabbinic leadership made strenuous efforts to suppress manifestations of sectarianism, they were powerless to capture the hearts of the populace to anything like the degree that would have been necessary to stem the growing tide of alienation.

At first Rabbi Israel ben Eliezer, the Baal Shem Tov (1698-1760) may have appeared as only one of a number of Torah leaders who were seeking to enhance the spiritual life of the people. To those who became close to him, however, it was clear that his service was on an entirely different plane. With the deepening alienation from Torah teachings the Jewish People were entering a new phase in their history. Chassidism, which was a higher stage in the revelation of Torah, was to reach out to those whom the traditional approaches were no longer able to inspire.

Chassidism has often been represented as a popular movement lacking the intellectual rigor of traditional Judaism. In fact some of the greatest talmudic scholars of the generation became devoted followers of the Baal Shem Tov. Their aim was not to develop some kind of "soft option" to rabbinic Judiasm but to invest the tradition itself with fresh vitality and joy and to bring it to those who were becoming estranged.

It was in the 1730's that the Baal Shem Tov first revealed himself. His teachings spread rapidly in Podolia and the adjacent districts. In his lifetime the Chassidic movement was consolidated by Rabbi Avraham Gershon of Kittov, Rabbi

Nachman of Horodenka (grandfather of Rabbi Nachman), Rabbi Pinchas of Koretz, Rabbi Yaacov Yosef of Polonnoye and Rabbi Dov Ber, the Great Magid of Mezritch. It was to the Magid that the leadership passed on the death of the Baal Shem Tov, and under his influence and that of his disciples the teachings of Chassidism were brought from Volhynia northwards into Belorussia and Lithuania, and westwards into Galicia and Central Poland. Tzaddikim like Rabbi Shneur Zalman of Liadi, Rabbi Levi Yitzchok of Berdichov, Rabbi Aaron "the Great" of Karlin and Rabbi Shmuel Shmelke Horowitz worked in their respective centers to instill their followers and communities with the joy and enthusiasm of Chassidism. It was they who were looked to as the senior leaders of the movement during the lifetime of Rabbi Nachman.

Division and Partition

History has proved that Chassidism, far from being in any sense the negation of Torah Judaism, was in fact an expression of its resurgence and indeed one of its strongest bulwarks. But many of the rabbinical leaders of the time, suspicious as they were of the recurrent activities of the sectarians, were unable to reconcile themselves with the new approach of the Baal Shem Tov and his followers. Under the influence of Rabbi Eliyahu, the Gaon of Vilna (1720-97), the *misnagdim* campaigned bitterly against Chassidism, even resorting to a *cherem* in 1772. The very movement which came to strengthen the attachment of Jewry to Torah tradition became cast in the role of a marginal, anti-establishment sect.

And as a seeming reflection of the divisions among the Jews, Poland itself was torn apart. Social changes had weakened the central government, leaving the country open to the ambitions of its neighbors. Russia's demand for complete religious and political liberty for all of Poland's Greek Orthodox subjects could only encourage the aspirations of the peasants and Cossacks in the Ukraine. In April 1768 bands of Haidemacks — rebels or rioters — began murdering Jews and Poles alike. Thousands of Jews from the surrounding areas fled to the town of Uman for safety, but after treachery on the part of the governor of the town the Haidemacks were able to enter the town. In a period of three days an estimated twenty thousand Jews were slaughtered.

Four years later in 1772 came the first partition of Poland. Russia took the larger part of White Russia, Austria took sections of Galicia and Podolia, while Prussia annexed Pomerania and the district of Posen. The Jews of Poland were henceforth split up between four different countries. Such was the crisis of Jewry as Rabbi Nachman started his life. For hundreds of years Poland had been the most thriving Jewish center in the diaspora, with by now close to a million souls. Now the community was divided not only by the redrawing of political borders but by spiritual fissures, bitter and profound.

The World of Rabbi Nachman

For the Jews of the Ukraine the details of day-to-day life were little different from what they had been in previous generations. Theirs was the old, pre-industrial world, a world without telephones, automobiles or televisions. Traffic was horse-drawn and the loudest sounds were thunder and gunpowder explosions. Armies went on foot and news was carried on horseback. But the world was in ferment, a ferment which was to shake Jewish life to its foundations.

The American Declaration of Independence in 1776 symbolized the emergence of a new image of man and new conceptions of government. Thirteen years later in 1789 the French Revolution swept away the *ancien regime* of king, aristocracy and church in the name of liberty, equality and fraternity. France saw herself as the standard-bearer of a revolutionary outlook, and by the 1790's, when Rabbi Nachman was in his twenties, French armies were advancing through Europe taking over Belgium (1792), Holland (1794) and large parts of Italy (1797).

The monarchs of Europe saw French republicanism as a threat not only to the principles on which they based their own regimes but also to the balance of power in Europe as a whole. Accordingly Austria, Prussia, Russia and Britain formed a succession of coalitions in the hope of thwarting French expansionism. For a while it seemed as though the conflict might attain even wider proportions. As Napoleon campaigned in Egypt and the Holy Land (1797-99) he dreamed of overwhelming the Ottoman Empire and emulating Alexander the Great in a career of world conquest. His dreams were not to materialize, however. The failure of the siege of Acco, which began just as Rabbi Nachman left Israel at the end of his pilgrimage, destroyed Napoleon's hopes of posing a significant threat to the Turkish Sultan. Thereafter the main theater of his operations was Europe.

Napoleon seized power in France in 1799. For the next fifteen years mass armies swept back and forth in Europe in a succession of wars which were to end only in 1815 with the surrender of Napoleon at Waterloo. Thus, the last ten years of Rabbi Nachman's life (1800-1810) were a period of recurrent warfare in Europe interrupted by abortive peace treaties and characterized by kaleidoscopic shifts of alliances.

The Haskalah Movement

The revolutions, wars and turbulence in the world at large seemed to mirror the changes and rifts within the Jewish People. More significant than anything was the growing tide of alienation from traditional Torah law and practice.

It was among the Jews of Germany, especially among the wealthy, that the neglect of Jewish law had gone furthest by Rabbi Nachman's time, and hand in hand with this neglect went a growing interest in gentile culture. A new school of Jewish intellectuals grew up, some of whom possessed extensive Torah knowledge but who saw the pursuit of secular culture as a supreme value and one which had more importance in their eyes than devotion to Torah law. They tried to represent their own approach as one which expressed authentic Jewish values more truly than that of the Torah-observant community, which they looked upon as archaic and outmoded.

The intellectuals of this new school, who later came to be known as the *maskilim* or "enlightened ones," understood that it was their distinctive customs and practices which had given the Jews their separate identity through the long years of exile in the lands of the gentiles. But far from seeing Jewish separateness as something of value, the *maskilim* regarded it as the source of gentile hostility and set out to break it down. Not content merely to pursue their secular cultural interests for themselves, they saw it as their mission to spread their approach among their fellow Jews and break their attachment to the traditional mode of Jewish life. The teachings of the *haskalah* (enlightenment) provided a rationalization for those who were already inclined to abandon the path of Torah.

One of the major initiators of the new movement was Moses Mendelssohn (1729-86). His translation of the Five Books of Moses into German (1779-83) was aimed at uprooting the traditional rabbinic approach to the interpretation of the written Torah. The translation was placed under a ban by leading rabbinical authorities, but this did not prevent thousands of students in the major yeshivot of Germany from studying it in private. Being familiar with the biblical text itself, many of them used the translation to learn German, with which they were hitherto unfamiliar, while absorbing the philosophical concepts contained in the accompanying commentary. From the ranks of these students there arose a whole band of exponents of secular culture.

Rabbi Nachman's lifetime saw the rapid spread of the influence of Mendelssohn and his followers amongst the Jews of Europe. In Western Europe and especially in France, with its sizeable Spanish and Portuguese Jewish community, leading Jewish figures campaigned for emancipation from the old restrictions and pressed for Jewish integration into gentile society. Further east, and especially in Poland and Russia, the bulk of Jews were still more traditionally inclined and rabbinic opposition to the new thinking carried more weight. Nevertheless there was a growing network of scholars and thinkers who were tempted by the apparent widening of horizons.

Mendelssohn's ideas had an effect on non-Jews as well, and under his influence a number of gentile writers and thinkers began campaigning for Jewish emancipation and devising plans for turning the Jews into "useful citizens" of the countries they lived in. The condition was that they were to abandon all the marks that distinguished them from the host population and embrace the dominant culture. They were to shave off their beards and cut off their side-curls; they were to give up their traditional costumes and cease speaking Yiddish. They were to be weaned from their traditional pursuits of trade and brokerage and be re-educated through being steeped in secular culture. Then, and only then, would they be integrated into the host society as equal citizens.

This was the strategy behind the *Toleranzpatent* promulgated in Austria in 1782, which removed a number of Jewish disabilities while encouraging the Jews to pursue secular education and begin mixing in Austrian society. A similar strategy was implicit in the approach of those who argued for Jewish emanicipation in France after the revolution. When civic freedom was conferred on the Jews in 1791 it seemed to be unconditional, at least on paper. But as the strong hand of Napoleonic autocracy began to reveal itself it was increasingly clear that the price of Jewish emancipation in France was to be the abandonment of all that had made them separate. The traditional loyalties of the

Jews were to be transferred to the nation in whose midst they were living. In 1768 the Jews of Uman had laid down their lives to sanctify God's name. Some forty years later Napoleon's Jewish *Sanhedrin* was asked if the Jews considered the land of their birth as their fatherland. Those present rose to a man with the cry *"Jusqu'à la mort!"* Unto death!

Russia

For centuries the Muscovy Empire had rigorously excluded Jews from her territories, seeing them as enemies of the faith and suspecting them of seeking to lead the Greek Orthodox pious astray. Yet the successive partitions of Poland in 1772, 1793 and 1795 brought the whole of the Ukraine, White Russia and Lithuania under Russian sovereignty. These territories contained about a million Jews, the largest Jewish center in the Diaspora. Their very presence was a glaring contradiction to traditional Russian policy.

Initially the authorities showed a liberal face to their new Jewish subjects, assuring them that their religious liberty and civil privileges would remain inviolate. The authorities showed themselves willing to preserve intact the apparatus of community autonomy inherited from the days of Polish rule. Within a few years, however, a succession of imperial decrees revealed the contours of far more repressive policies. It was in the mid-1780's that the concept of a special Pale of Settlement outside of which Jewish residence was to be forbidden first became established. The Jews were to be prevented from penetrating the Russian interior, being restricted to the Ukraine, White Russia and Lithuania. And within this Pale, far from leaving the Jews to live independently as they had for centuries under Polish rule, it soon became clear that the Russian authorities had plans for the total transformation of Jewish life — by imposing changes from above.

It was in 1795 that the areas of the Ukraine where Rabbi Nachman spent most of his life came under Russian sovereignty. One year later Czar Paul I acceded to the Russian throne. Although his reign (1796-1801) was bereft of any substantive measures affecting Jewish life, it was then that the policy-makers of St. Petersburg embarked on their search for a solution to what they saw as Russia's Jewish problem.

Between 1795 and 1800 the Governors of Lithuania, White Russia and the Ukraine were instructed to hold consultations with the leading figures in their regions — the aristocratic land-owners — regarding the role of the Jews. The material generated was submitted to the Russian Senate, where it came into the hands of the traditionalist Senator Gabriel Dyerzhavin. Taking advice from among others a number of "enlightened" Jewish intellectuals and businessmen who were followers of Moses Mendelssohn, Dyerzhavin wrote a voluminous "Opinion concerning the status of the Jews of Russia." This is significant as the fullest expression of the approach underlying subsequent Russian treatment of the Jews in her territories. Dyerzhavin proposed a vast scheme aimed at sweeping away Jewish autonomy and culture, inculcating the Jews with secular ideas and values, and integrating them into the stratification system of the Russian Empire.

The proposed methods of social engineering were opposed by a more liberal wing within the ruling circles in St. Petersburg, which was in favor of admitting the Jews to Russian society without imposing reforms from above. The debate between these two trends was in full swing when Czar Paul was assassinated in March 1801, and the fate of the Jews was still open.

During the last ten years of Rabbi Nachman's life the direction which Russian policy would take for the next century and more became increasingly clear under the rule of the new Czar, Alexander I (1801-25). In 1802 a new

Committee for the Amelioration of the Jews was set up and orders were given to draft new Statutes concerning the Jews. It was evident that the proposed regulations would threaten the distillery rights which were one of the main economic bases of Jewish life. The Committee finally reported in 1804 and on the basis of its proposals there was promulgated the notorious 1804 "Statute Concerning the Jews."

The Statute was intended as the concrete implementation of the interventionist approach, aiming at nothing less than a total transformation of Jewish political, social, economic and cultural life. The last vestiges of Jewish legal autonomy were to be swept away, with the rabbis henceforth confining themselves to "spiritual affairs." Hebrew and Yiddish were to be banned in business and public documents. Jews participating in civic life were to abandon their traditional costume. While secular culture was not to be imposed compulsorily as yet, it was offered on a voluntary basis with the admission of all Jews to public schools and universities in the Russian Empire. These educational and cultural provisions were a mere foretaste of the sustained efforts later on to force gentile culture on the Jews through compulsory secular education, forced conscription and so on. What was to have a far more immediate effect was the economic and social provisions of the 1804 Statute, which aimed a deadly blow at the traditional Jewish pursuits of land-tenure and inn-keeping. By January 1808 the Jews were to be expelled from the rural areas where they had lived for centuries and they would no longer be allowed to lease land or keep taverns. The aim was to convert the Jews into agriculturalists or factory workers, while trade and brokerage were to be given the lowest status of all.

The Leadership Crisis

The Jews of Russia were by no means unaware of the moves being taken to affect their entire destiny. Long before the promulgation of the 1804 Statue, in the 1780's, the *kahals* had petitioned the authorities to mitigate the force of a number of measures, and in 1798 the *kahal* representatives tried to send a deputation to St. Petersburg to put forth the Jewish point of view. In 1802 Rabbi Levi Yitzchok of Berdichov summoned a meeting there to discuss the situation confronting the Jews. The meeting was attended by representatives of other trends besides the Chassidic movement. Yet Russian Jewry lacked a forum with the authority of the old *va'ads* in Poland, whose revered rabbinic leaders had commanded the respect of the entire community. Instead, they were wracked by disputes and divisions, and the deepening crisis caught the Jews leaderless.

The opposition to Chassidism had been powerless to prevent its spread in the Russian south west, Podolia, Volhynia and the province of Kiev. In Rabbi Nachman's lifetime Chassidism was the predominating element in most communities in these areas, and the traditional rabbinate deferred to the authority of the Tzaddikim in the running of community affairs. Further north in White Russia, Rabbi Shneur Zalman had built up a strong following, but in the majority of towns the communities were split between Chassidim and *misnagdim*, and dissension and quarreling were rife in the *kahals* and synagogues. In Lithuania Chassidism had failed to take root as yet, and in Vilna itself the Chassidim were forced to pursue their activities in secret.

Even where the hold of Chassidism was secure, its triumph was not without its problems. There was a tendency towards institutionalization, and it sometimes happened that the older generation of Tzaddikim were succeeded by sons and grandsons who maintained the outer forms of Chassidic leadership while lacking the spiritual levels of their predecessors. At the same time there were serious divisions within the movement itself. Rabbi Shneur Zalman was opposed by Rabbi Avraham Kalisker, the leader of the Chassidic settlement in the Holy Land. And nothing was more bitter than the persecution of Rabbi Nachman by his opponents.

While the Chassidim were locked in strife among themselves and with the *misnagdim*, a medley of merchants, physicians and itinerant scholars were bringing the ideas of the "enlightened" thinkers of Berlin to the communities of Russia. Especially among the wealthier traders and brokers there were growing numbers who felt that the life they aspired to would only be possible if they could free themselves of the restrictions of Jewish law and custom, and in a number of places — notably Uman — there were some who openly flouted Jewish law.

Suddenly a bewildering variety of choices was opening up — choices which would affect the destiny of souls. Throughout Jewish history there had always been disputes between Torah leaders — disputes about how Torah law was to be fulfilled. But if the Sages had argued about which oils were suitable for kindling the Sabbath lights, no one had ever questioned the validity of kindling the lights themselves. If they had disagreed about the time for the evening *Shema*, no one ever doubted the binding obligation to recite it. For most of the period of exile, devotion to the Torah itself had never been an issue for the great majority of Jews. Now, however, not only were the Torah leaders locked in disputes with an unparalleled degree of bitterness, but new kinds of leaders were appearing who had placed themselves apart from Torah traditions. In the generations that were to follow, devotion to the Torah itself became the issue — an issue which could not but shake the Jewish People to the core of its being.

In such a situation, could there be a Torah leader acknowledged by all? Or must he be concealed and hidden because of the divisions within the people and their inability to accept him. "And they believed in God and Moses His servant" (Exodus 14:31). There was a time when the leader of the generation was visible and evident to all. But Jewish history had swung round, for "in that day I will surely hide My face" (Deuteronomy 31:18) — and even the face of the leader became hidden. Yet "there is no orphaned generation" (*Chagigah* 3b). Even "when they are in the land of their enemies I will not reject them, neither will I abhor them to destroy them utterly and to break My Covenant with them" (Leviticus 26:44). Our task is to *search* — and in the merit of that search may our righteous Redeemer be revealed, speedily in our time. Amen.

UNTIL THE MASHIACH

MEDZEBOZ

Medzeboz is a small town in Khmelnitsky oblast, latitude 49.26°N longitude 27.25°E, in the Ukrainian S.S.R. It was the home of the Baal Shem Tov and other great Chassidic masters. In 1770, there were approximately twenty one hundred Jews in Medzeboz and the surrounding villages.

Shabbos, Rosh Chodesh Nissan, 5532, Shabbos HaChodesh, Torah reading, Tazria; (April 4, 1772):

Rabbi Nachman was born (*Chayay Moharan* 25b #1, #104). Others say that he was born a year earlier in 5531 (March 16, 1771, Sabbath and Rosh Chodesh Nissan; Torah reading, Vayikra). See *Kochavey Or, Sichos VeSippurim* p. 128 #42, where the second opinion is supported.

Rabbi Nachman was born in Medzeboz (*Ibid.*) in the house which had belonged to his great-grandfather, the Baal Shem Tov (*Nevey Tzaddikim* p. 11).

His father was Rabbi Simcha, son of Rabbi Nachman Horodenker. Rabbi Nachman Horodenker lived with the Baal Shem Tov and was one of his closest disciples. Rabbi Simcha was brought up in the Baal Shem Tov's house. He followed the ways of the Tzaddikim of old, spending prolonged periods in seclusion.

Rabbi Nachman's mother was Feiga, a granddaughter of the Baal Shem Tov. Her mother was Adil, the Baal Shem Tov's only daughter. It was said that Feiga had divine inspiration (*Chayay Moharan* 27b #11, #114).

After his marriage to Feiga, Rabbi Simcha spent an extended period away from home. Worried about him, Feiga used her *ruach hakodesh* to locate him. He then returned home and it was afterwards that Rabbi Nachman was born (*Nevey Tzaddikim* p. 10; *Manuscript* p. 14).

His two uncles from his mother's side were Rabbi Baruch of Medzeboz and Rabbi Ephraim of Sudylkov, author of the *Degel Machaneh Ephraim*. His uncle from his father's side, Reb Shimshon, accompanied Rabbi Nachman Horodenker to Israel (see below, p. 41).

Rabbi Nachman had two brothers. One was Rabbi Yechiel Zvi, who later lived in Kremenchug (see letter in *Chayay Moharan* 36a, #165). This brother was most probably named after Rabbi Yechiel Ashkenazi, his grandfather, and husband of Adil (the Baal Shem Tov's daughter, see above).

The other brother was called Rabbi Yisroel Mes (the Dead). A long story involving the reason for this strange name is brought in the *Manuscript* p. 14. It also appears in a somewhat different form in the Introduction (*Meiras Eynayim*) to *Sefer HaBaal Shem Tov* #75; see also *Shemos HaTzaddikim*.

There are two conflicting traditions regarding who was the eldest of these three brothers. In *Nachal Novea*, we find a tradition that Rabbi Nachman was the eldest. In the *Manuscript* (*Ibid.*), however, we find that Rabbi Yisroel Mes was the first born.

Rabbi Nachman also had a sister named Perel (*Yemey Moharnat* p. 134b). In *Yemey Moharnat* p. 132a, she is identified as the widow of Reb Pinchas Meir. She is also mentioned in *Aveneha Barzel* p. 18, as having visited Rabbi Baruch while Rabbi Nachman was in Lemberg (see below, p. 152).

During this year the first partition of Poland took place, transferring nearly a third of Polish territory to Russia, Austria and Prussia, and about a quarter of a million Jews passed under the sovereignty of these countries.

Shabbos, 8 Nissan, 5532, Shabbos HaGadol, Torah reading, Metzora; (April 11, 1772):

Bris milah of Rabbi Nachman. He was then named Nachman, after his grandfather, Rabbi Nachman Horodenker. It was on that same day that a cherem was executed against the Chassidim. The text of this cherem was signed by Rabbi Eliyahu, the Vilna Gaon, and distributed in a pamphlet Zamir Aritsim (see Bais Rebbe #4; other sources say the cherem was executed shortly after that Pesach. It is possible that the reference in Bais Rebbe is to the letter from Vilna included in Zamir Aritsim and dated 8 Iyar, Cf. Igros Baal HaTanya, p. 178, note 16).

Thursday, 19 Kislev, 5533; (December 15, 1772):

Rabbi Dov Ber, the Magid of Mezritch, died (Chachmey Yisroel p.153).

Wednesday, 12 Tishrei, 5537; (September 25, 1776):

Rabbi Avraham "the Malach," son of the Mezritcher Magid and father of Rabbi Shalom Shachneh of Probisht, died (Chachmey Yisroel p.154).

As a child, living in the house of the Baal Shem Tov, Rabbi Nachman heard tales regarding the great Tzaddikim from the sages who came to visit his great-grandfather's grave, and from them he learned the way to serve God (Sichos HaRan #138).

Once a group of Tzaddikim intended to journey from Medzeboz to visit Rabbi Yaakov Yosef of Polonnoye, one of the Baal Shem Tov's closest disciples. The young Rabbi Nachman asked them to take him along, but they said the journey would be too much for him. As they sat in the coach ready to leave, Rabbi Nachman put his foot on the step of the coach and would not remove it. Rabbi Chaim Krasner (see below p. 15) then agreed to take responsibility for him (Rabbi Levi Yitzchak Bender).

Adar 5537; (February 1777):

A large group of Chassidic leaders set out on a pilgrimage to the Holy Land. They included Rabbi Menachem Mendel of Vitebsk, Rabbi Avraham Kalisker, Rabbi Yaakov Shimshon of Shepetevka, and Rabbi Shneur Zalman, author of *Tanya* and founder of Chabad Chassidus. They all passed through Medzeboz to pay respects to Rabbi Baruch (*Or HaGalil* p. 100). It is most probable that Rabbi Nachman, who was then about five years old, saw them at this time.

As a very young child, Rabbi Nachman tried to imagine God's name before him at all times. This distracted him from his studies, earning him punishment from his tutor (*Shevachey HaRan* #2; Cf. *Shulchan Arukh, Orach Chaim* 1).

He also found it very difficult to understand the *Mishnayos* which he was studying, but he cried and prayed to God until he was able to understand them (*Shevachey HaRan* #8).

5538; (1778):

When the Rebbe was six, he had already made up his mind to forgo all enjoyment of this world. He would no longer even derive any pleasure from his food (*Ibid.* #1). In the winter, when it was extremely cold, he would pray at the grave of the Baal Shem Tov, and then immerse himself in the freezing outdoor *mikvah* (*Ibid.* #19). Yet he managed to keep his service of God well hidden. Once, when he came to the synagogue with wet *peyos*, everyone wondered why he had washed his hair on such a cold morning (*Ibid.*).

Around this time, there was an occasion when he wanted to greet the Sabbath wholeheartedly. After much preparation he cried for several hours until he was convinced that he had perceived a light of the holiness of the Sabbath (*Shevachey Moharan* 3a #2, #231).

During this period, while he was searching for the path to the complete service of God, he began collecting the material which later became his *Sefer HaMidos* (*Nevey Tzaddikim* p. 48; also see Introduction to *Sefer HaMidos*).

His parents would give him small amounts of money for candy and the like (*Nevey Tzaddikim* p. 13). The Rebbe, however, would give this money to his teacher, three coins for each additional page of *Gemora* that he taught him (*Shevachey HaRan* #4). He would also donate much money secretly to charity (*Ibid.* #13).

Everything he did as a child was completely hidden (*Ibid.* #5). Outwardly he behaved like any other child his age (*Ibid.* #2).

He spent a great deal of time praying alone, often in a small room in the attic of his house (*Shevachey HaRan* #10).

He would recite all the optional prayers in the various prayer books that were available at the time. He would also pray in his native Yiddish (*Ibid.*). Furthermore, after eating, he would add extra thanks and praises in Yiddish besides the required blessings (*Shevachey Moharan* 3b #8, #237). Although he felt that God was not listening to him, he never gave up (*Shevachey HaRan* #12).

Thursday, 7 Teves, 5540; (December 16, 1779):

Rabbi Zvi, son of the Baal Shem Tov, died (*Chachmey Yisroel* p.156).

Shabbos, 15 Shevat, 5540, Shabbos Shirah; (January 22, 1780):

Rabbi Nathan of Nemirov, the foremost disciple of Rabbi Nachman, was born. His father, Reb Naftali Hertz of Nemirov (*Yemey Moharnat* 6a), was very wealthy, owning large stores in Nemirov, Berdichov and Odessa (*Kochavey Or* p. 9). His mother was the daughter of R. Yitzchok Danziger (*Tovos Zichronos* p. 113).

5540; (1780):

Publication of *Toldos Yaakov Yosef*, the first Chassidic work ever to be published.

5541; (1781):

Rabbi Baruch left Medzeboz and settled in Tulchin (*Chachmey Yisroel* p. 210; Cf. Letters of Rabbi Menachem Mendel of Vitebsk; *Igeres HaKodesh* p. 2; see below, p. 72).

Rabbi Nachman immersed himself in study in his father's house. He completed the Talmud, the *Shulchan Arukh*, the *Zohar* and all the *Mussar* books which he found there (*Shevachey HaRan* #7).

Whatever he desired to do in serving God came only with great difficulty. He found it very hard to remain alone in a room for several hours in secluded prayer, but overcame all obstacles and forced himself to do this (*Ibid.* #14). He was very easily angered, but this too he overcame (*Ibid.* #22). He fell many times in his devotions, but always lifted himself up again (*Ibid.* #5; *Sichos HaRan* #48). He was able to overcome all the obstacles and serve God with the utmost simplicity. Each day he would begin completely anew (*Shevachey HaRan* #6). He often accepted each day's undertakings with a vow (*Ibid.* #15).

When he was young, he was terrified of death. Nevertheless, he overcame this fear, and actually prayed that he would die a martyr's death (*Sichos HaRan* #57).

Before he was bar mitzvah, Rabbi Nachman was already finishing his *Sefer HaMidos* (*Nevey Tzaddikim* p. 15).

5545; (1785):

Under the influence of Alexander Koller and other admirers of Moses Mendelssohn, the Court of Vienna ordered that no Chassidic or Kabbalistic writings should be admitted to Galicia.

Shabbos, Rosh Chodesh Nissan, 5545, Shabbos HaChodesh, Torah reading, Vayikra; (March 11, 1785):

Rabbi Nachman's bar mitzvah. His uncle, Rabbi Ephraim of Sudylkov gave him a special blessing, quoting the verse (Psalms 2:7) "I have given birth to you today" which alludes to the bar mitzvah (*Shevachey HaRan* #3; according to the opinion that he was born in 1771, however, his bar mitzvah was on Thursday, March 24, 1784).

A short while later he married Sashia, daughter of R. Ephraim of Ossatin (*Shevachey HaRan* #3; *Chayay Moharan* 25b #2, #105). Her brother was R. Zvi of Tcherin (*Kochavey Or* p. 36). His wife's name is found in the end of a letter, dated Parshas Emor 5567, at the beginning of *Alim LeTerufah* (see Appendix, letter # 2). He had a *nadan* of three hundred rubles (*Chayay Moharan* 26b #7, #110). The wedding was in Medvedevka. On the wedding day Rabbi Nachman spoke to a number of young men about serving God, and it was then that he attracted his first disciple, Rabbi Shimon the son of Reb Ber (*Ibid.* 25b #2, 3, #105, 106). Rabbi Shimon later said, "I abandoned all the renowned leaders, and followed this young boy" (*Aveneha Barzel* p. 37 #51).

After his marriage Rabbi Nachman moved into his father-in-law's house.

2

OSSATIN

Reb Ephraim, Rabbi Nachman's father-in-law, lived in the village of Ossatin (*Chayay Moharan* 25b #2, #105). This village was on the outskirts of Medvedevka (*Sichos HaRan* #117), not far from Smela (*Shevachey HaRan* #20) and Alexanderevka (*Kochavey Or* p. 66 #47), on the bank of the Tyasmin River.

Thursday, 20 Iyar, 5546; (May 19; May 7 Julian, 1786):

An *ukase* of the Russian Senate forbade Rabbinical courts to decide disputes between Jews. It also restricted the extent of Jewish trade.

5547; (1787) approximately:

Rabbi Nachman's first child, a daughter, named Adil, was born about a year after his marriage.[1]

Sunday, 21 Adar, 5547; (March 1, 1787):

Rabbi Elimelech of Lizhensk died (*Chachmey Yisroel* p.164).

Although the journey from Ossatin to Medzeboz was more than two hundred miles, Rabbi Nachman made it a point to visit his parents and to be by the grave of the Baal Shem Tov quite often (*Chayay Moharan* 25b #2, #105). If he

---

1. Adil was married at the end of 5560, fifteen years after Rabbi Nachman's bar mitzvah. Assuming that she was about thirteen at the time of her wedding, as was the custom in those days, her birth can be set at around 5547.

From this we see that Rabbi Nachman's grandmother, Adil, the daughter of the Baal Shem Tov, must have died before this, since his daughter was named after her.

wished to speak to the Baal Shem Tov and could not reach Medzeboz, he would go to Smela, to the grave of Rabbi Yeshaya of Yanov, one of the Baal Shem Tov's great disciples, author of *Tzavo'as Rivash*, and send a message through him to his great-grandfather (*Shevachey HaRan* #20). He would also make him a messenger to his other grandfather, Rabbi Nachman Horodenker, who was buried in Tiberias, in Israel (*Chayay Moharan* 31b #5, #133). He would go very early in the morning, when no one could see him (*Aveneha Barzel* p. 25 #14).

Rabbi Nachman also traveled often from Ossatin to Medvedevka. The trip was through mountainous country. On one such journey together with Rabbi Shimon, the wagon they were traveling in began to overturn and it was only Rabbi Shimon's quick actions which saved them from probable death (*Aveneha Barzel* p. 36 #51).

In Ossatin, Rabbi Nachman spent much of his time praying alone in the forests. He once said that after such devotion, he saw all the world like new (*Chayay Moharan* 26a #4, #107). He would ride into the forests on a horse and pray by himself for hours (*Shevachey Moharan* 3a #1, #230), or he would take a small boat on the river and pray in the rushes (*Sichos HaRan* #117).

He would also pray by himself in bed, under the covers, at night. Once, when he was doing this, he was seen by a young boy, who later grew up to be Rabbi Shmuel Yitzchok, the Rabbi of Tcherin, one of his followers (*Aveneha Barzel* p. 31 #36; also see *Sichos HaRan* # 68, 275).[2]

At this time Rabbi Nachman was deeply engaged in the study of the Kabbalah. When he began, he found it extremely

---

2. Rabbi Shmuel Yitzchok was older than Rabbi Nathan, as stated in the *Manuscript* p. 8. Rabbi Shmuel Yitzchok saw this as a young boy. Rabbi Nathan was eleven years old when the Rebbe left Ossatin for Medvedevka. Therefore, it must have taken place in Ossatin.

difficult, but would cry and pray to God until the meaning was clear to him (*Shevachey HaRan* #8). In his youth, he already knew the entire *Zohar* and the writings of the ARI (*Sichos HaRan* #128; *Shevachey Moharan* 14b #25). In the same period, he went through all four sections of the *Shulchan Arukh* three times, the third time according to its Kabbalistic significance (*Sichos HaRan* #76).

It was during this time that the young Rabbi Nachman began his struggle to subjugate his sexual desires. He had many temptations in this matter (*Shevachey HaRan* #16; see also *Likutey Moharan* 257, which is related to one specific example; see *Nevey Tzaddikim* p. 207). He did not avoid temptations, however; rather he welcomed them, confident that he could overcome them (*Shevachey Moharan* 3a #3, #232).

He began by redirecting all his lusts into the desire for food (*Shevachey HaRan* #16; *Chayay Moharan* 22a, #12, #92). But the Baal Shem Tov appeared in a dream and indicated to him that if he wanted to see the Patriarchs, he must cast away this desire as well (*Ibid.*). He then discarded his appetite for food, and ate almost nothing (*Shevachey HaRan* #21). Very often he would fast from Sabbath to Sabbath, sometimes twice consecutively. He once fasted like this eighteen times in a single year. This occurred before he was twenty years old (*Shevachey HaRan* #9).

All this was done in utmost secrecy. Except for his wife, no one knew of his fasts, and he made her swear not to reveal his secret (*Ibid.* #19; Cf. see below p. 15).

During this period he also indulged in acts of self-mortification (*Ibid.* #24). He would sigh a great deal in order to subjugate his physical powers (*Sichos HaRan* #167; Cf. *Likutey Moharan* I, 8). He would imagine his own death, and how he would be mourned (*Sichos HaRan* #190).

At first, Rabbi Nachman was extremely strict in many practices, even where the law does not require it. He was so

careful regarding attending his needs before prayer that he
literally placed himself in danger (Sichos HaRan #30). He was
so stringent on Pesach that he avoided drinking even well-
water, for fear it had come in contact with chometz. But he
eventually realized that this type of stringency was not basic
to serving God (Ibid. #235).

Being a great-grandson of the Baal Shem Tov, young
Rabbi Nachman found himself treated with excessive
reverence. However, he did not welcome this kind of
attention (Nevey Tzaddikim p. 18). He would have preferred
to have gone somewhere where he was not known, and to
have hidden himself completely (Chayay Moharan 26b #8,
#111). Since this was not possible, he disguised his practices
even while in his father-in-law's house, gaining the reputation
of an ignoramus and playing with youngsters his own age
(Aveneha Barzel p. 23 #9).

Once, one of the great disciples of the Mezritcher Magid
visited Reb Ephraim's house and tested Rabbi Nachman in
his studies. The youth acted as if he did not know anything,
and the older Rabbi slapped him across the face. Later, he
found Rabbi Nachman praying fervently in the woods, and
understood that he was a great Tzaddik. He asked Rabbi
Nachman's forgiveness, but the latter replied that he would
only forgive him if the Rabbi promised not to reveal his
discovery during the Rebbe's lifetime (Ibid.).

Rabbi Yekusiel, the Magid of Terhovitza, became one of
Rabbi Nachman's most prominent disciples. Rabbi Yekusiel
was an older man and a leader in his own right, being Magid
over eighty-four communities in this area (Chayay Moharan
HaShmotos 46a). When Rabbi Nachman moved to Ossatin,
he found himself in the Magid's territory, and the Magid
therefore heard of him. Rabbi Yekusiel had been one of the
great disciples of the Magid of Mezritch (Nevey Tzaddikim p.
26). He was also a close friend of Rabbi Nochum of
Tchernoble (Chayay Moharan HaShmotos). Rabbi Shneur

Zalman (author of *Tanya*) received a *haskama* from him for his Siddur (*Ibid.*).[3]

Around this time, Rabbi Nachman prayed that he might see miracles and was answered three times. One was that his devotions outside would no longer be disturbed by a roadside cross which stood on the route he used to take. The cross suddenly fell. The second was that fish would come to him from the river without the use of a net. And the third was that he would see the soul of a dead person (*Chayay Moharan* p. 26a #7, #110).

His fame began to spread after he visited Alexanderevka with his father-in-law. His father-in-law had *yahrzeit* for his father, and Rabbi Nachman read *Mishnayos* for the sake of the dead. His father-in-law fainted and then said that he had seen the dead man standing next to the young Rabbi Nachman (*Kochavey Or* p. 66 #47).

Thursday, Rosh Chodesh Iyar, 5548; (May 8, 1788):

Rabbi Menachem Mendel of Vitebsk died (*Pri Etz l'Ashkavta DeRebbi*).

Tuesday, 20 Tammuz, 5549; (July 14, 1789):

In Paris, the storming of the Bastille marked the culmination of the French Revolution.

5550; (1790): approximately:

Around this time, Rabbi Nachman's mother-in-law died, and his father-in-law married a woman from Mohelov. At the wedding, Rabbi Nachman was given a little wine and revealed wondrous things, astounding everyone there. Among the people in Mohelov was the great Tzaddik, Rabbi Yissachar

---

3. This Siddur was first published in 5563 in Shklov, but because of numerous printing errors the copies were not distributed. No copies of this edition are known to exist; see *Igros Baal Tanya U-Vnei Doro*, p. 123 note 7. See also *Shaar HaKollel* Introduction. The Magid's *haskama* was printed in the Shklov edition.

Dov of Zaslov, known as Reb Ber ben Reb Binim, one of the close disciples of the Baal Shem Tov. Reb Ber said that Rabbi Nachman would be most remarkable (*Chayay Moharan, Ibid.* #5, #108).

Rabbi Nachman remained in his father-in-law's house in Ossatin for a short time after this. But his father-in-law's second wife took away his room, and he moved away, settling in nearby Medvedevka (*Ibid.*).

It was around this time that he gave his very first lessons, a few of which were later printed in *Likutey Moharan* (*Nevey Tzaddikim* p. 39).

Also, his second child, a daughter whom he named Sarah, was born around this time (for we find that she was married around the year 5563, at which time she would have been about thirteen, as was the custom at the time).

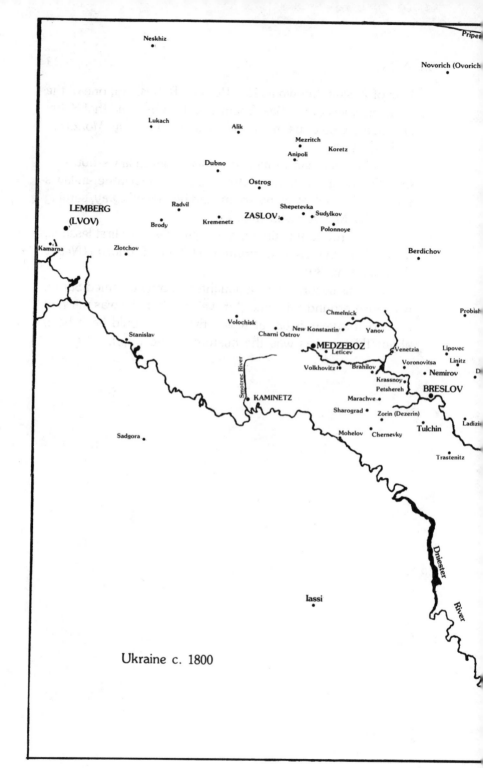

Ukraine c. 1800

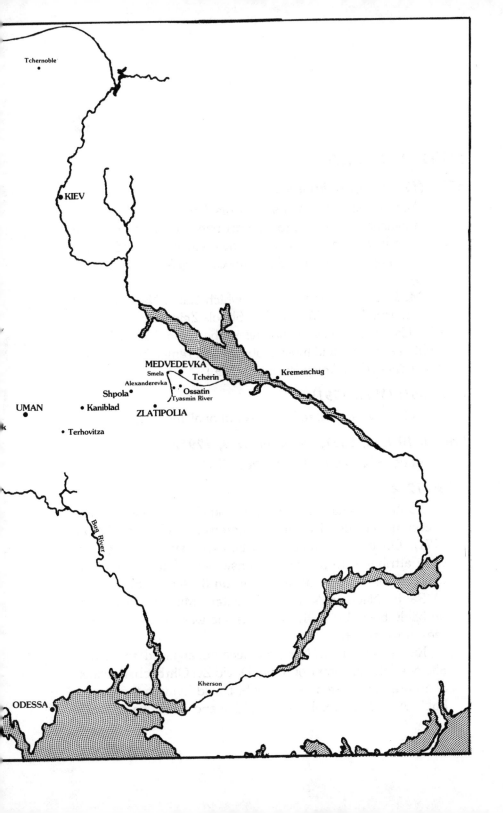

3

MEDVEDEVKA

5551; (1791) approximately:

After Rabbi Nachman set up residence in Medvedevka, the townspeople agreed to support him with the sum of one *rendel* a week. He lived there mostly undisturbed, and people began to become attracted to him (*Chayay Moharan* 26b #9, #112).

Medvedevka was the city in which Rabbi Nachman had been married (*Ibid.* 25b #2). The Shpola Zeida had lived there with his father-in-law, a *shochet* in the town. He had spent eight years there and most probably was remembered by the city elders (*Chachmey Yisroel* p. 209.)

Iyar 5551; (May, 1791):

Poland was declared a constitutional monarchy.

Friday, 10 Elul, 5551; (September 9, 1791):

Rabbi Pinchas of Koretz died (*Ibid.* p. 170).

5552; (1792):

Rabbi Nachman was 20 years old. By this age, he had overcome his physical desires completely (*Sichos HaRan* #171). Once his mother asked him why such great things were attributed to him and he answered, "I am truly totally devoid of evil" (*Shevachey Moharan* 3b #9, #238).

Rabbi Nachman's third daughter, Miriam, was most probably born during this year (as she was married in 5565; see above p. 13).

Rabbi Nathan of Nemirov became engaged to Esther Shaindel, the daughter of Rabbi Dovid Zvi Ohrbach, Rabbi of Sharograd and Kremenetz. Rabbi Dovid Zvi was the son of Rabbi Aryeh Leib, Rabbi of Stanislav and a relative of Rabbi

Nachman Horodenker (*Yemey Moharnat* 6a; *Nevey Tzaddikim* p. 28; *Shem HaGedolim HeChadash, Daled* 28; also see *Aveneha Barzel* p. 4).

11 Av, 5553, week of Shabbos Nachamu; (July 20, 1793):

Rabbi Nathan was married in Sharograd (*Yemey Moharnat, Ibid.*).

5553: (1793):

The second partition of Poland took place as a result of the Confederation of Targowice (Terhovitza). Russia annexed the Ukraine where Rabbi Nachman was living.

Tuesday, 14 Av, 5553; (July 23, 1793):

Rabbi Chaim Krasner died. He was a major disciple of the Baal Shem Tov and a close friend of Rabbi Pinchas of Koretz (*Chachmey Yisroel* p. 175).

This was a period of intensive fasting for Rabbi Nachman. He now hid his fasts so that even his wife was not aware of them. Only his attendant knew, and he was sworn not to divulge this (*Manuscript* p. 12; *Sichos HaRan* #160). This attendant would eat all Rabbi Nachman's food, so that no one would realize that he was fasting (*Manuscript, Ibid.*). Once Rabbi Nachman hemorrhaged from the mouth in the middle of a fast, but he told his attendant not to reveal this to anyone (*Sichos HaRan, Ibid.*). Another time he became so faint that he had to lie in bed with his feet raised (*Ibid.*). He did not prepare light foods with which to break his fast, and once was in severe danger (*Ibid.* #161).

Eventually his mother realized that her son was hardly eating anything at all. When she inquired, he replied that he was nourished the way that (Ecclesiastes 7:12) "Wisdom nourishes its possessor" (*Shevachey Moharan* 3b #9, #238).

During this same period, the mystery of the "Table" was revealed to him (*Ibid.* 27a #31, #476).

One of his earliest disciples was Rabbi Chaikel of Medvedevka. After he became a follower of Rabbi Nachman, he practically lived in his mentor's house. He was one of the few who learned about Rabbi Nachman's fasts (*Manuscript* p. 12). Rabbi Chaikel had a son by the name of Reb Leib of Medvedevka (*Yemey Moharnat* p. 98b #44). Rabbi Chaikel was a wonderful singer and the Rebbe asked him to become his regular cantor (*Manuscript, Ibid.*). Rabbi Nachman said of him that he knew the source of song in its divine roots (*Biur HaLikutim*, Introduction). It is also related that Rabbi Chaikel performed a miracle through which he made an individual rich (*Kochavey Or* p. 41). Another time the Rebbe showed him the soul of a dead man (*Ibid.* 56 #34). Rabbi Chaikel's faith in the Rebbe was so strong that he once held a snake by its head only because the Rebbe had told him to (*Aveneha Barzel* p. 46 #73).

In Medvedevka, Rabbi Nachman prayed alone in the mountains and fields (*Sichos HaRan* #162; see *Outpouring of the Soul* p. 42). When he had used up his dowry, he became very poor. He nevertheless had faith that even in the fields God would provide him with the necessities of life (*Chayay Moharan* 26b #7, #110).

Many of the great Chassidic leaders visited Rabbi Nachman in Medvedevka. Rabbi Yekusiel, the Magid of Terhovitza, brought his close friend Rabbi Nochum of Tchernoble to visit him. Rabbi Nochum said that the Rebbe had (Samuel I, 16:12) "beautiful eyes" (*Chayay Moharan HaShmotos* 46a). He also said that he could literally see the fear of God on the Rebbe's face (*Sichos HaRan* #168).

He once met Rabbi Aharon of Tetiev (*Tovos Zichronos* p. 24). Rabbi Aharon was a grandson of the Baal Shem Tov, a son of Rabbi Zvi.

In Medvedevka, Rabbi Nachman began to achieve a reputation as a miracle worker. He later said that he knew all twenty-four courts of Justice on High, and he also knew to which one a *pidyon* must be brought (*Sichos HaRan* #175). A man once came to him with his sick wife, and the Rebbe told him to quickly bring twenty-four *pidyonos* (*Chayay Moharan* 14a #55, #55; Cf. *Likutey Moharan* I:215).

By this time, the Rebbe also knew how each Jewish soul was rooted in the Torah (*Sichos HaRan* #185). He could not sleep at night, because the six hundred thousand letters of the Torah would pass before his eyes (*Ibid.* #176, 90).

In Medvedevka the Rebbe's following began to grow (*Chayay Moharan* 26b #9, #112).

Rabbi Meir of Medvedevka practically became a member of the Rebbe's household. He was very wealthy, but did not have any children. The Rebbe told him that he would have children but would lose his great wealth, which in fact happened (*Kochavey Or* p. 46, #12).

The Rebbe's brother, Rabbi Yechiel, also became one of his followers during this period (*Shevachey Moharan* 4a #11, #240).

Another person who joined his following was Rabbi Shmuel Yitzchok, later to become Rabbi of Tcherin, who had seen the Rebbe when he was still a child (see above, p. 9). Once there was a fire in Medvedevka, which Rabbi Shmuel Yitzchok had predicted to the Rebbe (*Chayay Moharan* 34a #1, #151).

Another early follower was Reb Avraham Peterberger. He wrote down many of the Rebbe's lessons before Rabbi Nathan became a follower (*Biur HaLikutim*, Introduction; *Nevey Tzaddikim* p. 27). Whenever we find in *Likutey Moharan* that something is in "the language of the companions," this means that it was written by Reb Avraham Peterberger (*Ibid.*). There are a number of lessons in *Likutey Moharan* said during this period, which were written by Reb Avraham (see *Shevachey Moharan* 16a #43, #382; *Ibid.* 27b #33, #479).[4]

---

4. We see that Lesson #73 was said as soon as Rabbi Nachman returned from Israel (*Chayay Moharan* 32b #15, #143), and this is in "the language of the companions." This would indicate that it was written by Reb Avraham

During this period, people from Dashev began to become attracted to the Rebbe (*Chayay Moharan* 26b #9, #112). Dashev was some one hundred and thirty miles (210 km.) from Medvedevka.

This came about through one of the disciples of the Mezritcher Magid, the saintly Rabbi Leib of Trastenitz (*Nevey Tzaddikim* p. 21; Cf. *Chayay Moharan HaShmotos* 46b #4). After he died, he appeared to the Rebbe, and asked him to attempt to attract his children (*Kochavey Or* p. 26 #23). At this same time, he revealed to the Rebbe part of lesson #96 in *Likutey Moharan* (*Parparaos LeChokhmah, ad loc.* This occurred a long time before his pilgrimage to Israel, as recorded in *Chayay Moharan* 15a #59, #59).

In the city of Dashev, there was a group of people dedicated to serving God (*Nevey Tzaddikim, Ibid.*). They were led by Rabbi Yudel, the son-in-law of this saintly Rabbi Leib, and a disciple of the great Rabbi Pinchas of Koretz (*Chayay Moharan HaShmotos, Ibid.* #3). Rabbi Yudel was extremely poor (*Alim LeTerufah* 163), but very wise (*Tovos Zichronos* p. 4). He was already an established Kabbalist (*Chayay Moharan HaShmotos, Ibid.* #4).

Another was the Tzaddik, Rabbi Shmuel Isaac. He would pray like an angel (*Nevey Tzaddikim, Ibid.*; Cf. *Tovos Zichronos* p. 31). He was also very strong (*Tovos Zichronos* #4), and very poor (*Alim LeTerufah, Ibid.*).

Among that same group was Rabbi Dov of Tcherin. For several years after his marriage, he lived with his father-in-law in Dashev, as was the custom. When this period ended, the couple returned to his father's home near Medvedevka. Before Rabbi Dov left Dashev, Rabbi Yudel had warned him not to go to Rabbi Nachman. However, Rabbi Dov became

---

Peterberger, and he must therefore have become one of the Rebbe's followers in Medvedevka before the Rebbe's pilgrimage to Israel.

very depressed in his father's home, since he could not have any children. He met with Rabbi Yeshaya Shalom, one of the Rebbe's early followers, and thus first came to meet the Rebbe (*Kochavey Or* p. 24 #20; Cf. *Nevey Tzaddikim* 23). The Rebbe told him that in order to have children, he must give a certain amount to charity. When he replied that he was dependent on his father and could not give charity, the Rebbe told him that faith was just like charity (*Ibid.* note 5; see *Shevachey Moharan* 27a #32, #477; *Sichos HaRan* #34).

Rabbi Dov also wanted to rise at midnight for *Tikkun Chatzos*, but it was extremely difficult for him, and he almost became sick in the attempt. The Rebbe told him that, in his case, three a.m. would be considered midnight. This was just one of the directives which the Rebbe gave him to balance Rabbi Dov's burning desire to serve God (*Kochavey Or* p. 25 #21).

Afterwards, Rabbi Dov found it necessary to travel to his father-in-law's house. Once there, he could not help but tell Rabbi Yudel of his relationship with Rabbi Nachman. Impressed by their friend's obvious spiritual development, the entire group went to visit the Rebbe. On the way, they stopped off in Terhovitza, and inspired some of the students of Rabbi Yekusiel, the Magid of that town, to join them on the trip (*Ibid.* p. 26; *Nevey Tzaddikim* pp. 23, 24, 34).

When Rabbi Yudel first met the Rebbe he was already renowned as a great scholar and Kabbalist, and was some fifteen years older than the Rebbe (*Chayay Moharan HaShmotos, Ibid.*). He began to speak to the Rebbe in the manner of prominent Chassidim: "Tell me the way to serve God." The Rebbe replied that Rabbi Yudel could not understand the way as long as he was insufficiently detached from his worldliness. The Rebbe then exposed Rabbi Yudel to a profound fear of Heaven for a few moments, and Rabbi Yudel was unable to withstand the intensity of the experience (*Sichos HaRan* #292; *Kochavey Or* p. 26 #23). He then became a follower of Rabbi Nachman, and one of his most important Chassidim.

Once, when he first began coming to the Rebbe, Rabbi Yudel asked to be shown a miracle. Rabbi Nachman then told him that he had promised a certain Chassid that God would give him a son if the Chassid gave the Rebbe a *rendel* every six months. He did this and a child was born. But now this follower was not going to keep his word and the child would not live. That same week, while Rabbi Yudel was still with Rabbi Nachman the Chassid came to the Rebbe. His son had died. Apparently, the Rebbe had used this *rendel* as a *pidyon* for keeping the child alive (*Kochavey Or* p. 26). There are likewise several other stories (*Ibid.* pp. 28, 29), including that of a woman in prolonged labor who was miraculously helped by Rabbi Yudel (*Aveneha Barzel* p. 45 #71). The Rebbe also told Rabbi Yudel to what extent he had overcome all his desires (*Sichos HaRan* #171).

The Rebbe told Rabbi Shmuel Isaac that he could lose both worlds because of a small amount of blood in his heart (*Shevachey Moharan* 23 #5, #441). He told him to groan and sigh in order to subdue the physical nature of his body (*Ibid.*), and to speak to each and every limb about the vanity of worldly desires (*Tovos Zichronos* #4; *Nevey Tzaddikim* p. 24). The Rebbe once compared him to the renowned Tzaddik, Rabbi Shalom Shachneh of Probisht (*Sichos Moharan, HaShmotos* p. 39a #9).

Soon after becoming followers of the Rebbe, Rabbis Yudel and Shmuel Isaac moved nearer to Medvedevka so they could always be close to him (*Shevachey Moharan* 8b #51, #291; *Chayay Moharan, HaShmotos* 46b #4).

After leaving his father's house, Reb Dov moved to Tcherin. He became a businessman and always gave a fifth of his income to charity, as ordered by the Rebbe. He was very wealthy and had a partner, Reb Yaakov Yosef (*Kochavey Or* p. 24 #19; *Yemey Moharnat* p. 95b #33, p. 96a #35).

It was also during this period that Rabbi Aharon became a

follower of the Rebbe. This Rabbi Aharon was later to be brought to Breslov by the Rebbe to be Rav of the town (*Sichos Moharan* 30a #63, #509; see below p. 90). In Medvedevka, the Rebbe lived three houses away from Rabbi Aharon's uncle. Rabbi Aharon, a young Rabbi already renowned as a brilliant scholar and rabbinic judge, was then living in Kherson. He once came to Medvedevka to adjudicate in a dispute and stayed with his uncle. The Rebbe sent for him and inspired him so greatly that Rabbi Aharon became the Rebbe's follower. It was at that time that the Rebbe said *Likutey Moharan* 34 (*Tovos Zichronos* #37).

In Medvedevka, the Rebbe told some of his followers to study the *Mesilas Yesharim* (*Sippurim Niflaim* p. 167).

Around that time, the wealthy Reb Leib Dubravner of Kremenchug told the Rebbe that he had a son, Yitzchok Isaac, who was the same age as the Rebbe's daughter, Sarah. He asked if a match could be arranged. The Rebbe did not desire this marriage, but Rabbi Chaikel pointed out that other great Rabbis had agreed to matches with Reb Leib's children. The Rebbe said that he would only agree if Reb Leib would provide a dowry of ten thousand *rendels*. Reb Leib agreed, and the match was made (*Manuscript* p. 12).[5]

In *Alim LeTerufah* (see Appendix letter #7), this Reb Leib is called Reb Aryeh Leib. However, in another letter (see Appendix letter #8) we find him called Yehuda Leib.

We find that Reb Leib lived in Kremenchug (*Yemey Moharnat* p. 101b #52; also see *Kochavey Or* p. 47). In *Shemos HaTzaddikim*, we find him called Reb Leib of Kremenchug (also see *Kochavey Or* p. 33 #30). He also had a son R. Shlomo (*Yemey Moharnat* p. 98a #41). His main

---

5. This took place before the pilgrimage to Israel, since we find in *Shevachey HaRan, Seder Nesiaso LeEretz Yisroel* #6, that the Rebbe said to his middle daughter, Sarah, that she could go to her in-laws. The reason why both Miriam and Sarah were engaged before Adil, the Rebbe's eldest daughter, is somewhat obscure.

business was in Nikolayev (*Yemey Moharnat, Ibid.,* cf. p. 85b and 86a; also see *Chayay Moharan* 28b #13, #116 and *Aveneha Barzel* p. 22 #8).

In Medvedevka the Rebbe met with some controversy (*Chayay Moharan* 26b #9, #112). Once, he chanted over and over the verse from the 124th psalm, "If God had not been with us." He then said to those around him that they would not merit to be called his followers unless the entire world stood up against them and they stood firm (*Ibid.* 30a #22, #124). Another time, after breaking bread for the Shabbos meal he sat in awesome *devekus* for the entire Friday night. It was only after sunrise that he recited *Birkhas HaMazon* and left the table (*Shevachey Moharan* 4a #11, #240).

Shabbos, 7 Tammuz, 5554; (July 5; June 23, Julian, 1794):

The Jewish Pale of Settlement was first instituted.

Summer-Autumn 5555; (1794):

Polish uprising against Russia and Prussia.

5556; (October 1795):

Third partition of Poland.

Succos 5556; (October 1795):

The days of Rabbi Nathan's agreement to live with his father-in-law ended, and he returned to his father's house in Nemirov (*Yemey Moharnat* 6a).

Winter 5556; (1795-96):

Rabbi Nathan began to study with a friend, Reb Lipa, who was a Chassid. His father and father-in-law were both *Misnagdim*, who opposed the Chassidic movement. Rabbi Nathan also saw some of the followers of Rabbi Zusia of Anipoli. Rabbi Nathan then traveled to see Rabbi Mordechai of Kremenetz and Rabbi Levi Yitzchok of Berdichov (*Aveneha Barzel* p. 6). He also saw Rabbi Baruch of Medzeboz and Rabbi Gedalia of Linitz (*Yemey Moharnat* 6a). Rabbi Nathan also said that he went to see Rabbi Shalom

Shachneh of Probisht and the Rabbi of Chmelnick, who later became an in-law of the Rebbe (see below p. 54; *Alim LeTerufah* #181).

Thursday, 16 Cheshvon, 5557; (November 17, 1796):

Katherine the Great, Empress of Russia, died and was succeeded by her son, Czar Paul.

In this year, *Likutey Amorim; Tanya*, by Rabbi Shneur Zalman of Liadi, was published.

Monday, 19 Tishrei, 3rd day of Chol HaMoed Succos, 5558; (October 9, 1797):

Rabbi Eliyahu, the Vilna Gaon, died (*Chachmey Yisroel* p.178). His followers were upset by what they saw as manifestations of disrespect by the Chassidim in Vilna and called a special meeting of the Vilna *kahal*. They renewed the *cherem* against the Chassidim and decided upon a number of secret measures, including denouncing Chassidic leaders to the government (*Igros Kodesh* pp. 126, 147)

Tuesday, 11 Cheshvon, 5558; (October 31, 1797):

Rabbi Nochum of Tchernoble died (*Chachmey Yisroel* p.179).

4

KAMINETZ — PODOLSK

Kaminetz is situated near the Smotrec River, latitude 48.41°N longitude 26.36°E, in the Ukraine. It was the capital city of Podolia, seat of the provincial government and an important trading and communications center. In 1750, King Augustus III expelled all Jews from Kaminetz.

5558; (1797-98):

Rabbi Nachman set out on a journey with Rabbi Shimon, his first disciple. The Rebbe said that he did not know how long he would be gone, nor did he know where his trip would lead him. They disguised themselves as merchants so as not to attract attention (*Chayay Moharan* 31a #1, #129; *Shevachey HaRan, Seder Nesiaso LeEretz Yisroel* #1).

They traveled through Volkhovitz, and were joined by a fellow traveler (*Chayay Moharan, Ibid.*).

They then traveled to Medzeboz, and visited Rabbi Nachman's parents. There the Baal Shem Tov appeared to him and told the Rebbe to go to Kaminetz. Rabbi Shimon fell ill and was left behind (*Ibid.*).

The Rebbe and the man from Volkhovitz arrived in Kaminetz and spent the day there. At that time, Jews were not allowed to stay overnight in the city. Rabbi Nachman sent his companion away. He, however, was resolved to spend the night in Kaminetz. In the morning, he was again joined by his companion and together they visited several houses there (*Shevachey HaRan, Ibid.*).

After having been gone for about a week and a half the Rebbe returned to Medzeboz, where Reb Shimon rejoined him (*Chayay Moharan, Ibid.*).

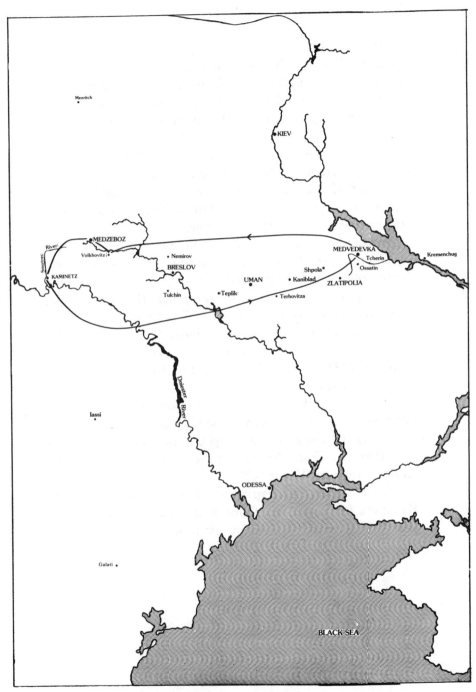

Journey to Kaminetz

Soon after this, the Jews were given permission to live in Kaminetz (*Ibid.* #1). In historical sources, we find that they were given this permission by Czar Paul in 1797. We do not, however, know in which month this occurred. It might have been at the beginning of 5558, corresponding to the latter part of 1797.

When he returned to Medvedevka, Rabbi Nachman taught a lesson on the verse "My soul longs for You," (Psalms 63:9) (*Ibid.* #2, #130). A young daughter of his had died, and he said that others like her would die because of the spiritual *tikkunim* he had undertaken to achieve (*Ibid.* #3, #131). This came true; he later lost another daughter and his two sons.

The purpose of the Rebbe's trip remains a deep mystery. Some interpreted it positively, saying that he went to Kaminetz to recover the writings which Reb Adam Baal Shem had given to the Baal Shem Tov (*Ibid.* #4, #132; Cf. *Shevachey HaBaal Shem Tov*, Jerusalem, 5729, p. 52). However, there were others who took an unfavorable view (*Ibid.* #3, #131). But the Rebbe said that both explanations were wrong (*Ibid.*).

The Rebbe later said, "Whoever knows why the Holy Land was first in possession of the Canaanites and only later settled by the Jews, will know why I first went to Kaminetz and then to *Eretz Yisroel*" (*Shevachey HaRan, Seder Nesiaso LeEretz Yisroel* #2)

There is also a story about how the Rebbe was in Kaminetz for Purim, but there is no indication as to which year this occurred (*Kochavey Or* p. 40 #4).

5

THE PILGRIMAGE

Shabbos 14 Nissan, Erev Pesach, 5558; (March 30, 1798):[6]

When the Rebbe left the *mikvah* he said that this year he would be in Israel (*Shevachey HaRan, Seder Nesiaso LeEretz Yisroel* #5).

Pesach; (April):

The Rebbe said a lesson on Psalm 77:20. From this lesson, it became obvious that he intended to go to *Eretz Yisroel* (*Shevachey HaRan, ibid.*). He said that he wanted to go there in order to keep all the commandments (i.e. to combine spiritually all the commandments which are kept outside the Land of Israel with those which can be kept only in Israel) (*Chayay Moharan*, 31b #5, #133). He also said that he wished to attain the higher wisdom — *chokhmah i'la'ah* (*Tikkuney Zohar* Introduction p. 6a; *Ibid.* #6, #134).

When the Rebbe told Rabbi Yudel that he wanted to go to *Eretz Yisroel*, Rabbi Yudel gave him a blessing (*Ibid.* #7, #135).

When his family heard that he wished to leave them they began to cry, but the Rebbe said that he had to go (*Shevachey HaRan, ibid.* #6).

After Pesach, the Rebbe's followers collected money for his trip (*Ibid.* #7). There was a wealthy man who wanted to travel with the Rebbe, but Rabbi Nachman told him that one should be willing to go on foot (*Yemey Moharnat* 110b #49).

---

6. Our source states that the Rebbe made this remark on Erev Pesach. Erev Pesach 5558 fell on Shabbos. "Erev Pesach" in the source could refer to Erev Shabbos.

He said that he could no longer send messages to his grandfather, Rabbi Nachman Horodenker, who was buried in Tiberias, through Rabbi Yeshaya of Yanov, who was buried in Smela (see above p. 9) and therefore had to go to Israel (*Chayay Moharan* 31b #5, #133). He told one of his followers that he had come to know how to see the Patriarchs when he wished and that this was connected with his forthcoming voyage on the sea, but that he did not have words to embody this in a lesson for his followers (*Ibid.* 33a #19, #147).

Apparently, the Rebbe had numerous reasons for his pilgrimage to the Holy Land — aside from the hidden intentions he did not reveal. In fact, he never undertook anything for just a single purpose and certainly not his journey to *Eretz Yisroel* for which he literally risked his life time and again (*Ibid.* 31b #5, #133).

Friday, 18 Iyar, Lag Be-Omer; (May 4):

The Rebbe left Medvedevka and began his pilgrimage to Israel with one of his followers[7] (*Shevachey HaRan, Ibid.* #8).

The Rebbe spent Shabbos along the way in the city of Sokila, where he saw Rabbi Menachem Mendel of Vitebsk in a vision. This Rabbi Menachem Mendel had been the leader of the Chassidim in Israel, and had died ten years previously in 5548 (1788). He told the Rebbe the secret meaning of the Name *Atah*, which is protective while traveling at sea (*Chayay Moharan* 9b #30, #30; 31b #8, #136; Cf. *Likutey Moharan* 256). The Rebbe foresaw that Sokila would become a large town in the future. Its name was later changed to Voznishensk (*Parparaos LeChokhmah, ad loc.*).

The Rebbe arrived in Nikolayev, fifty miles (80 km.) from

---

7. It is unclear who his attendant was. Some leading Breslover authorities have a tradition that this was Rabbi Shimon (Cf. *Chayay Moharan* 31b #6, #134; 32a #136). It is possible that he remained unidentified at his own request. Rabbi Shimon was known for his humility (Cf. *Kochavey Or* p. 23 #18).

Sokila along the Bug River. From there, he took a grain ship to Kherson (*Shevachey HaRan, Ibid.* #8). The journey from Nikolayev to Kherson by sea is forty-six miles (75 km.). In Kherson, Rabbi Nachman met several followers of Rabbi Shneur Zalman of Liadi (*Chayay Moharan* 31b #4, #132).

Tuesday, 22 Iyar; (May 8):

Captain Sidney Smith returned to London after having been held captive by the French. He was captain of the British ships which were in Acco when the Rebbe left Israel (see below page 46).

Shabbos, 4 Sivan, Torah reading, Bamidbar; (May 19):

Napoleon set off on his Middle East campaign.

Monday, 6 Sivan, Shavuos; (May 21):

On the first day of Shavuos, before prayers, the Rebbe heard the sounds of receiving the Torah on Mount Sinai (*Ibid.*).

The Rebbe spent Shavuos in Kherson. After the festival, he left for Odessa.

Upon his departure from Odessa he was escorted by several people. He told his companion to buy paper, and he wrote prolifically on board ship (*Shevachey HaRan, Ibid.* #9).

There was a violent storm on the Black Sea, and there he saw the soul of a dead man from Volkhovitz (*Chayay Moharan* 32a #9, #137). (This appears to have been the one who accompanied him to Kaminetz; see above p. 23).

The journey from Odessa to Istanbul lasted four days (*Shevachey HaRan, ibid.* #9).

The Pilgrimage

6

ISTANBUL

Istanbul, located at latitude 41.01°N longitude 28.58°E, was the capital of the Ottoman Empire. Situated on the Dardanelle Straits, it was the major junction for travel and commerce between Europe and Asia, and Russia and the Middle East. In 1778 the total population was one million. One-hundred and twenty thousand were Jews, most of whom lived in the Galati district.

When the ship arrived in Istanbul the travelers found themselves unable to communicate with the local inhabitants. They remained in the port until an interpreter arrived and guided them to a part of the city known as Galati. (Istanbul is divided into three parts and Galati is in the northwest, attached to the European mainland.) The Rebbe was not satisfied there and moved to the old city, known as Stambul (which is in the southwest) (*Shevachey HaRan, Seder Nesiaso LeEretz Yisroel* p. 23).

The Rebbe then met several emissaries from the Holy Land. They thought that he was going to foment controversy with Rabbi Avraham Kalisker, leader of the Chassidim in Israel (these emissaries were followers of Rabbi Avraham) (*Ibid.*).

At this time there was a fierce controversy between the followers of Rabbi Shneur Zalman and those of Rabbi Avraham. When *Tanya* was published, Rabbi Avraham wrote a very strong letter to Rabbi Shneur Zalman regarding it. This occurred in 5556 (1796). Reb Aharon ben Meir of Smela, who had been an attendant of Rabbi Menachem Mendel of Vitebsk (he signs himself thus in *Igeres HaKodesh* #13), was now one of the important followers of Rabbi

Avraham. He had been close to Rabbi Shneur Zalman, and
was also known as Aharon HaKatan. In 5557 (1797), Reb
Aharon visited Rabbi Shneur Zalman and was greeted very
coldly by the latter (*Ibid.* #37). In 5558 (1798) Rabbi Aharon
returned to Israel, and it became known that he had spoken
against Rabbi Shneur Zalman (*Igros Baal HaTanya U-Vnei
Doro* #103 p. 174). The emissaries from Israel furthermore
did not want to subjugate themselves to Rabbi Shneur
Zalman (*Ibid.* p. 176). Several followers of Rabbi Shneur
Zalman also went to Israel and began opposing Rabbi
Avraham (*Igeres HaKodesh* 39; Cf. *Igros Baal HaTanya* p.
178, note 9). Animosity began to burn between the followers
of these two great rabbis.

The Rebbe resolved to hide his identity from these two
emissaries. No matter how hard they tried, the Rebbe used
great wisdom in answering their questions. At one point, the
emissaries thought that the Rebbe was from Lagorna
(unidentified), but later realized that this was not so. On
another occasion they presumed that he was Yeshaya, son of
the Magid of Kamarna (*Shevachey HaRan* p. 25 #9). This
Magid was most probably Rabbi Yosef Moshe Likvornik, who
was Magid of Kamarna, and later Rabbi in Sadgora, where he
died on 24 Tishrei, 5562 (October 1, 1801). His son, Rabbi
Yeshaya, was also Rabbi in Sadgora, and died on 12
Cheshvon, 5589 (1828) (private communication from Rabbi
Shmuel Mendelson, a descendant of this Magid).

Frustrated in their attempts to discover his identity and
suspecting sinister intentions behind his journey, they began
insulting and cursing the Rebbe. He still did not give in to
their entreatments.

When they parted, the Rebbe told his attendant to give
them supplies for their journey. They refused, however, to
deliver a letter for the Rebbe (*Shevachey HaRan, ibid.* p.
26).[8]

---

8. We therefore see that they were planning to pass close by the Rebbe's

These two people insulted the Rebbe without knowing who he was. The Rebbe said that he had been afraid of Heavenly opposition to his reaching the Holy Land as had happened with other Tzaddikim, most notably the Baal Shem Tov and Rabbi Naftali Katz. The embarrassment he suffered at the hands of these two men had helped him overcome this obstacle. The one who had abused him the most died as soon as he returned home (Ibid. p. 27 and p. 52 #29).

These two men had told the ship's agent not to let the Rebbe continue to Israel (Ibid. p. 24). However, when the Rebbe revealed his identity to him, the agent was taken aback. The next day, the agent returned and treated the Rebbe with great respect (Ibid. p. 27).

The following day, the Tzaddik Rabbi Zev Wolf of Charni-Ostrov arrived in Istanbul.

Rabbi Zev Wolf was one of the great disciples of the Mezritcher Magid. He was also the mentor of the Gaon, Rabbi Dovid Shlomo of Soroke, author of Levushey S'rad and Arvey Nachal (Shem HaGedolim HeChadash, Vav 9; also see Chachmey Yisroel p. 202). He was with the Rebbe in Istanbul, and again in Haifa (see below p. 39). He returned to Europe and was in Berdichov in the summer of 5562 (see below p. 71, 72). He then returned to Israel, and was visited by Rabbi Nathan in Tiberias in 5582 (Yemey Moharnat 136b #153). He died on 5 Adar, 5583 (1823), and was buried in Tiberias (Tevor HaAretz).

The Rebbe spent the Sabbath with Rabbi Zev Wolf. He purposely acted against his host's will, but the love Rabbi Zev Wolf had for the Rebbe made him overlook Rabbi Nachman's seemingly foolish behavior. After Shabbos they spent almost the entire night talking together (Shevachey HaRan p. 28 #12).

At this time, the Rebbe engaged in childish acts (Ibid.;

home in Medvedevka. If one of these emissaries was Reb Aharon of Smela, this becomes very understandable.

Chayay Moharan 32a #11, #139). He was in very great danger, yet through the *tikkunim* he accomplished, he paved the way for others to get to Israel (*Ibid.* 6b #15, #15, note). The Rebbe said that the Baal Shem Tov was not able to come to Israel, because he could not descend to such a level of simplicity (*Ibid.* 32a #12, #140).

The story concerning the Baal Shem Tov involved the Tzaddik, Rabbi Yosef Safravildiver, father of Rabbi Yitzchok of Drovitch (Rabbi Yosef was the father-in-law of Rabbi Nachman Horodenker, hence the Rebbe's great-grandfather). He had heard that the Baal Shem Tov wanted to go to Israel, and told him, "You want to go like a king, and you will not arrive. But I will go like a beggar, and I will arrive." It turned out that way; the Baal Shem Tov's ship was destroyed and he was forced to return home (*Mazkeres Shem HaGedolim* 1a in note. Some other stories involving the Baal Shem Tov's pilgrimage to Israel, and why he was not successful, are told in *Kahal Chassidim* p. 10).

The Rebbe then visited the grave of Rabbi Naftali Katz of Pozen, who is buried in Istanbul (*Shevachey HaRan, Ibid.*).

Rabbi Naftali was the author of *S'michas Chachomim*. He set out on a pilgrimage to Israel but did not reach his goal and died in Istanbul on 26 Teves, 5479 (January 17, 1719) (Cf. *Chachmey Yisroel* p. 114; also see *Shem HaGedolim, Nun* 18). There is a story known to Breslover Chassidim regarding Rabbi Naftali. He wanted to go to Israel incognito. However, when he came to Istanbul, his identity became known, and the honor he received aroused Heavenly opposition. It was for this reason that he died (Cf. *Likutey Moharan* I, 67; 218; also see *Chayay Moharan* 32a #11, #139).

Upon his return from Rabbi Naftali's grave, the Rebbe suddenly fell critically ill. His illness lasted until the following afternoon. This was only one of the great dangers and countless obstacles that he faced each day he spent in Istanbul. The Rebbe said that it was the insults and childishness which sustained him (*Shevachey HaRan* p. 28 #12).

Tuesday, 28 Sivan; (June 12):

Napoleon and the French defeated the British and captured Malta in the Mediterranean.

Sunday, 17 Tammuz; (July 1):

Napoleon arrived in Egypt.

Monday, 18 Tammuz; (July 2):

Napoleon captured Alexandria.

Shabbos, 8 Av; (July 21):

The battle of the Pyramids, as a result of which Napoleon conquered all of Egypt.

Wednesday, 19 Av; (August 1):

Captain Nelson and the British defeated the French in the Battle of the Nile. The French lost all but two of their ships.

Elul; (September):

Turkey declared war on France (since Egypt had been under the dominion of the Turks).

When the Jewish community in Istanbul heard about the war in the Mediterranean, they refused to let any Jews embark on the sea (*Ibid.* p. 29 #14). However, a *chacham* from Jerusalem whose identity is unknown had come to Istanbul and had a revelation that he had to return to Israel to die there. He was allowed to hire a ship, and many, including the Rebbe, sailed with him (*Ibid.*). (This may have been Rabbi Avraham Azulai, son of the CHIDA, who in 5555 (1795), left Italy for Istanbul and the Holy Land. He died in Jerusalem in 5559 (1799); see *Shluchey Eretz Yisroel* p. 548).

Monday, 22 Elul; (September 3) approximately:

They set sail across the Mediterranean. There was a very violent storm, and everyone prayed fervently. The wife of the

Rabbi of Khottin criticized the Rebbe for not praying for them. The Rebbe told her that if they calmed down, so would the sea (*Ibid.*).

Tuesday, 23 Elul; (September 4):

At daybreak the sea calmed down (*Ibid.*).

The Rebbe had accustomed himself to eating practically nothing, using wisdom as his source of sustenance (see above p. 15). But now, at sea, he decided to change this practice and he began to eat a little (*Shevachey HaRan* p. 15 #21).

Thursday, 25 Elul; (September 6):

After a day or two, the supply of drinking water ran out, and they were in great danger (*Shevachey HaRan, Seder Nesiaso LeEretz Yisroel* p. 30 #15).

Friday, 26 Elul; (September 7):

They all prayed, and a strong wind came and brought them to Jaffa within forty-eight hours (*Ibid.* p. 31).

Sunday, 28 Elul; (September 9):

The ship docked at Jaffa, but the Rebbe was not allowed to disembark. Because of his dress and *peyos* the Turks refused him entry, fearing that he was a French spy (*Ibid.*).

7

HAIFA

Haifa is located at latitude 32.50°N longitude 35.00°E on the Mediterranean Sea coast of Israel. It has a deep natural bay and is thus an important port. The Jewish community at that time was relatively small.

Monday, 29 Elul, Erev Rosh HaShanah; (September 10):

That night the Rebbe sailed from Jaffa to Haifa. Before dawn, the ship stood near the foot of Mount Carmel, facing the cave of Eliyahu (Elijah's cave). After the morning prayers the passengers disembarked and the Rebbe was then able to stand on the Holy Soil for the very first time (*Shevachay HaRan, Seder Nesiaso LeEretz Yisroel* p. 31 #15). As soon as he had walked four cubits, the Rebbe attained the wisdom he had sacrificed so much for (*Ibid.* p. 32; *Chayay Moharan* 31b #6, #134; Cf. *Kesubos* 111b, 112a,b).

The Rebbe then went to the *mikvah* and to the synagogue, where he remained until after the Rosh HaShanah prayers (*Shevachey HaRan, Ibid.* p. 32).

5559 (1798-99)

Monday night, 1 Tishrei, 1st day of Rosh HaShanah; (September 10):

After services, the Rebbe went to his lodgings. He repeated "Happy are you." His followers, wanting him to pray for them in the Holy Land, had sent a list of their names. He now had his attendant read this list to him (*Ibid.* p. 32 #15).

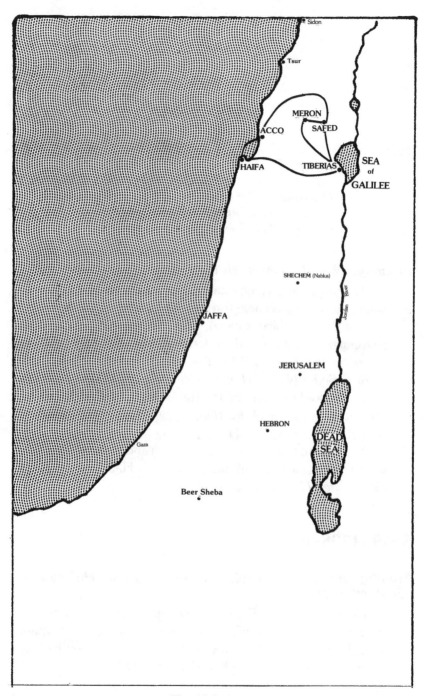

The Holy Land

Tuesday, 1 Tishrei, 1st day of Rosh HaShanah; (September 11):

After *davening* on the first day of Rosh HaShanah, he was very heartbroken and did not speak to anyone (*Ibid.*, *cf. Sichos HaRan* #21).

Thursday, 3 Tishrei, Fast of Gedalia; (September 13):

Right after Rosh HaShanah, the Rebbe wanted to return home. His attendant, however, wanted to go to Tiberias, and the Rebbe acquiesced. The attendant hired donkeys, but later fell sick, and their trip was delayed (*Shevachey HaRan, Ibid.* #16).

Tuesday, 8 Tishrei; (September 18) approximately:

Messengers were sent from the leading Rabbis in Tiberias, asking the Rebbe to visit them for Succos (*Ibid.* #17).

Thursday, 10 Tishrei, Yom Kippur; (September 20):

The messengers from Tiberias came to visit the Rebbe in Haifa, but he refused their request (*Ibid.*).

Sunday, 13 Tishrei; (September 23):

The Rebbe bought *esrogim* for Succos (*Ibid.*). There was an incident involving a Turk who befriended Rabbi Nachman. One day the Turk came with weapons angrily seeking the Rebbe. The Rebbe had to flee to the house of Rabbi Zev Wolf of Charni-Ostrov. The Turk later returned saying he wanted to help the Rebbe and that the Rebbe could have his horse and donkeys to make the trip to Tiberias. He need no longer fear him. Rabbi Nachman said later that this was Satan himself (*Ibid.*).

Thursday, 17 Tishrei, 1st day of Chol HaMoed Succos; (September 27):

Everyone went to the cave of Eliyahu where there was great rejoicing, but the Rebbe was very brokenhearted (*Ibid.* p. 33 #18). The Rebbe contemplated how the Prophet Eliyahu became worthy of his high level through *hisbodedus* (secluded prayer) (*Kochavey Or* p. 76 #23; *Aveneha Barzel* p. 61 #24; also see below, p. 130. Regarding *hisbodedus* by prophets, see *Yad, Yesodey HaTorah* 8:4, *Shaarey Kedusha* Introduction; *Kuntres HaHisbodedus*).

Wednesday, 23 Tishrei, Simchas Torah; (October 3):

The Rebbe's mood had not changed and he did not want to dance with the Torah (*Shevachey HaRan, ibid.* #18).

Thursday, 24 Tishrei; (October 4):

The day after the holiday, the Rebbe wanted to return home immediately. His attendant, however, again refused to go, since he wanted to visit Tiberias. The Rebbe agreed (*Ibid.*).

On this day, Rabbi Shneur Zalman was taken to prison. He had been denounced to the Prosecutor-General in St. Petersburg as a political agitator (*Tanya, Toldos Rabbenu HaZaken* p. 207; *HaTamim* p. 214a). (This might have been a reason why the Rebbe was so brokenhearted.)

Sunday, 27 Tishrei; (October 7) approximately:

The Rebbe left Haifa to go to Tiberias (*Shevachay HaRan, ibid.*).

8

TIBERIAS

Tiberias is situated on the western shore of the Sea of Galilee latitude 32.47°N longitude 35.32°E. At this time it was the site of the major Chassidic community in Israel. They were ruled by an intolerant Turkish governor and afflicted with severe debts.

Monday night, 29 Tishrei; (October 8):

The Rebbe arrived in Tiberias and stayed in the house of a cousin, a grandson of Rabbi Nachman Horodenker.[9] People came to him all that night dressed in their Sabbath garments (*Shevachay HaRan, Seder Nesiaso LeEretz Yisroel* #18).

Tuesday, 29 Tishrei; (October 9):

During the day, the Rebbe moved his lodgings to the house of Rabbi Zvi Harker (*Ibid.*).

That day, the Rebbe met for the first time with Rabbi Avraham Kalisker, head of the Chassidim in Israel (*Ibid.*).

Wednesday, 30 Tishrei, Rosh Chodesh Cheshvon; (October 10):

Rabbi Avraham Kalisker invited the Rebbe for the Sabbath (*Ibid.*).

---

9. It appears that this cousin was the son of R. Shimshon, the son of Rabbi Nachman Horodenker, mentioned in *Shevachey HaBaal Shem Tov* p. 126 (see text above p. 2). It is also possible that this R. Shimshon was the R. Shimshon Horshenki mentioned in *Igeres HaKodesh* #13 from the year 5546 (1786). Horshenki might have been meant to be Horodenki, since the letters Daled and Shin look somewhat alike in Rashi script. That letter mentions that he is the "old rabbi" and that he had a son and daughter in Tiberias.

Shabbos, 3 Cheshvon, Torah reading, Noach; (October 13):

The Rebbe spent the Sabbath with Rabbi Avraham Kalisker. The Rebbe asked Rabbi Avraham to bless him, but he declined. Rabbi Avraham then gave a wondrous lesson (*Ibid.*).

Sunday, 4 Cheshvon; (October 14):

Rabbi Avraham visited the Rebbe, and they spoke for a long time (*Ibid.* p. 35 #19). It is possible that they then discussed the dispute between Rabbi Avraham and Rabbi Shneur Zalman. The Rebbe promised Rabbi Avraham that, upon his return to Europe, he would go to Rabbi Shneur Zalman to try to make peace between them (*Aveneha Barzel* p. 34 #46). The Rebbe also met Rabbi Yisroel Eliezer, the grandson of Rabbi Avraham (Cf. the letter of Rabbi Avraham in *Chayay Moharan* p. 33b, #150. It is likely that this Rabbi Yisroel was the son of Rabbi Alexander, son of Rabbi Avraham, whose name is signed in letter #11 in *Igros Kodesh*).

Tuesday, 6 Cheshvon; (October 16) approximately:

The Rebbe fell sick and sent a *pidyon* to Rabbi Avraham. Rabbi Avraham visited him daily (*Shevachey HaRan, Ibid.*)

At this time, there was a Jewish informer who had been causing much trouble for the Tiberias community. His influence with the Pasha had won him the position of overseer of the city and he returned to Tiberias with an army of Turkish soldiers. Seeing the arrival of these troops, the men of Tiberias fled in terror. The Rebbe would have gone with them but, because of his infirmity, he was forced to stay behind. Using his great wisdom, Rabbi Nachman was able to subdue this informer, and the people were able to return in peace (*Ibid.*).

After this, the Rebbe visited the grave of his grandfather, Rabbi Nachman Horodenker (*Ibid.* Regarding the date of

Rabbi Nachman Horodenker's death, see *Pischey Chaim* p. 26.)

The Rebbe then went to the graves of Rabbi Shimon bar Yochai, and of Hillel and Shamai in Meron. He also visited the graves of Rabbi Kruspadai (mentioned in the *Zohar*; Cf. *Pischey Chaim* p. 27), and the holy child in Safed (*Ibid.*).

Upon returning to Tiberias, the Rebbe sent his attendant to Haifa to secure passage on a ship to return to Europe. There the attendant met Rabbi Yaakov Shimshon of Shepetevka (*Ibid.*). He had been sent by Rabbi Baruch, the Rebbe's uncle, to administer the distribution of the money he had sent to Israel (*Chachmey Yisroel* p. 186). Rabbi Yaakov Shimshon feared the Turkish troops who, because of the informer, were on the lookout for recently arrived foreigners carrying large sums of money. He therefore persuaded the Rebbe's attendant to return to Tiberias with the money he had brought (*Shevachey HaRan* p. 36. Regarding Rabbi Yaakov Shimshon, see *Pischey Chaim* p. 27).

The Rebbe saw that numerous obstacles were blocking his attempts to return home and understood that it was meant for him to stay a while longer in the Holy Land. He ordered his attendant to hire donkeys for a trip to Jerusalem, but Rabbi Avraham asked that he remain in Tiberias (*Shevachey HaRan, ibid.* p. 37).

Rabbi Yaakov Shimshon came to Tiberias and made a great feast in honor of the Rebbe, where they spoke together for a long time (*Ibid.* p. 37). Since Rabbi Shneur Zalman had already cast aspersions on Rabbi Avraham's handling of the charity funds, Rabbi Yaakov Shimshon's arrival as overseer was understandably not welcome. It also seems that there had been some earlier dispute between Rabbi Yaakov Shimshon and Rabbi Avraham (*Igeres Baal HaTanya* #98 p. 156). The Rebbe, however, made peace between them (*Shevachey HaRan, Ibid.*).

The Rebbe gave a lesson which was later incorporated into *Likutey Moharan* 117. This lesson was said in the company of several great Tzaddikim, including Rabbi Yaakov Shimshon (see *Parparaos LeChokhmah, ad loc.*).[10]

When the Rebbe had first come to Tiberias, a great Rabbi and Kabbalist who was said to be expert in the entire Talmud, knowing it almost by heart, had visited him. He asked the Rebbe to tell him the deeper reason for his pilgrimage. The Rebbe told him that it had to do with the concept of *tefillin*, but he was prevented from completing his explanation (*Shevachey HaRan* p. 53 #31; See *Likutey Moharan* I, 47; II, 40).

Around that time, the Rebbe also made a match between his third daughter Miriam and a son of Rabbi Moshe, son of Rabbi Menachem Mendel of Vitebsk. (In the introduction of *Likutey Amarim* of Rabbi Menachem Mendel, old edition, there is a reference to a son of Rabbi Moshe known as Reb Shmuel.) A great feast was made, and among the guests were all the leaders of the community. The great Rabbi, who had asked the Rebbe why he had come to Israel, was also there. The guests could not find the source of a *Rashi* that they needed for their discussion. The Rebbe told them that it was in *Zevachim*, and showed them the place (*Shevachey HaRan* p. 54 #11).[11]

Rabbi Moshe and his son died soon after the Rebbe left for Europe (*Ibid.*).

Tuesday, 19 Kislev; (November 27):

Rabbi Shneur Zalman was freed from prison (*Tanya, Toldos Rabbenu HaZaken* p. 207; *HaTamim* p. 214b).

---

10. Since this is the only time that it is recorded that the Rebbe was in the company of Rabbi Yaakov Shimshon, it is likely that this was said at that time (see next note).

11. There is a tradition that it was on p. 45a which speaks about "a law for the Messiah." This Rashi would connect up with the lesson in *Likutey Moharan* 117, discussed earlier. The "great Rabbi" might then be identified as Rabbi Yaakov Shimshon. It may be that his name was not mentioned out of respect.

Friday, 29 Kislev; (December 7):

Rabbi Mordechai of Lechovitz was freed from prison. He had been arrested together with Rabbi Shneur Zalman (*MiGedoley HaChassidim* 20:79). He was then made the overseer of the money sent to Israel. He was also a disciple of Rabbi Baruch (*Ibid.*).

Tuesday, 30 Shevat; (February 5, 1799):

Napoleon received a letter from Europe through a wine ship from Ragusa, a city state in Yugoslavia, today known as Dubrovnik. This was the first letter in five months to reach him through the British blockade (see below Thursday, 7 Adar II). This might be the reason why people thought it safe to sail on Ragusan ships through the blockade (see *Shevachey HaRan* p. 38 #20).

Around this time, a plague broke out in Tiberias, and the Rebbe had to flee from his lodgings (*Shevachey HaRan* p. 37 #19).

Thursday, 30 Adar I; (March 7):

Napoleon conquered Jaffa. There was also a plague there.

Sunday, 3 Adar II; (March 10) approximately:

The Rebbe had to leave Tiberias because of the plague. He was in great danger when he left. Climbing over the city's wall, he almost fell into the Sea of Galilee (*Ibid.*; also see *Sichos HaRan* #117).

Monday, 4 Adar II; (March 11) approximately:

The Rebbe arrived in Safed (*Ibid.*).

Thursday, 7 Adar II; (March 14):

Napoleon left Jaffa to go to Acco. When the Rebbe heard about this, he sent his attendant to book passage on a Ragusan ship. He also received letters from Rabbi Avraham and the community (*Ibid.* p. 38 #20).

Friday, 8 Adar II; (March 15):

The Rebbe left Safed on Thursday night and came to Acco three hours before the Sabbath. He was not permitted to board the ship on which his attendant had booked passage, because it was already filled to capacity. Instead, he spent Shabbos with one of the followers of Rabbi Avraham (*Ibid.*).

Shabbos, 9 Adar II, Shabbos Zachor; Torah reading, Vayikra; (March 16):

The gates of Acco were closed. There were fifteen thousand Turkish soldiers there (*Ibid.*) under the Turkish general, Jezar.

There were no more Ragusan ships on which to travel. The agent advised the Rebbe that it would be better to risk being taken captive on a Turkish merchant ship, than to remain in the city, where many people were sure to be killed (*Ibid.*).

Captain Sidney Smith had captured Napoleon's ships on the way to Acco. The name of Captain Smith's ship was the *Tigres*. He had two other warships with him, the *Thesius* and the *Alliance*.

Sunday, 10 Adar II; (March 17):

Napoleon came to Acco and laid siege to the city (*Ibid.* p. 41). The density of the crowds made it difficult for the troops to move efficiently and the Turks commanded that all who could not bear arms must leave the city or be killed (*Ibid.*). Amidst·the great panic and confusion, the Rebbe boarded a bark which he thought would bring him to his ship in Haifa, unaware that he was about to board a warship (*Ibid.* The British and Turks defeated Napoleon and he left Acco on 15 Iyar, May 20.)

9

THE RETURN VOYAGE

Monday, 11 Adar II; (March 18):

The ship carrying the Rebbe left Haifa. Neither he nor his attendant had been able to prepare provisions for the voyage, and they were very sick (*Shevachey HaRan* p. 42 #21).

Monday, 18 Adar II; (March 25) approximately:

The ship docked at Adalia (now known as Antalya) on the coast of Turkey. Rabbi Nachman and his attendant were in very great danger. It was a known custom in Antalya that any Jew falling into the hands of the natives would be killed as a human sacrifice. They remained hiding in their locked cabin for three days (*Ibid.*).

Wednesday, 20 Adar II; (March 27):

A strong wind swept the ship back to near Acco (*Ibid.*).

Thursday, 21 Adar II; (March 28):

The ship approached Acco in the morning. That afternoon saw the start of another strong wind which blew for several days (*Ibid.*).

Thursday, 28 Adar II; (April 4):

The ship was filling with water which could not be pumped out fast enough (*Ibid.*).

Friday, 29 Adar II; (April 5):

The ship continued filling with water and was in great danger of sinking. The Rebbe, for the first time in his life, prayed in the merit of his ancestors, the Baal Shem Tov, Rabbi Nachman Horodenker, and his grandmother Adil (*Ibid.*; see *Chayay Moharan* 29a #14, #117). The source of

The Return Voyage

the leak was then found, and the Rebbe said *Hodu* (Psalm 107) before *Minchah* with great joy (*Ibid.*; Cf. *Sichos HaRan* #270).

Nissan; April:

The ship continued on, passing several places. They had nothing to eat except for some rotten vegetables which the cook gave them (*Ibid.*). They were studying *Mishnah*. When they reached the words "Rabbi Yehoshua said, 'Who will remove the dust from your eyes, Rabbi Yochanan ben Zakai, that you were wont to say, *a future generation...*' " (*Sotah* 5:2), the Rebbe rejoiced and said that a great thing was revealed to him in this *Mishnah* (*Chayay Moharan* 32b #13, #141).

They were very worried that they would have nothing to eat for Passover. They reached an island and bought carobs. But they still did not have any *matzah*, which deeply disturbed them. They were also worried lest the captain sell them for slaves. The Rebbe then attained the understanding that he could fulfill the entire Torah even in a faraway land, just as the Patriarchs had done prior to the giving of the Torah (*Shevachey HaRan* p. 46; see *Chayay Moharan*, *Ibid.* #14, #142).

RHODES

The capital city at the northeastern corner of the Island of Rhodes in the Aegean Sea, latitude 36.26°N longitude 28.13°E. There was an important Sephardic community there. At that time the island was ruled by the Turks.

Thursday night, 14 Nissan; (April 19):

The ship approached Rhodes and anchored off the coast (*Ibid.* p. 46 #22).

On Friday morning — the morning before Pesach — the Rebbe and his attendant were overjoyed to learn that the ship's captain had unexpectedly given permission for the attendant to join a party which was to go ashore on a small boat and enter the city. There the attendant met with the Chief Rabbi. Telling him the whole story, the attendant suddenly remembered that Rabbi Zvi Harker's wife had a brother who was a *chacham* in Rhodes, though he could not remember the *chacham's* name. The Chief Rabbi knew who the *chacham* was and sent the attendant to him.

As soon as he arrived, the *chacham* assured him that the community would meet any ransom necessary to free them. When he heard that the attendant's companion was the great grandson of the Baal Shem Tov, and a very great sage in his own right, he was overjoyed at the opportunity to redeem someone so distinguished. He provided the attendant with all the Pesach necessities for himself and the Rebbe. The attendant then returned to the boat (*Ibid.* p. 47 #23).

Friday night, 15 Nissan, 1st night of Pesach; (April 20):

The Rebbe and his attendant made the *Seder* on board ship (*Ibid.* p. 49).

Shabbos morning, 1st day of Passover; (April 21):

The ship docked at Rhodes (*Ibid.*).

Saturday night, 16 Nissan, 2nd Seder night; (April 21):

This Seder was also held on board ship (*Ibid.*).

Sunday, 2nd day of Passover; (April 22):

The Rebbe's attendant prayed in the city. He was invited to the *chacham's* house for the festival meal and repeated some of the Rebbe's teachings. The *chacham* was deeply impressed (*Ibid.*).

When the attendant returned he appeared depressed and the Rebbe was deeply concerned that their situation might have taken a turn for the worse. The attendant did not reply to the Rebbe's questions but went to sleep. Later he explained that his host in the city had given him a lot of wine and this had made him appear depressed (*Ibid.*).

Monday, 17 Nissan, 1st day of Chol HaMoed; (April 23):

The Rhodes community redeemed the Rebbe, and his attendant for two hundred thalers and they were able to enter the city (*Ibid.* #24). The Rebbe gained the respect of the Jewish community there (*Ibid.* p. 50 #25).

After Passover, they booked passage on a ship to Istanbul. There was a plague on the ship, but after three days they arrived. The Rebbe did not have the proper papers, and therefore had to remain in Istanbul for ten days. A stranger got the necessary papers for them (*Ibid.*).

They then sailed on the Black Sea to Galatz, Walachei.

On the way they were imprisoned on an island in the Black Sea. They had to give four rubles per person before they were freed (*Ibid.* The only island in this part of the Black Sea is Seprans Island, also known as Ostrov Zmeinyj).

Friday, 4 Sivan; (June 7) approximately:

The Rebbe arrived in Galatz (since Erev Shavuos fell on Shabbos; *Ibid.*).

Sunday, 6 Sivan, Shavuos; (June 9):

The Rebbe spent the holiday in Galatz (*Ibid.*).

Tuesday, 8 Sivan; (June 11) most probably:

The Rebbe left Galatz and headed toward Iassi (Jasse) (*Ibid.* p. 51 #26. The distance between Iassi and Galatz is one hundred and eight miles (178 km.), a journey of some three days.)

Thursday, 10 Sivan; (June 13) approximately:

The Rebbe arrived in Iassi (*Ibid.*). There was a plague there at this time (*Ibid.*). It is possible that they spent Shabbos in Iassi.

They then crossed the Dniester River (*Chayay Moharan*

32b #17, #145). It was very difficult for them to cross the border because of the epidemic (*Shevachey HaRan, Ibid.*) and they had to change their clothing and disguise themselves as merchants (*Chayay Moharan, Ibid.*).

Friday, 18 Sivan; (June 21):

The Rebbe came to Teplik. He wanted to spend Shabbos with a certain *melamed*, but the latter would not allow him to, thinking him to be a thief (*Ibid.*)

Shabbos, 19 Sivan, Torah reading, Behaalosecha; (June 22):

They spent Shabbos in Teplik (*Ibid.*).

Sunday, 20 Sivan; (June 23):

The Rebbe came to Uman. The lodgings which had been arranged by their driver turned out to be a place of sin. Leaving quickly, the Rebbe remarked on the great temptations that exist in the world. He said that because of his presence there the immorality in that place would cease (*Ibid.* Uman is less than a day's journey from Teplik; Cf. *Yemey Moharnat* 34b.)

Monday, 21 Sivan; (June 24):

The Rebbe arrived in Kaniblad, and Rabbi Yekusiel, the Magid of Terhovitza, ran a half *parsa* (that is, about three miles or five kilometers) to greet him (*Chayay Moharan* 33a #21, #149). The distance between Uman and Kaniblad is twenty-seven miles (43 km.), a day's journey.

Tuesday, 22 Sivan; (June 25):

The Rebbe next came to Shpola and stayed with Rabbi Leib, the Shpola Zeida. They spoke together all that night (*Chayay Moharan* 32b #18, #146). From Kaniblad to Shpola is forty-seven miles (or 75 km.), a journey of a little over a day. In Shpola they finally had a chance to change their clothing.

Wednesday, 23 Sivan; (June 26):

The Rebbe returned home to Medvedevka (the distance from Shpola to Medvedevka was forty-four miles (or 70 km.), a day's journey).

When he arrived home, he did not even stop at his house, but immediately went to see Rabbi Shneur Zalman as he had promised Rabbi Avraham Kalisker (*Chayay Moharan* 26b #10, #113; *Aveneha Barzel* 34 #46).

Thursday, Rosh Chodesh Tammuz; (July 4) approximately:

The Rebbe came to Liozna, where Rabbi Shneur Zalman lived until his move to Liadi in 5561. From Medvedevka to Liozna was some four hundred and fifty miles (or 700 km.), a journey of some eight days.

They spoke together about the community in Israel (*Chayay Moharan, Ibid.*). In particular, they discussed the controversy involving the distribution of funds, and the Rebbe tried to calm the situation. But in the end, it did not help. (This was the Rebbe's trip to Reissin, which was the state in which Liozna was located, cited in the letter of Rabbi Avraham Kalisker, mentioned in *Chayay Moharan* 33b, #150; Appendix, letter #9.)

It was requested that the Rebbe give a lesson but he refused. Rabbi Shneur Zalman then spoke for eight hours (*Aveneha Barzel, Ibid.*).

Friday, 9 Tammuz; (July 12) approximately:

The Rebbe returned home to Medvedevka.

Shabbos, 10 Tammuz, Torah reading, Chukas; (July 13) most probably:

The Rebbe stayed in his room for several hours and did not come out to the Shabbos table. Rabbi Shimon entered his room and saw him crying. The Rebbe then came out and said, "I have brought you a present from Israel, and the present is strife!" (Oral tradition; Cf. *Manuscript* p. 18). The

Rebbe then said a lesson on the verse (Numbers 21:8) "Make yourself a serpent" (from the portion of Chukas) (*Chayay Moharan* 32b #15, #143).

At the third meal, the Rebbe said a lesson on the verse (Isaiah 43:2) "When you cross the waters, I am with you." This is printed in *Likutey Moharan* 73 (*Ibid.* 32b #15; Cf. *Parparaos LeChokhmah, ad loc.*). This lesson is marked "*leshon chaverim*," that is, it was written by Rabbi Avraham Peterberger (see above p. 17).

Friday, 22 Av, (August 23):

Napoleon, who was having great difficulty overcoming the British, was sent a European newspaper from Captain Sidney Smith. It stated that Italy had fallen and there was a precarious situation in France. Napoleon then abandoned his Middle East campaign and returned to France.

At about this time, the Rebbe made a match between his oldest daughter Adil and Yoska, the son of Rabbi Avraham Dov of Chmelnick (*Chayay Moharan* 26b #10, #113; also see *Shemos HaTzaddikim*. In a letter from the Rebbe from Zaslov, printed in *Alim LeTerufah*, the Rebbe calls him Reb Yoshe; see Appendix letter #4).

Rabbi Avraham Dov Ohrbach, the Rabbi of Chmelnick, was a disciple of both the Mezritcher Magid and Rabbi Yaakov Yosef of Polonnoye, author of the *Toldos Yaakov Yosef* (*Shem HaGedolim HeChadash, Aleph* 46). He married the granddaughter of Rabbi Yaakov Yosef, and helped print his book (see title page of original 1780 edition of *Toldos Yaakov Yosef*, printed in Koretz; also see *Chachmey Yisroel* p. 208). After Rabbi Yaakov Yosef died, Rabbi Avraham Dov became Rabbi in Polonnoye (*Shem HaGedolim HeChadash, Ibid.*).

Besides his son Reb Yoska who married the Rebbe's daughter, he had a son Reb Yaakov Pinchas, who married Adil, daughter of Rabbi Baruch of Medzeboz (*Chachmey Yisroel* p. 210). He was also related by marriage to Rabbi

Nissan, the father of Sarah, wife of Rabbi Aharon of Breslov (*Tzava'ah* of the Rav of Tcherin, in *Kochavey Or* p. 63).

Adil, the Rebbe's daughter, later had a son, Reb Avraham Dov, who was named after her father-in-law.

Before Rabbi Nathan came to the Rebbe, one of the Chassidic leaders he went to see was Rabbi Avraham Dov (*Alim LeTerufah* #181). Rabbi Nathan visited him in Shevat 5571, after the Rebbe died (*Yemey Moharnat* 48b). In 5581 after Passover, he was in Chmelnick for Rabbi Avraham Dov's *yahrzeit* (*Ibid.* 88b).

During this period, Rabbi Yekusiel, the Magid of Terhovitza, came to the Rebbe and the Rebbe discussed the generation and its preachers (*Chayay Moharan* 32b #16, #145).

The emissary from Israel that year was Rabbi Eliezer, and he visited the Rebbe bearing news from the Holy Land (letter from Rabbi Avraham Kalisker in *Chayay Moharan* 33b, #150; see Appendix, letter #9).

10

MEDVEDEVKA 5560 (1799-1800)

Tuesday, 2 Shevat; (January 28, 1800):

The saintly Rabbi Zusia of Anipoli died (*Chachmey Yisroel* p. 181). One of his disciples was Reb Yitzchok, the son-in-law of the Magid of Terhovitza. Before Rabbi Zusia died, he told Reb Yitzchok to find a mentor who prescribed *viduy*, i.e. a Rebbe who had his followers confess and to whom he would then prescribe spiritual practices through which they could rectify their souls. It was through this that Reb Yitzchok became a follower of the Rebbe, who practiced *viduy* and whose followers were known as *Viduynikers* — confessors (see below pp. 66, 68; *Kochavey Or* p. 29 #24).

Shevat; (January-February):

Emissaries came from Europe to Israel, and brought Rabbi Avraham Kalisker news from the Rebbe. Rabbi Avraham wrote to the Rebbe that he had not yet received the charity funds they had discussed during the Rebbe's stay in Tiberias (*Chayay Moharan* 33b, #150).

Friday, 2 Nissan; (March 28):

The Rebbe came to Neskhiz to visit Rabbi Mordechai, who was then very sick (*Chayay Moharan* 27a #10, #113; also see *Aveneha Barzel* p. 10). Rabbi Mordechai was one of the great Tzaddikim of his generation, a close disciple of Rabbi Michel of Zlotchov. He was also involved in collecting money for Israel (*Chachmey Yisroel* p. 182). Rabbi Avraham Yehoshua Heschel of Apta was then visiting the Chozeh of Lublin. When he heard how greatly the Chozeh praised Rabbi Mordechai, he wanted to go to Neskhiz but he delayed his visit since it was so close to Pesach. Before he could get there, Rabbi Mordechai had died (*Mazkeres Shem HaGedolim* p. 51b; *MiGedoley HaChassidus* 20:18).

Shabbos, 3 Nissan, Torah reading, Vayikra; (March 29):

Rabbi Mordechai had a special meal prepared for the Rebbe. Though he had not left his bed for over half a year, his love and respect for Rabbi Nachman were so great that he overcame his weakness and joined the Rebbe at this meal. The Rebbe spent Shabbos with Rabbi Mordechai in Neskhiz (*Chayay Moharan, Ibid.*).

Rabbi Mordechai was known for his *ruach hakodesh*. During this visit, the Rebbe differed with him over the interpretations of some of his visions (*Ibid.*).

Sunday, 4 Nissan; (March 30) most probably:

Rabbi Mordechai sent a *pidyon* of ten rubles to the Rebbe (*Ibid.*).

Wednesday, 7 Nissan; (April 2):

The Rebbe left Neskhiz and Rabbi Mordechai escorted him, despite his weakness (*Ibid.*).

Thursday, 8 Nissan; (April 3):

Rabbi Mordechai died (*Chachmey Yisroel, Mazkeres Shem HaGedolim, Ibid.*).

Soon after he left Neskhiz the Rebbe visited Rabbi Zvi Aryeh of Alik (*Chayay Moharan, Ibid.*).

Rabbi Zvi Aryeh was a disciple of Rabbi Michel of Zlotchov (*Chachmey Yisroel* p. 209, *Shem HaGedolim HeChadash, Tzadi* 1). Rabbi Nathan said of him that he was very pious, to which the Rebbe added that he was very wise (*Aveneha Barzel* p. 39 #59).

On this visit, the Rebbe disputed with him, as he had with Rabbi Mordechai, regarding the interpretation of visions (*Chayay Moharan, Ibid.*).

Tuesday, 17 Iyar; (May 12):

Rabbi Ephraim of Sudylkov, the grandson of the Baal

Shem Tov and uncle of the Rebbe, died. Before his death he had moved back to Medzeboz (*Chachmey Yisroel* p. 182).

Thursday night, 1 Elul; (August 21):

The marriage of the Rebbe's daughter Adil to Rabbi Yoska, son of Rabbi Avraham Dov of Chmelnick. The Rebbe's entire family, including his mother, was present (*Chayay Moharan* 27b #11, #114).

Friday, 8 Elul; (August 29):

The seven days of celebration for the wedding ended.

Right after the wedding, the Rebbe made a match between his daughter Miriam and R. Pinchas, son of Rabbi Leibush, Rabbi of Volochisk (*Ibid.;* Cf. *Shemos HaTzaddikim*). Miriam had already been betrothed to the grandson of Rabbi Menachem Mendel of Vitebsk, but he died before the Rebbe returned from Israel (see above p. 44).

Rabbi Leibush signed his name Aryeh Yehuda Leib ben Shalom Segel (Segel, indicating that he was a Levite) (*haskama* to *Amud HaAvodah*). He originally came from Zbarez (see his *haskama* to *Ginzey Yosef*). He was a major disciple of the Mezritcher Magid (*Shem HaGedolim HeChadash, Lamed* 15).

In 5550 (1790) he gave a *haskama* to the book *Ginzey Yosef*, by Rabbi Yosef of Halshitz. In 5552 (1792) he gave a *haskama* to *Ahavas Dodim*, by Rabbi Binyamin of Zlazitz. He was then Rabbi in Iassi. On 28 Sivan, 5555 (1795), he gave a *haskama* to *Amud HaAvodah* by Rabbi Baruch Kassover. Finally in the year 5558, he gave a *haskama* to the book *Meiras Eynayim* by Rabbi Nochum of Tchernoble.

In the summer of 5565 he settled in Israel, (see below p. 115f). While on the way, he gave a *haskama* to the book *Taharas HaKodesh* (Cf. *Mishnas Yoel* p. 88; *Shem HaGedolim HeChadash, Sefarim, Tes* 2).[12]

---

12. Besides R. Pinchas, the son-in-law of the Rebbe, Rabbi Leibush had another son by the name of Yosef Yoska, who was also Rabbi in Iassi. He

Rabbi Leibush was the author of the book *Ahavas Shalom*. He died on 23 Nissan, 5573 in Safed (*Igros Baal HaTanya* p. 188, note on letter #108). He was buried in a cave between the grave of the ARI and the Bais Yosef, where Rabbi Dovid Shlomo, Rabbi of Soroke, author of the *Levushey S'rad* and Rabbi Avraham Dov Ohrbach of Ovorich, author of the *Bas Ayin* were later buried (*Toldos Chachmey Yerushalayim*, by Reb Aryeh Leib Frumkin, Jerusalem, 5529 3:76; also see *Yemey Moharnat* p. 135b #142).

Sunday, 10 Elul; (August 31) approximately:

The Rebbe left Chmelnick, and moved to Zlatipolia (*Ibid.*).

---

also had a son, Reb Sh., who was married in 5562 (*Chayay Moharan* 29b #19, #122) and a daughter who was married to the grandson of the Chozeh of Lublin. (In a letter to Rabbi Levi Yitzchok from the Chozeh printed in *Igros Baal HaTanya*, Letter #108, and in *Mishnas Yoel* p. 87, it is mentioned that they were *mechutonim*. In addition, in *Niflaos HaRabbi* 157, mentioned in *MiGedoley HaChassidim* 19:123, we find that Rabbi Zvi Hirsh, son of the Chozeh, married the daughter of Rabbi Leibush. We also find there that his daughter Tzirel married Rabbi Shmuel, Rabbi of Resha. It is possible that this is Reb Sh. mentioned earlier.) It could be because of this that the Chozeh mentions that the Rebbe is related to him by marriage in his *haskama* to *Likutey Moharan*. That is, he is related through Rabbi Leibush.

Rabbi Leibush had another son, Reb Feivish, who saw Rabbi Nathan when the latter was in Safed in 5582 (*Yemey Moharnat* 134b #137). One of his sons was in Europe in 5571 when the Rebbe died (*Ibid.* 46a). Rabbi Leibush's grandson, Rabbi Avraham Yosef, married the daughter of Rabbi Naftali Zvi, grandson of the Baal Shem Tov (*Igeres HaKodesh* 63, letter of Rabbi Aharon the Second of Karlin).

ZLATIPOLIA; 5560 (1800)

Zlatipolia is located at latitude 49.00°N longitude 32.10°E, about seventy-five miles (135km.) east of Uman, close to Shpola.

Wednesday, 13 Elul; (September 3) approximately:

The Rebbe came to Zlatipolia with his family directly from the wedding. He came into the city without having informed anyone, and had not asked for permission. He merely rented an apartment, and settled there (*Chayay Moharan* 27b #11, #114. The Rebbe left Chmelnick on Sunday, approximately, and the distance was one hundred sixty three miles (or 263 km.), a journey of four days).

Zlatipolia was seventeen and a half miles (28.5 km.) from Shpola. The Shpola Zeida had also spent eight years as *shamesh* in the synagogue in Zlatipolia (*Chachmey Yisroel* p. 209).

The Rebbe rented an apartment in Zlatipolia from Reb Yekusiel, one of his followers, who lived there (*Yemey Moharnat* 93b). The Rebbe lived on the second floor, facing a courtyard with several other houses (*Tovos Zichronos* # 6 p. 119).

Friday, 29 Elul, Erev Rosh HaShanah; (September 19):

Around a hundred people came to Zlatipolia to be with the Rebbe for Rosh HaShanah. Though the Rebbe had not made any previous arrangements, the people of the community accommodated all these guests. They urged the Rebbe to pray in the large synagogue with all his followers. He was told that everything in the synagogue would be conducted in accordance with his wishes (*Chayay Moharan, Ibid.*).

11

ZLATIPOLIA; 5561 (1800-1801)

Shabbos, 1 Tishrei, Rosh HaShanah; (September 20, 1800):
The Rebbe worshiped in the great synagogue with his followers. He had been received with great respect by the inhabitants of Zlatipolia and he was at ease there (*Chayay Moharan, Ibid.*).

At *sholosh se'udos* (most probably), the Rebbe said a lesson on the verse (Samuel I, 2:10) "He gives strength to His king" (which is in the *haftorah* of the first day of Rosh HaShanah). This is in *Likutey Moharan* 78 (*Chayay Moharan* 15a #59, #59, *Parparaos LeChokhmah, ad loc.*). This lesson refers to speech, and also alludes to *viduy*.

Monday, 10 Tishrei, Yom Kippur; (September 29):
A certain man led the *Minchah* service. His son-in-law then began to lead the *Neilah* prayer. The Rebbe, however, did not approve, and the man lost his voice in the middle of the prayers. The Rebbe wanted to pray for the retraction of the Russian decrees endangering Jewish distillery rights — one of the main bases of Jewish economic life (see Introduction) but the way the man prayed caused much opposition on High (*Chayay Moharan* 27b #11, #114).

That night, the Rebbe made a joke about these men, and said that they were praying to impress their wives (*Ibid.*).

Tuesday, 11 Tishrei; (September 30):
The cantor went to the Shpola Zeida, complaining about the Rebbe. He also slandered about the Rebbe (*Ibid.*). Some also say that he complained that the Rebbe had changed a number of customs that the Shpola Zeida had instituted when he was in Zlatipolia.

There is another legend that a follower of Rabbi Shneur Zalman from Byela Cherkov (Sadeh Lavan), who was very learned and rich, became extremely jealous of the Rebbe. He made amulets, and hired false witnesses to testify before the Shpola Zeida that these were distributed by the Rebbe. They also concocted stories that the Rebbe was making use of Sacred Names for incantations. These stories were at least partly responsible for the great opposition of the Shpola Zeida to the Rebbe (*Meoros HaGedolim* p. 6a).

A short time after Succos, the Shpola Zeida came to Zlatipolia and spoke very strongly against the Rebbe (*Chayay Moharan* 28a, #114). (The Shpoler was also a close friend of Rabbi Shneur Zalman. Even today, the Lubavitcher Chassidim sing *Kol BaYaar* and *Hap Kazak*, two of his songs.)

When the dispute began, the Rebbe said, "I knew that the Evil One would stand up against me, but I am very surprised that this one was placed in his hand" (*Chayay Moharan* 29b #211; also see *Ibid*. 33a #18, #146).

A fierce conflict broke out between the followers of the Rebbe and those of the Shpola, and they came close to stoning one another (*Meoros HaGedolim* 6b). The latter also made up various stories about the Rebbe (*Ibid*. 6a; *Chayay Moharan, Ibid.*; also see *Sichos Moharan* 17a #1-4, #392-395; *Sichos HaRan* #182, 211, 212, 213).

This dispute caused nearly the whole town of Zlatipolia to turn against the Rebbe (*Chayay Moharan* 27b #11, #114).

When Rabbi Yaakov Shimshon of Shepetevka heard of the slander against the Rebbe, he cursed them with the Talmudic curse (*Sotah* 35a), "May their tongue become stretched to their belly" (*Chayay Moharan* 33a #18, #146).

Monday, 24 Tishrei; (October 13):

The day after Simchas Torah, Rabbi Shneur Zalman was arrested and brought to St. Petersberg (*Rabbi Shneur Zalman of Liadi* p. 231). His arrest was brought about through Rabbi Avigdor ben Chaim, who was Rabbi in Pinsk. One of Rabbi Avigdor's complaints was that Rabbi Shneur Zalman was sending large sums of money to the Chassidim in Israel (*Igros Baal HaTanya* 69, 70; 83 #10).

The news of Rabbi Shneur Zalman's second arrest caused a great stir in the Chassidic community in general. It appears that his followers suspected that Rabbi Avraham Kalisker's followers were involved in his arrest. Right after this, Reb Elazer of Disna denounced Rabbi Avraham Kalisker in Israel, and Rabbi Avraham wrote and complained about this to Rabbi Shneur Zalman. Reb Aharon, the Cantor of Pakshan, and Reb Yisroel Kosianier were also involved in this (*Ibid*. 94).

That winter, Rabbi Shmuel Isaac had a dream, and because of it, he visited the Rebbe in Zlatipolia for the first time.[13] From the way the Rebbe received him, Rabbi Shmuel Isaac knew that Rabbi Nachman was already aware of all the details of his dream. That Shabbos, the Rebbe said *Likutey Moharan* 2. In it he discussed the importance of binding oneself to the greatest Tzaddik in each generation when praying. He also explained the meaning of the dream (*Tovos Zichronos* #2).

Adar; (February 1801):

The Rebbe's fourth daughter, Chaya, was born.[14] She was born just before the death of the Rebbe's mother, and he wanted to give her his mother's name. Word had not yet

13. Rabbi Shmuel Isaac had become attached to the Rebbe together with Rabbi Yudel. Rabbi Yudel moved from Dashev nearer to Medvedevka to be closer to the Rebbe, as we find in *Chayay Moharan, HaShmotos* 46b #4. Rabbi Shmuel Isaac also wanted to move to Medvedevka, as we find in *Shevachey Moharan* 8b #1, #291. From *Tovos Zichronos*, however, it appears that he was living in Dashev when the Rebbe was in Zlatipolia. Cf. above text, p. 18-20. Rabbi Yudel remained in Medvedevka even after the Rebbe's move to Zlatipolia as is apparent from *Yemey Moharnat* p. 95b.

14. In *Yemey Moharnat* 52a, we find that she was about twelve years old when the Rebbe died. According to *Tovos Zichronos* p. 27, however, she

come from Medzeboz about Feiga's passing. The Rebbe, who knew with *ruach hakodesh* that his mother had passed away, waited, not yet giving a name to his newborn daughter. When Reb Chaikel pointed out to the Rebbe that delaying would bring further talk against him, Rabbi Nachman, whose way it was never to be obstinate, agreed to give her a name. It was only later, when news of Rabbi Nachman's mother's death reached Zlatipolia, that Reb Chaikel realized the mistake he had made (*Manuscript* p. 12).

Wednesday, 19 Adar; (March 3, 1801):

Feiga, the Rebbe's mother, died.[15]

In her will, his mother expressed the wish that the Rebbe should not allow anyone near him whom he could not tolerate (*Likutey Moharan* 257).

Sunday, 22 Nissan; (April 4; March 23 Julian):

Czar Paul was killed. He had two sons, Alexander and Nikolai, and there was some question as to who would be his successor.

was only ten when the Rebbe died. We also find, in *Yemey Moharnat* p. 54b, that she was married on 2 Elul, 5574 (1814). If she was twelve when the Rebbe died in 5571, then she would have been close to fifteen when she was married, which was considered fairly old for marriage in those days. However, if she was born in 1801, then she was married according to the prevailing custom, around her thirteenth birthday.

15. We find that her *yahrzeit* was on 19 Adar (*Chayay Moharan* 6b #14, #14). However, our sources do not give the year of her death. The fact that the Rebbe kept both *yahrzeits* (Adar I and Adar II), makes it evident that she did not die on a leap year, for in that case the *yahrzeit* is only observed in the Adar in which death occurred (Cf. *Shach, Yoreh Deah* 402:12). We know that his mother was still alive when his daughter Adil was married in 5560 (see above p. 58). We find that at the beginning of the dispute between the Rebbe and Rabbi Baruch in the summer of 5563, his mother was already dead (Cf. *Aveneha Barzel* p. 17 #15; *Yemey Moharnat* 7a; below p. 100). She did not die in 5563, since the Rebbe's daughter Sarah would have been married just two weeks after her death on the first of Nissan (Cf. *Chayay Moharan* 28b #13, #116). She did not die in 5562, since this was a leap year. Therefore she must have died in 5561 (1801).

Of these brothers, Nikolai was a religious zealot whose policies were certain to result in persecution of the Jews under his rule. The other brother, Alexander, was not religious and this was seen as a possible benefit for the Jewish community. It was feared, however, that liberal policies might present a more dangerous spiritual problem in that it would open Russian schools to the Jewish populace. Even the leading Tzaddikim of the time were split as to the preferable choice (*Manuscript* p. 19).

Around this time, Rabbi Shmuel Isaac visited the Rebbe. When he arrived, the Rebbe was in the middle of a discussion on the subject of the new Czar. The Rebbe then said to those around him, that in Heaven they were also asking Rabbi Shmuel Isaac which of the two brothers should rule (*Ibid.*).

Alexander eventually became the new Czar.

Friday, 3 Sivan; (May 14):

Rabbi Yaakov Shimshon of Shepetevka died (*Chachmey Yisroel* p. 186).

Monday, 6 Sivan, Shavuos; (May 17):

The Rebbe had a dream about one of his followers who was always contemplating the World to Come. After Shavuos, this individual came to Rabbi Nachman and was astonished to hear that the Rebbe knew his thoughts (*Sichos Moharan* 25a #7, #450; also see *Sichos HaRan* #96).

In the evening, between the first and second days of Shavuos, the Rebbe told the story of how the Baal Shem Tov had told someone to confess to him (*Chayay Moharan* 14b #58, #58). He then said the lesson *Anochi* in *Likutey Moharan* 4.[16] This lesson speaks of *viduy* before a Tzaddik

---

16. In *Chayay Moharan* it is mentioned that this lesson was given on Shavuos in Zlatipolia. Although no year was given, it seems obvious that it was in 5561, since shortly after Shavuos 5562 the Rebbe was in the process of moving to Breslov. However, when Rabbi Yitzchok, the son-in-law of the Terhovitza Magid, joined the Rebbe's followers, which happened during the Rebbe's stay in Zlatipolia, they were already known as *Viduynikers*.

(*Chayay Moharan* 14b #59, #59). Rabbi Yudel, Rabbi Shmuel Isaac and Rabbi Aharon were also there at the time. After hearing this lesson, they began the practice of confessing to the Rebbe each time they came (*Tovos Zichronos* #4).

After this, the Rebbe's followers became known as *Viduynikers* (*Kochavey Or* p. 29 #24).

Around that time, the Rebbe began to study the *Etz Chaim* for its *mussar* implications. He gave many lessons involving the Kabbalistic meaning of *tefillin* during this period (*Shevachey Moharan* 14b #22, #362; *Ibid.* 30a #64, #510; see end of Lesson #38).

Shabbos, 1 Av, Rosh Chodesh, Torah reading, Matos Masai; (July 10) most probably:

Rabbi Yekusiel, the Magid of Terhovitza, came to the Rebbe and asked him why he had not allowed him to make arrangements for him before he came to Zlatipolia. The Rebbe answered that he had not had time to wait, having been obliged by Heaven to go to the town. The Rebbe then said *Likutey Moharan* II, 62, which speaks of rectifying the sin of idolatry through the "journeys" of the Jewish people (*Chayay Moharan* 28a #11, #114).

Monday, 10 Av; (July 19; July 3 Julian):

Rabbi Shneur Zalman was freed from prison in St. Petersberg (*Rabbi Shneur Zalman of Liadi*, p. 234).

Friday, 14 Av; (July 23):

Rabbi Shneur Zalman settled in Liadi (*Ibid.*).

He said that he supported the Rebbe in his conflict with his opponents (*Bais Rebbe* #25 p. 66 in note, brought in *Nevey Tzaddikim* p. 207).

That summer, about a year before he met Rabbi Nachman, Rabbi Nathan was in Berdichov with followers of Rabbi Levi Yitzchok. Feeling depressed at the lack of spiritual encouragement he had found even in Chassidism, he entered the empty women's section of the *Beis HaMedrash* and said the first fifty psalms. He anguished over each verse until he became exhausted and fell asleep. Someone (whom he later recognized to be the Rebbe) appeared to him in a dream and encouraged him (*Aveneha Barzel* p. 6 #3).

Early one morning, while in Zlatipolia, the Rebbe called for a certain man to accompany him into the fields. The Rebbe remarked on how beautiful it is to hear the songs of praise which each blade of grass sings to God and how good it is to serve Him in the fields. They then entered a cave and spent the entire day there. The Rebbe read from the *Shaarey Tzion* siddur, praying and crying until the sun had just about set (*Sichos HaRan* #163).[17]

17. There (in *Sichah* #163) the Rebbe speaks of "Y.Y.," most probably R. Yaakov Yosef of Zlatipolia, to whom the Rebbe said he would eventually become related by marriage. This came true: after the Rebbe died, R. Yaakov Yosef's son, R. Zalman, married the Rebbe's daughter Chaya (*Yemey Moharnat* 52a; Cf. *Shemos HaTzaddikim*).

12

ZLATIPOLIA 5562 (1801-1802)

Tuesday, 1 Tishrei, Rosh HaShanah; (September 8):
The Rebbe said *Likutey Moharan* 35.[18]

Tishrei, Succos; (September):
It appears that the lesson in *Likutey Moharan* 33 was said then, for this is also among the lessons that were given at this time. It also alludes to the concept of the *lulav*. It furthermore mentions the verse (Zechariah 14:7) "And a day will come, known to God," which is in the *haftorah* of the first day of Succos.

In the winter of this year, R. Yitzchok, son-in-law of the Terhovitza Magid, became a follower of the Rebbe. After Rabbi Zusia of Anipoli, his mentor, died, he went to many Tzaddikim, but could not find a Rebbe (*Chayay Moharan, HaShmotos* 46a #1). He heard that the followers of Rabbi Nachman were called *Viduynikers* and he went to visit the Rebbe (see above page 56). He then confessed before the Rebbe, and became one of his followers (*Kochavey Or* p. 29 #24). He returned to his father-in-law and told him that he now realized that without Rabbi Nachman's words his prayer and Torah study were without inspiration (*Tovos Zichronos* #6 p. 21).

Friday, 2 Cheshvan; (October 9):
Alexander I issued an *ukase* giving orders to draft new "Statutes Concerning the Jews" aimed at reforming Jewish life in Russia.

---

18. For we find in *Shevachey Moharan* 14b #22, #362 and 30a #64, #510 that this was said during the same period as Lessons #4 and #38, which

Shabbos, 13 Shevat, Shabbos Shirah; (January 16):

The Rebbe said *Likutey Moharan* 38 which speaks about the concept of *tefillin* (*Chayay Moharan* 15a #59, #59).

It seems likely that this lesson was given in Medvedevka. We later find that the Rebbe had a custom of traveling to Medvedevka for Shabbos Shirah, and it is possible that this custom had begun at this time.

It is also possible that it was on this occasion that the Rebbe became upset with Rabbi Shimon and said that he wanted to send him away over the Don River in Eastern Russia. Not long afterwards, Rabbi Shimon traveled there intending to stay for only a short while. He remained there for about three years, living amongst non-Jews and resisting many temptations (*Sichos HaRan* #173). [19]

Friday, 19 Shevat; (January 22):

The Rebbe finished saying *Kaddish* for his mother.

Shabbos, 20 Shevat, Torah reading, Yisro; (January 23):

Rabbi Yekusiel, the Terhovitza Magid, visited the Rebbe, who at this time said *Likutey Moharan* 15 (*Tovos Zichronos* #6 p. 21). The verse (Exodus 19:6) "You shall be a kingdom of priests," upon which this lesson is based, is in the reading of Yisro.

A person who was very jealous of the Rebbe because

were known to have been said in Zlatipolia. According to the topic, we see that this lesson speaks of Rosh HaShanah.

19. In *Sichos HaRan* #173, we find that Rabbi Shimon returned to the Rebbe after the latter had been in Breslov for two or three years. It further states that he was away from the Rabbi Nachman more than three years. This sets the time around half a year before the Rebbe moved to Breslov, namely in the winter of 5562. We also find it clearly stated that this took place in Medvedevka, even though the Rebbe then lived in Zlatipolia. We must therefore assume that this occurred during one of the set times that the Rebbe went to Medvedevka. The most likely time was Shabbos Shirah (Cf. *Chayay Moharan* 30a #24, #126).

Rabbi Yekusiel had visited him, denounced the Rebbe to Rabbi Yekusiel. Rabbi Yekusiel then asked his son-in-law, R. Yitzchok, to show him one of the Rebbe's lessons. Upon seeing *Likutey Moharan 2*, which the Rebbe had said the previous winter, he became so impressed that he called Rabbi Nachman's teachings greater than even the *Zohar* and the *Tikkuney Zohar*. This prompted him to ridicule severely those who had denounced the Rebbe (*Aveneha Barzel* p. 74).

Around this time, Rabbi Yitzchok Isaac, a follower of Rabbi Yekusiel, joined the Rebbe's following (*Chayay Moharan* 28a #11, #114). He was originally a businessman. The Rebbe was aware of the greatness of Rabbi Yitzchok Isaac's soul and provided him with specific practices accordingly, the most difficult of which was not to speak to anyone for an entire year (*Shevachey Moharan* 10a #23; *Kochavey Or* p. 31 #25-26; see below p. 104).

Shabbos, 15 Nissan, Passover; (April 17):

Rabbi Nathan visited Kremenetz, where his father-in-law was Rabbi. He brought a letter to Rabbi Mordechai of Kremenetz. When Rabbi Nathan became involved in Chassidus, he would occasionally visit Rabbi Mordechai (*Aveneha Barzel* p. 7 #4). Rabbi Mordechai was the son of the famed Rabbi Michel of Zlotchov, and was related by marriage to Rabbi Nochum of Tchernoble (*Chachmey Yisroel* p. 219; *Shem HaGedolim HeChadash, Mem* 113).

The Chassidic leaders called a meeting in Berdichov to discuss the impending decree against the Jews by the Russian government. It was attended by representatives of other trends in Jewish life as well, including Menachem Mendel Levin (1741-1819) who is regarded as the father of the *haskalah* in Galicia, although he himself was opposed to those who deviated from traditional Jewish observance.

That summer, before this meeting, the Shpola Zeida sent letters to a number of Chassidic leaders, urging them to place the Rebbe in *cherem*. The majority, however, replied by writing to the Rebbe offering encouragement. They also wrote strongly against the Shpola Zeida (*Chayay Moharan* 29b #19, #122). Among those supporting the Rebbe were:

Rabbi Levi Yitzchok of Berdichov
Rabbi Gedalia of Linitz
Rabbi Baruch of Medzeboz, the Rebbe's uncle
Rabbi Zev Wolf of Charni-Ostrov
Rabbi Avraham Kalisker
Rabbi Leibush of Volochisk, in-law of the Rebbe
Rabbi Avraham Dov of Chmelnick, in-law of the Rebbe (*Ibid.*).

Before the Rebbe left for Berdichov, he gathered ten men and argued with the Evil One in their presence. Rabbi Nathan adds that he was not informed of all the details involved in this incident, saying only that this was the beginning of an everlasting confrontation (*Ibid.* #20, #123).

The Rebbe then went to the meeting at Berdichov with his father, Rabbi Simcha (*Ibid.* #19).

In Berdichov the Shpola Zeida gathered a number of leaders in Rabbi Levi Yitzchok's house, with the intention of placing the Rebbe in *cherem.* He also accused the Rebbe of distributing amulets and of having committed an act akin to idolatry on his pilgrimage to Israel. But Rabbi Baruch stood by his side. Rabbi Levi Yitzchok's Rebetzin said, "How can you forget that Rabbi Nachman is a great-grandson of your leader, the Baal Shem Tov?" They then refrained from placing the Rebbe in *cherem* (*Meoros HaGedolim* 6a).

The dispute did not subside, however. When Rabbi Levi Yitzchok found out that the accusations against the Rebbe were based on slander, he cursed the slanderer that his lips should be cut off, and his curse came true (*Ibid.*).

After the Rebbe had seen the Shpola Zeida, he said that he now understood him. Until this time the Rebbe had not discussed him, saying that he did not want to speak about him until he completely understood his essence. He then began to speak of him a little, but even then only infrequently (*Chayay Moharan* 30a #23, #125).

Around that time, Rabbi Leibush of Volochisk married off his son, Rabbi Sh. (see below p. 59 footnote #12). After the wedding, several leaders were ready to place a *cherem* on the Shpola Zeida (*Chayay Moharan* 29b #19, #122). This group included:

> Rabbi Leibush of Volochisk
> Rabbi Yosef Yoska, Rabbi of Iassi, son of Rabbi Leibush
> Rabbi Zev Wolf of Charni-Ostrov
> Rabbi Moshe of Krassnoy, son of Rabbi Chaim of Krassnoy
> Rabbi Yitzchok of New Konstantin

Rabbi Levi Yitzchok, however, did not approve of this *cherem*, and did not want it to be applied in his city (*Ibid.*).

The Rebbe then visited his uncle, Rabbi Baruch, in Tulchin.

Rabbi Baruch had lived in Medzeboz, the city of his grandfather, the Baal Shem Tov, until 5541 (1781). He then moved to Tulchin, and remained there until 5548 (1788), when he returned to Medzeboz, but would visit Tulchin for a month in the summer and a month in the winter (Introduction to *Biur HaLikutim*).

The Rebbe saw that it was impossible to remain in Zlatipolia, which was so close to Shpola. He asked Rabbi Baruch's advice on where to move. Rabbi Baruch said that near Tulchin there was a city named Breslov, which was in his own territory. There, Rabbi Nachman would not be troubled by the followers of the Shpoler (*Ibid.*; also see *Chayay Moharan* 29b #19, #122). Rabbi Baruch told the Rebbe that he himself had wanted to settle in Breslov, but it had not been possible (*Ibid.* 28b #12, #115).

The heads of the Breslov community were the partners, Moshe Chenkis and Avraham Pais. Rabbi Baruch sent for them to come to Tulchin. They agreed to the Rebbe's moving to Breslov and promised him a *rendel* each week (*Biur HaLikutim, Ibid.*).

While with Rabbi Baruch, the Rebbe met R. Moshe Zvi of Savran, one of his uncle's disciples. The Rebbe wanted to draw him closer to his school of thought, but R. Moshe Zvi refused. After the Rebbe died, he became a strong opponent of Rabbi Nathan (*Manuscript* p. 3; also see *Yemey HaTalaos* p. 19).

There are several other incidents that occurred in Zlatipolia, with no date given.

Once in Zlatipolia, the Rebbe fasted from Sabbath to Sabbath. On Friday, he became very weak. He said that this was because others had found out about his fasting (*Sichos HaRan* #162).

It was in Zlatipolia that the Rebbe began to learn how to rectify souls (*Chayay Moharan* 34b #2, #152).

There was the story of a woman who was very sick, and the Rebbe told them to bring a coin of a certain weight for a *pidyon* (*Kochavey Or* p. 62 #44).

Sunday, 24 Av; (August 22) approximately:

The Breslov community sent wagons to Zlatipolia to transport the Rebbe to Breslov (*Chayay Moharan* 28a #12, #115). The Cantor of Breslov also went to help the Rebbe. He was suspected of adultery, and wanted to gain the Rebbe's favor (*Biur HaLikutim, Ibid.*).

Wednesday, 27 Av; (August 25) approximately:

The wagons arrived at Zlatipolia, and the Rebbe left with them. The Rebbe said that he had suffered double hell in the two years he was in Zlatipolia, i.e. double the twelve-month period of the wicked in Gehenom (*Rosh HaShanah* 17a) (*Chayay Moharan* 28a #12, #115).

Friday, 29 Av; (August 27) approximately:

The Rebbe came to Uman on his way to Breslov. As soon as he entered the city, he passed through the old cemetery

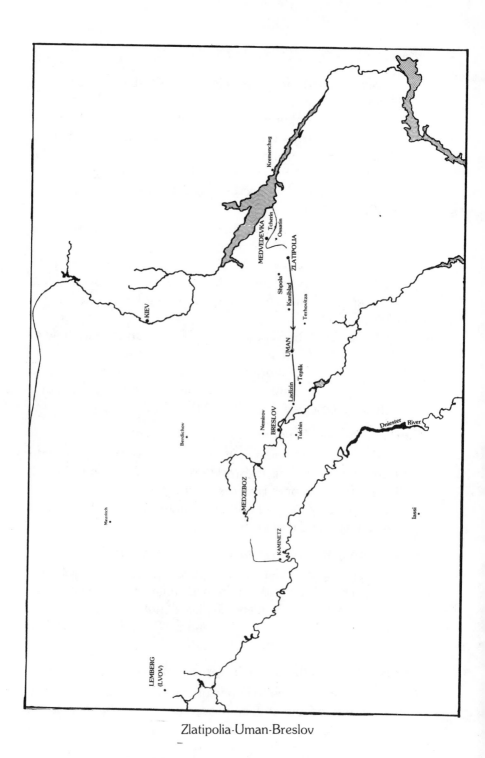

Zlatipolia-Uman-Breslov

there. In this cemetery were buried all the martyrs killed by Gunta and the Haidemacks on 5-7 Tammuz, 5528 (1768). The martyrs numbered about twenty thousand (see below p. 186-187). The Rebbe said, "It would be good to be buried here" (*Chayay Moharan* 44a #33, #217; also see *Sippurim Niflaim* in *Kochavey Or* p. 3).

The Rebbe stayed in the hotel of Reb Avraham Chaim in Uman (*Manuscript* p. 7; also see *Yemey Moharnat* 90b #21, #24). This was opposite a house where a Russian general was staying (*Sippurim Niflaim, Ibid.*).

Three renowned heretics, Chaikel Hurwitz, Hirsh Ber Hurwitz and Moshe Landau, who were heads of the Russian *haskala* movement, lived in Uman (*Ibid.*).

Chaikel (Chaim) Hurwitz, born in 5510 (1750), was a lumber merchant, and his travels brought him to the German forests. It was in Germany that he came in contact with the followers of Moses Mendelssohn. In 5577 (1817) he published a book, *Tzofnas Poneach*, dealing with the discovery of America. (Only one copy of this is known to exist, in the British Museum.) He died in 5582 (1822).

Hirsh Ber Hurwitz had governmental contacts, and had received a sword from the Czar (*Sippurim Niflaim* p. 3). According to *Sippurim Niflaim* he was the son-in-law of Chaikel and after Rabbi Nathan died, he went to America, where he passed away with the Rebbe's name on his lips (*Ibid.* p. 10). However, according to other sources, he was the son of Chaikel, and son-in-law of Nachman Nathan Rappaport, another of the heretics of Uman (see below p. 166). Upon becoming bankrupt he fled to England where he changed his name to Herman Bernard and became professor of Hebraica at Cambridge University. There are also indications that he became an apostate (Cf. *Ohel Rochel*; *The Book of Job* by Herman H. Bernard, London, 1864; *Reshumoth* Vol. 1, edited by A. Druyanov, Tel Aviv, 5685-1925).

His brother-in-law, Moshe Landau, was, according to

Sippurim Niflaim, another son-in-law to Chaikel and a doctor in Uman (*Sippurim Niflaim, Ibid.*). Other accounts, however, make him a banker and son-in-law of Nachman Nathan and grandson of Rabbi Yechezkel Landau, the renowned *Nodeh BiYehudah* (*Ohel Rochel*). He helped Rabbi Nathan in the opposition he faced after the Rebbe died (*Sippurim Niflaim, Ibid.*; see *Alim LeTerufah*, letter dated Sunday, Kedoshim, 5595).

Hirsh Ber and Moshe Landau were students of Naftali Hertz Wiesel, author of *Yain Levanon* and one of the chief disciples of Mendelssohn (see *Kochavey Or* p. 53 #27). In 5582 (1822) they founded a school in Uman.

On Friday, Chaikel came to visit the Rebbe. The Rebbe dismissed him, saying that if he wanted to meet an important person he should go to the Russian general staying across the way (*Sippurim Niflaim, Ibid.*).

Friday night, 30 Av, 1st day of Rosh Chodesh Elul, Torah reading Re'eh; (August 27):

On Friday night, these three *maskilim* came to the Rebbe when he was in the middle of speaking. The Rebbe turned the focus of his lesson to a geometrical problem found in the Talmud (*Succah* 8a; Cf. *Tosefos, s.v. al*). He probed deeply into the mathematics involved, greatly surprising them (*Sippurim Niflaim* p. 4).

Sunday, 1 Elul, 2nd day of Rosh Chodesh; (August 29):

The heretics came to the Rebbe and discussed this mathematical problem with him. They were highly impressed by him and wanted him to stay in Uman. The Rebbe told them, "When you will send me the book *Yain Levanon...*" (*Ibid.*).

In Uman there was a *shochet*, who wanted to travel to the Rebbe for Rosh HaShanah by Kabbalistic means. The Rebbe told him that he must come by natural means (*Aveneha Barzel* p. 47 #75).

Shabbos, 7 Elul, Torah reading, Shoftim; (September 4):

The Rebbe stayed in Ladizin for the Sabbath on the way to Breslov. (This was some 19 miles or 30 km. from Breslov.)[20] There was then an incident involving the cantor, and, as a result, *Likutey Moharan* 3 was said which speaks of the sources of holy and profane song (*Tovos Zichronos* 3).[21]

That summer, Rabbi Nathan had planned to settle in Berdichov. However, he waited in Nemirov for his father-in-law. This delay enabled him to become a disciple of the Rebbe (*Kochavey Or* p. 10 #3).

20. Although he had sufficient time to reach Breslov, it is possible that they were not prepared for him. It is also possible that he remained in Uman for a few days.

21. In *Chayay Moharan* 14b #59, #59, however, we find that this lesson was said on the first Sabbath that the Rebbe was in Breslov. We find the same in the introduction of *Biur HaLikutim*, where the entire story is brought in connection with the Cantor of Breslov (see text p. 73). However, since they were so near Breslov, and likewise, since many people from Breslov had come to Ladizin to see the Rebbe, this may have been counted as his first Sabbath there. There is some evidence that this was said on the Sabbath when Shoftim is read. This lesson speaks of the Mishnah "Make yourself a Rabbi, buy yourself a friend" (*Avos* 1:6). According to the usual order of saying a chapter of *Avos* on each of the Sabbaths between Pesach and Rosh HaShanah, this chapter was said on that particular Sabbath.

13

BRESLOV: End of 5562 (1802):

Breslov is on the Bug River, latitude 48.50°N longitude 28.55°E, midway between Tulchin to the south and Nemirov to the north; 9 miles or 15 km. from each. Breslov was about half the size of Nemirov and a major staging post for trade with Odessa. By the end of the eighteenth century, Breslov had a Jewish population of just over a thousand. It had a main synagogue and six small prayer houses. One of them was known as the Baal Shem Tov's synagogue, and the community gave the Rebbe a house nearby. However, a new synagogue was later built in the Rebbe's house. His house was open to the west. On the way into the Rebbe's room, there was a large room where guests could stay.

Tuesday, 10 Elul; (September 7):

The Rebbe arrived in Breslov. (*Chayay Moharan*, 28a #12, #115 states that the Rebbe came to Breslov in the week of Ki Tetze, which was this week. In *Aveneha Barzel* p. 8 #6, we also find that he came on a Tuesday, which was market day.)

After he came to Breslov, the Rebbe instituted three fixed times for saying a lesson. The times when his followers all came together were on Rosh HaShanah, Shabbos Chanukah, and Shavuos. On Rosh HaShanah and Shavuos he would give the lesson at nightfall between the two days of the holiday. On Shabbos Chanukah, he would speak at the third meal. He would also travel to Tcherin, Terhovitza and Medvedevka, on Shabbos Shirah, Shabbos Nachamu, and another Sabbath during the year (*Chayay Moharan* 30a #24, #126; also see *Sippurim Niflaim* p. 168).

The Rebbe did not have a permanent cantor in his

synagogue, but he would provide a list of those who were to lead each service (*Manuscript* p. 12).

When the Rebbe came to Breslov, the cantor asked him if he should sing like a cantor or like a prayer leader, and the Rebbe answered, "like a cantor" (*Biur HaLikutim*, Introduction). The Rebbe later invited R. Chaikel to Breslov to be cantor, for he said that R. Chaikel could draw song from its roots on high (*Ibid.*). Although Reb Chaikel did not agree to be permanent cantor, he would often lead the services (*Manuscript, Ibid.*). Rabbi Aharon, the Rav of Breslov, would also often lead the Rosh HaShanah *Mussaf* services in the central synagogue (*Tovos Zichronos* p. 25). One of the three things that the Rebbe desired was a cantor with a good voice, who would be acceptable both below and on high (*Sichos VeSippurim* p. 138 #48). [The other two were a fine woolen "Turkishe" *tallis* and a *Sefer Torah* written in order from beginning to end without corrections (*Ibid.*)].

Shabbos, 14 Elul, Torah reading, Ki Tetze; (September 11) most probably:

A cup was poured for the Rebbe for *Kiddush*, but it spilled on the ground. A second cup was filled upon which the *Kiddush* was said. The Rebbe said, "Today we have planted ourselves in Breslov." He then said that his followers would always be known as Breslover Chassidim (*Chayay Moharan* 28b #12, #115). He also said that the name BReSLoV had the same letters as *LeV BaSaR* — a heart of flesh (Ezekiel 36:26) (*Shevachey Moharan* 12a #49, #339).

The Rebbe said to Rabbi Yudel, "I see a soul in the Ukraine, near Breslov" (*Aveneha Barzel* p. 8 #5).

Word reached nearby Nemirov that the Rebbe had come to Breslov. Rabbi Nathan said, "Now I can travel to Rabbi Nachman" (*Ibid.*; Cf. *Kochavey Or p. 11 #3*).

After Sabbath, reports came to Nemirov that the Rebbe did not behave like some other Chassidic leaders. He did not place emphasis on Chassidic gatherings centered on eating

Rabbi Nachman's Kiddush Cup

and drinking, but instead spoke of Godliness and directed his followers to confess their sins. Valtchi Nasanels, a Jew from Nemirov, saw one of Rabbi Nachman's followers and called him a *Viduynik*. Rabbi Naftali cursed him for this and then said, "Is this something to ridicule? This is what I want!" (*Ibid.* #6).

Shabbos, 21 Elul, Torah reading, Ki Tavo; (September 18):

Reb Lipa, Rabbi Nathan's friend, spent Shabbos with the Rebbe in Breslov (*Ibid.* p. 9).

That *Motzoai* Shabbos, Rabbi Nathan saw Reb Lipa, who had just spent Shabbos with the Rebbe in Breslov, saying *Selichos* very fervently. He decided then and there to go to Breslov to meet the Rebbe (*Ibid.*).

Sunday, 22 Elul, 1st day of Selichos; (September 19):

Rabbi Nathan then hired a coach to Breslov. He was accompanied by Rabbi Naftali and Reb Lipa (*Ibid.*), and by Reb Zalman HaKatan (*Kochavey Or* p. 11 #3). When Rabbi Nathan's wife and father heard that he was preparing to go, they became very angry at him (*Ibid.* p. #4).[22]

On the way they stopped at the house of Reb Berel Dovrishis, where they heard tales about the Rebbe. They then came to the Rebbe. Rabbi Nathan pointed out to Rabbi Nachman that they were related. The Rebbe commented, "Then I am not alone" (*Aveneha Barzel* p. 9). He also told Rabbi Nathan "I know you from before, but it's a long time since we've met" (*Shevachey Moharan* 11a #43, #333). The Rebbe told them three stories, about Rabbi Mordechai of Neskhiz, Rabbi Shneur Zalman of Liadi, and Rabbi Michel of Zlotchov, in which he illustrated the proper relationship

---

22. See *Kochavey Or* #4, however, where it seems to indicate that Rabbi Nathan met the Rebbe the week before *Selichos*. In *Tovos Zichronos* p. 7 #5, we find, nevertheless, that it was during the week of Netzavim, which agrees with our account.

between Chassidim and their Rebbe (*Kochavey Or* 11, 12 #3; *Aveneha Barzel* p. 9). He said that he had three types of Chassidim: "One in whose heart I am engraved, another who comes to hear my lessons, and a third who comes to eat my left-overs" (as is the custom of Chassidim with their Rebbe). The Rebbe then blessed Rabbi Nathan that he would be of the first type (*Nevey Tzaddikim* p. 35).

The Rebbe invited Rabbi Nathan to eat with him. Rabbi Nathan was bashful and declined, a decision he regretted all his life (*Aveneha Barzel* p. 11 #77; see also introduction to *Biur HaLikutim*, re: *Likutey Moharan* I,62).

Rabbi Nathan heard of the importance the Rebbe placed on being with him on Rosh HaShanah (*Kochavey Or* p. 12 #4; *Aveneha Barzel, Ibid.*). The Rebbe stressed on many occasions that the most important part of his path of devotion is to be together with him on Rosh HaShanah, despite all obstacles (Cf. *Shevachey Moharan* p. 18a, b, #403-406). Even after his physical death, Breslover Chassidim continued to assemble in Uman (the site of his grave) on Rosh HaShanah.

Rabbi Nathan left for home immediately in order to be able to return for Rosh HaShanah (*Aveneha Barzel, Ibid.*).

The Rebbe had always wanted someone like Rabbi Nathan, who was both a scholar and a writer (*Shevachey Moharan* 14b #23, #363). After meeting Rabbi Nathan, he remarked, "Not one more word of mine will be lost" (*Ibid.* #28, #367). He spoke to his daughter, Adil, of Rabbi Nathan's greatness (*Ibid.* 12a #48, #338). Rabbi Yitzchok, son-in-law of the Terhovitza Magid, also heard the Rebbe praise Rabbi Nathan's humility (*Ibid.*).

During this week, two chassidim were at a meal with the Rebbe. They made fun of a man who clapped his hands during his prayers. The Rebbe disapproved of their attitude and spoke of hand-clapping during prayer on the following Sabbath. This became *Likutey Moharan* 44 (*Chayay Moharan* 17b #19, #19).

Friday, 27 Elul; (September 24) most probably:

Rabbi Nathan returned to Breslov. The Rebbe stood with Rabbi Nathan near the synagogue and complained that people no longer prayed fervently (*Tovos Zichronos* #5). He said that Chassidic enthusiasm was declining (*Chayay Moharan* 17b #19, #19).

That afternoon, the Rebbe told Rabbi Nathan and Rabbi Naftali that he would lead them on a new path (*Tovos Zichronos, Ibid.*).

Rabbi Nathan's father expected him to return for the Sabbath, but Rabbi Nathan was determined to remain in Breslov (*Ibid.*).

That Friday night, Rabbi Nathan was at the Rebbe's Shabbos table for the first time (*Ibid.*; a complete description of the event is given there).

That night, the Rebbe said *Likutey Moharan* 44, which speaks of clapping hands during prayer. This was the first lesson that Rabbi Nathan heard from Rabbi Nachman (*Chayay Moharan* 17b #19, #78, 15a #59, #59). After the meal was over, Rabbi Nathan ran into the field and cried out, "A fire is burning in Breslov. Kindle this fire in my heart" (*Nevey Tzaddikim* p. 36).

Shabbos, 28 Elul, Torah reading, Netzavim; (September 25):

In the morning Rabbi Nathan was again at the Rebbe's table and received encouragement, preparing him for all the difficulties he would have to overcome (*Tovos Zichronos, Ibid.*).

Right after Shabbos, Rabbi Nathan wrote down the lesson which he had heard, *Likutey Moharan* 44 (*Chayay Moharan* 17b #19, #78).

Sunday, 29 Elul, Erev Rosh HaShanah; (September 26):

Rabbi Nathan's family expected him back for Rosh HaShanah. Sunday was market day in Breslov and some of Rabbi Nathan's acquaintances from nearby Nemirov were there. Upon meeting Rabbi Nathan they asked him if he planned to return home for the holiday. He replied, "My market day is not over" (*Tovos Zichronos, Ibid.*).

14

BRESLOV 5563 (1802-1803)

Monday, 1 Tishrei, 1st day of Rosh HaShanah; (September 27):

The Rebbe *davened* the *Amidah* prayer for four hours. Everyone went home, but when they returned, the Rebbe was still praying (*Manuscript* p. 17).

That evening, the Rebbe said *Likutey Moharan* 5, which speaks of decrees. This was because the decree of drafting Jewish children, which later came into effect in Czar Nikolai's time, was now being mooted (*Chayay Moharan* 4a #1, #1; *Parparaos LeChokhmah, ad loc.*). This lesson also answered for Rabbi Nathan a question which his father-in-law had often raised: "Why are there disputes between Tzaddikim?" Rabbi Nathan had brought Reb Zalman HaKatan who also posed a question regarding the Chassidic custom of drinking whiskey, a custom disapproved of by Rabbi Nachman (*Aveneha Barzel* p. 12 #8).

Wednesday, 3 Tishrei; (September 29):

On the day after Rosh HaShanah, the Rebbe directed Rabbi Nathan to begin recording his lessons (*Yemey Moharnat* 6b).

During the week after Rosh.HaShanah, Rabbi Nathan had a conversation with the Rebbe. The Rebbe told Rabbi Nathan to study eighteen chapters of *Mishnah* each day, not to eat any animal produce for a twenty-four hour period each week, and to stay up two days and one night in a row (*Aveneha Barzel* #9; see *Sichos HaRan* #184). They walked back and forth in front of the synagogue, and the Rebbe told him that it is good to speak to God (*Kochavey Or* p. 13 #4; cf. *Aveneha Barzel ibid.*).

After talking to the Rebbe, Rabbi Nathan went alone into the synagogue and prayed (*Ibid.* #5). He also went to the fields at night and prayed (*Ibid.* p. 14 #5).

All this time, while Rabbi Nathan remained in Breslov, his wife had to care for their store (*Tovos Zichronos* p. 8).

Shabbos, 6 Tishrei, Shabbos Shuvah, Torah reading, Vayelech; (October 2):

The Rebbe said *Likutey Moharan* 6. This speaks of "The Man on the Chair" (see Ezekiel 1). The Rebbe then grasped his chair and said, "When one sits on a chair, one is a man" (*Chayay Moharan* 4a #2, #2). Upon hearing this lesson, Rabbi Nathan was deeply moved (*Aveneha Barzel* p. 12 #9). This lesson was said at the third meal. After *havdalah*, the Rebbe explained the Kabbalistic meaning of Elul according to this lesson (*Chayay Moharan, Ibid.*).

Wednesday, 10 Tishrei, Yom Kippur; (October 6):

Rabbi Nathan was with the Rebbe.

Thursday, 11 Tishrei; (October 7):

Rabbi Nathan returned home after having been in Breslov since before Rosh HaShanah (*Shevachey Moharan* 6a #23, #263). His wife was very angry at him when he returned (*Tovos Zichronos* p. 8). He began praying as he had learned in Breslov, clapping his hands with emotion (*Ibid.* p. 9). He still lived in his father's house, and had no quarters for *hisbodedus* there. He therefore went out into the fields at night to pray (*Kochavey Or* p. 13 #5).

Sunday, 14 Tishrei; (October 10):

Rabbi Shalom Shachneh of Probisht, grandson of the Mezritcher Magid, died (*Chachmey Yisroel* p. 190).

Monday, 15 Tishrei, Succos; (October 11):

Rabbi Nathan gathered ten of the Rebbe's followers and prayed in his father's large *succah*, using his father's Torah (*Tovos Zichronos* p. 9).

Rabbi Nathan also began studying eighteen chapters of *Mishnah* a day as the Rebbe had prescribed (*Aveneha Barzel* p. 13 #9).

During that Succos, Rabbi Yekusiel had a dream. It indicated that BReSLoV had the letters of *LeV BaSaR* (see above page 80), and that Zlatipolia was connected with the concept of money (in Russian it means city of gold) (*Shevachey Moharan* 12a #49, #339).

Sunday, 21 Tishrei, Hoshana Rabbah; (October 17):

The Rebbe said, "What can I do if two murderers stand over me and insist that I am a leader?" When he said "two murderers," he indicated Rabbi Yudel and Rabbi Shmuel Isaac, who were present at the time. Rabbi Nathan explained that this meant they were very strongly attached to him (*Shevachey Moharan* 6a #23, #263).

Monday, 22 Tishrei, Shemini Atzeres; (October 18):

Many of the towns people came to the Rebbe, and he danced for a long time. He then told Rabbi Yudel and Rabbi Shmuel Isaac about the wedding customs mentioned in *Sichos HaRan* #86 (*Ibid.; Chayay Moharan* 15b #59, #59).

Tuesday, 23 Tishrei, Simchas Torah; (October 19):

The Rebbe danced a great deal (*Yemey Moharnat* 7a, *Chayay Moharan* 28b #13, #116).

Meanwhile, in Nemirov, people gathered around Rabbi Nathan, and he spoke about the Rebbe (*Aveneha Barzel* p. 12 #9). His father, however, told him that if he went back to Rabbi Nachman he should not return home again (*Ibid.* p. 13).

That night Rabbi Nathan and a friend hired a wagon and went to Breslov. They were wearing their holiday clothing, which got soaked in a sudden downpour. They arrived in Breslov around 11 p.m., singing in the streets, "Rejoice, dwellers of Breslov" (paraphrase of Isaiah 12:6).They then came to the Rebbe (*Tovos Zichronos* #5; *Aveneha Barzel* p. 13). The Rebbe was sitting with members of the community, but Rabbi Yudel and Rabbi Shmuel Isaac were not present (*Aveneha Barzel, ibid.*).

Wednesday, 24 Tishrei; (October 20):

The next morning Rabbi Nathan went to the *mikvah* with the Rebbe, and prayed using the Rebbe's *tallis* and *tefillin* (one of the Rebbe's pairs of *tefillin* was written by the Tzaddik, Rabbi Ephraim the Scribe; see *Yemey Moharnat* 29a). He then sat outside the Baal Shem Tov's synagogue with the Rebbe. The Rebbe told him *Likutey Moharan* 48 which discusses how the reading of the conclusion of *Devarim* and the beginning of *Bereshis* on *Simchas Torah* is connected with the concept of Succos and fervent prayer (*Tovos Zichronos* #5; Cf. *Chayay Moharan* 15a #59, #59; in *Aveneha Barzel* p. 13, however, it appears that *Likutey Moharan* 48 was said the previous night).

Rabbi Nathan's wife, who had previously suffered several miscarriages, was pregnant at the time. The Rebbe told Rabbi Nathan to bring him a *pidyon*. Rabbi Nathan said that he anyway had in mind to make new chairs for the Rebbe. The Rebbe told him to bring a gift of six chairs, which he did. Rabbi Nathan eventually had six children, five sons and a daughter (*Tovos Zichronos, Ibid., Aveneha Barzel* p. 60 #22, p. 26 #19). The Rebbe then told him *Likutey Moharan* 169 which speaks of dancing (*Aveneha Barzel* p. 60 #22). They ate a meal together, and the Rebbe told him that he must return to Nemirov (*Tovos Zichronos, Ibid.*).

Wednesday night, 25 Tishrei:

That night Rabbi Nathan returned to his father's house. His wife was visiting his grandfather. Rabbi Nathan changed his ruined clothing and began the *Maariv* prayers. In the meantime, his wife returned, but before he had finished praying she fell asleep and did not have the opportunity to question him about where he had been (*Ibid.*).

Thursday, 25 Tishrei; (October 21):

In the morning some merchants arrived to take Rabbi Nathan to Berdichov and his wife was again unable to question him (*Ibid.*).

On the same day (October 9 in the Julian calendar), Alexander's *ukase* "A Statute Concerning the Jews" was proclaimed.

Shabbos, 27 Tishrei, Shabbos Bereshis; (October 23):

Most probable date for saying of *Likutey Moharan* 52.[23] (Since Rabbi Nathan was present at the time, he must have stopped in Breslov on the way to Berdichov.)

When he heard this lesson from the Rebbe, Rabbi Nathan said that he would run in the streets to tell everyone about it. The Rebbe grabbed him and restrained him (*Kochavey Or* p. 19 #12; Cf. *Chayay Moharan* 7b #23, #23). Rabbi Nathan then left Breslov and went to Berdichov for merchandise.

When Rabbi Nathan returned from Berdichov, it was agreed that his wife was to care for the store and in the evenings he would keep the accounts and set prices (*Tovos Zichronos, Ibid.*). However, he did not advise his wife how to sell the merchandise and she did not know (*Kochavey Or* p. 20 #13). His wife then sent his brother-in-law to speak to him about earning a livelihood, and Rabbi Nathan replied that a person must prepare himself for the day of his death. His

---

23. *Chayay Moharan* 15a #59, #59 states that it was said at the beginning of this year; it furthermore speaks of Creation. In *Kochavey Or* p. 17 #10 and 11, however, it appears that it was said the following summer, on Rabbi Nathan's next trip to Berdichov.

brother-in-law died soon after, but only after first conceding to Rabbi Nathan's foresight (Aveneha Barzel p. 19).

Rabbi Nathan then returned to Breslov. The man who had mocked the worshiper who had clapped his hands during prayer (see above p. 82) asked Rabbi Nathan to request the Rebbe to pray for his son, who was very sick. The Rebbe had said Likutey Moharan 46 (which speaks of clapping hands), and told this person a story about a stubborn lord. The man in question was a follower of one the Rebbe's opponents, however, and had not followed the Rebbe's advice. When Rabbi Nathan mentioned the man's request to the Rebbe, the Rebbe said, "The child is still alive?" The child died shortly after this (Chayay Moharan 18a #19, #78).

Around this time, Rabbi Nathan borrowed a Shevachey HaARI from the Rebbe. What struck Rabbi Nathan about the book was the account of the relationship between the ARI and his closest pupil, Rabbi Chaim Vital. When he mentioned this to the Rebbe, the latter said this was what he intended him to get from the book. (Aveneha Barzel, Ibid.).

Rabbi Nathan was finding it very difficult to pray. He decided to go the Rebbe, but was delayed by a heavy rain. When he finally arrived, the Rebbe told him, "It is difficult to reach the truth." The Rebbe said Likutey Moharan 112 which discusses how with truth, one can pray well. Rabbi Nathan then returned to Nemirov. He went to his grandfather's house because he was no longer welcome in his father's home (Ibid. #11; Cf. Chayay Moharan 4b #3, #3).

The Rebbe had told him to record his accounts only once a week. Rabbi Nathan therefore began to keep his accounts only on Saturday nights. After two weeks, he returned to the Rebbe. This time the Rebbe told him to keep his accounts only once a month (Tovos Zichronos #5).

Around this time the Rebbe brought Rabbi Aharon to Breslov to assume the post of Rav. He became a close friend of Rabbi Nathan (Tovos Zichronos p. 24).

Also during this period, the Czar appointed a Committee for the Amelioration of the Jews.

Friday, 1 Kislev; (November 26):

Rabbi Nathan's first son was born (*Yemey Moharnat* 7a).

Friday, 8 Kislev; (December 3):

Bris milah of Rabbi Nathan's son. He was given the name Shachneh (*Ibid.*).

Sunday, 10 Kislev; (December 5):

Rabbi Nathan arrived at Breslov and remained there for three weeks until after Shabbos Chanukah (*Yemey Moharnat* 6b, *Tovos Zichronos* p. 13).

About this time, the congregation of Minsk protested the *ukase* against the Jews.

Tuesday, 26 Kislev; (December 21, December 9 Julian):

Jews became eligible for municipal office in Russia.

Shabbos, 30 Kislev, Shabbos Chanukah, Torah reading, Miketz; (December 25):

The Rebbe said *Likutey Moharan* 8, which discusses subduing evil people. After the lesson he danced. When Rabbi Nachman's followers from Nemirov had come to be with him for Chanukah, they had told him about an evil person who had been causing them much trouble. Right after Chanukah this evil-doer suffered a fall (*Chayay Moharan* 4b #4, #4; 28b #13, #116; *Yemey Moharnat* 7a). During Chanukah the Rebbe also said, "I am a beautiful, wondrous tree, with wonderful branches, and below I reach into the ground" (*Shevachey Moharan* 4b #5, #245).

Sunday, 1 Teves, 7th day of Chanukah; (December 26):

Rabbi Nathan began writing the lessons under the Rebbe's direct supervision. He wrote *Likutey Moharan* 8, reviewing it sentence by sentence with the Rebbe. He then returned home after having been in Breslov for three weeks (*Yemey Moharnat* 6b).

When Rabbi Nathan came home, his wife threw the keys of the store at him. His father threw him out of his house, and he had to stay with Rabbi Yitzchok Danzig, his mother's father. His wife, however, stayed with his father (*Yemey Moharnat* 6b, *Tovos Zichronos, Ibid.*). Rabbi Nathan's father would not even give him the two thousand rubles which he was holding for him (*Kochavey Or* p. 15a #7; from *Aveneha Barzel* p. 13 #10, however, it appears that this took place on 25 Tishrei, but all the other accounts seem to conflict with this).

Rabbi Nathan's wife then went to her father to ask him if she should request a divorce. When she informed him that Rabbi Nathan was studying much more than previously, her father told her that she should even stand with a sack of salt in the street and sell it for a livelihood in order to support him (*Tovos Zichronos, Ibid.*; See *Aveneha Barzel* p. 14 #10).

In this period, Rabbi Avraham Kalisker had sent Reb Chaim Meshares to Rabbi Shneur Zalman on behalf of the community in Israel, but Rabbi Shneur Zalman forced him to comply with his own demands (*Igeres Baal HaTanya* 98, 103). Rabbi Zvi Harker was also there, but the author of the *Tanya* alleged that he said he did not want any money from him (*Ibid.* p. 176).

Monday, 1 Shevat, Rosh Chodesh; (January 24):

Around this time, Rabbi Nathan returned to Breslov (*Yemey Moharnat* 6b). He accompanied the Rebbe when he went to Tulchin to visit Rabbi Baruch, with whom he was still on good terms (see below pp. 99-100; *Ibid.* 7a). For the period of *Shovavim*, Rabbi Nachman advised Rabbi Nathan not to eat any animal products (*Manuscript* p. 16).

During that winter, Rabbi Nathan heard the Rebbe say that he knew the supernal sources of the Torah, which transcend even the loftiest concepts that are expressed anywhere in the Torah (*Shevachey Moharan* 8b #47, #287).

Also during that winter, the Rebbe said *Likutey Moharan* 23 which reveals the harm brought about by the desire for money (*Chayay Moharan* 15a #59, #59). He said it in relationship to Reb Lipa, who had developed a strong desire for wealth. The Rebbe then told him, "I don't want you to have any money." Shortly afterwards a storm destroyed Reb Lipa's property (*Kochavey Or* p. 54 #30). (Rabbi Nathan was present when this lesson was said, see end of *Likutey Moharan* 23, but the main part was written by the Rebbe himself.)

The Rebbe then set off for Medvedevka where his daughter, Sarah, was to be married (*Kochavey Or* 15a #8, *Yemey Moharnat* 7a; in *Tovos Zichronos* p. 14, we find that this was at the *end* of Shevat). Rabbi Nathan accompanied him as far as Linitz, where the Rebbe visited Rabbi Gedalia and gave a lesson (*Yemey Moharnat, Ibid.*). Rabbi Nathan did not know, however, that the Rebbe was continuing to Medvedevka, and he returned home. It was only after he had been home for a while that he heard that the Rebbe was continuing his journey to Medvedevka (*Tovos Zichronos, Ibid.*).

Shabbos, 13 Shevat, Shabbos Shirah; (February 5):

Likutey Moharan 9 was said while traveling (*Chayay Moharan* 4b #3, #3). In it, the Rebbe discussed prayer (based on the verse in Exodus 15:5), connecting it to that day's Torah reading. It was written down by the Rebbe himself (*Likutey Moharan, ad loc.*). During this period, the Rebbe saw the Baal Shem Tov and said that the concepts in *Likutey Moharan* 9 and 112 were connected with this vision (*Chayay Moharan, ibid.,* and 14b #59, #59).

After this he began to say *Likutey Moharan* 7 (on Parshas Mishpatim) which was given in sections over a period of time. Later, he wrote it down himself (*Ibid.*).

Shabbos, 27 Shevat, Shabbos Shekalim, Torah reading, Mishpatim; (February 19):

Most probable date for the saying of *Likutey Moharan* 10. It was said before Purim (*Sichos HaRan* #131) in Terhovitza (*Chayay Moharan* 14b #59, #59, 28b #13, #116). Rabbi Nathan found a brief manuscript of it, which is printed at the end of the lesson (*Likutey Moharan, ad loc.*).

The Rebbe's wife then sent to Nemirov from Breslov to buy cake for the wedding. This is how Rabbi Nathan heard that the Rebbe had left for Medvedevka (*Aveneha Barzel* p. 15 #12). Rabbi Nathan told his family that he wanted to go to Berdichov to consider taking a position managing the affairs of his wealthy aunt there (*Tovos Zichronos* #5). He wanted to sell his wife's expensive kerchief for his expenses but Reb Lipa advised him not to, but rather to trust in God. Not knowing the way, he decided to go to Linitz to ask for directions to Medvedevka. His father sent a note to Rabbi Gedalia there to ask that his son honor his father and return home. The note reached there before Rabbi Nathan. When Rabbi Nathan arrived Rabbi Gedalia was sleeping and Rabbi Nathan heard about the note. He immediately asked for directions to Medvedevka and left before Rabbi Gedalia awoke[24] (*Aveneha Barzel, Ibid.*).

Monday, 13 Adar, Erev Purim; (March 7):

Rabbi Nathan met Rabbi Yudel (*Aveneha Barzel* p. 16 #12) in a village some eight miles from Medvedevka. There were only nine men there, and they completed the *minyan*. Rabbi Yudel read the *Megillah* (*Tovos Zichronos* #5). He did so after having studied the *ARI's Siddur* which Rabbi Nathan had brought along (*Aveneha Barzel, Ibid.*).

That evening, in Medvedevka, the Rebbe said, "My disciple 'Joshua' — whose name is Nathan — wants to come

---

24. In *Tovos Zichronos* #5 it appears that Rabbi Nathan went to Breslov and from there to Medvedevka.

and celebrate with us here, but he will finish the Purim celebrations on Shushan Purim" (*Tovos Zichronos Ibid.*).

At midnight, Rabbi Nathan came to Medvedevka (*Ibid.*).

Tuesday, 14 Adar, Purim; (March 8):

Before morning, Rabbi Nathan went to the *mikvah*, and prayed with the sunrise *minyan*. He then came to the Rebbe for the morning Purim meal, where the Rebbe gave him to drink and told him to fight Amalek. Rabbi Nathan understood that this referred to his doubts (the Hebrew word for doubt — ספק, *safek* — has the numerical value of 240, the equivalent of עמלק, *Amalek*.) Rabbi Nathan then took a nap (*Ibid.*; Cf. *Yemey Moharnat* 7a).

At the afternoon Purim meal, the Rebbe told Rabbi Nathan, "I have a lot to say to you." He then spoke about Joshua and Moses as brought in *Likutey Moharan* 6 and said that the concept of "Joshua" who fought Amalek was an allusion to Rabbi Nathan. The Rebbe told Rabbi Nathan to be happy always (*Ibid.*).

Wednesday, 15 Adar; (March 9):

Rabbi Nathan said that he hadn't danced on Purim as much as he should have. The Rebbe told him that Shushan Purim is also called Purim. He spoke about the three mitzvos connected to the Land of Israel, but said he would not discuss them then. They danced and rejoiced all day (*Ibid.*; Cf. *Chayay Moharan* 28b #13, #116; *Aveneha Barzel* p. 16 #12).

Rabbi Nathan then wrote down *Likutey Moharan* 6. The Rebbe read it from his notebook, and Rabbi Nathan transcribed. The Rebbe then spoke of the three mitzvos mentioned at the end of this lesson (*Chayay Moharan* 4a #2, #2). The Rebbe told Rabbi Nathan to offer his own interpretation (*Tovos Zichronos, Ibid.*). Later that night, Rabbi Nathan wrote down some of his own ideas, and showed them to the Rebbe the next day (*Chayay Moharan, Ibid.*).

After Purim, the Rebbe was involved in preparations for his daughter's wedding, but Rabbi Nathan saw him almost every day (*Tovos Zichronos, Ibid.*). He showed Rabbi Nathan the fields around Medvedevka where he used to go and meditate as a young teenager (*Sichos HaRan* #162).

In Medvedevka, the Rebbe saw the child of Reb Meir, a follower of his. The boy was born as a result of the Rebbe's blessing. After testing him in his studies, the Rebbe said of the child that it was a great loss. A short time later, the Rebbe went to Kremenchug to speak to the groom's parents. While he was there, Reb Meir's child died (*Kochavey Or* p. 47. For more regarding this Reb Meir see *Ibid.* p. 46).

Thursday night, 1 Nissan, Rosh Chodesh; (March 24):

Wedding of the Rebbe's daughter Sarah to Reb Yitzchok Isaac, son of the wealthy Reb Leib Dubravner of Kremenchug (*Yemey Moharnat* 7a; *Chayay Moharan* 28b #13, #116). The wedding took place in Medvedevka, in the house of Reb Meir. Feiga, the wife of Reb Meir, gave the couple a golden candlestick as a wedding present (*Kochavey Or* p. 47).

At the wedding, the Rebbe sang a melody with which he summoned the Patriarchs (*Aveneha Barzel* p. 16 #12). There was a non-Jewish drummer at the wedding, and the Rebbe sent him away (*Ibid.* p. 32 #40).

After the wedding, the Rebbe told Reb Meir's wife, Feiga, that she would give birth to a son, and that she should call him Nachman (*Kochavey Or* p. 47).

Shabbos, 3 Nissan, Torah reading, Vayikra; (March 26):

At the third meal, the Rebbe began in a loud voice, "And he, like a groom, leaves the *chupah*" (Psalms 19:6). With this he began *Likutey Moharan* 49. After the lesson, he danced with his daughter Sarah (*Shevachey Moharan* 6a #23, #263; Cf. *Yemey Moharnat* 7a). He said that this lesson was said to prevent the *ukase* known as "points" (*Chayay Moharan*

28b #13, #116) and that it was also the reason he danced so much (*Shevachey Moharan* 6a #23, #263; *Yemey Moharnat* 7a; *Sichos HaRan* 88 #131; *Chayay Moharan* 28b #13, #116; Cf. *Likutey Moharan* 10, 41). He said that he had delayed the decree for some twenty odd years. In fact, it took effect twenty-five years later (*Kochavey Or* p. 43 #5).

Wednesday night, 15 Nissan, Pesach; (April 6):

The Rebbe remained in Medvedevka for Pesach. After praying, Rabbi Nathan saw the Rebbe sitting at the *Seder*. This was the only time that Rabbi Nathan ever saw the Rebbe at a *Seder* (*Aveneha Barzel* p. 16 #13). He also ate with the Rebbe all Pesach (*Tovos Zichronos, Ibid.*).

After Pesach, the Rebbe returned home to Breslov, and Rabbi Nathan accompanied him as his attendant (*Yemey Moharnat* 7a). They stopped over at Rabbi Gedalia of Linitz, and Rabbi Nathan, in particular, prayed loudly. The Rebbe explained to Rabbi Gedalia why his followers did so (*Aveneha Barzel* p. 16 #14). On the way home, realizing Rabbi Nathan's fear of facing his family, the Rebbe said, "A person walks on a very narrow bridge, but the main thing is not to be afraid" (*Tovos Zichronos, Ibid.*; Cf. *Likutey Moharan* II 48; *Meshivas Nefesh* 35).

Upon returning from Sarah's wedding, the Rebbe said *Likutey Moharan* 132 and 133 which discuss why the Tzaddik is famous in some places while his greatness remains unrecognized in others (*Chayay Moharan* 15a #59, #59; Cf. *Parparaos LeChokhmah, ad loc.*).

After Rabbi Nathan returned, his wife left his father's house (*Yemey Moharnat* 7a). His father had thrown him out and he had to set up his own household (*Tovos Zichronos, Ibid.*).

Rabbi Nathan returned to Breslov shortly before Shavuos. He wanted to remain with the Rebbe for Shavuos, but the Rebbe told him, "Better to desecrate one Sabbath..." (a reference to *Shabbos* 151b, *Yoma* 85b) (*Yemey Moharnat*

27a). Rabbi Nathan wanted to move to Breslov, but the Rebbe told him not to.

Thursday night, 6 Sivan, 1st night of Shavuos; (May 26):

The Rebbe said *Likutey Moharan* 51 (*Chayay Moharan* 15a, #59, #59; *Parparaos LeChokhmah ad loc.*).

Likutey Moharan 11 was also said on this Shavuos (*Chayay Moharan* 14b #59, #59). We have no details of any of the incidents relating to the saying of the lesson, but Rabbi Nathan said, quoting the Rebbe, that the subject "Understanding the Torah in depth" includes three separate concepts (*Parparaos LeChokhmah, ad loc.*).

Sunday, 8 Sivan; (May 29):

Rabbi Nathan came to the Rebbe, and the Rebbe reviewed *Likutey Moharan* 51 with him (*Chayay Moharan* 7b #23, #23; *Parparaos LeChokhmah, ad loc.*).

During the summer, Rabbi Nathan's father began making peace with him. He returned all Rabbi Nathan's money. Rabbi Nathan would not need to be involved in business except to go to Berdichov for merchandise. Otherwise he was to be free to study Torah (*Kochavey Or* pp. 15, 16 #9; *Aveneha Barzel* p. 19).

Shabbos, 5 Tammuz, Torah reading, Korach; (June 25):

Around this time, Rabbi Nathan started out for Berdichov for merchandise. On the way he stopped off in Breslov. Near a stream close to the Rebbe's house, the Rebbe talked with him for a long time (*Kochavey Or* p. 17 #10).

Rabbi Nathan became very poor, since his store was not making enough money. After his wife complained about their difficult situation, he prayed that God would provide him with a livelihood. Around this time his father had a meeting with his business partners. They rebuked him for having abandoned such a precious son. They advised him to take Rabbi Nathan's remaining merchandise and sell it in their stores, giving Rabbi Nathan the profits (*Kochavey Or* p. 21 #14).

Summer:

A large number of the Rebbe's followers unexpectedly came to visit him for a Shabbos. On Friday night he said *Likutey Moharan* 24. It was said with so much emotion that his words were hardly audible (*Parparaos LeChokhmah, ad loc.; Chayay Moharan* 7a #18, #18). The next morning he said *Likutey Moharan* 16 and 166 (*Chayay Moharan* 4b #6, #6; Cf. *Parparaos LeChokhmah, ad loc.*). The table broke under the weight of the crowd and the Rebbe complained, saying, "Are gentiles sitting at my table as in the times of the Mashiach, when gentiles will come to the Tzaddikim?" He quoted the verse, "And all nations shall flow unto Him" (Isaiah 2:2), which is mentioned in *Likutey Moharan* 16. *Likutey Moharan* 166 speaks of the additional power the Tzaddik has when his followers are with him. Both lessons 16 and 24 were written down by the Rebbe himself.

During this summer, Rabbi Dov Chayalas, who had been Rabbi in Ladizin, gave up his position to settle in Breslov. He told the Rebbe a story involving the letters of the *Aleph-Bais*. This prompted Rabbi Nachman to reveal *Sefer HaMidos*, which is arranged alphabetically (*Sefer HaMidos*, Introduction, p. 15; *Nevey Tzaddikim* p. 50). Soon after this, Rabbi Nathan began transcribing the *Sefer HaMidos* at the Rebbe's dictation (*Yemey Moharnat* 10b).

That summer, the Rebbe planned a trip to his uncle, Rabbi Baruch, in Tulchin. Before this trip Rabbi Baruch asked one of the Rebbe's followers, "What is my nephew doing?" and the follower told him of Rabbi Nachman's greatness (*Aveneha Barzel* p. 17). Rabbi Nathan heard that the Rebbe was planning a trip to Rabbi Baruch and wanted to accompany him, but the Rebbe would not let him come (*Ibid.*).

When he was with Rabbi Baruch the Rebbe sighed. When

Rabbi Baruch asked him why, he said he wanted to achieve very great levels. Rabbi Baruch tried to console him, mentioning various Tzaddikim whose levels Rabbi Nachman had attained. The Rebbe said he had passed them all. Then Rabbi Baruch mentioned the Baal Shem Tov. The Rebbe said of himself that he had surpassed the Baal Shem Tov when he was thirteen. His uncle then pushed him and he nearly fell from the landing. He was saved through the intervention of his mother's soul (*Ibid.*; see above p. 64).

The Rebbe remained with his uncle over Shabbos (*Ibid.* p. 18). People slandered the Rebbe and gossiped about him to his uncle, and from then on a conflict developed between them (*Yemey Moharnat* 7a).

During her lifetime, the Rebbe's mother had asked Rabbi Baruch why people thought he rejected her son. Rabbi Baruch answered that it was his intention to conceal the Rebbe because the world was not yet ready for his light (*Tovos Zichronos* p. 9).

On the Shabbos that the Rebbe was away, Rabbi Nathan remained in Breslov. He visited Rabbi Yudel and saw the Rebbe's teachings from before his arrival in Breslov. Rabbi Nathan spent that entire Friday night reading these notes (*Ibid.*). When the Rebbe returned from Tulchin, Rabbi Nathan went home (*Ibid.* #15).

On another Sabbath that summer, while sitting at the Shabbos table, the Rebbe embarrassed Rabbi Nathan (*Yemey Moharnat* 7a). Rabbi Nathan kept eating. The Rebbe told him, "When a man is shamed, he doesn't eat." What the Rebbe wanted was to make sure that Rabbi Nathan could accept rebuke sincerely (*Biur HaLikutim*, Introduction, with reference to *Likutey Moharan* II, 7).

Shabbos, 11 Av, Shabbos Nachamu, Torah reading, Va'eschanan; (July 30):

The lesson *Likutey Moharan* 12 was said (*Chayay Moharan* 14b #59, #59). It was most probably said in Tcherin,

since the Rebbe usually went there for Shabbos Nachamu
(*Ibid.* 30a #24, #126; see above p. 79). This lesson was written
down by the Rebbe himself (Cf. *Parparaos LeChokhmah, ad
loc.*). It speaks of the difference between the *Tzaddik* and the
Lamdan. When the Rebbe said this *Torah* he connected it to
(Isaiah 40:1) "*Nachamu, Nachamu,*" but when he wrote it
down, he left this out.

When the Rebbe returned from a trip (most probably this
one), he acted especially kindly to Rabbi Nathan, after having
previously embarrassed him (*Yemey Moharnat* 7a).

15

BRESLOV 5564 (1803-1804)

Shabbos, 1 Tishrei, Rosh HaShanah; (September 17):

Likutey Moharan 13 was said (Chayay Moharan 14b #59, #59). In it Rabbi Nachman spoke of overcoming the desire for money, and of coming to a Tzaddik.

Rabbi Aharon wanted to pray with the Rebbe, and did so for Shacharis. For Mussaf, however, he went to the main synagogue, and led the service there (Tovos Zichronos #7).

Thursday, 2 Kislev; (November 17):

Rabbi Nathan's mother died (Yemey Moharnat 7b). During the mourning period, Rabbi Nathan went to see the Rebbe and asked him what he could do to benefit her soul. The Rebbe answered that he should make a blessing with sincerity (Aveneha Barzel p. 71 #57).

Wednesday, 29 Kislev, 5th day of Chanukah; (December 14):

Rabbi Gedalia of Linitz died (Chachmey Yisroel p. 160).[25] Rabbi Gedalia was a student of Rabbi Yehuda Leib, the Magid of Polonnoye, who in turn was a major disciple of the Baal Shem Tov. He was also a disciple of Rabbi Yaakov Yosef of Polonnoye, author of the Toldos. He was among those who supported the Rebbe in his dispute with the Shpola Zeida (Chayay Moharan 29b #19, #122). The Rebbe

---

25. There, however, we find the year of his death given as 5545. This is clearly in error since Rabbi Nathan visited him in 5563 as above. Similarly, in Hillulah Rabbah, we find the year given as 5548, and this is also incorrect. The correct year is learned from Sichos HaRan #132; see below, p. 103.

credited him with the creation of *Shevachey HaBaal Shem Tov* (*Aveneha Barzel* p. 29 #30). Its editor, Rabbi Dov Ber ben Shmuel, the *shochet* of Linitz, in his introduction, also credited his decision to compile the stories to the statement he had heard from "Rabbi Gedalia as told to him by Rabbi Schmerel of Varchivka" that before the Mashiach comes, there will be no more miracles. Rabbi Gedalia was also the author of *Teshuos Chen* (*Chachmey Yisroel, Ibid.*; see also *Shem HaGedolim HeChadash, Gimel* #6).

Friday, 1 Teves; (December 16; December 4 Julian):

The "Statute Concerning the Jews," first proposed in October 1802, became law.

Shabbos, 2 Teves, Shabbos Chanukah, Torah reading, Miketz; (December 17):

Likutey Moharan 14 was said on Shabbos Chanukah, after the death of Rabbi Gedalia of Linitz (*Chayay Moharan* 14b #59, #59; *Sichos HaRan* #132; *Parparaos LeChokhmah, ad loc.*). In a sense this lesson was a eulogy for Rabbi Gedalia. It therefore mentions that one does not eulogize on Chanukah (§13) (Cf. *Shabbos* 21b, *Orach Chaim* 670:1). It speaks of how one's studying the Torah in purity brings people to repent and convert to Judaism. Most of it was written down by the Rebbe himself. (When there were two Sabbaths in Chanukah, the Rebbe's regular Chanukah lesson was given on the second.)

After Shabbos Chanukah, the Rebbe told Rabbi Nathan to study the *Shulchan Arukh* at the rate of five pages a day. He continued this study for half a year (*Shevachey Moharan* 22b #6, #435).

Before Shabbos Shirah, the Rebbe set off for Tcherin. On the way he said *Sichah 58*. Rabbi Nathan was with him. Rabbi Nachman then said *Likutey Moharan* 192 (*Chayay Moharan* 16b #10, #69).

During this winter, Rabbi Nathan continued work on the *Sefer HaMidos*, which he had begun transcribing at the

Rebbe's dictation in the summer of 5563 (*Yemey Moharnat* 10b). However, the work was often interrupted and took two years to complete (*Shevachey Moharan* 22a #5, #434).

That winter, the Rebbe spoke of "good life." He then outlined *Likutey Moharan* 18 (*Chayay Moharan* 5a #8, #8). The lesson itself was given in Terhovitza later that winter (*Chayay Moharan* 14b #59, #59).

One Friday night that year, the Rebbe dreamt of a big city where there was a great Tzaddik whom no one would greet (*Chayay Moharan* 20b #7, #87).

Rabbi Yitzchok Isaac became sick and died (Cf. *Shevachey Moharan* 10a #23, #313; *Kochavey Or* 31 #26). When the students lamented the death of Rabbi Yitzchok Isaac, the Rebbe said, "Now we have Rabbi Nathan" (*Shevachey Moharan* 10a #23, #313).

Spring:

Rabbi Avraham Dov of Chmelnick visited the Rebbe. The meal was delayed while Rabbi Avraham Dov was preparing himself. While they waited, the Rebbe told the story of his vision of a circle (related in *Chayay Moharan* 18b #3, #83). The Rebbe then commented, if his guest were to tell such a story he would have to make many preparations (*Aveneha Barzel* p. 24 #12).

Wednesday, 6 Sivan, Shavuos; (May 16):

Shortly after the visit of Rabbi Avraham Dov the Rebbe said *Likutey Moharan* 19 (*Chayay Moharan* 5b #10, #10; 14b #59, #59). In it, he spoke of the importance of coming to the Tzaddik to hear him say Torah. The Rebbe himself wrote down this lesson.

Summer:

During that summer, when Rabbi Nathan came with Rabbi Naftali, the Rebbe announced that he was giving him a "new practice." The Rebbe told Rabbi Nathan to study

Kabbalah (*Shevachey Moharan* 22b #6, #435; *Yemey Moharnat* 7b).

The Rebbe had a young daughter, Feiga, named after his mother. She was being raised by a nurse in Ladizin (*Chayay Moharan* 5b #12, #12). When this daughter fell ill, the family turned to a gentile who used charms to try to cure her (*Ibid.* 6a #13, #13).

After Shavuos, the Rebbe began to reveal some of the concepts of *Likutey Moharan* 21 (*Chayay Moharan* 5b #10, #10).

Sunday, 29 Tammuz, Erev Rosh Chodesh; (July 8):

Rabbi Nathan found the Rebbe lying on his bed. After remaining silent for a long time, the Rebbe said, "This Shabbos I cried about how everything I do is with great effort. Even to pray is very difficult for me" (*Chayay Moharan* 5b #10, #10). He also told him that "On Shabbos, a question was asked on High about 'transcendental light' and I answered it" (see end of *Likutey Moharan* 21). When his attendant came and asked for money for candles, the Rebbe said, "This is also an answer to the question [which was asked on High]" (*Ibid.* #11, #11).

Shabbos, 13 Av, Shabbos Nachamu, Torah reading, Va'eschanan; (July 21):

The Rebbe was away from Breslov. (His custom was to spend Shabbos in Tcherin and Medvedevka.) He then said *Likutey Moharan* 21, which is connected to (Isaiah 40:1) "*Nachamu, Nachamu*" and speaks of how through efforts in this world, one can perceive "transcendental light" in the Future World (§11). It also speaks about Miriam, who had shown disrespect for Moses, and how her punishment was an "aspect" of *yibum* (§6). This was an allusion to his own daughter Miriam, who later went to Israel and had to undergo *yibum* (*Chayay Moharan* 7a #16, #16; Cf. *Ibid.* 5b #10, #10; #12, #12).

Around this time, the Rebbe's daughter Feiga died. He

indicated to those around him that he was aware of this through *ruach hakodesh*. Upon his return to Breslov, the family hid the bad news from him, and since he had not heard the news by natural means he did not mourn her until later (see below p. 108; *Yemey Moharnat* 7b; *Chayay Moharan* 5b #12, #12).

16

BRESLOV 5565 (1804-1805)

Thursday, 1 Tishrei, Rosh HaShanah; (September 6):

The Rebbe said *Likutey Moharan* 20, which speaks of the Supernal Beard. Before beginning the lesson, he repeated the words "Nine *Tikkunim*" a number of times, and grasped his own beard (*Shevachey Moharan* 14a #21, #361). He said that his soul goes out each time he begins to say *Torah*. After the lesson, he also spoke of the greatness of the Land of Israel and the soul through which explanations of the Torah are revealed. He said that he did not mean an abstract concept, but literally the physical Land of Israel — "with these houses and these buildings" (*Chayay Moharan* 6b #15, #15; Cf. *Yemey Moharnat* 83b #2). He also said that the vision of the circle (in *Chayay Moharan* 18b #3, #83; see above p. 104) is explained in this lesson (*Chayay Moharan* 5b #9, #9).

After the lesson, the Rebbe said, "Today I have spoken of fire and water." The lesson discusses (§1) "Is not Thy word like fire?" (Jeremiah 23:29) and (§2) "He opened the rock and water gushed out" (Psalms 105:41) (*Chayay Moharan* 7a #15, #15). Rabbi Nathan said that when the Rebbe said this lesson, he felt thunder and lightning in his mind (*Aveneha Barzel* 45 #68).

On that Rosh HaShanah the Rebbe saw a vision in which he was given one thousand rubles for expenses, with which he paid to hear a lesson. This was *Likutey Moharan* 22 (see below p. 108; *Chayay Moharan* 29a #14, #117).

Shabbos, 3 Tishrei, Shabbos Shuvah, Torah reading, Haazinu; (September 8):

The group was waiting to see if the Rebbe would come to the third meal. Suddenly he entered and asked his oldest daughter about the death of Feiga. She was forced to tell him the truth (*Chayay Moharan* 6a #12, #12).

That Saturday night, he sat for an hour in mourning for his daughter Feiga (see *Yoreh Deah* 402:1. If one hears of a relative's passing after thirty days from the day of death, then the *shivah* is reduced to one hour.) He then related *Likutey Moharan* 175, which speaks of crying. He told his disciples that his daughter Feiga had come to him complaining that a gentile sorcerer had been used to try to cure her (*Chayay Moharan* 6a #13, #13; see above p. 105).

Monday, 5 Tishrei; (September 10):

That afternoon, the Rebbe was talking with his followers. He lit an oil lamp and said part of the *Selichos* from Yom Kippur. He said *Likutey Moharan* 22 (*Chayay Moharan* 6a #13, #13; 7a #17, #17) taking over four hours to do so. All the shopkeepers closed their stores and ran to listen (*Manuscript* p. 20).

Afterwards, the Rebbe said that a person must become so completely one with God that his study and prayer will be in the category of the (*Avodah Zarah* 19a) "Torah and prayer of God" (see end of lesson) (*Aveneha Barzel* p. 44 #67).

Shabbos, 1 Cheshvon, Rosh Chodesh, Torah reading, Noach; (October 6):

The Rebbe's daughter Miriam was soon to be married in Volochisk. On that Shabbos they made the *forshpiel*, and the Rebbe danced nearly all day. At *sholosh se'udos* the Rebbe told his disciples that he had paid one thousand rubles for *Likutey Moharan* 22, and then the Rebbe said *Likutey Moharan* 177. This lesson was said very rapidly, and could not be copied down exactly. It speaks of *Kaddish* (see *Likutey Moharan*, note at end of lesson; *Chayay Moharan* 29a #14, #117; *Ibid.* 15a #59, #59; *Yemey Moharnat* 7b).

Sunday, 2 Cheshvon; (October 7):

Rabbi Nathan stopped saying *Kaddish* for his mother (*Chayay Moharan* 29a #14, #117; she died on 2 Kislev, 5564, and this was the end of 11 months, cf. *Yemey Moharnat* 7b).

Rabbi Nathan went with the Rebbe to Volochisk for his daughter's wedding (*Yemey Moharnat* 7b). The distance from Breslov to Volochisk is 130 miles. On the way, the Rebbe took a side trip with Rabbi Shmuel Yitzchok of Tcherin. The Rebbe told the driver to give the horses free rein. They came to a house in a strange city several hundred *parsos* away, but the Rebbe would not eat any of the food that was prepared there (*Aveneha Barzel* p. 47 #74, *Sippurim Niflaim* p. 153 #6).

The wedding took place that week. At the wedding, Rabbi Leib of Volochisk mentioned to the Rebbe that he had bad eyes. The Rebbe replied, "If you had good eyes, you would have come and had the wedding in Breslov" (*Aveneha Barzel* p. 24 #11).

Rabbi Leib did not let Miriam dance with the Rebbe at the wedding. It was the reason why Miriam never had any children (*Aveneha Barzel* p. 33 #44; Cf. *Likutey Moharan* 21).

Friday, 7 Cheshvon; (October 12):

The Rebbe and Rabbi Nathan remained in Volochisk for Shabbos after the wedding. The *mikvah* was very crowded, and it was difficult to keep one's clothes from getting soiled. Rabbi Nathan, knowing how the Rebbe always spoke of keeping one's clothing clean, was worried that he might not be able to do so. But the Rebbe told him that he must go anyway but to be careful (*Manuscript* p. 4).

Around this time, the Rebbe told Rabbi Nathan to begin thinking of his own lessons, and said that at a later date he would tell him to write them down. He told Rabbi Nathan and his other followers to say *Tikkun Chatzos* (*Yemey Moharnat* 7b).

Kislev; (November):

Before Shabbos Chanukah, the Rebbe spoke of how everything created is embodied in the letters of its Hebrew name (*Sichos HaRan* #306; *Chayay Moharan* 17b #16, #75; see *Sefer HaMidos II Daas* #1). He also spoke of the types of wisdom that can sustain a man without his eating or drinking (*Sichos HaRan, Ibid.,* Cf. *Ibid.* 181, *Sippurey Maasios* 78b; see above pp. 15, 36).

Shabbos, 28 Kislev, Shabbos Chanukah, Torah reading, Miketz; (December 1):

The Rebbe said *Likutey Moharan* 54 (*Chayay Moharan* p. 15a #59, #59). This lesson speaks about the power of imagination. When the Rebbe said this lesson, he also said, "Sometimes one can heal a headache by drawing blood from the feet" (*Parparaos LeChokhmah, ad loc.*). At the end of the lesson, the Rebbe connected the concepts he had explained to *Tikkun Chatzos* and kindling the Chanukah lights (*Likutey Moharan, ad loc.*).

It was around this time that Rabbi Nathan started composing *Likutey Halachos.* His first piece was based on *Likutey Moharan* 54 (*Nevey Tzaddikim* 89). However, it was only thought out at this time, and not actually written down until the winter of 5566, when the Rebbe told him to record his ideas (*Yemey Moharnat* 10b). He told his followers that he had given them a good power of imagination (*Shevachey Moharan* p. 31a #75, #521). This alludes to *Likutey Moharan* 54 (§5, 6), given that Shabbos Chanukah (*Sichos VeSippurim* p. 87 #13; *Biur HaLikutim* 54,4).

Friday, 19 Teves; (December 21; December 9 Julian):

Statute of Jewish Organizations signed by Czar Alexander. Under the provisions of the Statute, by January 1808 no Jews were to be permitted to lease land, keep taverns, sell wine or even live in any village or hamlet in any part of the Pale of Settlement. They were offered the option of buying unoccupied land in certain areas or settling on crown lands. Encouragement was to be given to manufacture and handicrafts. The *kahals,* which had been the principal agency of Jewish self-government, were to become mere tax-collecting agencies. The Rabbis were to restrict themselves to "spiritual affairs." The election of the *kahals* and Rabbis was to be subject to ratification by the Russian governors.

Shabbos, 12 Shevat, Shabbos Shirah; (January 12):

The Rebbe was in Medvedevka. His daughter Chaya was staying there at the time. She was then four years old (see above p. 63). She had a stye in her eye which caused her considerable distress. The Rebbe then said *Likutey Moharan* 62 (§5), which speaks of the "beautiful maiden who has no eyes" (see *Zohar* II, 96a). Through this she was healed (*Chayay Moharan* 8b #26, #26). This lesson was dictated to one of his followers by the Rebbe. However, he himself wrote a somewhat different version which was given to Rabbi Nathan on Wednesday, 24 Adar II, 5584 (March 24,1824) by someone from a nearby town (see end of *Likutey Moharan, Hosafos*).

Sunday night, 19 Adar; (February 18):

Yahrzeit of the Rebbe's mother, Feiga. (However, this might also have taken place in Adar II.) Rabbi Nachman was dictating *Likutey Moharan* 20 to Rabbi Nathan, when the Rebbe's mother came and reminded him that it was her *yahrzeit*. He immediately called a *minyan*, learned *Mishnayos*, said *Kaddish* and lit a candle for her. The next morning the Rebbe led the congregation in prayer. He said it was the first time he had ever done so (*Chayay Moharan* 6a #14, #14).

Thursday, 29 Adar; (February 28):

Naftali Hertz Wiesel, a leading *maskil*, died. He was the mentor of Chaikel Hurwitz, et al. (see above p.75).

During this winter, the conflict intensified between Rabbi Shneur Zalman and Rabbi Avraham Kalisker (*Igeres Baal HaTanya* #96ff). It appears that it was in this year that Rabbi Mordechai of Lechovitz was appointed administrator of charities in Israel, taking Rabbi Shneur Zalman's place (*Ibid.* #106).

It was at this time too that the Rebbe told Rabbi Nathan to ask his father-in-law to provide him with a rabbinical post (*Yemey Moharnat* 10b; *Shevachey Moharan* 23b #1, #444).

Around the beginning of Adar II, Rabbi Nathan began organizing the lessons of *Likutey Moharan*. He had originally written the Rebbe's lessons in many separate notebooks. The Rebbe told Rabbi Nathan to copy them in order. Rabbi Naftali read the lessons, and Rabbi Nathan wrote them (*Yemey Moharnat* 8b; *Chayay Moharan* 38a #17, #184).

The Rebbe also told Rabbi Nathan to collect the practical advice which could be derived from each lesson. His first attempt at writing this anthology did not satisfy the Rebbe, but then he compiled them in *Kitzur Likutey Moharan*, and the Rebbe said that it was a nice *tzetel*. Both projects took around three months until before Shavuos (*Yemey Moharnat, Ibid.*; cf. *Advice* p. 4).

During this year the Rebbe had a dream in which he was standing over a table and bending into the sea, and all the nations and kings stood and watched in wonder (*Chayay Moharan* 18b #1, #81).

Around Rosh Chodesh Nissan, the Rebbe's first son, Shlomo Ephraim, was born (*Yemey Moharnat* 7b). Rabbi Nathan came to Breslov the day after the birth (*Yemey Moharnat, Ibid.*). During that week, the Rebbe said *Likutey Moharan* 72 which speaks of mastering the evil inclination (*Chayay Moharan* 15a #59, #59; *Parparaos LeChokhmah, ad loc.*).

Shabbos, 29 Adar II; (March 30) (most probably, but possibly 7 Nissan; April 6):

The Sabbath after the birth of Shlomo Ephraim was the *sholom zochor*. The Rebbe spoke of Rabbi Nathan's bent shoe and this led to his saying *Likutey Moharan* 63, which connects "bent shoe" to *bris milah* (*Chayay Moharan* 9a #27, #27; *Yemey Moharnat* 8a).

On the night before the *bris* of Shlomo Ephraim, the Rebbe spoke about his own greatness. He said that even though other leaders spoke of themselves in similar terms, nevertheless, every person can only understand where the truth is according to his own heart (*Shevachey Moharan* 5b #21, #261).

At the *bris*, the Rebbe himself served as *sandek* and *mohel*. Rabbi Nathan was given the mitzvah of *periah* (*Yemey Moharnat* 7b).

On the third day after the *bris*, the Rebbe spoke about how plants die in the winter, and the importance of praying in a field with plants when they awaken in the spring (*Sichos HaRan* #98, *Chayay Moharan* 17a #13, #72; see also *Sichos HaRan* #227; *Likutey Moharan* II, 11). Right after this, Rabbi Nathan went home (*Yemey Moharnat* 7a).

Thursday, 12 Nissan; (April 11):

Russia joined England, Austria and Naples in a war coalition against France.

After Passover:

The Rebbe said that he knew two things: the meaning of "Man does not sin unless he thinks that no one sees him" (*Berachos* 28b), and "The culmination of all knowledge is to realize the extent of one's incomprehension" (*Bechinas Olam* 33:13; Cf. *Kuzari* 5:21; *Aylimah Rabasi* p. 3b; *Keser Shem Tov* p. 3a #3). The Rebbe said he had now attained new levels in understanding the profundity of these statements (*Sichos Moharan* 8a #42, #282; Cf. *Sichos HaRan* #3).

Between Pesach and Shavuos, the Rebbe suddenly went to Sharograd (*Yemey Moharnat* 8a). Sharograd is about 28 miles from Breslov. He stayed there for two weeks, and said that he had saved them from the plague (*Chayay Moharan* 29b #18, #121). There were, however, numerous fires in Sharograd (*Chayay Moharan, Ibid.*).

Rabbi Nathan was in Breslov many times between Pesach and Shavuos (*Yemey Moharnat* 8b), and the Rebbe seemed annoyed with him and Rabbi Naftali for coming too often (*Shevachey Moharan* 36b #142, #594).

Before Shavuos, Rabbi Nathan finished the project of copying the lessons that would make up *Likutey Moharan* (*Yemey Moharnat* 8b).

Rabbis Nathan and Naftali came to the Rebbe before Shavuos and he told them, "I know nothing. But of late I have learned that when there is *lashon hara* (slander) in the world, Tzaddikim cannot be humble." He said *Likutey Moharan* 197 which speaks of the same concept (*Chayay Moharan* 7b #24, #24; *Ibid.* 15a, #59).

He told them that he had had a dream that the Chassidim were with him for Shavuos as usual but he was unable to give a Torah lesson because of their coarseness (*Ibid.*).

Monday, 6 Sivan, Shavuos; (June 3):

The Rebbe said *Likutey Moharan* 56, which speaks of how everyone rules to some extent both openly and in a concealed way. He said, "I rule over all Tzaddikim" (*Chayay Moharan* 8a #24, #24). After Shavuos, Rabbi Nathan returned to Nemirov (*Yemey Moharnat* 9a).

Thursday, 16 Sivan; (June 13):

Rabbi Nathan decided to return to Breslov, in spite of some hesitations about whether the Rebbe would be annoyed with him for coming (*Ibid.*).

Friday, 17 Sivan; (June 14):

Rabbi Nathan arrived in Breslov that morning. The manuscript of *Likutey Moharan* was then given to be bound (*Ibid.*).

The Rebbe usually went to the *mikvah erev Shabbos*, at noon, but was delayed speaking to his followers. He said, "It is difficult to be a leader" (*Ibid.* 9b).

He spoke of the importance of the binding of the book

(*Ibid.; Shevachey Moharan* 13b #12, #351; *Chayay Moharan* 38a #17, #184). He then began to reveal the mystery of the Ten Psalms, known as *Tikkun HaKlali* (see *Rabbi Nachman's Tikkun*), as outlined in *Likutey Moharan* 205 (*Sichos HaRan* #141; *Yemey Moharnat, Ibid.; Chayay Moharan, Ibid.* 15a #59, #59).

During that week, the Rebbe's granddaughter, Adil's child, was very sick. The Rebbe said that he could feel her every groan (*Yemey Moharnat* 10a). The Rebbe then told the story of how the ARI's son had died because he had revealed a secret (*Sichos HaRan* #189, Cf. *Shevachey HaARI,* Warsaw, 1875, p. 11b f.). The lesson revealed that Shavuos, *Likutey Moharan* 56, discusses a number of these concepts, including the subject of health and suffering (§9).

Thursday, 23 Sivan; (June 20):

The binding of *Likutey Moharan* was finished, and when the Rebbe received it, he spoke about joy (*Yemey Moharnat, Ibid.; Chayay Moharan* 38a #17, #184; Cf. *Sichos HaRan* #43). Rabbi Nathan had been in Breslov all week. It was about this time that the Rebbe first told Rabbi Nathan about the "Burned Book" (*Yemey Moharnat, Ibid.;* see pp. 118-119, 155).

Rabbi Shimon now returned to the Rebbe after having been away for almost three and a half years (*Sichos HaRan* #173; see above p. 69). The Rebbe spoke of his name, and said that the letters SHiMON — שמעון, spell out avON MaSH — מש עון (free of sin) (*Sichos HaRan* #44). Rabbi Shimon asked the Rebbe to promise him that he would be his attendant in the World to Come and reminded him of the incident in Ossatin when he had saved the Rebbe's life (see above p. 9). The Rebbe said that, although that was a great thing, it was not enough to merit being his attendant. But the Rebbe later agreed after his mother appeared to him in a dream and urged him to consent (*Aveneha Barzel* p. 36 #51).

Around this time, Rabbi Leib of Volochisk decided to go

to Israel. He wanted to take all his children with him (*Chayay Moharan* 7a #16, #16). He also wanted his son, Reb Pinchas, Miriam's husband, to go with him to study (while still a teenager; *Shevachey HaRan* p. 55 #32). The Rebbe did not want Miriam to go, and at one point a divorce seemed imminent (*Yemey Moharnat* 28a).

Before this trip, the Volochisker was visited by the Chozeh of Lublin. A daughter of the Volochisker was married to a grandson of the Chozeh, and the couple was also going to Israel. On the way, he heard that Rabbi Baruch wanted to see him, and he visited him (*Igros Baal HaTanya* p. 87 #108).

There was inflation that summer.[26] It seemed there would be a good crop, and that the inflation would decrease. The Rebbe, however, said that it would last another year (*Sichos HaRan* #186; also see #62, where inflation is mentioned).

26. The Chozeh of Lublin refers to the inflation in his letter, printed in *Igros Baal HaTanya*, p.87 #108.

17

BRESLOV 5566 (1805-1806)

Tuesday, 1 Tishrei, Rosh HaShanah; (September 24):

Likutey Moharan 58 and 59 were said (Chayay Moharan 15a #59, #59). They were both written down by the Rebbe. Originally, they were given as one lesson on the verse, "Happy is the people who know Teruah" (Psalms 89:16).The Rebbe himself divided the lesson into two parts, and gave them to Rabbi Nathan in the manner in which they are now written (see end of Likutey Moharan 59).

Lesson 58 speaks about the religious people of the generation. Through "repentance from love" (allusion to Yoma 86b) which the Tzaddik brings into the world, they are healed and gain the respect of the generation (§8). It is important, though, that they not fall into pride because of this (§10).

Lesson 59 speaks of those who want to bring others close to God, and the danger that they will fall into the power of the klipah (§1). Some people are so wicked that it is forbidden to try to bring them back [because of their adverse influence] (§6). (See Likutey Halachos, Taaruvos 5:3, which explains that this does not exclude their returning by themselves).

On one of the days between Rosh HaShanah and Yom Kippur, when the Rebbe was leaving the mikvah, he said that he had been told from Heaven about how his followers should conduct themselves with regard to fasting (Shevachey Moharan 28a #45, #491).

After the holidays, the Rebbe told his followers about the fasts each one should undertake. Every year, they were to accept these fasts before the Rosh HaShanah lesson. Anyone who was not with the Rebbe on Rosh HaShanah was not to fast at all (Ibid.).

Cheshvon; (November):

A son, Meir, was born to Rabbi Nathan (*Yemey Moharnat* 10b, 27b).

After Meir's *bris*, Rabbi Nathan went to Breslov. It was at this time that the Rebbe showed him the "Burned Book" (see above p. 115; *Ibid.* 10b). He also told Rabbi Nathan to begin writing down his own *chidushim* (*Ibid.*).

Around this time also, the Rebbe completed the "Hidden Book" (it was completed about five years before his death; *Chayay Moharan* 37b #9, #175).

Kislev; (December):

For about three weeks, Rabbi Nathan remained in Breslov. During this period, he finished transcribing *Sefer HaMidos*, Part I, which he had begun in the summer of 5563 (*Yemey Moharnat, Ibid.*; *Shevachey Moharan* 22a #5, #434).

Shabbos, 30 Kislev, Shabbos Chanukah, Rosh Chodesh Teves, Torah reading, Miketz; (December 21):

The Rebbe said *Likutey Moharan* 17. It discussed, among other things, the many people who had recently converted to Judaism. In general, this lesson speaks of gentiles converting because of the contradictions to their faith which they find in their own books (§6). It also contained allusions to many recent events (*Chayay Moharan* 5a #7, #7). After the lesson, the Rebbe danced (*Yemey Moharnat, Ibid.*).

Shortly after that, a priest in a nearby village converted to Judaism. He later came to the Rebbe and told him that he had found contradictions to his faith in gentile literature. A woman and her children in a nearby town also converted (*Chayay Moharan* 5a #7, #7).

Shabbos, 13 Shevat, Shabbos Shirah; (February 1):

The Rebbe was expected in Medvedevka for that Shabbos. He was delayed and spent the Sabbath in nearby Halavkievka, without food or dishes (*Chayay Moharan* 30b #25, #127).

Monday, 15 Shevat; (February 3):

The Rebbe finally arrived in Medvedevka. He gave the lesson that he was supposed to have given that Shabbos[27] (*Ibid.*).

During this winter, Rabbi Nathan continued writing down the "Burned Book" at the Rebbe's dictation (*Yemey Moharnat* 11a; *Chayay Moharan* 37b #9, #175).

Nissan; (April):

After Passover, the Rebbe sent Rabbi Nathan with a *kvittel* to Reb Yehoshua of Zorin (Dezerin) (mentioned in *Kochavey Or* p. 33 #29) just before he died. The *kvittel* contained holy names which the Rebbe wanted Reb Yehoshua to have in mind. He also wanted Reb Yehoshua to think of him every day until his death. The Rebbe said that it would do him good in the next world (*Yemey Moharnat, Ibid.*; *Chayay Moharan* 37b #12, #178).

Rabbi Nachman then sent Rabbis Yudel and Shmuel Isaac to read the "Burned Book" in various towns. They left pages of the manuscript of *Likutey Moharan* behind in each community (*Chayay Moharan* 37a #8, #174). While they were there they read from the copy of the "Burned Book" which Rabbi Nathan had made (*Ibid.* 37b #9, #175). Rabbi Yudel and Rabbi Shmuel Isaac had many troubles along the way. They ran out of money and could not get any more. They were furthermore suspected of being thieves (*Kochavey Or* p. 52 #25).

After Passover, the Rebbe said to Rabbi Nathan, "I have given you a great mitzvah with this book (the *Likutey Moharan*); it has already begun to make an impression in the world." He then entreated Rabbi Nathan to pray for his son Shlomo Ephraim. (*Yemey Moharnat, Ibid.*; *Chayay Moharan* 37b #11, #177).

27. We know from the story in *Chayay Moharan* that 15 Shevat fell on a Monday. This occurred only in 5563 and 5566. We can eliminate the former date, since it is well documented.

Friday, 6 Sivan, Shavuos, (May 23):

The Rebbe wore white clothing for the first time. A man had come with his epileptic daughter, and had brought the Rebbe some wine.

On this Shavuos the Rebbe said *Likutey Moharan* 29. The lesson speaks of the rectification of speech (§1), and its being accepted through praising Tzaddikim (§2), rectification of the Covenant (§3) (see *Rabbi Nachman's Tikkun*; *Advice* p. 32ff), white clothing (§3), epilepsy (§7) and wine (§8). The Rebbe said that this lesson also pertains to France (*Chayay Moharan* 7b #20, #20).

This girl had her epileptic fits at regular intervals. During this lesson, when the Rebbe quoted the verse, "She has fallen but will no more; rise, O virgin of Israel," (Amos 5:2, according to the Talmudic interpretation *Berachos* 4b) the expected period passed without incident. From then on she was cured (*Rabbi Gedaliah Koenig*).

One of the Rebbe's wealthy followers had filled an order of flour for some aristocratic army officers. They were not satisfied with the merchandise and he was in financial and physical danger. When the Rebbe said this lesson, which explains that speech can be perfected through praising Tzaddikim, the Rebbe's follower realized that this would solve his problem (which depended on persuasion). The day after Yom Tov he traveled to Venetzia (a city some 40 miles from Breslov) where the officers were. All along the way he told stories of the Rebbe. When he arrived, his explanations were accepted and he was saved (*Chayay Moharan, Ibid.*).

Around this same time, after Shavuos, Reb Avraham Pais, one of the Rebbe's wealthy followers, arranged a match for his son with a granddaughter of the Baal Shem Tov. On the way to the wedding, Reb Avraham stopped in Breslov to see the Rebbe. That night the Rebbe went with another of his followers Reb Chaim Saras to the forest for *hisbodedus*. Then the Baal Shem Tov appeared to the Rebbe. The Baal

Shem Tov did not approve of the match and said that the groom should die. The Rebbe convinced him that he could live but would not have children and would divorce his wife. Soon a messenger arrived saying that the groom had fallen ill on the way, but the next day the Rebbe said that everything would be all right (*Kochavey Or* p. 62 #43).

This Reb Chaim Saras was a businessman in Breslov (*Kochavey Or* p. 33 #30). He would fast twice a year from Sabbath to Sabbath, on Ki Tetze and Ki Tavo, as the Rebbe told him (*Sippurim Niflaim* 63). The Rebbe himself made use of Reb Chaim Saras' devotions to accomplish great things (*Aveneha Barzel* 32 #37). His daughter, Chaya Leah, married Rabbi Zvi Aryeh, son of Rabbi Aharon of Breslov (*Sippurim Niflaim, Ibid.*; Cf. *Kochavey Or* p. 65). Later, he told Reb Avraham Pais not to join the Savraner (who was to become Rabbi Nathan's chief adversary in 5595-5599 (1835-39); see *Yemey HaTalaos*) (*Kochavey Or* p. 62). Before his death, he saw the Rebbe in a dream (*Sippurim Niflaim, Ibid.*).

At a gathering, the Rebbe said, "A person is so foolish that even when the angel of death is behind him, he continues in his folly." No one understood what the Rebbe meant, but Reb Chaim Saras felt that it meant that he would die. The Rebbe confirmed this, but told him that he could save his life by coming to Medzeboz and praying at the grave of the Baal Shem Tov, where the Rebbe was planning to go to pray for his ailing son, Shlomo Ephraim (*Kochavey Or* p. 61 #43).

The Rebbe went with Reb Chaim Saras to Medzeboz and they prayed at the Baal Shem Tov's grave. Afterwards, the Rebbe said, "I succeeded for you, but not for me" (*Ibid.*).

In Sivan, soon after Shavuos, the Rebbe's son, Shlomo Ephraim, died. The Rebbe later spoke of the greatness that this child could have achieved (*Yemey Moharnat* 11a; *Chayay Moharan* 33b #1, #151).

On the way back from Medzeboz, the Rebbe said, "The child is dead." He would not come into Breslov for Shabbos, but spent Shabbos in a village outside the city with Reb Chaim Saras (*Kochavey Or, Ibid.*).

He also sat *shivah* in this village, accompanied by Reb Chaim Saras (*Ibid.*).

The Rebbe said, "The ARI only revealed one secret, and was punished with the loss of his son. But I have revealed many great secrets" (*Sichos HaRan* #189; see above p. 115).

The next Thursday, Rabbi Nathan and Rabbi Naftali were with the Rebbe. The Rebbe's wife had complained on three counts: that the Rebbe did not take care of himself, that he traveled too much, and that he had let the child die. The Rebbe said to his two disciples, "You be the judges if she is the one who suffered from the loss of the child" (*Aveneha Barzel* p. 30 #32). He said, "I suffer inside and outside," and began to cry. His two disciples ran in embarrassment (*Yemey Moharnat* 11b; *Chayay Moharan* 9a #28, #28).

The next day, Friday, the two disciples returned. The Rebbe told them, "If you had not run out, I would have told you something beautiful." He then said *Likutey Moharan* 65 (*Yemey Moharnat, Ibid.; Chayay Moharan, Ibid.*).

In this lesson, the Rebbe speaks about a beautiful field of souls and about the "keeper of the field," and the suffering that the "keeper" must endure.

After the lesson he said that every lesson had a story. He began to tell the story of how "Azus" had a daughter, which corresponded to that lesson, but he did not finish the story (*Ibid.* 22b #14, #94).

During this time, the Rebbe began to speak more openly about rectifying souls. He had begun to comprehend this, however, while in Zlatipolia (*Chayay Moharan* 34b #2, #152).

Before this, the Rebbe also said *Likutey Moharan* 242, which speaks of *Arikh Anpin* of *klipah* (*Chayay Moharan* 9b #31, #31).

The next day was Shabbos, and the Rebbe said *Likutey Moharan* 262, which speaks of "from crying rivers" (Job

28:11); that is, from "crying" come rivers of Torah (*Yemey Moharnat, Ibid.*; *Chayay Moharan, Ibid.*).

During the summer, the Rebbe sent Rabbi Nathan and Rabbi Naftali to Medzeboz to pray at the Baal Shem Tov's grave. He told them first to go to Berdichov (*Yemey Hatalaos* p. 44). They visited Rabbi Levi Yitzchok in Berdichov, and spent Shabbos there. The Shpola Zeida was also there for that Shabbos (*Ibid.* 44, 46). When the Shpoler returned from Berdichov, he met a man from Nemirov, and called Rabbi Nathan and Rabbi Naftali (Psalms 47:10) *Maginey Eretz* — protectors of the earth (*Ibid.* p. 5).

Sunday, 5 Av; (July 19):

The Rebbe set out on his usual summer journey to Medvedevka and Tcherin, accompanied by Rabbi Nathan and Rabbi Naftali. On the way to Ladizin, the Rebbe spoke about the Mashiach. He said that if his son had not died, the Mashiach would have come. At that time, on the way between Ladizin and Teplik, he revealed the *Megilas Sesarim*, which contained many secrets concerning the Mashiach. Rabbi Nathan and Rabbi Naftali later told the Rebbe they had been very happy after hearing what he had related, and the Rebbe said he too had been very joyous (*Yemey Moharnat* 11b-12a; Cf. *Aveneha Barzel* 30 #32). Two men from Teplik and the Rebbe's son-in-law, Reb Yoske, were also on the wagon, but were not aware of what the Rebbe was saying when he spoke to Rabbi Nathan and Rabbi Naftali[28] (*Kochavey Or* p. 50 #21; *Aveneha Barzel* p. 30 #31).

Shabbos, 11 Av, Shabbos Nachamu; (July 25):

The Rebbe was in Medvedevka. It was here that he told the first of his stories (*Yemey Moharnat* 12a; *Chayay*

---

28. This *Megilas Sesarim* was known to Rabbi Avraham beReb Nachman of Tulchin (*Nevey Tzaddikim* p. 78). It was written to a large extent in abbreviations in order to conceal the secrets. Some Breslover Chassidim still possess copies today.

Moharan 15b #59, #59). Before he told it, he said, "Now I will begin to tell stories!" (*Chayay Moharan* 33b #1, #151).

When he returned, he repeated the story to Rabbi Nathan, saying, "On my trip, I told a story and everyone who hears it will have a thought of repentance" (*Sippurey Maasios*, story #1).

This story, The Lost Princess, is about a king who had six sons and a daughter (see *Rabbi Nachman's Stories* #1 p. 31).

Monday, 13 Av; (July 27):

The Rebbe gave a lesson which speaks of how one can accept suffering with love. The lesson is printed in *Likutey Moharan* at the end of the volume. (See *Shevachey Moharan* 35a #124, #575; also see *Likutey Halachos, Geviyas Milveh* 3:10.)

Monday, August 17 (4 Elul):

The Rebbe told the story, Trust in God, as printed in *Maaseh Bitachon* (Nevey Tzaddikim p. 83; see *Rabbi Nachman's Stories* #29 p. 485).

During this month of Elul, Rabbi Nathan's wife went with her children to Mohelov, one of the cities where her father was the Rabbi (*Yemey Moharnat* 12b).

18

BRESLOV 5567 (1806-1807)

Shabbos, 1 Tishrei, Rosh HaShanah; (September 13):
At *sholosh se'udos* the Rebbe said *Likutey Moharan* 60 which speaks of stories in general, and is related to the first story told the previous summer (*Yemey Moharnat* 12a; *Chayay Moharan* 34a #1, #151; 22b #14, #94).

This lesson speaks of the role of wealth (§1), followed by the attainment of fullness of days through the fear of God (§2, §3). This fear can only come when barren women conceive (§5), which in turn comes about by arousing people from their "sleep" through telling stories (§6) and requires good students (§7) (see above p. 117, regarding lesson 59).

After finishing this lesson, the Rebbe said, "It was a beautiful 'wedding' " (*Shevachey Moharan* 13b #17, #356). The Rebbe then said lightheartedly, "Today I said three things which are contrary to popular belief. People say that stories help one to fall asleep, but I said stories awaken one from sleep; people say that from talk one doesn't become pregnant, but I said that through the Tzaddik's stories, which awaken people from sleep, barren women conceive; people say that the true Tzaddik does not need worldly possessions, but I said that the Torah has depths which can only be reached through the greatest wealth" (*Chayay Moharan* 8b #25, #25). Everyone present was highly aroused by this lesson. Even as the Rebbe was still preparing to begin the lesson, many of those present suddenly began thinking of some of the concepts the Rebbe was to explain such as (*Ta'anis* 23a) "Can a person sleep for seventy years?" (§6).

When the Rebbe said that the *shofar* awakens many who sleep (§9) several people cried, and he did not continue until they had stopped. The Rebbe said that he could have held the entire group for three straight days with this lesson, and they would not have known the difference between day and night (*Parparaos LeChokhmah, ad loc.*).

Between Rosh HaShanah and Yom Kippur the Rebbe said that there would be much sickness during the year (*Yemey Moharnat* 16b; *Sichos HaRan* #186). This premonition was so strong that on Erev Yom Kippur, when the Rebbe left the *mikvah*, he put his hand on his head to see if he was alive (*Ibid.*). Later that year, he was to contract tuberculosis.

Sunday night, 10 Tishrei, Yom Kippur; (September 21):

During the *Kol Nidrei* prayers, when the *chazan* began the *piyut* "*Yaaleh*," there was a fire in Breslov and all the congregants went home to save their possessions (*Chayay Moharan* 34a #1, #151). The Rebbe said that despite the sanctity of the day they need not observe unnecessary stringencies with regard to saving their possessions (*Shevachey Moharan* 33a #100, #547; Cf. *Shulchan Arukh, Orach Chaim* 334). After the fire, soldiers came into the synagogue and beat some of the people there to force them to extinguish what remained of the fire (*Yemev Moharnat* 12b).

Monday night, 11 Tishrei, Motzoai Yom Kippur; (September 22):

The Rebbe said he knew of the fire in advance because of Rabbi Shmuel Yitzchok, and remarked that the numerical value of the name "Shmuel Yitzchok" — שמואל יצחק (585) is equal to that of the Hebrew word "*srefah*" — שרפה (fire). He also said that he had wanted to achieve great things on High that *Kol Nidrei*, viz. that God grant him a knowledge of the Torah equal to Moses', but was prevented by the fire (*Chayay Moharan* 34a #1, #151; *Hashmotos, ad loc.; Yemey Moharnat, Ibid.*; see above p.17; below p. 157).

Tuesday, 11 Tishrei; (September 23):

Rabbi Nathan returned to Nemirov (*Chayay Moharan* 34a #1, #151). From there, he continued to Mohelov where his family was waiting (*Yemey Moharnat, Ibid.; Chayay Moharan, Ibid.*). On the way to Mohelov, he saw much sickness (*Yemey Moharnat* 15b).

Thursday, 13 Tishrei; (September 25):

Rabbi Nathan came to Mohelov (some 65 miles from Nemirov). His father-in-law was in Kremenetz, so he waited for him to return. He was to remain in Mohelov for nearly two years (*Yemey Moharnat* 13a). He did not visit Breslov again until Chanukah (*Ibid.* 13b).

In Tishrei of that year, the *Sefer HaGanuz* (The Hidden Book) was completed. Rabbi Nachman said that this book contained much deeper mysteries than any of his others and that the Mashiach would explain it (*Chayay Moharan* 37a #5, #171).

Shabbos, 7 Cheshvon, Torah reading, Noach; (October 18):

The Shpola Zeida heard about the Rebbe's stories. He spoke of why stories were needed in later generations (*Sippurey Chassidim*, Rabbi Shlomo Yosef Zevin, Tel Aviv, 1959 #10).

Reb Avraham Peterberger went to St. Petersberg around this time. He wrote the Rebbe that he had fears about remaining a religious Jew. When the Rebbe received his letter, he remarked that this fear itself would save him (*Chayay Moharan* 34a #1, #151; Cf. *Biur HaLikutim*, Introduction).

During that Cheshvon, the Rebbe bought stores in Medzeboz (*Yemey Moharnat* 12a). He sent Reb Shmuel of Teplik to Medzeboz to buy up the stores that had belonged to the Baal Shem Tov. Rabbi Baruch also wanted these stores. When he saw Reb Shmuel walking in an arrogant manner to acquire the stores, he cursed him with a fever. The

Rebbe said that this curse was in reality a blessing for it
extended his life (*Biur HaLikutim*, Introduction). The Rebbe
owned these stores, and also a house in Medzeboz, for the
rest of his life. After he died, we find that Rabbi Nathan went
to see about them (*Yemey Moharnat* 47a, 48b). Involved as
business partners with the Rebbe were Reb Yisroel, Reb
Moshe BeHarav and Moshe ben HeAni (*Alim LeTerufah*; see
Appendix letter #1).

Shabbos, 11 Kislev; (November 22) most probably:

A son, Yaakov, was born to the Rebbe. (He was born on a
Shabbos and the *bris* was before Chanukah; *Yemey
Moharnat* 14a).

**Friday night, 18 Kislev, Torah reading, Vayishlach;
(November 28):**

On *vach nacht*, Reb L. Dayin brought the Rebbe fish for
the *bris*. The Rebbe then said *Sichah* 93 (*Yemey Moharnat,
Ibid.; Aveneha Barzel* 33 #41; Cf. *Chayay Moharan* 15b #59,
#59).

Sichah 93 speaks of a "light that shines in one thousand
worlds." It discusses how a Tzaddik must be as vengeful and
vindictive as a snake (*Yoma* 23a), and that such a Tzaddik
can divide the thousands into hundreds so that everyone can
receive this light.

The next day, after the *bris*, the Rebbe said to those
present, "Why do you come to me? I hate you" (*Aveneha
Barzel, Ibid.*).

Wednesday, 29 Kislev; (December 10) approximately:

Rabbi Nathan left Mohelov for Breslov, a trip of some
sixty miles. Even though he had no money for expenses or
for a coach, his strong desire enabled him to overcome the
obstacles (*Yemey Moharnat, Ibid.*).

Friday, 1 Teves; Chanukah; (December 12):

Rabbi Nathan arrived in Breslov. The Rebbe told him
about a man who said terrible things about him (the Rebbe),

and how much he suffered because of this (*Yemey Moharnat* 14b).

Shabbos, 2 Teves, Second Shabbos of Chanukah, Torah reading, Miketz; (December 13):

At the third meal, the Rebbe said *Likutey Moharan* 30. He began with the opening verse of *Miketz*, but did not elaborate on how it was connected with the lesson. On Saturday night, he said that he would have to give an entire new lesson in order to connect this lesson to the verse (*Chayay Moharan* 7b #7, #7; see end of lesson in *Likutey Moharan*).

Sunday, 3 Teves; (December 14) approximately:

Rabbi Nathan returned to Nemirov. His father greeted him warmly, and gave him a present. Rabbi Nathan remained there for several days, trying without success to find a coach going to Mohelov. When he saw that this was not possible, he decided to return to Breslov and wait there for a coach.

Around this time, the Rebbe went to Tulchin to visit his uncle, Rabbi Baruch. Rabbi Baruch mentioned that the Mezritcher Magid had not completely understood the concept of left-handedness. Shortly afterwards the Rebbe explained it in *Likutey Moharan* 66 (*Aveneha Barzel* 46 #72; see *Likutey Moharan* 66 end of §1).

Tuesday night, 13 Teves; (December 23):

Rabbi Nathan returned to Breslov. He had not yet said *Kiddush Levanah*, and this was the last night that it could be said. The Rebbe said that he could say it as long as the moon could be seen through the clouds (Cf. *Magen Avraham* on *Orach Chayim* 426:a; *Yemey Moharnat* 15a; *Shevachey Moharan* 27b #37, #483).

After Rabbi Nathan had said *Kiddush Levanah*, he sat down with the Rebbe and his son-in-law, Reb Yoske. The Rebbe then told them a story about birds which had helped an army, ending with cries of *mazal tov* (brought in *Chayay Moharan* 18b #2; *Ibid.* 15a #59, #59; *Yemey Moharnat* 15a). They then ate together (*Ibid.*).

During the meal, they heard another of Rabbi Nachman's followers say *Kiddush Levanah* with great feeling. The Rebbe spoke of his satisfaction from this. The conversation led to his saying the first part of *Likutey Moharan* 66 (*Yemey Moharnat, Ibid.*). This lesson speaks of how important it is to be with a Tzaddik when he leaves this world, as Elisha was with Eliyahu (see Kings II, 2:9-11), and how a follower can sometimes apply the power of the Tzaddik more than the Tzaddik can himself.

Shabbos, 16 Teves, Torah reading, Vayechi; (December 27):

Rabbi Nathan remained in Breslov until after Shabbos. Guests from the Land of Israel were there. The Rebbe spoke of the strong yearning one must have for *Eretz Yisroel*, and the importance of breaking down barriers. This was incorporated into *Likutey Moharan* 66 §4 (*Yemey Moharnat, Ibid.; Chayay Moharan* 15a #59, #59).

Motzoai Shabbos, 17 Teves:

The Rebbe spoke about bringing the "spirit of the Mashiach," thus completing *Likutey Moharan* 66 (§2; *Chayay Moharan, Ibid.*).

The Rebbe told the story of the cave of Eliyahu, and how Eliyahu also had *hisbodedus* (see *Outpouring of the Soul*, p. 10; *Kochavey Or* 76 #23). He said that Eliyahu attained all his spiritual achievements in this way. The Rebbe said he had thought about this while in the cave in Haifa (see above p. 39). Rabbi Nathan then ran into the empty women's section of the synagogue for *hisbodedus*. A man was celebrating the engagement of his daughter and wanted Rabbi Nathan to be present, but he could only be found after they called his name (*Aveneha Barzel* p. 61 #24).

That night Rabbi Nathan took leave of the Rebbe and returned to Mohelov. His father-in-law was there, and was very angry because Rabbi Nathan had gone to Breslov (*Yemey Moharnat* 15b).

Rabbi Nathan could not return to Nemirov that winter, because the weather was so severe. He and his wife each fell ill three times. His children also suffered from illness. Their maid died, and the maid of his father-in-law was very sick. It was a time of great sickness and epidemics in the world (*Ibid.*; *Chayay Moharan* 34a #1, #151). Rabbi Nathan wrote the Rebbe a letter, and the Rebbe answered him. This gave Rabbi Nathan the strength to overcome his illness (*Yemey Moharnat, Ibid.*).

Shabbos, 15 Shevat, Shabbos Shirah; (January 24):

The Rebbe went to Medvedevka and Tcherin for Shabbos Shirah, as was his custom (*Yemey Moharnat* 16a states that he was in Medvedevka. In *Chayay Moharan* 34a #1, #151, however, we find that he was in Tcherin).

After that, he went to Kremenchug, where his daughter Sarah lived. She was pregnant and he waited there for several weeks until she gave birth. During this time, he was very distressed (*Ibid.*).

Sarah finally had a son, and he was named Yisroel. The Rebbe was then very happy, especially at the *bris*. On the third day after the *bris*, however, Sarah fell ill, and the Rebbe rushed back to Breslov. He said that the tremendous grief had devitalized his spirit (*Ibid.*).

Thursday, 25 Adar I; (March 3; February 19 Julian):

The Czar signed a law appointing Jewish deputies.

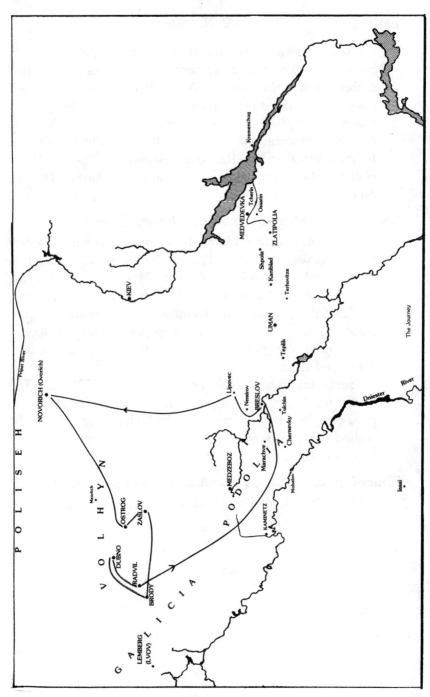

The Journey

19

THE JOURNEY

In late winter 5567 (1807), Rabbi Nachman set off on his mysterious journey to several cities northwest of Kiev, in the Poliseh, Volhyn and Galicia regions. Ostrog, latitude 50.20°N longitude 26.31°E, was famous for its outstanding Rabbinical leaders. Novorich (or Ovorich), a large city to the north of Kiev at 51.21°N 28.49°E, had leading Chassidic masters in its Rabbinical seat. Very little is known about Zaslov, 50.07°N 26.51°E. Dubno, 50.26°N 25.44°E, is famous for the Dubnor Magid, Rabbi Yaakov Krantz. Brody, latitude 50.06°N longitude 25.10°E, was one of the largest cities in Galicia. It was at one time the seat of the Vaad Arba Artzot – Council of the Four Lands – and home of many leading codifiers and Kabbalists.

Before Purim, the Rebbe set off on his trip to Novorich (*Chayay Moharan* 34b #3, #153). This was in the district of Poliseh (the area northwest of the Pripet River towards Pinsk) (*Yemey Moharnat* 16a).[29]

Before the trip, the Rebbe gave Reb Shmuel of Teplik thirty *rendels* to buy a horse and wagon and to hire a driver (*Sippurim Niflaim* p. 151). He made a condition with Reb Shmuel's wife that her husband could be away for a year (*Manuscript* p. 18).

Before setting off the Rebbe clapped his hands and said, "Now something new is beginning. We can be compared to someone who is playing and everyone is dancing. To anyone who doesn't understand and can't hear the music, it appears

---

29. It seems most probable that Novorich mentioned in our sources is identical to the town known as Ovorich. Rabbi Nota of Novorich, mentioned in *Shemos HaTzaddikim* (p. 58) would be Rabbi Nota of Ovorich, the father-in-law of Rabbi Avraham Dov Ohrbach, the *Bas Ayin*.

very strange — so people don't understand why you run after me. When I return from my trip, I'll be able to play and you'll be able to dance" (*Chayay Moharan* 34b #7, #157). He said that if people knew the reason for this trip, they would kiss his footsteps. "With every footstep I tilt the balance of the world towards the side of merit" (Cf. Talmud *Kiddushin* 40b). He also said (like King David; *Berachos* 4a), "My hands are soiled with blood and afterbirths in order to purify a woman for her husband" (*Chayay Moharan* #4-5, #154-155; *Yemey Moharnat* 16b).

In general, however, no one knew the reason why the Rebbe took this trip to Novorich. He did not collect any money, but spent a considerable amount (*Chayay Moharan, Ibid.* #4, #154; *Ibid.* 29a #15, #118; *Yemey Moharnat* 16a). He traveled disguised as a merchant. He warned the men with him not to reveal his identity to anyone (*Sippurim Niflaim* p. 150; Cf. *Chayay Moharan* 29a #15, #118).

The two men who started off with the Rebbe were Reb Shmuel of Teplik and Rabbi Naftali. Rabbi Naftali, however, was weak and sick and could only travel as far as Lipovec (approximately thirty miles north of Breslov) because of the cold (*Sippurim Niflaim* p. 150). Rabbi Naftali took with him the manuscript of *Sefer HaMidos*, and the Rebbe praised it very highly, saying, "*Mein liber hartzeker chaver, mein liber getrayer chaver. Ot dos hot mich gemacht far ein Yid*" — My dear beloved friend, my dear loyal friend. This is what made me a Jew (*Shevachey Moharan* 15b #40, #379).

Along the way, the Rebbe said, "I have the power to change the whole world for the better, not just simple people but even Tzaddikim, and I could even bring non-Jews close to God" (*Shevachey Moharan* 5a #11, #251).

They finally arrived in Lipovec, where Rabbi Naftali left them, and they were joined by Reb Isaac Yosef of Lipovec (*Sippurim Niflaim* p. 150). This Reb Isaac Yosef was a follower of the Rebbe and a businessman (*Kochavey Or* p. 33 #30).

In Lipovec the Rebbe asked his followers how they thought they could repent for even one of their sins. He told them he was repenting for all of them (Cf. *Yoma* 86b, "Great is repentance for even if a single individual repents, the entire world is forgiven"). He said he had the power to rectify everything, as long as they refrained from intentional sins in the future (*Shevachey Moharan* 9b #14, #304). He also said, "I am a wonder, and my soul is very wondrous" (*Ibid.* 5b #16, #256).

Between Lipovec and Novorich, they did not know where they were going. At each crossroads the Rebbe indicated to them which road to take (*Sippurim Niflaim* p. 151).

On the way, Reb Shmuel of Teplik would sleep near the Rebbe. Once the Rebbe asked him if he had heard anything that night. He replied, "No, but I couldn't sleep the whole night." The Rebbe then said, "Even though he didn't see, his *mazal* (soul) saw" (*Megillah* 3a), for the Rebbe had seen lofty things that night (*Kochavey Or* p. 57 #37).

Another time the Rebbe said, "How did you sleep and how did I sleep? My sleep was in the mystery of 'left-handedness' " (*Sichos HaRan* #152; see above, p. 129).

In Poliseh, on the way to Novorich, the Rebbe spoke with merchants as if he knew their business as well as they did. There was a case where he read a man's mind (*Sippurim Niflaim* p. 152 #5; *Kochavey Or* p. 57 #36).

There was also an episode during this journey where a child recognized the Rebbe through his disguise. The child later died (*Kochavey Or* p. 48 #13; *Aveneha Barzel* p. 35 #50; *Sippurim Niflaim* p. 151-52 #3, 4).

Tuesday, 14 Adar II, Purim; (March 24):

The Rebbe was in Novorich for Purim. He originally planned to travel further (*Yemey Moharnat* 16b). He stayed there with the Rabbi of the town who was related to him by marriage[30] (*Chayay Moharan* 34b #3, #153).

---

30. According to our assumption that Novorich is identical to Ovorich, this

Soon after this, the Rebbe left Novorich and went to Ostrog. He then sent a letter to his followers in Breslov (see Appendix, letter #1).

Thursday, 8 Nissan; (April 16):

Rabbi Nathan received a copy of this letter from Rabbi Naftali, while still in Mohelov. He immediately wrote the Rebbe an answer (reprinted in *Alim LeTerufah* #1).

Rabbi Nathan then left Mohelov and traveled to Nemirov. He and his family had recuperated from their illness. Rabbi Naftali had written to him about the Rebbe's trip. When he arrived in Nemirov, he had a long conversation with Rabbi Naftali, and the latter told him details of what had happened to the Rebbe on the way to Novorich (*Yemey Moharnat* 16b).

Meanwhile, the Rebbe sent Reb Shmuel of Teplik to Breslov to bring the Rebetzin. The Rebbe hired another man to attend him (*Yemey Moharnat* 17a; *Chayay Moharan, Ibid.*).

Friday, 9 Nissan, Erev Shabbos HaGadol; (April 17):

Reb Shmuel and the Rebbe's wife arrived in Ostrog. It is possible that the Rebbe's daughter Miriam was with them (Appendix, letter #2).

Shabbos, 10 Nissan, Shabbos HaGadol, Torah reading, Metzora; (April 18):

The Rebbe and his wife were in Ostrog. The Rebbe wanted his wife to be treated by Dr. Gordon, who lived in Ostrog at the time (*Ibid.*). Although the Rebbe did not in general hold physicians in high esteem, this Dr. Gordon was a very special individual. He was originally non-religious, and was a physician to the court, but through a remarkable series of events, he became a follower of the Mezritcher Magid (see

---

Rabbi would be Rabbi Avraham Dov Ohrbach, the *Bas Ayin*, who appears to have been a relative of the Rabbi of Chmelnick, the Rebbe's *mechutan*.

Adas Tzaddikim p. 42, in *Chayay HaTzaddikim U'Fa'alam*; *Kahal Chassidim* pp. 55-56). He was also known as Rabbi Aharon ben Shimon Rofey. After the Magid's death, he lived in Vilna and Ostrog, until he died on 27 Adar II, 5570 (*Chachmey Yisroel* p. 204. In *Ir Vilna* it is suggested that all Jewish Gordons are his descendants.)

The Rebbe's wife, however, did not want to be attended by Dr. Gordon, but preferred to go to Zaslov where she had family (*Yemey Moharnat*, *Ibid.*; *Chayay Moharan*, *Ibid.*). Zaslov was the original home of Reb Ephraim, the Rebbe's father-in-law (*Chayay Moharan* 25b #2, #105).

Sunday, 11 Nissan; (April 19):

The Rebbe, his wife, and Reb Shmuel of Teplik left Ostrog and traveled to Zaslov (*Ibid.*). The journey was just twenty-five miles, and they arrived there in the evening.

They only had Reb Shmuel to attend to their needs. He had to find them lodgings and *matzah* and the other Passover necessities, all in one day. The only place that they could find was an old, delapidated house, and they had to fix the roof (*Yemey Moharnat*, *Ibid.*).

Thursday, 15 Nissan, Passover; (April 23):

Passover was spent in Zaslov.

Subsequently, a wealthy man opened his house for the entire family (*Ibid.*).

Rabbi Nathan stayed in Nemirov until after Pesach. He went to Breslov and told Reb M. (Moshe Chenkes?) to send money to the Rebbe in Novorich, and Reb M. sent twenty-five rubles. The Rebbe had told them to send all moneys to Novorich (*Yemey Moharnat* 16b). Rabbi Nathan then returned to Mohelov.

In Mohelov Rabbi Nathan heard that the Rebbe had sent a letter to Breslov saying that he was very sick and that they should pray for him. Rabbi Nachman later said that their prayers helped him (*Yemey Moharnat* 17a; *Chayay Moharan* 35a #9, #159).

Sunday, 2 Iyar; (May 10):

The Rebbe received a letter from his son-in-law Reb Yoske and daughter Adil (see unnumbered letter at the beginning of *Alim LeTerufah*; Appendix, letter #2).

Thursday, 6 Iyar, Emor; (May 14):

The Rebbe sent a letter from Zaslov (Appendix, letter #2).

Monday, 17 Iyar, Bechukosai; (May 25):

The Rebbe wrote a letter (Appendix letter #3) to his brother Rabbi Yechiel in Kremenchug.

Around this same time, the Rebbe also sent another letter (Appendix, letter #4) to the community in Breslov.[31] This letter is also alluded to in *Yemey Moharnat* 17a, which quotes the Rebbe as saying that his health had improved without recourse to medicine.

One of the people whom Rabbi Nathan saw while in Mohelov was Rabbi Yisroel Shochet, brother of Reb Avraham, and uncle of Rabbi Nachman of Tulchin (who later became Rabbi Nathan's leading disciple). Rabbi Yisroel visited Rabbi Dovid Zvi, Rabbi Nathan's father-in-law, since he was accustomed to visit many sages and ask them questions concerning *shechitah*. It was there that he met Rabbi Nathan, and was impressed with his scholarship and sincerity in prayer. It was through this that he met the Rebbe (*Biur HaLikutim*, Introduction).

Thursday, 27 Iyar; (June 4):

Rabbi Nathan had heard that men from Nemirov, Teplik and Dashev were planning to go to Zaslov to be with the Rebbe for Shavuos. His father-in-law was planning to go to Kremenetz, and leave him in charge of his Rabbinical post in

---

31. This also speaks of the Rebbe spending a further three months in Zaslov, as does his letter to his brother Rabbi Yechiel, and therefore they were most probably written around the same time (see below, p. 144; cf. *Chayay Moharan* 35a #9, #159).

Mohelov. Rabbi Nathan, however, begged him to let him go to Breslov. Suddenly two people appeared who lent him some money, and he found a coach that was returning to Nemirov (*Yemey Moharnat* 17b).

Around 2 p.m., Rabbi Nathan left Mohelov to go to Breslov, and from there to Zaslov (*Ibid.* 18a). He was only to travel two and one-half *parsos* before nightfall (*Ibid.* 18b). (A *parsa* is ten *verst*, or 6.629 miles (10.67 km.). He had therefore traveled some 16.6 miles.) This would place him around Chernevky for the night.

Friday, 28 Iyar; (June 5):

Rabbi Nathan remained in this city overnight. By noon, he had reached Marachve, but was still some five *parsos* (33 miles, or 53 km.) from Nemirov. At this rate he would not be able to reach even as far as Nemirov, let alone Breslov, before Shabbos. But he had to be in Breslov before Sunday, where his friends were hiring a coach to journey to Zaslov. He was disappointed and prayed for a coach with four horses to take him to Breslov. Suddenly his prayer was answered and just such a coach came and took him to Breslov (*Yemey Moharnat* 18b, 19a).

Shabbos, 29 Iyar, Torah reading, Bamidbar; (June 6):

Rabbi Nathan was in Breslov.

Sunday, 1 Sivan, Rosh Chodesh; (June 7):

Rabbi Nathan left Breslov for Zaslov on the coach his friends had hired (*Ibid.* 19a).

Wednesday, 4 Sivan; (June 10):

Rabbi Nathan and his companions arrived in Zaslov (*Ibid.*).

Around this time, one of the Rebbe's followers, who had not been particularly close to him, died. The Rebbe said "Who knows what is happening with him in the next world? But if he had been a true follower, he would have been under the impression that he was preparing to come to me for Shavuos, and consequently he would have to be informed that he was already dead" (Cf. below, p. 170). After Shavuos, the Rebbe said that the man had been with him (*Shevachey Moharan* 11b #46, #336).

The Rebbe told them that R. Yaakov, the son of Rabbi Yudel, had had a son in Breslov. The Rebbe knew about it in Zaslov (*Kochavey Or* p. 50 #17).

The men of Zaslov were gathered around the Rebbe, and they told him about a rich man who had given Rabbi Baruch a large sum of money. Also present was a poor man from Nemirov. The Rebbe said that he was a teacher, and had sacrificed the opportunity of employment for half a year in order to come to him. Therefore, relative to his position, he had given more than the wealthy man (*Shevachey Moharan* 12a #47, #337).

Thursday, 5 Sivan, Erev Shavuos; (June 11):

In the morning, Rabbi Nathan visited the Rebbe, and the Rebbe told him a lesson which had been revealed to him in Zaslov. Some followers from Teplik brought him some new silver articles (*Yemey Moharnat* 19b).

Late that afternoon, the people gathered for *Minchah*. The Rebbe, however, was at his wife's side. She died shortly before the holiday, and was buried just before the holiday began (*Ibid.* 19b; Cf. *Chayay Moharan* 34b #3, #153). The Rebbe later said that if he had known the importance of a first wife, he would have made sure she lived in spite of her great suffering (*Aveneha Barzel* p. 39 #58).

Thursday night, 6 Sivan, Shavuos:

The first night, the Rebbe did not speak. Between the courses of the meal, he studied. Then he joined his followers and said *Tikkun lail Shavuos* throughout the rest of the night (*Yemey Moharnat, Ibid.*).

Friday, 6 Sivan, Shavuos morning; (June 12):

The Rebbe went to the *mikvah*, and prayed with Rabbi Nathan and the other followers who had come there (*Ibid.*).

The first day of Shavuos, he still did not speak. He sat at the meal, studying the *Idra Rabbah* out loud in a beautiful voice. The people kept bringing him food, and later he explained that they were "arguing" with him: they wanted him to end the meal with food like the great Tzaddikim who learn in order to know how to serve God through eating, but he wanted to end the meal with Torah like the simple Tzaddikim who eat in order to be able to learn Torah (*Yemey Moharnat, Ibid.; Chayay Moharan* 35a #8, #158).

Friday night, 7 Sivan:

The Rebbe put on his *shtreimel* for the first time that holiday. After *Birkas HaMazon* he sang *Atah Niglesa*. He then sat until morning with Rabbi Nathan and a few other men (*Yemey Moharnat* 19b-20a).

A discussion ensued regarding one of the group who lived in a large non-Jewish city, and each time he wanted to leave, he stayed a while longer thinking that he could accomplish more. This led to the Rebbe telling the story of "The Horse and the Pump" (*Rabbi Nachman's Stories* #15 p. 444; *Chayay Moharan* 15b #59, #59).

Shabbos, 7 Sivan; (June 13):

The Rebbe was happy at the morning meal. People from the city sent drink, and he distributed it (*Yemey Moharnat* 20a).

At the third meal, the Rebbe engaged Rabbi Yisroel Shochet in a conversation. The Rebbe said, "You are a *lamdan*, and therefore, I shall tell you a scholarly lesson." He then said *Likutey Moharan* 67 (*Yemey Moharnat, Ibid.; Chayay Moharan* 34b #4, #154; *Biur HaLikutim*, Introduction).

The Rebbe sat up with the entire group all that night (*Yemey Moharnat, Ibid.*).

The Rebbe had a lengthy conversation with Rabbi Yisroel Shochet. Among other things, they discussed Rabbi Yisroel's strictness. The Rebbe asked, "Who then should be a *shochet*? One who has no fear of God?" Rabbi Yisroel then asked the Rebbe to make him one of his followers. The Rebbe told him that he was too old, and it was hard to make old people his followers (*Biur HaLikutim*, Introduction; Cf. *Shevachey Moharan* 32b #96, #543).

Sunday, 8 Sivan; (June 14):

Rabbi Nathan wrote down the lesson (*Yemey Moharnat, Ibid.*).

The Rebbe asked Rabbi Nathan, "How does one merit becoming a real Jew?" Rabbi Nathan was dumbfounded. The Rebbe then explained, "When I began serving God, I had no idea that I would achieve what I did. There are things that I know now that I did not even realize existed. I could not even begin to yearn to perceive what I know now, for I had no idea that such levels of understanding and knowledge even existed. I therefore did not have any concept of what to strive for. But the same thing may still be true. Who knows what I have still to comprehend, what understanding I have still to perceive? My only comfort is the fact that I spend the entire day in Torah and prayer" (*Sichos HaRan* #159; see also *Shevachey HaRan*, p. 55 #33). Rabbi Nathan then spoke at length with the Rebbe, and left for home (*Ibid.*).

Wednesday, 11 Sivan; (June 17) approximately:

Rabbi Nathan returned to Nemirov. His father was very angry at him for refusing the Rabbinical position that his father-in-law had offered him, and he had to stay with his sister over the Sabbath (*Ibid.*).

Sunday, 15 Sivan; (June 21):

Rabbi Nathan went to Breslov, and stayed there several days, trying to get a coach back to Mohelov. After a few days, he finally found a wagon, and returned home to Mohelov. He was to remain there until Rosh HaShanah (*Ibid.* 20a-b).

Shabbos, 12 Tammuz, Torah reading, Chukas; (July 18):

Most probable time that *Likutey Moharan* 55 was said (since it speaks about the Red Heifer in §4-5). The lesson came to be said after a young man told the Rebbe that he had completed the study of tractate *Niddah*. The Rebbe asked him what was the connection between yawning (discussed in *Niddah* 63a) and the evil eye, and then said *Likutey Moharan* 55 to answer it[32] (*Aveneha Barzel* p. 45 #67).

After this, the Rebbe visited Brody and Dubno with Reb Shmuel of Teplik (*Chayay Moharan* 34b #7, #157). The Rebbe went into Brody alone. He disguised himself completely (*Ibid.* 29a #15, #118). He visited the houses of many rich people there and said, "I heard them crying out in their lust for money" (*Ibid.* 34b #7, #157). In each house, he gave a different name, but said that when he called himself Isaac that was the most appropriate (*Aveneha Barzel* p. 50 #6). In one house he saw a man and woman playing chess. The man ran out of the city after the Rebbe, and R. Shmuel of Teplik saw tears running down the man's cheeks (*Manuscript* p. 18; according to *Aveneha Barzel* p. 47 #74 this incident took place on the trip to Lemberg).

Many women had come who had wanted to marry the Rebbe (*Shevachey Moharan* 37a #143, #595). The Rebbe became engaged to a woman from Brody (*Chayay Moharan* 35a #10, #160; *Yemey Moharnat* 20b). He had visited the house of Reb Yechezkel Trachtenberg just as Reb Yechezkel's wife and daughter were talking about marriage. When the Rebbe entered the house the daughter saw him and said, "I want such a man" (*Manuscript* p. 18).

32. See *Parparaos LeChokhmah, ad loc.*, that it was written in Zaslov.

The *tana'im* were made in nearby Radvil. The bride was given a dowry of three hundred *rendels* (*Manuscript*, Ibid.). The Rebbe had completely separated himself from all sexual desires. He made a condition with her that they would not live as man and wife (see next paragraph; *Manuscript, Ibid.*; Cf. *Yemey Moharnat* p. 44a). She said of him, "I imagine you, I call you, but I never knew you" (*Shir HaKavod*). She eventually arranged for the building over his grave (*Sippurim Niflaim* p. 8).

Right after the engagement, the Rebbe contracted tuberculosis (*Chayay Moharan* 29a #15, #118; 35b #14, #164). With the first cough, he said that this disease would take his life (*Yemey Moharnat* 31a; *Chayay Moharan* 35a #12, #162). Before his death he said that it was a miracle that he had lived for the last three years (*Chayay Moharan* 35a #11, #161).

Shabbos, 26 Tammuz, Torah reading, Matos Masai; (August 1) most probably:

On the Sabbath after returning to Breslov, the Rebbe was with Rabbi Naftali. He cried for a while. He then said, "I will tell you the reason for my trip," and then he told the story of the Spider and the Fly (*Rabbi Nachman's Stories* #7 p. 138) (*Yemey Moharnat* 20b; *Chayay Moharan* 35a #10, 12, #160; *Rimzey HaMaasios* p. 3b).

Soon after this, the Rebbe told the story, The Rabbi's Son (*Rabbi Nachman's Stories* #8 p. 154) (*Yemey Moharnat* 20b; *Chayay Moharan* 15b #59, #59).

Shortly after his return, the Rebbe said, "Your prayers helped heal me in Zaslov" (*Chayay Moharan* 35a #9, #159). He also spoke about *shiduchim* (*Shevachey Moharan* 37a #143, #595).

Sunday, 5 Av; (August 9) most probably:

The Rebbe left for Tcherin for Shabbos Nachamu. In Ladizin he said he was going to die and that he wanted "sixty warriors" (Song of Songs 3:7) like the Baal Shem Tov had

had. He also said that he would have liked to return to the Land of Israel to die there, but he was too weak to undertake the journey. Secondly, he said, in Israel no one would be able to come to his grave. But if he was buried in Russia, he would be there with them so that they would visit his grave. He said that he would derive great pleasure from his followers' prayers and Torah study at his graveside (*Yemey Moharnat* 20b; *Chayay Moharan* 35a #12, #162; 40b #13, #197).

Shabbos, 11 Av, Shabbos Nachamu; (August 15):

The Rebbe was in Tcherin[33] (*Chayay Moharan, Ibid.*).

Tuesday, 28 Av; (September 1):

The Rebbe wrote a letter to his future father-in-law, Reb Yechezkel Trachtenberg (Appendix, letter #5).

Elul; (September):

The Rebbe married his second wife (*Ibid.*). The wedding was in Vatchak, near Breslov (*Manuscript* p. 18). It was to have been in Tshikov, but the plan was changed because of rain (*Kochavey Or* p. 59 #41). The Rebbe said that everyone at the *chupah* was forgiven all his sins (Cf. *Yerushalmi, Bikurim* 3:3). Rabbi Nathan, however, was not there at the time (*Yemey Moharnat* 20b; also see *Chayay Moharan* 29a #15, #118).

Friday, 22 Elul; (September 25):

Rabbi Nathan arrived in Nemirov. He had been in Mohelov since his return from Zaslov (*Yemey Moharnat, Ibid.* 20b).

---

33. In *Yemey Moharnat* 20b, however, it states that he was in Medvedevka and that he said a lesson there. We find the same contradiction as to whether he went to Tcherin or Medvedevka in the winter of 5567; see above, p. 131. They are very near each other on the outskirts of Kremenchug.

Shabbos, 23 Elul, Torah reading, Netzavim Vayelech; (Septemer 26):

Rabbi Nathan stayed at his sister's home in Nemirov but also visited his father, and made peace with him (*Ibid.*).

Motzoai Shabbos, 24 Elul; (September 26):

That Saturday night, Rabbi Nathan left Nemirov and arrived in Breslov in time for *Selichos*. After *Selichos*, he spoke with the Rebbe for a long time. Rabbi Nathan then remained in Breslov until after Rosh HaShanah (*Ibid.*).

Around this time the Rebbe told Rabbi Nathan *Likutey Moharan* II, 86, that only one who is weak in faith must serve God with fasts and self-mortification. He then told Rabbi Nathan the importance of having faith in oneself, as outlined in *Sichos HaRan* #140 (*Parparaos LeChokhmah* 61:8).

Shortly before Rosh HaShanah, the Rebbe also said *Likutey Moharan* 211, which speaks of why people must visit a Tzaddik on Rosh HaShanah. Rabbi Nathan writes that the same applies to visiting graves of Tzaddikim (*Ibid.*; *Chayay Moharan* 15a #59, #59).

20

BRESLOV 5568 (1807-1808)

Shabbos, 1 Tishrei, Rosh HaShanah; (October 3):
The Rebbe said *Likutey Moharan* 61 (*Chayay Moharan*
15a #59, #59; *Yemey Moharnat* 20b), which speaks of belief in
our sages (§1), about improper leaders, and about the reason
why Jews must undergo exile from their homes (§2). He also
spoke about how holy books come to be written because of
disputes (§5). This was an allusion to *Likutey Moharan*,
which would be printed that year (*Yemey Moharnat, Ibid.*). It
also speaks about belief in oneself (§5), which the Rebbe had
earlier discussed with Rabbi Nathan (see above, p. 146) and
the importance of traveling to Tzaddikim for Rosh HaShanah
(§7).

There was one member of the group who was not present
at the gathering that Rosh HaShanah. The Rebbe said, "I will
therefore have to go to Lemberg" (*Aveneha Barzel* p. 27
#21).

After Rosh HaShanah, Rabbi Nathan wrote down *Likutey
Moharan* 61 under the Rebbe's supervision. He wanted to
return to Nemirov but was unable to do so and remained in
Breslov until after Yom Kippur (*Yemey Moharnat* 21a).

Shabbos, 8 Tishrei, Shabbos Shuvah; (October 10):
Rabbi Nathan's wife was very sick in Mohelov, and there
was no one to take care of her. On Friday night, Rabbi
Nathan was told about it, and he told the Rebbe.

The next morning, the Rebbe said a lesson relating to the
illness of Rabbi Nathan's wife. He said that Shabbos is the
wife of all Israel (part of *Likutey Moharan* 277; *Yemey
Moharnat* 23b, 24a).

Tuesday, 11 Tishrei; (October 13):

After Yom Kippur, Rabbi Nathan left Breslov, and got as far as Tulchin (Cf. *Chayay Moharan* 10a #33, #33). He wanted to continue to Mohelov, but there was no way to go. Some merchants had offered to take him there but then said they were not going. This was because they had received false information about their buisiness affairs. As a result Rabbi Nathan returned to Breslov that evening (*Yemey Moharnat* 21a,b; Cf. below, p. 151, "The whole world is working for you ...").

Tuesday night, 12 Tishrei:

It became known that the Rebbe was intending to journey to Lemberg after the holidays. Rabbi Nathan was glad that circumstances had caused him to return to Breslov, giving him the opportunity to see more of the Rebbe before his journey. Rabbi Naftali was also in Breslov. He and Rabbi Nathan sat together with the Rebbe and it was a joyous occasion (*Yemey Moharnat* 21b).

Wednesday, 12 Tishrei; (October 14):

On Wednesday morning, as Rabbi Nathan was *davening*, Reb Michel, the Rebbe's attendant, came and told him to hurry to the Rebbe. Rabbi Nathan immediately took off his *tallis* and *tefillin* and quickly went to him. The Rebbe told him to bring his manuscript of *Likutey Moharan* and to write a table of contents for it. He also finished writing the "Burned Book," sitting many hours while the Rebbe dictated it (*Ibid.* 21b, 22a).

Thursday, 13 Tishrei; (October 15):

Rabbi Nathan went to Nemirov. Then he returned to Breslov, where he remained until after Simchas Torah (*Ibid.* 22a).

Friday night, 15 Tishrei, Succos; (October 16):

The Rebbe asked the meaning of the Russian word *hust* (which in Yiddish means cough or tuberculosis). He said it meant "guest," indicating a connection between his coughing and the *ushpizin* — the seven visitors to the *succah* (*Chayay Moharan* 35b #14, #164).

Shabbos, 22 Tishrei, Shemini Atzeres; (October 24):

The Rebbe said *Likutey Moharan* 277, 278, and the first part of *Azamra*, Lesson 282 (see bibliography). *Azamra* speaks of looking for the good points in each individual (*Chayay Moharan* 15a #59, #59; *Parparaos LeChokhmah* on *Likutey Moharan* 277, 278).

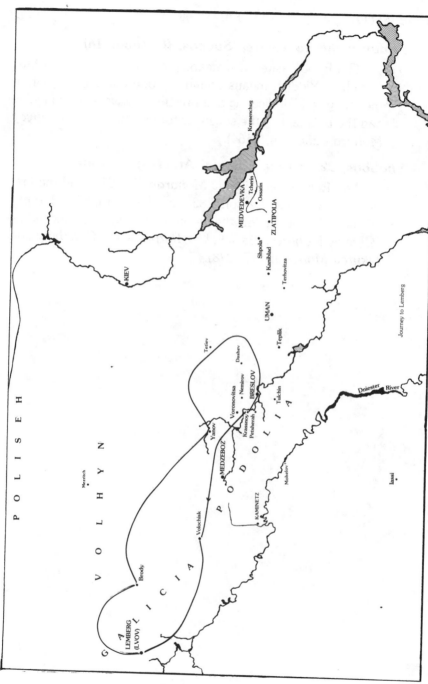

Journey to Lemberg

21

LEMBERG (LVOV)

The largest city in east Galicia, Lemberg is located at latitude 49.50°N longitude 24.00°E. Its population was approximately one hundred and fifty thousand of which about twenty percent were Jews. Lemberg was for many centuries the seat of some of the leading Rabbis of Europe. During Rabbi Nachman's lifetime the haskalah movement found a foothold there.

Monday, 24 Tishrei, Day after Simchas Torah; (October 26):

The Rebbe prepared to go to Lemberg. He took along the bound manuscript of *Likutey Moharan*. The people accompanied him as far as Krassnoy (some 20 miles from Breslov). Rabbi Nathan was delayed, and in his rush forgot the writings in his trunk in Petshereh, and had to have them sent to him. He caught up with the Rebbe in a small village, but by the time he had fed the horses the Rebbe had left and it was already night (*Yemey Moharnat* 22a-b; Cf. *Chayay Moharan* 29a #16, #119).

Monday night, 25 Tishrei:

Rabbi Nathan reached Krassnoy and found the Rebbe. Rabbi Nathan was very depressed. The Rebbe said, "Why are you depressed?! The whole world is working for you. One travels to Breslau and another elsewhere just for you. We will see each other again and again" (*Yemey Moharnat* 22b, 23a; *Chayay Moharan* 36b #1, #167).

Tuesday, 25 Tishrei; (October 27):

On Tuesday morning, the Rebbe hurriedly left Krassnoy. Rabbi Nathan and Rabbi Naftali ran after his coach, and met him by the bridge, where another follower, Reb M., came to meet Rabbi Nachman. The Rebbe then completed *Likutey Moharan* 282, telling how Tzaddikim build the "*Mishkan* on High," saying that this explained the reason for the trip (see *Parparaos LeChokhmah ad loc.*; below, p. 153). They took leave of the Rebbe, who then journeyed on (*Yemey Moharnat* 23b; *Chayay Moharan* 9b #33, #33; 36b #1, #167; 15a #59, #59).

After this, Rabbi Nathan returned to Mohelov. His father-in-law was very angry, since he had been away while his wife was so sick (*Yemey Moharnat* 23b, 24a).

Friday, 28 Tishrei, Erev Shabbos Bereshis; (October 30) approximately:

The Rebbe arrived in Volochisk (110 miles from Krassnoy, a little over two days' journey). He had to stay there two weeks before he could cross the Austrian border. One night he had a dream in which the Emperor gave his permission to cross. The next morning he received permission (*Chayay Moharan* 29a #16, #119).

Monday, 15 Cheshvon; (November 16) approximately:

The Rebbe left Volochisk and crossed the border. He was then able to continue to Lemberg (*Ibid.*).

Thursday, 18 Cheshvon; (November 19) approximately:

Upon his arrival in Lemberg, the Rebbe was so sick that he could only lie on his left side. Rabbi Aharon of Tetiev came to him and ordered him to turn over (*Chayay Moharan* 36b #2, #168). This Rabbi Aharon was the son of Rabbi Zvi, and the grandson of the Baal Shem Tov. He died on 5 Teves, 5589 (1829) (*Hillulah Rabbah*; see above, p. 16).

Rabbi Baruch asked Perel, the Rebbe's sister, about Rabbi Nachman's health. He told her that when he had decided to stop opposing the Rebbe he was able to understand a certain saying in the *Zohar*. The Rebbe's sister later told the Rebbe about this (*Aveneha Barzel* 18).

A wealthy man who had many guests begged the Rebbe to eat at his home. The Rebbe, however, only ate there once (*Ibid.* 26 #18).

In Lemberg there was a large community of doctors. The Rebbe spoke to many of them and they admitted their ignorance of medicine. He heard them defend two opposing views (*Sichos HaRan* #50).

The Rebbe once heard a *badchan* in Lemberg refer in his repartee to "the old old old God." The Rebbe later repeated this to his followers to emphasize our belief in God's primordiality (*Shevachey Moharan* 20a #8, #413).

Rabbi Nachman said that he worked in Lemberg to destroy heresy (*Parparaos LeChokhmah* 282). This was one of the reasons why the Rebbe took medicines in Lemberg (*Chayay Moharan* 38a #14, #181; also see *Sichos HaRan* #50).

In Lemberg, the Rebbe was with Reb Shmuel Yitzchok of Teplik. They saw troops of soldiers marching and the Rebbe showed Reb Shmuel Yitzchok that one of them was wearing shrouds. He explained that this was the path where angels drive people to Hell (*Aveneha Barzel* p. 47 #74).

The Rebbe lodged near a certain Rabbi in Lemberg, whose son later became Rabbi in Iassi. On one occasion, the Rebbe told a story of the Land of Israel, and because of his *devekus* he almost died. The Rabbi's son brought a candle which revived him. The Rebbe thanked him and said, "Oh, do I have a Nossele (a reference to Rabbi Nathan), and if you will come to me in Breslov I will make you unique like him" (*Aveneha Barzel* p. 59).

The Rebbe told Reb Yaakov of Medvedevka to see about printing *Likutey Moharan* (*Chayay Moharan* 38a #17, #184 states that it was somebody from Medvedevka. In a letter, *Alim LeTerufah*, we find that his name is Yaakov; see Appendix, letter #6).

Sunday, 24 Teves; (January 24) approximately:

The Rebbe sent out Reb Zalman HaKatan to all the gedolim of Poland for haskamos to Likutey Moharan. The Rebbe had once told him that a journey is tikkun habris (Biur HaLikutim, Introduction; Cf. Likutey Moharan 31 §4). When Reb Zalman HaKatan went to the Chozeh of Lublin, he had kvittels from Rabbi Nathan and Rabbi Naftali (Aveneha Barzel p. 91). He had been with Rabbi Nathan on his first trip to the Rebbe (see above, p. 81; Kochavey Or p. 11 #3; Aveneha Barzel p. 12 #8; also see Kochavey Or p. 33 #29).

Tuesday, 26 Teves; (January 26):

Date of haskama of Rabbi Yaakov Yitzchok, the Chozeh of Lublin. He called the Rebbe his mechutan (see above, pp. 59 footnote #12, 116).

Tuesday, 4 Shevat; (February 2):

Haskama from Rabbi Yisroel, the Koznitzer Magid.

Thursday, 20 Shevat; (February 18):

Haskama of Rabbi Avraham Chaim of Zlotchov. Also, on the same day, a haskama from Rabbi Meir ben Zvi Hirsh, Rabbi of Brody.

That same week, a haskama was obtained from Rabbi Ephraim Zalman Margolies of Brody. He signs that it is in the week of "and I will remove sickness from you" (Exodus 23:25), which is the week of Mishpatim. This was the week of 23-29 Shevat (February 21-27). He also writes that the year is "And the count of your days I will fill" (U'mispar yamecha amale) (Exodus 23:26). This adds up to 568, alluding to the year 5-568.

The haskamos of Rabbi Avraham Chaim, Rabbi Meir and Rabbi Ephraim Zalman were first printed in the second edition in 5581 (1821) in Rabbi Nathan's private printshop. The haskamos of the Chozeh and the Koznitzer Magid were first printed in the fifth edition of Likutey Moharan in 5636 (1876) by Rabbi Nachman of Tcherin.

Reb Zalman HaKatan's journey had taken about a year, during which time he had received many *haskamos* for *Likutey Moharan*. But when it came to printing the book, the Rebbe, because of his humility, did not want to have these approbations included. In time all but the five mentioned were lost (*Biur Halikutim*, Introduction; *Likutey Moharan*, *haskamos*).

In the winter, before Purim, a certain Reb D. came to Breslov with the information that the Rebbe wanted to print *Likutey Moharan*. Rabbi Naftali gave this information to Rabbi Nathan (*Yemey Moharnat* 24a).

After this, there was a rumor that the Rebbe had died in Lemberg (*Ibid.*). The truth was that he was very sick (*Ibid.* 31a).

When they heard that the Rebbe was alive, the *shochet* of Teplik began making a chair for the Rebbe. He was to spend six months working on it (*Aveneha Barzel* p. 27 #20; see below, p. 160).

Before Purim, a coach was sent to Mohelov to bring Rabbi Nathan to Breslov to edit the *Likutey Moharan* (*Yemey Moharnat* 24a).

Sunday, 14 Adar, Purim; (March 13):

Rabbi Nathan was in Breslov. He edited *Likutey Moharan*, and then returned to Mohelov (*Ibid.* 24a, b).

Reb Yaakov then brought *Likutey Moharan* to Ostrog to be printed (*Ibid.* 24b).

Between Purim and Pesach, the Rebbe cried a great deal (*Chayay Moharan* 36b #3, #169; Cf. *Nevey Tzaddikim* p. 81).

Around this time, the Rebbe made up his mind to destroy one of his manuscripts (the "Burned Book"). Rabbi Shimon had come to Lemberg and he was sent on this assignment. Rabbi Shimon fell ill in Dashev. He continued on to Breslov lying on a wagon, however, and burned both copies of this book, the Rebbe's original, and Rabbi Nathan's copy (*Yemey Moharnat, Ibid.; Chayay Moharan* 37a #3, #169).

This "Burned Book" contained many secrets, and was only fit for the greatest and most learned Tzaddik of the generation (*Chayay Moharan* 37a #6, 7, #172-173). It included the mystery of the mitzvah of *hachnasas orchim* — providing hospitality (*Shevachey Moharan* 35a #123, #574).

Monday, 14 Nissan, 1st day of Pesach; (April 11):

Bris milah of Rabbi Nathan's son, Yitzchok. His father-in-law was too sick to be the *sandek* (*Yemey Moharnat, Ibid.*).

Sunday, 11 Iyar, Emor, 26th of Omer; (May 8):

The Rebbe sent a letter to Reb Yaakov regarding the printing of *Likutey Moharan* (Appendix, letter #6).

Monday, 19 Iyar; (May 16):

Rabbi Dovid Zvi, Rabbi Nathan's father-in-law, died. Rabbi Nathan was by his side at the time (*Yemey Moharnat, Ibid.*).

Sunday, 17 Sivan; (June 12) approximately:

The Rebbe left Lemberg and went to Brody (*Chayay Moharan* 38a #16, #183). (The journey from Lemberg to Brody is some sixty miles, or two days' journey.)

Tuesday, 19 Sivan; (June 14) approximately:

The Rebbe arrived in Brody. He was to stay there for two weeks (*Ibid.*).

Tuesday, 3 Tammuz; (June 28) approximately:

The Rebbe left Brody for Yanov (a journey of one hundred-fifty miles or three to four days).

Shabbos, 7 Tammuz, Torah reading, Chukas; (July 2):

The Rebbe remained in Yanov for Shabbos (*Ibid.*).

Sunday, 8 Tammuz; (July 3):

The Rebbe rose early Sunday morning and left for Breslov. He traveled all that day.

From Yanov to Breslov was a journey of some fifty miles.

On the way, the Rebbe said, "I am like Choni HaMaagel, who slept seventy years and everyone forgot about him" (see *Ta'anis* 23a). When he came to Voronovitsa, some fifteen miles from Nemirov and twenty-five miles from Breslov, one of his followers jumped aboard his wagon. This gave the Rebbe a new spirit (*Chayay Moharan* 37b #13, #179).

Before dark that same day, the Rebbe returned to Breslov (*Chayay Moharan* 38a #16, #183; 29a #16, #119; *Yemey Moharnat* 24a).

Friday, 13 Tammuz; (July 8):

Rabbi Nathan arrived in Breslov. Word had reached him in Mohelov that the Rebbe had returned (*Yemey Moharnat* 25a).

Shabbos, 14 Tammuz, Torah reading, Balak; (July 9):

Rabbi Nathan was in Breslov. He greeted the Rebbe, who was extremely weak (*Ibid.*).

After returning from Lemberg, the Rebbe spoke at length about rectifying souls (*Chayay Moharan* 33b #1, #151). He also spoke of what he had wanted to do on Yom Kippur of 5567, which had been disturbed by the fire. He implied that it was because of this that he was suffering (*Ibid.* 34a #1, #151; see above p. 126). He then told a story about the son of Rabbi Yaakov Shimshon of Shepetevka. This son was sick as a punishment for acting disrespectfully towards his father. Although he realized this, he did not regret it. Rabbi Nachman was suggesting that he also did not regret his attempts that Yom Kippur (*Ibid.*).

The Rebbe said that he would have been content to be buried there in Lemberg, since many Tzaddikim were buried there.[34] But this would be far from his followers, and he wanted them to visit his grave (*Yemey Moharnat* 31a).

---

34. Some of the better known are: Rabbi Dovid Halevi, author of the *Turei Zohov* (*Taz*); Rabbi Chaim Cohen Rappaport; Rabbi Zvi Ashkenazi, author of *Chacham Zvi*; his son, Rabbi Ephraim Ashkenazi; and Rabbi Meir Teumim, father of the "*Pri Megodim*".

The Rebbe told his followers not to fast any more (see above, p. 117). He said that it was enough that they came to him on Rosh HaShanah, and that anyone who did not come on Rosh HaShanah would not be helped by the fasting (*Shevachey Moharan* 28a #45, #491).

After returning from Lemberg, the Rebbe emphasized the importance of faith more strongly than ever before. From this time on, Rabbi Nachman repeatedly stressed how his teachings would endure for future generations. The Rebbe then said, "My fire will burn until Mashiach comes" (*Chayay Moharan* 45b #45, #229; *Shevachey Moharan* 9b #16, #306; *Sippurim Niflaim* p. 70 #3).

Sunday, 22 Tammuz; (July 17):

After Shabbos Rabbi Nathan returned to Nemirov and arranged housing there. He then returned to Mohelov. Since his father-in-law had died, his wife and mother-in-law wanted to move to Nemirov (*Yemey Moharnat* 25a).

After Tisha b'Av; (Summer):

Rabbi Nathan left Mohelov, and moved back to Nemirov. He was then able to be with the Rebbe a number of times in Av and Elul (*Ibid.*).

Early in Elul, the *Likutey Moharan* was printed in Ostrog by Reb Shmuel ben Yissacher Ber Segel (see title page of the first edition; Cf. *Yemey Moharnat* 25a).

After the book was printed, the Rebbe discussed it and praised it, saying that people must study it until they are fluent in its teachings (*Yemey Moharnat* 25b; Cf. *Shevachey Moharan* 13a #7, #346). He said that they must also make another volume (*Yemey Moharnat, Ibid.*).

After that, the Rebbe spoke about people who follow their own intellect. In particular, Reb Reuven Yosef, son of Reb Yisroel Shochet, discussed a number of questions with the Rebbe. The Rebbe told him that these conundrums could drive him to Hell. He also spoke about the importance of a beard (*Chayay Moharan* 13a #51, #51; *Biur HaLikutim*, Introduction). The Rebbe then said *Likutey Moharan* II, 12 — *Ayeh* (see bibliography) — which speaks about following one's own intellect (*Ibid.*, Cf. *Chayay Moharan, Ibid.*).

Likutey Moharan II, 10 was said as the Rebbe sat by the south wall of the synagogue foundation. He spoke about joy, and how God had separated our paths from His opposers' and from those of the Rebbe's opposers' (*Chayay Moharan* 13a #50, #50).

During this time, the Rebbe went for many walks in the fields, and often said lessons on the way. *Likutey Moharan* II, 11, 12, 15 and 16 were said on such walks (*Chayay Moharan* 13a #40, #40; *Yemey Moharnat* 25b; *Sichos HaRan* #144). *Likutey Moharan* II, 11 was said after they had prayed *Minchah*, and the grass seemed to be praying along with them (*Sichos HaRan, Ibid.*; see also *Chayay Moharan* 15b #59, #59).

One Shabbos that summer, the Rebbe spoke about how one must be happy on the Sabbath (*Chayay Moharan* 13a #50, #50; Cf. *Sichos HaRan* #155). The Rebbe then said *Likutey Moharan* II, 17 (*Ibid.*).

One day the Rebbe went for a ride for fresh air together with Rabbi Nathan, Reb Moshe Chenkes and Reb Avraham Pais. They got out to walk but the Rebbe could not keep up with them. He spoke about how God is above time and space, incorporating it in *Likutey Moharan* II, 61 (*Biur HaLikutim*, Introduction).

Perel, The Rebbe's sister, convinced the Rebbe that he should visit Rabbi Baruch that summer because of her conversation with him the preceding winter (see above, p. 152), but the Rebbe said that even if an angel came and told him that his uncle, Rabbi Baruch, was at peace with him he would not believe him. Nevertheless, he did go to visit him (*Aveneha Barzel* p. 18).

During that month, Reb Avraham Peterberger returned to the Rebbe (*Biur HaLikutim*, Introduction).

Shortly before Rosh HaShanah, the *shochet* of Teplik brought the Rebbe the beautiful chair that he had carved for him. The Rebbe related a dream he had had involving that chair, and later said that *Likutey Moharan* II, 1 (which was said the following Rosh HaShanah) explained it. Rabbi Nathan was not there at the time (*Chayay Moharan* 20a #4, #84; *Yemey Moharnat* 26a). The Rebbe asked the *shochet* how long it had taken him to make the chair, and he replied that he had worked an hour a day for the last six months. The Rebbe said, "Then for half a year you spent an hour each day thinking of me" (*Aveneha Barzel* p. 27 #20). (According to tradition, Rabbi Nachman's chair which is presently in the Breslov synagogue in Jerusalem, is the chair made by the *shochet* of Teplik.)

The Rebbe gave several sheets of *Sefer HaMidos* II to some of his followers to copy. Rabbi Nathan had still not arrived. They put the material in alphabetical order. When Rabbi Nathan came, they gave him what they had and the Rebbe also gave him a number of additional sheets (*Yemey Moharnat, Ibid.*).

During that summer, Rabbi Nathan and Rabbi Naftali were with the Rebbe on a journey. They stopped at an inn. Rabbi Naftali had begun to develop tuberculosis and did not want to eat cheese, which aggravates the disease. Rabbi Nathan said that if he ate the cheese it would cure him, and the Rebbe confirmed this. Rabbi Naftali did so and was cured (*Kochavey Or* p. 51 #24). This is also alluded to in *Likutey Moharan* II, 1 (§10-11).

The Rebbe also told them about a dream regarding "I am God who heals you" (Exodus 15:26). He then said *Likutey Moharan* II, 43, about how weakheartedness produces fear in a person (*Chayay Moharan* 13b #53, #53).

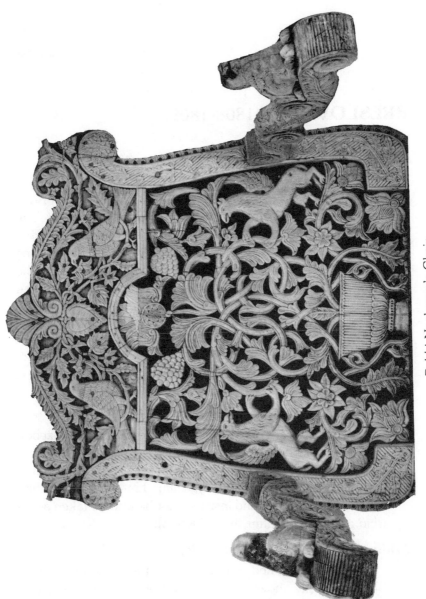

Rabbi Nachman's Chair

22

BRESLOV 5569 (1808-1809)

Thursday, 1 Tishrei, Rosh HaShanah; (September 22):
Hundreds of people came to Breslov for that Rosh HaShanah. The Rebbe said *Likutey Moharan* II, 1. The lesson speaks of recognizing true Tzaddikim (§3), overcoming evil desires (§4) through wisdom (§5), healing sicknesses (§11), prayer (§9) and Rosh HaShanah (§14). The Rebbe was so weak that it was a miracle he could speak (*Yemey Moharnat* 26a; *Chayay Moharan* 15b #59, #59).

Sunday, 4 Tishrei; (September 25):
Rabbi Nathan could not review the lesson with the Rebbe because of the Rebbe's weakness. He wrote it down anyway, as best he could (*Yemey Moharnat* 26b).

Monday, 5 Tishrei; (September 26) probably:
The Rebbe sent his brother, Rabbi Yechiel, to Medzeboz to pray for his health. Rabbi Yechiel had a weak horse, and wanted to go alone. Nevertheless, he agreed to Rabbi Naftali's request to accompany him. Later, Rabbi Nathan heard about the trip and insisted that he also be taken along (*Ibid.*; *Biur HaLikutim*, Introduction).

Friday, 9 Tishrei; (September 30):
Rabbi Nathan and others were at the grave of the Baal Shem Tov. He showed some of the distinguished people in Medzeboz the newly printed *Likutey Moharan* and they were greatly impressed (*Yemey Moharnat, Ibid.*).

Shabbos, 10 Tishrei, Yom Kippur; (October 1):

Rabbi Nathan, Rabbi Naftali and Rabbi Yechiel were in Medzeboz (Ibid.).

Sunday, 11 Tishrei; (October 2):

Rabbi Nathan returned to Nemirov (Ibid.).

Motzoai Shabbos Chol HaMoed, 18 Tishrei; (October 8):

Rabbi Nathan returned to Breslov. He would remain there until after Simchas Torah (Ibid.).

Upon his return, Rabbi Nathan reviewed *Likutey Moharan* II, 1 with the Rebbe. The Rebbe said, "This is what I said." Reb Avraham Peterberger had also written down this lesson, but the Rebbe said, "This is not what I said" (*Biur HaLikutim, Ibid.*).

During Chol HaMoed Succos, the Rebbe asked, "Where are we in the prayers?" He explained that all his lessons corresponded to and explained part of the daily prayers (*Shevachey Moharan* 14b #27, #366).

Sunday, 25 Tishrei; (October 16):

After Simchas Torah, Rabbi Nathan returned to Nemirov.

Friday, 13 Kislev, Vayishlach; (December 2):

The Rebbe sent a letter to his daughter, Sarah, and her husband, Rabbi Yitzchok Isaac (Appendix, letter #7).

Tuesday night, 25 Kislev, Chanukah; (December 13):

After lighting the menorah, the Rebbe had a dream about a guest with very special powers (*Chayay Moharan* 20a #5, #85).

Shabbos, 28 Kislev, Shabbos Chanukah, Torah reading, Miketz; (December 17):

The Rebbe said *Likutey Moharan* II, 2. A young man from Brahilov was on his way to the Rebbe but was delayed in Nemirov for Shabbos. He arrived on *Motzoai* Shabbos in the middle of the lesson. The Rebbe then wove this into the lesson. There was another part that he did not say until his brother Rabbi Yechiel, who was also delayed, arrived later (*Chayay Moharan* 18a #21, #80; *Parparaos LeChokhmah* on *Likutey Moharan* II, 2:2).

After that, Rabbi Nachman had those present sing *Luley HaShem* (Psalm 124) for a long time (*Ibid.* 30a #22, #124). Rabbi Nathan writes that this lesson was meant as a *korban todah* (a thanksgiving offering) that he was able to return from Lemberg (*Chayay Moharan* 18a #20, #79).

Shabbos, 11 Shevat, Shabbos Shirah; (January 28):

The Rebbe spoke about how he used to celebrate Shabbos Shirah in previous years (*Chayay Moharan* 31a #26, #128).

Shabbos, 18 Shevat, Torah reading, Yisro; (February 4):

Rabbi Yekusiel visited the Rebbe for Shabbos. His son-in-law, Reb Yitzchok, was also there. The Rebbe then told a story about the Baal Shem Tov and a hidden Tzaddik (*Chayay Moharan* 13b #52, #52). Rabbi Yekusiel, the Terhovitza Magid, had a question as to why all the books that were written in earlier generations were not preserved. The Rebbe answered this with *Likutey Moharan* II, 32, which also discusses hidden Tzaddikim (*Shevachey Moharan* 38a #155, #607). Rabbi Yekusiel said that the Rebbe was unique and the Rebbe agreed, saying, "Indeed there was never anyone so unique" (*Ibid.*).

After Shabbos, Rabbi Nathan showed the Magid how he had recorded this lesson, and Rabbi Yekusiel was astonished that it could be put into writing (*Parparaos LeChokhmah* on *Likutey Moharan* II, 32).

Somewhat later, the Magid visited his son-in-law, Reb Yitzchok, in Kherson. He told him of this question and the Rebbe's answer (*Shevachey Moharan* 46a #1, #607).

Adar; (March):

Before Purim, the Rebbe told the story, The Sophisticate and the Simpleton (*Rabbi Nachman's Stories* #9 p. 160). After Purim, he told the story, The Burgher and the Pauper (*Rabbi Nachman's Stories* #10 p. 197; *Chayay Moharan* 15b #59, #59; *Ibid.* #1).

One Saturday night, the Rebbe said "Even if a great soul came to us, we would still be important." He then told a story about a man who built a tower to protect himself from his enemies and how he had become king over them by means of a precious stone. The "stone" alluded to the great soul (*Shevachey Moharan* 8a #41, #281).

Sometime that year, he also had a dream about a leader who thought that he had to disguise himself as a gentile (*Chayay Moharan* 20b #6, #86).

Nissan; (April):

During Chol HaMoed Pesach, Reb Lipa returned to the Rebbe after having stayed away for several years. He had refrained from coming because of his preoccupation with money, but the Rebbe told him that a wind would blow away his money (*Kochavey Or* pp. 54, 55 #30; *Shevachey Moharan* 10a #25, #315; see above p. 93). It was through Reb Lipa that Rabbi Nathan originally came to Breslov (*Kochavey Or* p. 11 #3; see above p. 81).

Between Pesach and Shavuos, the Rebbe planned to return to Lemberg. Rabbi Nathan heard about this and hurried back to Breslov, but he found that the Rebbe had changed his mind and Rabbi Nathan returned home. The Rebbe once said that trips like this that are planned and later canceled are connected with *gilgulim*, and he spoke about naked souls (*Yemey Moharnat* 26b, 27a; see *Chayay Moharan* 34a #1, #151, *Sichos HaRan* #195).

Several days before Shavuos, Rabbi Nathan came to Breslov (*Yemey Moharnat* 27b).

Around this time, a group of followers arrived from

Ladizin to be with the Rebbe for Shavuos. They told him about Reb Getzel of Ladizin who had been forced to stay behind because of an anal infection, which the doctors had given up all hope of curing (*Shevachey Moharan* 16b #51, #390).

Friday, 4 Sivan; (May 19):

The Rebbe heard that Rabbi Nathan was in Breslov and that his family was opposed to his being there for Yom Tov. The Rebbe would have sent him back, but Rabbi Nathan avoided speaking with him until right before Shabbos (*Yemey Moharnat, Ibid.*).

Motzoai Shabbos, 6 Sivan, 1st night of Shavuos; (May 20):

The Rebbe said the first part of *Sichah* 51, "This world is nothing" (*Chayay Moharan* 15b #59, #59; *Parparaos LeChokhmah* II, 4 §6, §10). He also said *Sichah* 17 about the importance of learning Torah (*Biur HaLikutim, Likutey Moharan*, 4). This *Sichah* was said in reprimand of Reb Lipa (*Kochavey Or* p. 55 #30).

The second night of Shavuos, the Rebbe said *Likutey Moharan* II, 4. This lesson discusses the value of *tzedakah* (§1), and the battle between David and Goliath (§11). It also details how a wound is healed (§12). When the men from Ladizin returned home, they found that, to everyone's astonishment, Reb Getzel had recovered. The wound had cleaned itself at the exact time that the Rebbe had given this lesson (*Chayay Moharan, Ibid.; Parparaos LeChokhmah* II, 4 §9).

The Shpola Zeida had predicted frosts. The Rebbe commented, "Frosts?! — *CHoReF*?! (חרף — winter) — 'CHeReF ma'archos Elohim chayim' – חרף מערכות אלהים חיים — 'he taunted the hosts of the Living God' (Samuel I, 17:36). But King David said that 'he had conquered the lion and the bear' " (*Ibid.*). The lion refers to the Shpoler, whose name was Leib (lion in Yiddish), and the bear — Hirsh Ber of

Uman. The Rebbe said of the Shpoler that he made his nest in Judaism, and spoke of his charitable activities (*Biur HaLikutim*, Introduction).

After Shavuos, the Rebbe said *Sichah* 7, which relates a story about his grandfather, Rabbi Nachman Horodenker (*Chayay Moharan* 15 #59, #59). This involved the verse, "I have commanded the ravens to feed you" (Kings I, 17:4), which is also the opening line of *Likutey Moharan* II, 4.

Reb Tevia Kramer of Terhovitza came to the Rebbe who said, "It is better to lose your money than to die (see *Sichah* 51 mentioned above p. 165). The Rebbe continued, "Nachman Nathan would rather become poor than lie under the ground." When Reb Tevia came home, his house had burned down, but no one had died (*Sippurim Niflaim* p. 12).

Nachman Nathan Rappaport, one of the *maskilim* in Uman (see above p. 75), had been in St. Petersberg and was returning with a large sum of money. He died on the way and the corpse had to be brought back quickly for burial because of its decaying odor (*Sippurim Niflaim, Ibid.*; See *Yemey Moharnat* 31b, 35a).

During this summer, the Rebbe completed *Sichah* 51, which speaks of subduing the impurities of the mind (*Chayay Moharan* 15b #59, #59). Also during that summer, the Rebbe said *Sichah* 24, which speaks of giving charity to a true Tzaddik (*Ibid.*).

Also during that summer, Rabbi Nathan's son Meir died (*Yemey Moharnat* 27b).

Friday, 1 Av; (July 14):

There was a great fire in Ostrog, and many people died (*Shevachey Moharan* 26b #21, #466).

Miriam left Breslov for the Land of Israel with her brothers-in-law, the sons of the Volochisker. The Rebbe accompanied them a long distance out of the city on foot, saying, "One must go on foot to *Eretz Yisroel*" (*Yemey Moharnat* 27b, 28a; *Shevachey Moharan* 25b #13, #456 —

that it was during the "Three Weeks"; *Shevachey HaRan* p. 55 #32). Sarah also came to Breslov from Tcherin to see Miriam off (see Appendix, letter #8).

Around this time, the Rebbe sent Rabbi Nathan to Berdichov to collect a debt from the Rebbe's brother-in-law. Rabbi Nathan was therefore away when the Rebbe's daughter left for the Land of Israel (*Yemey Moharnat* 27b).

Thursday, 7 Av; (July 20):

Miriam left Odessa for the Land of Israel (*Ibid.*).

Friday, 8 Av; (July 21):

The Rebbe spoke of the *Megilas Sesarim* a second time (see above p. 123). Rabbi Aharon was in the *Beis HaMedrash* and the Rebbe did not want him to listen (*Aveneha Barzel* p. 30 #32).

Friday night, 9 Av, Shabbos Chazon, Torah reading, Devarim:

The Rebbe spoke about the recent fire in Ostrog, where many people had died. He related it to the melody of the *Unesaneh Tokef* prayer (*Shevachey Moharan* 26b #21, #466).

Tuesday, 12 Av; (July 25):

The Rebbe sent a letter to his daughter Sarah (Appendix, letter #8).

Sunday, 17 Av; (July 30):

A funeral passed the Rebbe's house. The Rebbe said, "The dead man is laughing at the people who are crying over him as if it were better for him in this world than in the next." He told Rabbi Nathan to repeat *Likutey Moharan* II, 32 (which he had said the previous Shabbos Yisro, see above p. 163; *Shevachey Moharan* 24a #3, #466) in the presence of Reb Yitzchok Segel, son-in-law of the Terhovitza Magid (*Ibid.*).

During this summer Rabbi Levi Yitzchok of Berdichov traveled through Walachei (Moldavia), although this was not his usual custom (*Yemey Moharnat* 28b). He was in Iassi and collected money there (*Shevachey Moharan* 35b #133, #585). Also during this year, he visited the Chozeh of Lublin (Bromberg 19:70).

Wednesday, 4 Elul; (August 16):

The Rebbe was in Breslov and he spoke about his humility (*Shevachey Moharan* 6b #29, #269). He told Reb Yaakov, his *sofer*, to examine his *tefillin* (*Yemey Moharnat* 28b-29a). The Rebbe said that he wanted this done because the Berdichover was traveling and he is the *pe'er* — glory — of Israel and *tefillin* are called *pe'er* (*Kesubos* 6b) (*Shevachey Moharan* 6b #30, #270; Cf. *Sichos HaRan* #196).

During this month of Elul, people — many of them ill — came to the Rebbe and complained about their lack of faith (*Chayay Moharan* 10b #41, #41; *Parparaos LeChokhmah* II, 5 §5). The Rebbe also discussed with Rabbis Nathan and Naftali the fact that the Shpola Zeida had called them *Maginey Eretz* (see above, p. 123). All this was included in the lesson of the next Rosh HaShanah (*Chayay Moharan* 10b #41, #41).

Sunday, 29 Elul, Erev Rosh HaShanah; (September 10):

Reb Abba Shochet of Tcherin and his son, Reb Shmuel were coming to the Rebbe for Rosh HaShanah, and they had a golden cup which they planned to give the Rebbe as a present. There was heavy rain and they had to sell the golden cup and other valuables in order to pay for the passage to Breslov, but they reached there for Rosh HaShanah. The Rebbe said, "I will knock out the teeth and eyes of the Evil One because of this golden cup" (*Aveneha Barzel* p. 48 #76).

23

BRESLOV 5570 (1809-1810)

Sunday night, 1 Tishrei; (September 10):

On the first night of Rosh HaShanah, the Rebbe spoke to Reb Abba Shochet saying that he could not pay Reb Abba in this world. To his son, Reb Shmuel, he said, "You, Shmuel, take the soup." He then gave Reb Shmuel some soup (*Aveneha Barzel* p. 48 #76).

Soon after Rosh HaShanah, Reb Abba Shochet went home and died. His son, Reb Shmuel, later became very rich (*Ibid.*).

Monday, First day of Rosh HaShanah; (September 11):

On the way to *Tashlich* the Rebbe fell into the mud. He cleaned himself off and changed his clothing. He then said *Tashlich* near the synagogue, where he had a view of the river. That night, he alluded to this when he said *Likutey Moharan* II, 5 (§15) that one must cast oneself in the mud for God (*Yemey Moharnat* 28a; *Chayay Moharan* 10b #41, #41).

Monday night, 2 Tishrei:

The Rebbe said *Likutey Moharan* II, 5. This was a very long lesson, speaking of many things that had happened around that time. The Rebbe spoke of lack of faith and illness (§1), seeking correct advice (§2), false leaders (§6) and of *Maginey Eretz*, the appellation that the Shpola Zeida had used for Rabbi Nathan and Rabbi Naftali (§7). He also spoke of *shofar* (§13), Rosh HaShanah, Yom Kippur and Succos (§14), why people should go to Tzaddikim for Rosh HaShanah (§15) and lungs (§16) (*Yemey Moharnat, Ibid.*).

Thursday, 4 Tishrei, Vayelech; (September 14):

The Rebbe had a dream about one of his followers who had recently died. The Rebbe did not know of this until then. In his dream, he reprimanded him for not coming to him on Rosh HaShanah in spite of his death. He told a story of a follower of Rabbi Menachem Mendel of Vitebsk who came to his Rebbe after he died (*Chayay Moharan* 23b #21, #101). This last story is also mentioned in the Introduction to *Asifas Zekenim* on *Rosh HaShanah*, where the follower is identified as Rabbi Noach (the grandfather of the Tzemach Tzedek, not his father as printed there). The Rebbe also spoke of a man who had died and had come to him, and had lifted himself to the sun (*Ibid.* 11a #41, #41).

Motzoai Shabbos, 7 Tishrei; (September 16):

There was a rumor that the Mashiach would come. The Rebbe said that he could not come, since before the Mashiach comes there will be great heresy in the world (*Sichos HaRan* #126; Cf. *Ibid.* #35, #220; also see *Shevachey Moharan* 31a #81, #527).

Rabbi Nathan left Breslov after Yom Kippur and did not return until after Simchas Torah (*Yemey Moharnat* 29a).

Before Succos, there were no *esrogim* available. Many cities did not have *esrogim* at all, and in some communities *esrogim* were being sold for as much as sixty or seventy rubles each (*Ibid.* 28b; *Sichos HaRan* #125).

Thursday, 11 Tishrei; (September 21) probably:

The Rebbe told how a Tzaddik must do repentance for all Israel, *Likutey Moharan* II, 66 (see above, p. 135). In this lesson, he also discussed why the day after Yom Kippur is called "the Name of God." The Rebbe also spoke about the *esrog*, and said that the crying of the Jews on the High Holydays brings about our having a beautiful *esrog* (*Sichos HaRan* #87; *Chayay Moharan* 15b #59, #59; *Yemey Moharnat* 29a; see also *Sichos HaRan* #125 which would suggest that this was repeated on Succos).

Motzoai Shabbos, 14 Tishrei, Erev Succos; (September 23):

Some esrogim arrived in Nemirov, and a number were despatched to Breslov. Rabbi Naftali was sent to bring them, and he returned with them before morning (Yemey Moharnat 28b). Thus, almost by a miracle, the Rebbe acquired a beautiful esrog (Sichos HaRan #125).

Sunday morning, 14 Tishrei; (September 24):

The Rebbe told Rabbi Naftali, "When you came into the city, I saw a great light in all the worlds. And though I knew that there would be esrogim — because I had trusted in the prayer of the Berdichover, who is the glory of our leaders — still I am amazed that they reached Breslov, the factory of Judaism." The Rebbe said that he was so happy at receiving the esrog that he wanted to send for musical instruments (Yemey Moharnat, Ibid.; Chayay Moharan 12a #45, #45; Sichos HaRan, Ibid.).

Monday, 15 Tishrei; (September 25):

The Rebbe spoke further about the mitzvah of esrog (Sichos HaRan, Ibid.). For three days he did not feel his sickness, so great was his joy with his esrog (Yemey Moharnat, Ibid.; Sichos HaRan, Ibid.).

Wednesday, 24 Tishrei; (October 4):

Rabbi Nathan arrived in Breslov the day after Simchas Torah. He heard from his friends what the Rebbe had said earlier and wrote it all down. Afterwards he came to the Rebbe, who discussed the greatness of the mitzvah of esrog (Yemey Moharnat 29a). He said that Jews are wise in spending much money on an esrog (Ibid. 28a; Sichos HaRan, Ibid.).

Wednesday night, 25 Tishrei:

Rabbi Levi Yitzchok of Berdichov died that night. News did not arrive in Breslov for several days (Sichos HaRan #196).

Rabbi Nathan had written down *Likutey Moharan* II, 66 and brought the writings to the Rebbe. The Rebbe sat there without speaking with tears in his eyes (*Yemey Moharnat* 29a,b).

Friday night, 27 Tishrei, Shabbos Bereshis; (October 6):

Rabbi Aharon of Breslov came to the meal. It was raining and Rabbi Aharon's house did not have a good roof. The Rebbe commented on this and said there is no *baal habayis*. There were also other discussions that evening. He then said that followers of other Tzaddikim feel Shabbos Bereshis, but it was not felt there. Rabbi Nathan said others connected the beginning and the end of the Torah. The Rebbe said he would also but then said, "I can't." This was repeated several times. Then, movingly, he said *Likutey Moharan* II, 67. This lesson contained a eulogy for the Berdichover, even though the news of his death had not yet reached Breslov (*Yemey Moharnat, Ibid.; Chayay Moharan, Ibid.*).

Sunday, 28 Tishrei; (October 8):

Word first reached Breslov that the Berdichover had died. Rabbi Nathan was writing *Likutey Moharan* II, 67 when he heard the news, but he did not believe it (*Yemey Moharnat* 29b; *Sichos HaRan* #196).

Sunday night, 29 Tishrei:

Rabbi Nathan brought *Likutey Moharan* II, 67 to show to the Rebbe. The Rebbe sat astounded, and said, "My lessons are very great. With them you can see the future," and "The *mussar* of my lessons is very wonderful and inspiring" (*Yemey Moharnat, Ibid.; Sichos HaRan, Ibid.*).

Monday, 29 Tishrei; (October 9):

Rabbi Nathan heard again that the Berdichover had died. He then saw how it was alluded to in *Likutey Moharan* II, 67, even though the Rebbe had not yet been told about it. The Rebbe had said that with his lessons one can predict the future, and now he realized that the report was true. He discussed it with Rabbi Naftali, who agreed, but they did not tell the Rebbe (*Yemey Moharnat, Ibid.*).

During this week, Rabbi Nathan and the others came to the Rebbe one night. He said, "What I am doing with you is a small accomplishment for me." The great accomplishment was what he was doing for the "naked souls" (*Sichos HaRan* #195; see above, pp. 122, 157).

Friday night, 4 Cheshvon, Torah reading, Noach; (October 13):

The Rebbe had still not been told about the death of the Berdichover. The Rebbe asked what portion it was, and was told that it was the portion of Noach. He then said, "Bereshis is a eulogy for Noach" (end of *Likutey Moharan* II, 67; *Yemey Moharnat* 30a; Cf. *Chayay Moharan* 15b #2, #61). He said that he would say a lesson every Shabbos, but only if Rabbi Nathan was present (*Biur HaLikutim*, Introduction).

Motzoai Shabbos, 5 Cheshvon; (October 14):

On Saturday night, the Chassidim came as usual to speak with the Rebbe. The Rebbe sent the group away, and they went to Rabbi Aharon. Later, the Rebbe sent his attendant to call Rabbi Nathan and Rabbi Naftali. When they came, he asked them to tell him about events in the world and they discussed the Napoleonic Wars. He spoke of the place where souls are exchanged, and of Napoleon's rise to power. He then told the story, The Exchanged Children (*Rabbi Nachman's Stories* #11 p. 231) (*Yemey Moharnat* 30b; *Chayay Moharan* 15b #2, #61; 15b #59, #59).

It is significant to note that on October 14, 1809, the same day that this story was told, the Treaty of Schönbrun was signed, giving Napoleon control of Austria's share of Poland, including the Warsaw area. Napoleon had defeated Austria, and negotiations had been going on since August 11 (Baron C.F. de Meneval, *Memoirs of Napoleon Bonaparte*, Collier,

New York, 1910, p. 585). This brought Napoleon's influence into Eastern Europe.

A man eventually came from Berdichov and the Rebbe asked him about Rabbi Levi Yitzchok's death. The man did not want to tell him, but the Rebbe urged him, saying, "How can I not know about it, when they know about it already in the Land of Israel?" He then said how bitter the world is when a Tzaddik dies (*Yemey Moharnat* 30a; *Parparaos LeChokhmah* II, 67). He said that every man must feel the death of the Berdichover. As to the rumor that people had seen a pillar of fire at his funeral, the Rebbe said he doubted that the people in the generation were worthy of seeing it, though the Berditchover certainly merited it (*Sichos HaRan* #197; Cf. *Kesubos* 17b).

The Rebbe said that the death of a Tzaddik could lead to sorcery and fires. Soon after that, a sorcerer was exposed in Chvastivetz and there were many fires, particularly in Breslov. This was all a result of the death of the Berdichover (*Chayay Moharan* 12a #45, #45).

Soon after this, Rabbi Nathan had a death in his family and had to sit *shivah*. It was almost as if he were sitting for the Berdichover. This occurred again after the Rebbe's death the following year (*Yemey Moharnat* 46a).

Shabbos, 11 Cheshvon, Torah reading, Lech Lecha; (October 21):

Rabbi Nathan was not there for this Sabbath. The Rebbe said that there was no one for whom to say a lesson and stopped saying them weekly. But a lesson had been prepared. It is included among outlines for a number of lessons the Rebbe wrote, presented in *Likutey Moharan* II, 79. This extends from *Toldos* up to *Yisro*, with the exception of *Beshalach* (*Biur HaLikutim*, Introduction; see above p. 173).

Reb Yehuda Eliezer became a follower of the Rebbe and started to confess to him (see above, p. 56). The Rebbe, however, stopped him since he had discontinued the practice of having his followers confessing. Later Reb Yehuda Eliezer was to travel to the Land of Israel with Rabbi Nathan (*Sippurim Niflaim* p. 143).

The Rebbe asked Rabbi Aharon of Breslov why he did not analyze his *sefer Likutey Moharan*, finding difficulties and solving them (the way the Talmud is studied) (*Ibid.* 129).

The Rebbe had spoken about his desire to visit Uman and stay at the house of Nachman Nathan who had died the previous year (see above, p. 166). The men of Teplik, who often traveled to Uman, came and asked the Rebbe if he now wanted to come to Uman, telling him that he would receive great honor there. The Rebbe did not agree to leave at this time (*Yemey Moharnat* 31b; see below, p. 182).

Kislev; (November):

Around this time, the Rebbe had a dream that he was in his small room and no one came to him. Then he went to the second room, the large room and then to the *Beis HaMedrash* and in each place there was no one to be found (*Chayay Moharan* 21b #11, #91).

During that winter, workmen were digging in Breslov to put up a new building. A girl was severely injured and several others were hurt. The Rebbe then said *Sichah* 60, regarding the dangers in building (*Sichos HaRan* #60; *Chayay Moharan* 15b #59, #59).

Motzoai Shabbos, 4 Kislev; (November 11):

The Rebbe spoke of how his service of God grows and becomes more refined with each season (*Chayay Moharan* 21a #9, #89).

That winter, the Rebbe reprimanded his son-in-law, Reb Yoske, who was lax in his study of Torah. He encouraged him to study regularly before engaging in his daily business. The Rebbe then said, "Do I not study? Indeed, my learning is extraordinary... I can show even the most outstanding scholar that he does not understand even the basics of

Talmudic study. In contrast, I can show the lowest that they are close to God and the Torah" (*Chayay Moharan* 12b #46, #46).

He then said that the inspiration which other leaders had brought to the world, faded with the passing of time. However, his followers must work so that his fire would never be extinguished. He then said *Likutey Moharan* II, 68 (*Ibid.; Parparaos LeChokhmah* II, 7:7).

Shabbos, 2 Teves, Shabbos Chanukah, Torah reading, Miketz; (December 9):

The Rebbe said *Likutey Moharan* II, 7 at the third meal. It follows the same theme as *Likutey Moharan* II, 68 , viz. that the Tzaddik must show the lowest Jews that they are still close to God, and the highest that they are still far from Him. He said that the end of this lesson was specifically meant for those who attend the supernal "third meal" (*Chayay Moharan* 11a #42, #42). Then he said *Sichah* 32, regarding strengthening one's faith (*Ibid.* 15b #59, #59).

That Chanukah, the Rebbe also said *Sichah* 40, which speaks of philosophy and the deeper meaning of the *dreidel* (*Ibid.*).

During this winter Rabbi Nathan was again in Berdichov to collect a debt from the Rebbe's brother-in-law (see above, p. 167; *Yemey Moharnat* 27b). After Chanukah, when Rabbi Nathan returned from Berdichov, the Rebbe said, "I have a story that was told by a prophet in the time of the First Temple, and only he and I understand it." Soon after that, he told the story of the Master of Prayer, but he said that this was not the story to which he had referred (*Sichos HaRan* #198).

Motzoai Shabbos, 2 Shevat; (January 6):

Reb Yosef, the cantor of Breslov, was amongst the Rebbe's followers and he had on a torn coat. The Rebbe then told the story, The Master of Prayer (*Rabbi Nachman's*

Stories #12 p. 278) (*Chayay Moharan, Ibid.*). In the story, the Master of Prayer did not pay attention to clothing. The Rebbe told the story in one sitting, and at first everyone there thought that he was recounting an incident which had actually occured (*Ibid.* 16a #2). After telling the story the Rebbe asked those present, "Who told the story written in their Chronicles?" He wanted to make sure that they appreciated the significance of each detail (*Sichos HaRan* #148).

Tuesday, 4 Shevat; (January 9):

Rabbi Avraham Kalisker died (*Chachmey Yisroel* p. 202).

Shabbos, 15 Shevat, Shabbos Shirah; (January 20):

On Friday night the Rebbe had a discussion regarding the conflict over the money being sent to the Land of Israel by Chassidic leaders. This in particular involved Rabbi Shneur Zalman, Rabbi Baruch, and a number of others. At this time Rabbi Shneur Zalman was forced to change his procedure for sending the money as a result of the death of the Berdichover (*Igros HaKodesh* p. 453). The Rebbe then said *Likutey Moharan* II, 71 which discusses the roots of this conflict. He said its source was from outside the Land of Israel, unlike Rabbi Shneur Zalman who had said (in the name of Rabbi Menachem Mendel of Vitebsk) that its roots were in the Land of Israel (*Igros HaKodesh* p. 120; *Chayay Moharan* 12b #47, #47).

Tuesday night, 19 Shevat; (January 23):

The Rebbe had a dream which he said was stranger than any he had had before (*Hashmotos Chayay Moharan* p. 6).

Shabbos, 22 Shevat, Torah reading, Yisro; (January 27):

Rabbi Shneur Zalman of Liadi visited Breslov on his way to Tulchin. The Rebbe came to meet him outside the city, greeting him with great honor, and brought him to his house (*Rabbi Shneur Zalman of Liadi* p. 370).[35]

The Rebbe said, "Give glory to the lord of thousands." Hearing of Rabbi Shneur Zalman's dispute with Rabbi Baruch, the Rebbe said, "You have overcome Petersberg (*Pheters-berg*; see above p. 66), but you will not overcome *Pheter* Baruch (Uncle Baruch) " (*Aveneha Barzel* p. 34 #46).

That Friday night, the Rebbe did not give a lesson. On Shabbos morning, after *Birkas HaMazon*, the Rebbe said *Likutey Moharan* II, 72 (*Chayay Moharan* 12b #48, #48). This lesson speaks of the "lord of thousands," the title by which the Rebbe called Rabbi Shneur Zalman.

Before Purim, Rabbi Shneur Zalman visited Rabbi Baruch (*Rabbi Shneur Zalman of Liadi* p. 255; see *Igros Baal HaTanya*, letter 113 p. 192, and note quoting *Kovetz Ksav Yad*; *Igros HaKodesh* p. 141 #60). Then ensued the famous dispute between them, where Rabbi Shneur Zalman showed that Rabbi Baruch's *tefillin*, which he had inherited from his grandfather the Baal Shem Tov, were unfit. They cast insults at each other. Upon Rabbi Shneur Zalman's departure, he was informed that a number of manuscripts of his *Shulchan Arukh* had been burned in his home. Soon after, Rabbi Baruch's daughter died (see *Kahal Chassidim* pp. 80-81; *Butzina DeNehorah HaShalem* pp. 12a,b).

Wednesday, 3 Adar I; (February 7):

The Rebbe told Rabbi Nathan a story, saying that a certain concept of the Torah had been withheld from him, and without that knowledge he had no desire to live (*Shevachey Moharan* 12b #5, #344). He exclaimed, "We do not belong to this world at all" (*Ibid*. 13a #6, #345).

---

35. Cf. *Igros HaKodesh* p. 139, Rabbi Shneur Zalman's letter #58 dated 23 Shevat, 5570 in the city of Rohtshov, but see footnote that the name of the city was not clear in the manuscript and was completed according to the context.

Shabbos, 27 Adar I, Shabbos Shekalim, Torah reading, Vayakhel; (March 3):

While the Rebbe was in the synagogue for the Torah reading, Rabbi Nathan entered the Rebbe's private room and saw a paper upon which the Rebbe had listed the Ten Psalms (see above, p. 115; *Sichos HaRan* #141 p. 96; in *Parparaos LeChokhmah* II, 92, however, it states that this was in 5569).[36]

Sunday, 28 Adar I; (March 4):

Rabbi Nathan returned home. Before leaving Breslov, he asked the Rebbe about the Ten Psalms, but the Rebbe was not yet ready to reveal them (*Sichos HaRan, Ibid.*).

Soon after this Rabbi Nathan was in Berdichov (*Sichos HaRan* #149 p. 103).

Tuesday, 14 Adar II; (March 20):

(From the sequence in *Chayay Moharan,* the year is most probably this one.) On Purim the Rebbe spoke about how the mysteries of the Torah are revealed to him and discussed Korach (*Chayay Moharan* 21a #10, #90).

Shabbos, 18 Adar II, Shabbos Parah, Torah reading, Tzav; (March 24):

The Rebbe said lesson *Likutey Moharan* II, 74, which speaks of *Parshas Parah* being a preparation for Pesach

---

36. According to *Parparaos LeChokhmah,* end of II, 5 and beginning of II, 92, this took place close to Passover 5569. He writes that there is a question whether it was before or after the holiday. However, in a letter, Rabbi Nachman of Tulchin, a disciple of Rabbi Nathan, writes that the teaching of the Ten Psalms was revealed between the lesson appearing in *Likutey Moharan* II, 74 and the story of the Seven Beggars, shortly before the Rebbe left Breslov for Uman (unnumbered letter, dated 18 Adar, 5633, at the end of *Alim LeTerufah* p. 215a,b). This sets the year as 5570. The lesson deals with *Parshas Parah* and most probably was revealed on that Sabbath, 18 Adar II (March 23, 1810). The story of the Seven Beggars was begun on 25 Adar II (March 30), also on a Friday night, as discussed below. The Ten Psalms were therefore revealed during the intermediate week.

(*Alim LeTerufah*, letter from Rabbi Nachman of Tulchin, end).

During the following week the Rebbe revealed the secret of the Ten Psalms (*Alim LeTerufah, Ibid.*). Rabbi Nathan was not in Breslov at the time, but the Rebbe called in Rabbi Aharon and Rabbi Naftali, and revealed it to them (*Sichos HaRan* #141). He appointed them as witnesses and said, "If someone comes to my grave, gives a *prutah* to charity and says these Ten Psalms, I will pull him out from the depths of Gehenom by his *peyos*" (*Chayay Moharan* 45a #41, #225; see also *Nevey Tzaddikim* p. 66).

Friday night, 25 Adar II, Parshas HaChodesh, Torah reading, Shemini; (March 30):

Rabbi Nathan had sent a letter to a friend telling him to be happy even in depressing circumstances. The Rebbe, who had seen the letter, said: "What do you know about becoming happy after depression? I will tell you how people were once happy." He then began telling the story, The Seven Beggars (*Rabbi Nachman's Stories* #13, p. 354), and reached the end of the First Day in the story (*Sichos HaRan* #149; *Chayay Moharan* 15b #59, #59; 16a #4, #63). Rabbi Nathan was not there at the time (*Yemey Moharnat* 31b).

Monday, 27 Adar II; (April 2):

Dr. Gordon, Rabbi Aharon ben Shimon, died in Ostrog (*Chachmey Yisroel* p. 204).

Tuesday, 28 Adar II; (April 3):

Rabbi Naftali arrived in Nemirov and told Rabbi Nathan about the story. Rabbi Nathan immediately set off for Breslov. He arrived there that night (*Sichos HaRan* #149 p. 103; *Yemey Moharnat* 31b).

Wednesday, 29 Adar II; (April 4):

Rabbi Nathan came in to the Rebbe after *davening*. The Rebbe spoke about many things, and then Rabbi Nathan asked the Rebbe to review the story. The Rebbe then corrected some of the details which had not been accurately transmitted. The Rebbe said, "I am very anxious to hear the end." The Rebbe's attendant came and Rabbi Nathan had to leave while the Rebbe took a nap (Ibid.).

After the Rebbe awoke, Rabbi Nathan spoke to him again. He had recently been in Berdichov and he told of how the wealthy people in Berdichov were constantly in debt. He quoted the verse, "[God] has set the world in their heart, so that men cannot find out God's deeds from the beginning to the end" (Ecclesiastes 3:11), which the commentaries explain as referring to the deficiencies of the world. The Rebbe said, "Is this not our tale? Where are we holding now?" The Rebbe then told the story of the Second Day. A few other people were also present to hear it (Sichos HaRan #149 p. 104; Yemey Moharnat 32a).

Friday night, 3 Nissan; (April 6):

Adil's son was very sick. The Rebbe was extremely distressed about this. He said Birkas HaMazon before those who had come to hear him speak had entered, and said a Sichah regarding his anguish. He then told the story of the Third Day, about the Heart and the Spring, and that of the Fourth Day, involving the two birds. He then immediately left the table. Rabbi Nathan concentrated so much on remembering each detail of the story that he forgot the Sichah which preceded it, remembering only that it was related to the Heart in the story of the Third Day (Sichos HaRan #151; Cf. Ibid. #149 p. 104; Yemey Moharnat 32b).

Sunday, 4 Nissan; (April 8):

The Rebbe told the story of the Fifth Day, about the "little which holds much" (Sichos HaRan, Ibid.; Yemey Moharnat, Ibid.; Chayay Moharan 16a #5, #64).

Tuesday, 6 Nissan; (April 10):

The Rebbe's house was being plastered (Aveneha Barzel p. 21 #5). The Rebbe went out to Rabbi Aharon's house and his followers spoke with him there. He told the story of the Sixth Day about "healing the Princess" (*Sichos HaRan* #151 p. 105). A follower told the Rebbe a story. The Rebbe said, "This is the story of the Seventh Day. The world is already telling my stories." He did not finish it, and after Pesach, on the way to Uman, he said that it would not be finished until Mashiach came (*Sichos HaRan* #149 p. 104; *Yemey Moharnat, Ibid.*; see p. 176).

Friday night, 10 Nissan, Shabbos HaGadol, Torah reading, Metzora; (April 13):

Adil's son, the Rebbe's grandson, who had been sick for some time, died (*Yemey Moharnat* 32b).

Motzoai Shabbos, 11 Nissan; (April 14):

Rabbi Nathan returned to Nemirov.

Before Pesach the Rebbe said that he wanted to go to Uman, and live in the house of Nachman Nathan (*Yemey Moharnat* 31b; see above, pp. 166-167, 175). Several men from Teplik came to the Rebbe and asked him if he would like to move to Uman. This time, he answered in the affirmative (*Ibid.* 32b).

Thursday, 15 Nissan, Pesach; (April 19):

Throughout the week of Pesach there were many fires in Breslov (*Ibid.*).

During Chol HaMoed, Rabbi Nathan was in Breslov with Rabbi Naftali and Reb Lipa, and heard a wondrous lesson (*Ibid.*).

Friday, 23 Nissan; (April 27):

The day after Pesach, Rabbi Nathan went to Breslov, and spent the Sabbath there (*Ibid.*).

Motzoai Shabbos, 25 Nissan; (April 28):

The Rebbe told Rabbi Nathan how the Baal Shem Tov revealed new concepts to the world. He also praised highly the revelation of the ARI in *Likutey Torah* which he was then studying, and spoke of the uniqueness of both the ARI and the Baal Shem Tov (*Shevachey Moharan* 7b #40, #280). Rabbis Nathan and Naftali then returned to Nemirov (*Yemey Moharnat, Ibid.*).

Towards the end of Nissan, the Rebbe sent a man to Uman to arrange lodgings for him in the house of Nachman Nathan (*Chayay Moharan* 38b #1, #185).

Tuesday, 27 Nissan; (May 1):

Rabbi Nathan returned to Breslov, where he would remain until after Shabbos (*Yemey Moharnat, Ibid.*).

Friday night, Rosh Chodesh Iyar; (May 4):

The Rebbe was sitting at the Sabbath table and said, "I know nothing." Suddenly there was a great fire in the street near his house. The Rebbe said, "*Shoin, shoin*" (already, already) [he had known earlier that there would be a fire and had spoken about it at length]. The house burned down, but the people escaped and saved everything (*Ibid.* 33a; *Chayay Moharan*, 38b #1, #185; 42b #26, #210; *Sippurim Niflaim* p. 4).

The Rebbe said that the people should be lenient about saving things from a fire on Shabbos (see above, p. 126; *Shevachey Moharan* 33a #100, #547). The *Beis HaMedrash* in the Rebbe's house was also burned. (It was rebuilt two years after the Rebbe's death in 5573 when Rabbi Nathan moved to Breslov; *Yemey Moharnat* 52b).

With the fire still burning, they waded through the river and sat on the hill with the *sifrei Torah*, looking at the ruins of the house and synagogue. Rabbi Nathan was with the Rebbe, who was very happy. The Rebbe sat there all night (*Yemey Moharnat* 33a; *Chayay Moharan* 42b #26, #210).

Rabbi Nathan returned to the Rebbe just before morning. They crossed the bridge but did not go to the house. They went to Rabbi Shimon's house which had been saved from the fire and spent the rest of Shabbos there. It was at the end of town, at the crossroads to Uman (*Yemey Moharnat, Ibid.*; *Chayay Moharan* 43a #26, #210).

Sunday, 2 Iyar; (May 6):

In the morning, the Rebbe moved from Rabbi Shimon's house to that of Reb Zelig at the other end of town, where the Rebbe's property had been placed (*Yemey Moharnat* 33a; *Chayay Moharan, Ibid.*). A man who owed him money spoke to him in the afternoon (*Yemey Moharnat, Ibid.*). Rabbi Naftali then left for home (*Ibid.* 34a). A man arrived from Uman with a reply to the Rebbe's message of the previous week (*Chayay Moharan* 38b #1, #185). He had been sent by Chaikel, Hirsh Ber and Landau, the *maskilim* of Uman with the book, *Yain Levanon*, by N.H. Wiesel. This was the agreed upon sign (*Sippurim Niflaim* p. 4, see above p. 76). The Rebbe's face became red, for he knew that he was being called to die (*Yemey Moharnat* 33a).

Rabbi Nathan then began to make preparations for the journey to Uman. They could not find any wagons and finally hired one for an exorbitant price. Adil did not want the Rebbe to leave Breslov (*Yemey Moharnat* 34a).

Tuesday, 4 Iyar; (May 8):

In the morning the Rebbe prayed, drank some coffee and then left Breslov. Rabbi Nathan had not yet prayed, and he did so on the wagon. The Rebbe thus left Breslov with his attendant, Rabbi Nathan, and the man from Teplik who had brought the message from Uman (*Ibid.*).

On the way out of Breslov, the Rebbe put his hand on the *mezuzah* and said that his followers should pray together and, if they prayed earnestly, they could bring him back (*Chayay Moharan* 38b #3, #187). He said it was proper that he was leaving since he accepted his misfortune (the burning of his house) joyfully and could not commiserate with the townspeople in their sorrow over their own losses (*Yemey Moharnat, Ibid.*; *Chayay Moharan* 38b #2, #186).

Three *parsos* (20 miles) outside of Breslov, the Rebbe met Rabbi M. of Teplik who had been sent to find lodgings for the Rebbe. He told the Rebbe how anxious they were for him to arrive in Uman (*Yemey Moharnat, Ibid.*; *Shevachey Moharan* 8a #43, #283; *Chayay Moharan* 38b #1, #185). The Rebbe said, "Isn't everything ours? For a person must say, 'The world was created for me' " (*Sanhedrin* 37a). He remarked on the coincidence that Rabbi Nachman and Rabbi Nathan were traveling to the house of Nachman Nathan and how he would be making *Kiddush* in a house where care was taken that God's Name not be mentioned (*Chayay Moharan, Ibid*; *Yemey Moharnat, Ibid.*). He then spoke about the limitlessness of God's greatness, and how the culmination of all knowledge is realizing the extent of one's incomprehension (see above, p. 113, where he discussed this after Passover, 5565, but now he said that he understood this on a higher level) (*Yemey Moharnat* 34a; *Chayay Moharan* 16b #8).

They traveled another seven miles to Ladizin, which was nineteen miles from Breslov.

Many people accompanied the Rebbe on the way out of Ladizin. He said, "No generation is an orphan" (*Chagigah* 3b). "Rabbi Shimon bar Yochai said that the Torah would never be forgotten," (*Shabbos* 138b) as brought in the opening piece in *Likutey Moharan*. "Now," the Rebbe continued, "there is a **N**achal **N**ovea **M**ekor **CH**okhmah — A flowing brook, a source of wisdom" (Proverbs 18:4) (an acronym for NaCHMaN). He also once said, "I am a river which purifies all blemishes" (*Chayay Moharan* 39a #5, #189; *Yemey Moharnat* 34b), and "God is always good" (*Chayay Moharan* 38b #4, #188). He mentioned that the story of the Seventh Day, in the story of The Seven Beggars, will not be told until the time of the Mashiach (*Yemey Moharnat* 32b).

That evening, as they approached Teplik, the Rebbe was met by several men who urged him to stay in Teplik. The Rebbe refused and continued traveling, even though it began to rain. He stayed in a nearby village, and many people from Teplik came there. Rabbi M. was made Rabbi of Teplik (*Yemey Moharnat* 34b). This Rabbi M. was most probably

Rabbi Mordechai of Teplik (*Kochavey Or* p. 33 #29; *Shemos HaTzaddikim* p. 80).

Wednesday, 5 Iyar; (May 9):

After *davening*, they traveled to Uman. The Rebbe spoke of the death of the Tzaddik, mentioned in *Likutey Moharan* II, 67. He said the end of that lesson, regarding "Rachel crying for her children" (Jeremiah 31:14) and spoke of the Berdichover. He told a story of the Baal Shem Tov, and about souls in need of rectification three hundred years after their death, and how they could only be rectified through the Tzaddik's death. He later said that the reason that he was going to Uman was because of the many souls there awaiting rectification, particularly those killed in the massacre which had taken place there in 5528 (1768) (*Yemey Moharnat, Ibid.* 34b; *Chayay Moharan* 39a #6, #190).

24

UMAN 5570 (1810)

Uman, latitude 48.44°N longitude 30.14°E, a city in Kiev oblast, was part of Poland until the 1793 partition. In 1749 the Haidemacks massacred many Jews there and burned part of the city. Count Felix Potacki, the landlord of the city, rebuilt it in 1761, held fairs there, and fostered its development in many other ways. He also built the famous Sophiefka Park, for his wife Sophia, where Rabbi Nachman used to go for walks.

In 5528 (1768), the Haidemacks wiped out the Jewish population of Uman, along with other Jews who had sought refuge there. It was on 5 Tammuz (June 19), that the peasant revolutionary Maxim Zelieznak attacked the city together with Ivan Gunta, the Cossak commander. Despite the Jews' courageous defense, the city fell. The massacre went on for three days, and some twenty-thousand Jews were killed. Rabbi Naftali said that the massacre was a punishment for the opposition to the Baal Shem Tov.

Uman later became a stronghold of the haskala under Chaikel Hurwitz and Hirsh Ber Hurwitz. Both Rabbi Levi Yitzchok of Berdichov and Rabbi Yaakov Shimshon of Shepetevka wanted to be Rabbi in Uman, but Chaikel would not permit them. Rabbi Yaakov Shimshon was eventually Rabbi there for a while, but he was forced to leave.

Rabbi Nachman, however, was readily accepted by all the factions in the city. Uman remained the focal point of Breslover Chassidim from generation to generation.

Wednesday, 5 Iyar; (May 9):

The Rebbe arrived in Uman. He stayed in the house of Nachman Nathan (*Yemey Moharnat* 35a; *Chayay Moharan* 43b #33, #217).

The Rebbe said that this was the first time that he had ever lived in a rooming house, and that this could cure him (*Chayay Moharan* 42b #23, #207). The Rebbe later discussed this in *Likutey Moharan* II,8 §6 (*Ibid.*).

When the Rebbe arrived in Uman, one of his supporters came to apologize to him for the people of the *Beis Medrash* who had not received him fittingly. The Rebbe then said, "I don't need any new Chassidim. It's enough if the old Chassidim are good Jews. If not, I alone am enough" (Cf. *Succah* 45b, Rabbi Shimon bar Yochai) (*Sippurim Niflaim* 141; *Chayay Moharan* 43a #27, #211).

Monday, 10 Iyar, BeHar; (May 14):

In *Hashiva Shoftenu*, the Rebbe thought about Nachman Nathan and wanted to rectify his soul (*Chayay Moharan* 41a #19, #203).

Friday, 21 Iyar; (May 25):

Rabbi Nathan was with the Rebbe. The Rebbe spoke of the fear of God and said, "We are at the boundary of Jewishness." He repented for having spoken lightly about Nachman Nathan on the way to Uman (*Chayay Moharan* 39b #11, #195).

Monday, 24 Iyar; (May 28):

The Rebbe said, "I want to throw the world aside [and be alone]." He then said that he would like to remain in Uman, even after his death, because of the holiness of the martyrs. He also explained that the reason why there were so many heretics in Uman was because of the impurities left behind by the death of the martyrs (Cf. *Etz Chaim* 39, 3; *Chayay Moharan* 40a,b #12, #197).

The Rebbe told Rabbi Nathan about a dream involving a wedding which was attended by a dead man (*Ibid.* 22a #13, #93).

One reason why the Rebbe chose Uman was to show Rabbi Nathan and Rabbi Naftali what heretics were, so that they would comfort themselves that they were not like them

(*Sippurim Niflaim* p. 8). He told Rabbi Naftali only to speak to Landau, while Rabbi Nathan could speak even to Hirsh Ber (*Ibid.* p. 5).

Hirsh Ber said that each conversation with the Rebbe was as if he were telling him, "There is a God." The Rebbe would not discuss Torah in front of them (*Ibid.*p. 5).

The heretics thought that the Rebbe was wise, but they did not consider him as wise as Wiesel, who was their mentor (*Ibid.*). Once, however, Hirsh Ber wanted to ask the Rebbe a question raised in *Yain Levanon* which Wiesel did not answer. Before he could ask the question, the Rebbe read his thoughts and provided him with an answer (*Ibid.*; *Kochavey Or* p. 53 #27).

The three heretics spoke of a Greek book and the Rebbe demonstrated that he was conversant with it. Once they said that they wanted to make the Rebbe the Mashiach. Another time they said that the old Czar (Paul I, died 1801; see above p. 64) would have placed a crown on the Rebbe's head, but the new Czar (Alexander I) did not appreciate wisdom. They also played chess with the Rebbe often (*Sippurim Niflaim* p. 6; regarding the wicked coming to a Tzaddik, see *Chayay Moharan* 39b #9, #193).

All this time Rabbi Nathan remained in Uman with the Rebbe. The Rebbe was searching for new quarters when a stranger suddenly appeared and offered him free accommodation in the Lukacher's home, but this did not work out at the time (*Chayay Moharan* 43b #33, #217; *Yemey Moharnat* 35a). This Lukacher (after the city of Lukach, the birthplace of the Mezritcher Magid) was a well known sinner but was in St. Petersberg. His family later on took in the Rebbe (*Yemey Moharnat* 36a).

Sunday, 1 Sivan; (June 1):

The Rebbe told Rabbi Nathan that on the journey to Uman Rabbi Nathan, and later Rabbi Naftali and Rabbi Y.(Yudel?) had each said something to the Rebbe which implied a prediction. When that prediction materialized, they could destroy heresy (*Chayay Moharan* 41a #15, #199).

Before Shavuos the Rebbe rented a house from Reb Yosef Shmuel. He did not move in, however, until after Shavuos (*Yemey Moharnat* 35a).

Friday, 6 Sivan, Shavuos; (June 6):

The Rebbe was still in the house of Nachman Nathan. Many people gathered there, but the Rebbe did not give a lesson (*Yemey Moharnat, Ibid.; Chayay Moharan* 41b #18, #202).

Shabbos, 7 Sivan, 2nd day of Shavuos; (June 7):

Rabbi Nathan asked the Rebbe to give a lesson, but the Rebbe refused (*Yemey Moharnat* 35a).

Motzoai Shabbos, 8 Sivan:

The Rebbe said jokingly that some Torah lessons result from sins (cf. *Nedarim* 22b), and "You have not sinned so much that I should give you a lesson" (*Ibid.; Chayay Moharan, Ibid.*).

Sunday, 8 Sivan; (June 8):

The Rebbe moved from Nachman Nathan's house to that of Reb Yosef Shmuel, where Rabbi Nathan had rented an apartment (*Yemey Moharnat, Ibid.; Chayay Moharan* 43b #33, #217). The Rebbe said a lesson regarding false leaders (*Ibid.* 43a #28, #212).

Rabbi Nathan then returned home. He had been in Uman since the Rebbe's arrival (*Yemey Moharnat, Ibid.*).

Around this time it happened that the Rebbe's landlord saw him on the floor prostrate before God. In spite of his illness the Rebbe continued his simple devotions (*Sichos HaRan* #164).

The Rebbe also spoke of the opposition to him, quoting the verse (Hosea 7:13), "I will redeem them [and they spoke lies against me]" (*Shevachey Moharan* 17b #5, #396).

After Shavuos, Rabbi Naftali sent Rabbi Nathan a message that the Rebbe wanted him to return to Uman. Rabbi Nathan returned and remained there until Shabbos Nachamu (*Yemey Moharnat, Ibid.*).

Friday night, 12 Tammuz, Torah reading, Chukas-Balak; (July 13):

The Rebbe spoke of how he did strange and unfathomable things and why he moved so often and had dealings with heretics and sinners (*Chayay Moharan* 41b #20, #204).

On Shabbos morning the Rebbe discussed the same question (*Ibid.*).

During this summer the Rebbe visited Terhovitza. On the way, he discussed how the contemporary leaders did not comprehend his great achievements in Uman (*Chayay Moharan* 41b #21, #205).

Rabbi Naftali told the Rebbe that the Magid of Terhovitza had asked why the Rebbe was in Nachman Nathan's house first, and only later in the house of Reb Yosef Shmuel, and why he attracted the wicked. He answered, "The first paradox is an old one, viz. why the world was created in a state of chaos and only later put in order; as for the second, if the Tzaddikim don't follow me, I must appeal to the wicked. Perhaps I can make them into good Jews" (*Chayay Moharan* 42b #24, #208).

Beginning of Av; (August):

Shortly before Shabbos Nachamu, the Rebbe moved from Reb Yosef Shmuel's house, which was somewhat cramped, to the house of the Lukacher (*Yemey Moharnat* 35a, 38b; *Chayay Moharan* 43b #33, #217; *Sichos HaRan* #153 p. 107).

Friday night, 11 Av, Shabbos Nachamu, Torah reading, Va'eschanan; (August 10):

The Rebbe received several visitors that night. He was very weak when he made *Kiddush*, but he spoke before *netilas yadayim.* He asked, "Why do you come to me? I know nothing. I am a *prostock* (simple) and can give no lessons. Only from 'the way to the Land of Israel' do I draw encouragement" (Cf. *Sichos HaRan* #11). This conversation led to him saying *Likutey Moharan* II, 78, which speaks of the simplicity of Tzaddikim, and how this is connected to "the way to the Land of Israel." He then asked the company to sing *Azamer BiShevachin*, unlike his usual custom of singing this after *HaMotzi*.[37]

The Rebbe became very happy, and then he washed for the meal. At the meal he told those present to sing a lot and rebuked Rabbi Naftali who was ashamed to sing. He then said, "We have nothing to be ashamed of. The world was made for us" (see above, p. 185). He then spoke of lust for women and poetry, alluding to the Lukacher (*Yemey Moharnat* 35b, 36a; *Sichos HaRan* #153). He continued, "Never give up" (*Ibid.*; *Chayay Moharan* 13a #49, #49).

Sunday, 12 Av; (August 12):

Rabbi Nathan wrote down *Likutey Moharan* II, 78, and brought the manuscript to the Rebbe. The sheet fell out of the window. Rabbi Nathan retrieved it and handed it to the Rebbe. After reading it, the Rebbe said, "This is what I myself said" (*Sichos HaRan* #153 p. 109).

Shortly after this, Rabbi Nathan returned to Nemirov (*Yemey Moharnat* 36a).

In Uman, Adil gave a dinner where many Chassidim were present in one room and the women in another. The women thought that the Chassidim had already said the *Birkas HaMazon*, but Adil said, "When my father's followers say this blessing, one hears it." Right after that they heard them say

---

37. This may also be connected to the concept of *prostock*. The ARI, composer of *Azamer BiShevachin*, meant it to be sung after *HaMotzi* and the reason it is printed in the Siddur before the kiddush is for simple Jews who do not know the Kabbalistic meditations connected with the Shabbos meal, as explained in *Torah Lishmah* #80.

the Grace in a loud voice (*Aveneha Barzel* p. 34 #47).

While in the Lukacher's house, the Rebbe heard a woman crying to her father, who was buried in the nearby cemetery. The Rebbe's daughter was with him. He remarked that perhaps her father's soul was not then near his grave, but told her that for a Tzaddik, death is like going from one room to another, and that anyone who came to his grave would surely find him there (Cf. *Zohar* I:218b *Nitzutzei Oros*; *Shevachey Baal Shem Tov* p. 161, where the Baal Shem Tov said before his death, "I know for sure that I will go out this door and will immediately enter another door") (*Sichos HaRan* #156).

Each day, the Rebbe would ride out of the city for fresh air. One day he could not find a coach for his daily ride, and he rode a horse like an expert horseman. Reb Avraham Peterberger saw him, and the Rebbe said, "I am so sick that I have lost my voice, and when one loses one's voice, the merit of one's fathers doesn't help" (this was alluded to in *Likutey Moharan* II, 5 said the previous Rosh HaShanah; see above p. 169) (*Aveneha Barzel* p. 79 #66).

A man asked the Rebbe if one could learn Kabbalah without fasting. The Rebbe answered that Kabbalah is a form of intellectual study. He said, "Where the wisdom of philosophy ends, that is where Kabbalah begins" (*Sichos HaRan* #225).

Tuesday, 26 Elul, 3rd day of Selichos; (September 25):

Rabbi Nathan returned to Uman (*Yemey Moharnat* 36a).

Rabbi Aharon of Breslov had come with the Rebbe to Uman, and had remained there all summer. The people of Breslov wrote that they needed him for the High Holydays. Every Rosh HaShanah he led the *Mussaf* services in the main synagogue. Rabbi Aharon discussed it with the Rebbe, and decided to return to Breslov (*Manuscript* p. 8; *Tovos Zichronos* p. 26; *Shevachey Moharan* p. 18a #4, #406). On the way back to Breslov he met Rabbis Nathan and Naftali, who were on their way to Uman. Rabbi Nathan said, "Even if he had chased us with a club, we would have stayed with the Rebbe for Rosh HaShanah" (*Manuscript, Ibid.*).

Before Rosh HaShanah, the Rebbe moved out of the Lukacher's house, back to the house of Nachman Nathan. He remained there until after Yom Kippur (*Yemey Moharnat* 38b).

Friday, 29 Elul, Erev Rosh HaShanah; (September 28):

The Rebbe spoke of the importance of Rosh HaShanah (*Chayay Moharan* 44b #36, #220). He also spoke about those, including Rabbi Aharon of Breslov, who were not there for Rosh HaShanah. He made special mention of a man from Nemirov (*Shevachey Moharan* 18a #4, #406). This man was Reb Lipa, who was busy obtaining *esrogim* for the Ukraine. The Rebbe said, "Above all, there is nothing greater than my Rosh HaShanah" (*Kochavey Or* p. 55 #30; according to the *Manuscript* p. 9, this was Reb Berel).

On this same day the Rebbe said, "An angel is created from each step of your journeys to me. I should only see the radiant light of the paths that you travel upon to me" (*Shevachey Moharan* 8b #1, #291).

On this day too a man asked the Rebbe how to achieve diligence in study. The Rebbe told him not to speak badly against any Jew, as outlined in *Sichah* 91 (*Chayay Moharan* 10a #34, #34; 15b #59, #59).

Before Rosh HaShanah the Rebbe told Rabbi Naftali, "An awesome mountain stands before us, but I don't know whether we are going to the mountain or the mountain is coming to us" (*Chayay Moharan* 45b #43, #227).

Rabbi Nathan came to the Rebbe's room. The Rebbe said, "Such troubles, Temma — big pearls, Sarah — small pearls." Reb Leib Dubravner, Sarah's father-in-law, had given his other daughter-in-law (the daughter of a famous Rabbi) a large pearl, but had given Sarah a small pearl (*Aveneha Barzel* p. 22 #8).

25

UMAN 5571 (1810)

Shabbos, 1 Tishrei, Rosh HaShanah; (September 29):
On the first day of Rosh HaShanah, the Rebbe prayed with the congregation, and ate together with his followers (*Yemey Moharnat* 37a). Hirsh Ber and his group also prayed with the Rebbe. Hirsh Ber showed signs of becoming religious. He had begun to grow a beard, and would not drink coffee before the blowing of the *shofar* (*Sippurim Niflaim* p. 7).

The Rebbe prayed in the *hambar* (summer house) of Nachman Nathan (*Chayay Moharan* 44b #37, #221). Rabbis Yudel and Shmuel Isaac wanted to pray there also the following year (*Sippurim Niflaim* p. 141).

The Rebbe's grandson Yisroel, son of his daughter Sarah, was with him. The Rebbe asked the child to pray for him, and Yisroel said, "Give me your watch." The child was three and a half at the time, and the Rebbe said, "He is already a *guter Yid* (since he asked for a present in order to pray, as is the custom of Rebbes). Then the child said, "God, let him be well," and the Rebbe commented that this is the way to pray — with simplicity (*Shevachey Moharan* 23a #3, #439). About ten years later this grandson married the daughter of Rabbi Aharon of Tchernoble (*Yemey HaTalaos* p. 47).

After the morning services, the Rebbe became very sick and coughed up a great deal of blood (*Yemey Moharnat* 36a).

That evening a very large crowd gathered. The Rebbe was extremely sick, but he called Rabbi Nathan and finally decided to speak. They put his chair near the door in case he should have to leave because of his illness. In a faint voice, the Rebbe said *Likutey Moharan* II, 8 speaking for several hours (*Yemey Moharnat* 36a,b; *Chayay Moharan* 44a #35, #219). This lesson speaks of rebuke (§1), prayer (§2), faith (§8) and the Land of Israel (§10). *Parparaos LeChokhmah* (*ad. loc.*, §3) connects this to how Moshe Rabbenu admonished the Jewish people before his death. It also states there that in this lesson Rabbi Nachman indicated to his Chassidim that they were to continue following him after his death. The lesson also discusses: cures (§6), looking for a leader and the errors of heresy (§8), the lungs, and the holiness of the Jewish encampment (§12). Rabbi Nathan and Rabbi Yudel were very close to the Rebbe, while the others sat further away. Hirsh Ber was able to hear the lesson well, since the people were afraid to push him (*Sippurim Niflaim* p. 7). The Rebbe said, "My followers, no matter from what city, should come home and say: 'Whoever believes in God should come to Rabbi Nachman for Rosh HaShanah' " (*Tovos Zichronos* p. 25, 26).

After the lesson, the Rebbe told the group to sing. He then went to his room. He was very sick and they wanted to call the doctor, but the doctor did not come. Rabbi Nathan was not there at the time. The Rebbe said not to bring the doctor. He said not to call a doctor, even if he himself asked for one (*Chayay Moharan* 44b #38, #222; *Yemey Moharnat* 37a).

Motzoai Shabbos, 2 Tishrei:

The Rebbe was with Reb Avraham. He said, "I am not afraid of death." He then tapped Reb Avraham on the shoulder and said, "Avraimel, we have done something in the world" (*Chayay Moharan* 45a #38, #222).

On the second day of Rosh HaShanah, the Rebbe did not pray with the congregation, but nearby, in his own room. He also did not eat with his followers (*Yemey Moharnat, Ibid.*).

Monday, 3 Tishrei; (October 1):

The Rebbe spoke to each one who took leave from him. His daughters and sons-in-law also left (*Ibid.*).

Between Rosh HaShanah and Yom Kippur, Rabbi Nathan reviewed the lesson, especially with Hirsh Ber, who had a very keen mind. It was brought to the Rebbe, who helped complete it. This was Rabbi Nathan's only opportunity to see the Rebbe before Yom Kippur (*Ibid.* 37b; *Sippurim Niflaim* p. 7).

Sunday, 9 Tishrei; (October 7):

All the Chassidim went in to the Rebbe, and he blessed each of them, as was his custom. His face was shining (*Yemey Moharnat* 37b).

Monday, 10 Tishrei, Yom Kippur; (October 8):

The Rebbe did not pray with the *minyan*, but in his own room (*Ibid.*).

At *Neilah*, there was a question about who would lead the prayers. Rabbi Nathan felt that this would be an opportunity to see the Rebbe. He and Rabbi Naftali asked the Rebbe, who made a sign as if to say, "Go, I have no more to do with this. Do as you wish" (*Ibid.*).

Monday night, 11 Tishrei:

After Yom Kippur, Rabbi Nathan went with the the other followers to see the Rebbe, who appeared weak and unhappy (*Yemey Moharnat* 37b).

Tuesday (October 9):

In the morning the Chassidim went in to see the Rebbe and he was in good spirits. Rabbi Nathan went in later, after he had prayed. The men of Teplik were already there. The Rebbe spoke warmly to them and encouraged them. Rabbi Nathan went outside and spoke with the Rebbe's brother, Rabbi Yechiel, about how he wanted to review the lesson of Rosh HaShanah with the Rebbe (*Ibid.* 38a).

After receiving encouragement from Rabbi Yechiel, Rabbi Nathan returned to see the Rebbe alone. The Rebbe told him to close the door and they reviewed and corrected the lesson. The Rebbe then connected the lesson to the opening verse, "Blow a *shofar*..." (Psalms 81:4). This was to be his last lesson (*Ibid.*). The Rebbe said, "Don't ask me for money to print it" (*Biur HaLikutim*, Introduction).

After reviewing the lesson, the Rebbe told how his lessons were woven together. Rabbi Nathan left and wrote this down. The Rebbe was then in a very good mood and met with several people (*Yemey Moharnat* 38b; *Shevachey Moharan* 16b #50, #389).

In the afternoon, the Rebbe moved from Nachman Nathan's house back to that of the Lukacher. He was very particular that his bed be put in a specific place, for he was choosing the place where he would die. Rabbi Nathan reviewed with him his corrected notes of the lesson. The Rebbe's earlier exuberance was gone (*Yemey Moharnat* 38b).

During the rest of the week, from Yom Kippur to Succos, Rabbi Nathan did not have much chance to visit the Rebbe, being very involved in writing the lesson. The Rebbe, however, asked about him (*Ibid.* 39a).

Thursday, 13 Tishrei; (October 11):

In the late afternoon, shortly before *Minchah*, Rabbi Nathan came to the Rebbe and found Rabbi Naftali and others. The Rebbe was very sick.

That night, against Rabbi Nathan's wishes, they called the doctor. Rabbi Nathan later said that it appeared that the doctor only made matters worse and brought the Rebbe's death closer (*Ibid.* 37a, 39a; *Chayay Moharan* 45a #38, #222).

Thursday night, 14 Tishrei:

Rabbi Nathan spent the night with the Rebbe. The Rebbe made his will, leaving three hundred rubles to his daughter Chaya (for her dowry; Cf. *Yemey Moharnat* p. 52b, that he left her pearls) and the *kesubah* payment to his wife. Rabbi Nathan did not want to discuss it saying, "You will certainly live to see your daughter married." The Rebbe said, "Everything is possible with God. It is a miracle that I lived for the past three years." The Rebbe was very sick, and coughed up much blood. At this time, the Rebbe told Rabbi Nathan to tell Reb Moshe Chenkes that if he divorced his wife and married someone else, he would have children. This he did, and later married a woman named Elka, the sister of the Rabbi of Tomashpol, and had a son and daughter (*Yemey HaTalaos* p. 5,6). Before morning they called the doctor again, against Rabbi Nathan's wishes (*Yemey Moharnat* 39a, b).

Around this time a mysterious, short, old man came to Reb Avraham Chaim's hotel. He made some miraculous predictions. Some said that he was Rabbi Mordechai of Neskhiz (whom the Rebbe had seen shortly before he died nine and a half years previously; see above, pp. 56-57). Others said that he was the Koznitzer Magid (*Manuscript* p. 7) who was then seventy-three years old, and was usually bedridden because of his chronic illness. He died exactly four years later on Erev Succos (*Eser Oros* pp. 35a, 42a; *Chachmey Yisroel* p. 214).

On Friday morning, the Rebbe asked for a chair. He remained there until Saturday night. They put his *tallis* and *tefillin* on him. He coughed very much and asked Rabbi Nathan to hold his head. Rabbi Nathan begged the Rebbe to intercede to save himself, but the Rebbe said, "I have no desire to" (*Yemey Moharnat* 39b).

The strange old man came in to *daven Minchah* with the Rebbe. The Rebbe greeted him joyously, and they spoke for several hours (*Manuscript* p. 7).

26

THE LAST DAYS

Shabbos, 15 Tishrei, Succos; (October 13):

The Rebbe sat in the chair all day and did not go into the *succah*. The Chassidim took turns staying with him. In the morning, the Chassidim helped him don his *tallis* and he prayed sitting in the chair (*Yemey Moharnat* 40a).

Motzoai Shabbos, 16 Tishrei, Eve of 2nd day of Succos:

The Rebbe asked to be taken from his chair to the bed. He reminded Rabbi Nathan of the story of the Baal Shem Tov, which he had told on the way to Uman (above, p. 186). He said, "There are many tens of thousands of souls here in Uman which have long been waiting to bring me here" (*Yemey Moharnat* 40a).

Before he passed away, the Rebbe said, "I have already reached such a level that I can no longer advance while still clothed in this earthly body. I yearn to put this body aside, for I cannot remain on one level" (*Sichos HaRan* #179).

The Rebbe alternated sitting in the chair and lying in bed (*Yemey Moharnat* 41a). Once when he was sitting he had a coughing attack and was very weak. But, in spite of his weakness, the Rebbe made a fist as if to say, "I still have strength." He then grasped Reb M.'s coat and said with a gesture, "What strength I have" (*Chayay Moharan* 45a #39, #223).

Monday night, 18 Tishrei; (October 15):

Until after midnight, it was the turn of Rabbi Naftali and Rabbi Shimon to be with the Rebbe. The Rebbe then repeated what he had said *Motzoai* Shabbos, "Many

judgments were made here; there were many martyrs."
Rabbi Naftali said, "Didn't you say (in *Likutey Moharan* 65)
that the greatest Tzaddik could do it (i.e. rectify everything
necessary) in his lifetime?" The Rebbe replied, "There are
many other concepts involved" (*Chayay Moharan* 39a #7, 8,
#191, 192). He then gave them the keys to his chest,
instructing them to burn all his manuscripts as soon as he
passed away, while he was still lying on the ground. Rabbi
Naftali and Rabbi Shimon were shocked to hear the Rebbe
preparing to die, and whispered to each other. The Rebbe
said, "There is no need to whisper. I am not afraid of death. As
for yourselves, you have nothing to fear since I am going
before you. It is difficult to rectify the souls of those who died
before, but you have nothing to fear" (*Yemey Moharnat* 40b).

Around 1 a.m., Rabbi Nathan came in. The Rebbe was
sitting in his chair. Rabbi Naftali told him about the key. Rabbi
Nathan was shocked at how the Rebbe was preparing for his
death but still refused to believe that it was truly imminent.
The Rebbe sat in silence. Rabbi Naftali then went out to sleep
(*Yemey Moharnat* 41a).

From about 2 a.m. until daybreak Rabbi Shimon lay down
to sleep on the floor in the Rebbe's room. Rabbi Nathan was
the only one attending the Rebbe. Rabbi Nathan did not want
to believe that the Rebbe would soon be taken from the world
and was unwilling to ask him any questions. The Rebbe did
not speak, but looked intently at Rabbi Nathan. He then put
the Rebbe to bed. The Rebbe said, "Slowly, slowly" and then
explained that he was heavy now [because the life was going
out of him] (*Ibid.* 41b).

Tuesday morning, 18 Tishrei; (October 16):

In the early morning Rabbi Nathan gave the Rebbe some
tea with egg yolk (which relieves coughing). The Rebbe's
attendant awoke and he came in. Rabbi Nathan then went to
the *mikvah* and when he returned the Rebbe was sitting up

in bed with his *tallis* on, praying. He then said the blessing over the *esrog* and *lulav*, and took the ARI's Siddur on his lap. He completed *Hallel* and said *Hoshanos* quite loudly until everyone in the house heard. The others prayed in a nearby room (*Ibid.* 42a, b).

After the prayers, Rabbi Nathan passed by the Rebbe's room. The Rebbe looked at Rabbi Nathan. Rabbi Nathan spoke with Rabbi Yechiel saying that he was starting to believe that the Rebbe's death was close and asked Rabbi Yechiel to help him overcome such thoughts. Rabbi Yechiel strengthened him. He then went back to his lodgings, rested a little, went over the last lesson and ate. In spite of his tiredness, he then returned to the Rebbe (*Ibid.* 42b).

When he came into the Rebbe he found a commotion in the room. The Rebbe was in a chair, but the life was draining from him. A man who had suddenly arrived from Terhovitza stood by him. More than anyone else he saw to the Rebbe's needs. The Rebbe had promised him long before this that he would do this. Together with the man from Terhovitza, they put the Rebbe into bed. Rabbi Nathan held the Rebbe's hand (*Ibid.* 43a).

Tuesday afternoon, 18 Tishrei; (October 16):

In the early afternoon the Rebbe lay in bed, dressed in his best robe. He told Rabbi Shimon to arrange his clothing and wash the blood from his beard. He then lay on the bed in a free state of mind. He rolled a ball of wax between his fingers with the utmost delicacy, composing his thoughts. Then he drank some soup. Later, however, he would not eat (*Ibid* 43a).

While the Rebbe lay in bed, there was an unusually strong gale which tore out rocks in the hills. It blew down the *succah* near the Rebbe's house and a fire broke out in Uman. Everyone, including Rabbi Nathan, ran to the fire, but miraculously it went out by itself before Rabbi Nathan reached it.

Rabbi Nathan returned to the Rebbe and stood near his bed. Many people came to be with the Rebbe in his last hour and started saying the verses in *Maaver Yabok* for a Tzaddik approaching death (*Ibid.* 43b).

The people then thought that the Rebbe had died. Rabbi Nathan started crying and shouted, "Rebbe! Rebbe! To whom have you left us?" The Rebbe heard and lifted up his head with an expression that said, "I am not leaving you, God forbid!"

But the end came soon afterwards. The Rebbe died in a state of serenity and with the utmost composure. All those present, including the *chevra kadisha*, said that although they had seen people die calmly, they had never seen anything like this (*Yemey Moharnat* 43b).

The Rebbe thus passed away on Tuesday afternoon, on the second day of Chol HaMoed Succos, 18 Tishrei (October 16) (*Chayay Moharan* 39a #7, #191; *Yemey Moharnat* 44a).

There was a great commotion in the room and people began crying loudly. No woman was in the room at the time of his death to cry over him. His wife remained in the other room. His daughters had gone home after Yom Kippur, not realizing that his death was so imminent (*Manuscript* p. 18; *Yemey Moharnat, Ibid.*).

During the commotion, Rabbi Shimon quickly took the key the Rebbe had given him and burned the manuscripts as he had been instructed (*Yemey Moharnat, Ibid.*).

Meanwhile, they undressed the Rebbe and laid him on the floor with his feet to the door, according to custom. It was already night and it was agreed that it would not be fitting for the funeral of a great leader like this to take place before the morning (*Ibid.*; see *Yoreh De'ah* 357:2, 242:1).

Wednesday, 19 Tishrei; (October 17):

Everyone was told to go to the *mikvah* and afterwards they prayed. Rabbi Nathan was asked how to perform the burial, and he replied, "Treat the Rebbe like any other Jew."

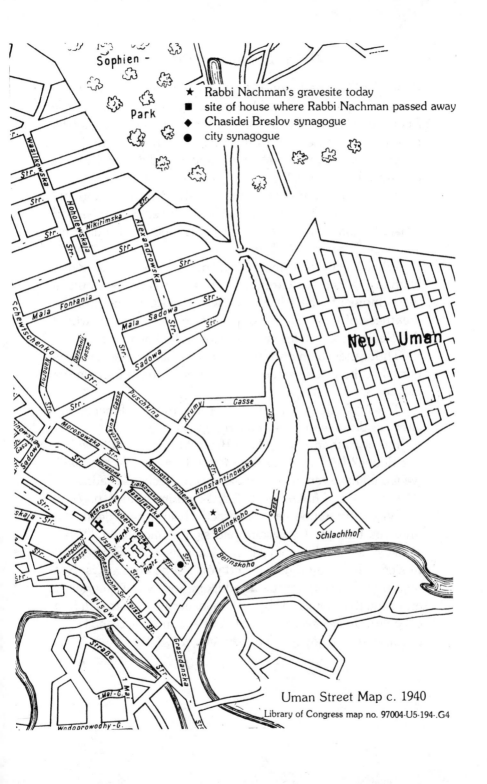

Sophien - Park

★ Rabbi Nachman's gravesite today
■ site of house where Rabbi Nachman passed away
◆ Chasidei Breslov synagogue
● city synagogue

Neu - Uman

Schlachthof

Uman Street Map c. 1940
Library of Congress map no. 97004-U5-194-.G4

Rabbi Nathan had not yet prayed *Mussaf* or made the blessing over the *esrog*. He sat on the ground next to the Rebbe and spoke into his ear, crying. The *chevra kadisha* then came and performed the *taharah*, preparing the body for burial. They wrapped him in his *tallis* and placed the body on the table (*Ibid.* 44b).

There was a problem burying the Rebbe in the old cemetery since it was no longer in use. Rabbi Nathan insisted, and Hirsh Ber helped arrange it through his influence (*Sippurim Niflaim* p. 7).

When they took the Rebbe out of the house, Rabbi Nathan grasped his garment and helped carry him out. In these moments, he felt an overwhelming awareness of the greatness of God. They made a bier out of the chair where the Rebbe had sat for his last Rosh HaShanah lesson.

Thousands of mourners attended the funeral. He was buried in the place he had chosen, among the martyrs in the old cemetery in Uman (*Ibid.*).

The mysterious old man was at the Rebbe's funeral, and later he disappeared (*Manuscript* p. 7).

Rabbi Nathan cried. Hirsh Ber told him, "*You* have lost the Rebbe? *We* have lost the Rebbe! If the Rebbe had lived, we would have repented completely and become Tzaddikim" (*Parparaos LeChokhmah* 215:2; *Sippurim Niflaim* p. 7).

When the Rebbe had discussed his imminent death the previous Elul, the Chassidim had sighed and asked, "What shall we do?! With whom will you leave us?" The Rebbe then replied, "Just stay together and you will be good Jews. Not only that, but you can be Tzaddikim, for God will certainly grant me that things will be as I have always wanted. *Ich hob ois gefirt, un vell ois firren!* — I have accomplished and I shall accomplish" (*Chayay Moharan* 44a #34, #218).

APPENDICES

APPENDIX A
LETTERS

Letter #1

[Zaslov, 5567 (1807)]
To my good friends, my beloved friends, the amicable partners,
I earnestly ask you to give my wife 100 rubles. I need a great deal [of money] for expenses, which are very high here, as the bearer of this letter will attest. Not only double, but four times as much [as at home]. I do not have even a single *prutah*.

I ask you, Reb Moshe BeHaRav, Reb Yisroel and Reb Moshe ben HeAni, to send me this money. When I come home, please God, I will settle things as you desire. I repeat again and again, do not act otherwise, just send 100 rubles.

Also encourage my wife to come immediately.

Also tell my good friend, Rabbi Nathan of Nemirov, and all our group that they should pray that God heal me completely. I shall not write details of my sickness, in order that it not make my *mazal* worse.[1] I only ask that you pray for me in each and every prayer, and not forget all the good that I have done for each of you until now. It is possible that God will allow me [to live] and you will be able to receive even more good from me. My beloved brethren and friends, I beseech you that you pray for my anguished soul. Pray with feeling of the heart.

Remember how I found each of you when I came to Breslov, and how much energy, both spiritual and physical, I expended for you. It is therefore only proper that you should now likewise pray to God for me, that He heal me and show me the pleasure of His splendor.[2]

Rabbi Nachman's Handwriting

Also encourage my wife to come to me, for a wife of one's youth is impossible to replace.

Particularly as the expenses are so great here, I beseech you that none of you should attempt to come here. Soon, God willing, I shall return home.

Thus are the words of he who truly loves you all, that each of you sits in the chambers of my heart.

> Nachman, son of my master Rabbi Simcha, may God protect him.

Greetings to our entire group, each according to his lofty standing. I repeat, encourage my wife to leave quickly but do not inform her or the children of this.

> Nachman, son of my master Rabbi Simcha (the aforementioned)

1. Cf. *Berachos* 55b.
2. Cf. *Y'did Nefesh*, "I beseech thee O God, heal her, showing her the presence of Your splendor."

Letter #2

With the help of God, Thursday [week of] Torah reading Emor, [6 Iyar] 5567, [May 14, 1807] Zaslov
To my beloved son-in-law, the scholarly, princely Rabbi Yoske, may his light shine and spread, and his wife, my modest, wise daughter Adil, may she live, Amen.

I received your letter on Sunday, the week of Emor, [2 Iyar].

The 100 rubles also arrived.

I should like to inform you that I am now residing in Zaslov. Your mother-in-law has taken a great turn [for the better].

I also want to tell you that I shall not be in your home for Shavuos, but shall remain here in Zaslov.

Nothing else, just blessings of life and peace.[1]

Your father-in-law who deeply loves you and always wishes your good welfare.

> Nachman, son of my master Rabbi Simcha, may God watch him.

I should also like to inform you that I am not making use of medicine, for God has helped me and has not taken His beneficence and truth from me.[2]

> Nachman (the aforementioned)

Give my regards to my friend, Reb Moshe BeHaRav, and to his neighbor, my friend, Reb Yisroel, and my partner, my friend Reb Moshe ben HeAni. He has written me asking if he should make use of medicine, but my mind is not clear now, and I do not know what to answer.

> Nachman (the aforementioned)

Regards to our entire group

> Nachman (the aforementioned)

When you write to me send your letter to Zaslov, to the house of the Rabbi of the Tailors' [Synagogue] as mentioned in a note included in the letter.

My wife, Sashia, and my daughter Miriam send regards.

I beseech you, my son-in-law, make yourself fixed times every day to study Talmud and the Codes. Do not make the secondary the main thing[3], but "Fear God...for this is all of man."[4]

> Nachman (the aforementioned)

My friend, Reb Shmuel [of Teplik], sends regards to you all.

---

1. Malachi 2:5
2. Genesis 24:27
3. Cf. *Berachos* 6:7
4. Ecclesiastes 12:13

Letter #3

With God's help, Monday, [Week of] Torah reading Bechukosai [17 Iyar; May 25]
To my dear beloved brother and friend, the very learned, scholarly, altogether wise Rabbi Yechiel Zvi, may his light shine and spread,

I received your letter here in Zaslov, and was greatly pained to hear how these wicked people took it upon themselves to act so brazenly against you. I am very surprised that there was no good opposite the bad[1] — against them to destroy the evil.

My beloved brother, my heart and soul, do not be afraid or dismayed[2] before them. Be strong and firm[3] in Torah and in awe of God all the day.[4]

As we have already spoken...

The merit of your fathers will help you.[5] For all this is only to help you wax, to increase your honor, and to develop your mind. It is impossible for plants to grow unless the seed is first placed in the earth. The seed then decomposes, and only then does it sprout and then grow and become a great tree. The same is [true] here. For through their casting you in the dust, you will grow and sprout and bloom in the world. If these wicked men realized this, they would certainly not insult you. For all their intentions are evil.

I am honorably informing you that it is my intention to remain here in Zaslov for approximately three months. After that, I'll know where to turn.

I should also like you to know that my wife had at first taken a turn [for the better], but now this continues to be reversed, and her strength is diminishing daily.

My expenses here are tremendous. I have already spent 54 rubles.

There is nothing else[6] [to write], just [hope for] life. From your brother and devoted friend who awaits to hear good tidings, and to see you in life and peace.[7]

Nachman, son of my master Rabbi Simcha, may God protect him.

My wife sends regards to your wife. My daughter Miriam also sends regards to you all. Send regards to all your supporters. Be strong and firm,[8] for there is a reward for all your work[9] in this world and in the next.

Nachman (the aforementioned)

1. Cf. Ecclesiastes 7:14
2. Deuteronomy 31:8
3. Deuteronomy 31:7
4. Proverbs 27:17
5. Avos 2:2
6. Eruvin 103b
7. Malachi 2:5
8. Deuteronomy 31:6
9. Chronicles II, 15:6

Letter #4

[Zaslov, 5567 (1807)]

I am informing our entire gathering that I am weary of living in Breslov, because of all the troubles and difficulties that have passed over me and I am now going from tent to tent.[1] I have no intention of settling, but am sojourning.[2]

My petition and request[3] of you is that all the effort that I put into each one of you not be in vain. I placed my soul in my hands[4] for the good of your souls. God is righteous and I have wronged.[5] My own deeds caused my suffering, and the death of my darling children, as well as all the strife and denunciation. Nevertheless, I certainly know, that for all the trouble that I have taken for you, to snatch you out from the teeth of the evil one, also for all this, his eyes glare and he grits his teeth over me.

Therefore, my friends, brothers and companions, strengthen and encourage yourselves in the fear of God, each one according to his ability and his quality, and my efforts will not be in vain. Keep the Torah of Moshe the servant of God, as I have taught you,[6] and know that although I am now distant from you, it is only a distance of the bodies and this distance is not, Heaven forbid, between our souls, for we are very near.

My beloved brothers and friends, please see that these words which I have beseeched you, be close to you day and night.[7]

Let me inform you that I am now staying in Zaslov, and will remain here, with God's help, around three months.

These are the words of your devoted friend, who is writing in tears[8] of joy that God has given me iron strength to bear the yoke of these sufferings and travels.

> Nachman, son of my master Rabbi Simcha, may God watch and keep him.

Let me also tell you, that I am now quite healthy without having resorted to any physical cures.

> Nachman (the aforementioned)

1. Chronicles II, 4:5
2. paraphrase from Passover Haggadah
3. Esther 5:7
4. Psalms 12:3
5. Exodus 9:27
6. Cf. Malachi 3:22
7. Kings I, 8:59
8. *Bava Basra* 15a

Letter #5

With the help of God, the day when *ki tov* was repeated[1] [Tuesday, 28 Av; September 1], the end of Av 5567
To my honored brother and *mechuten*, the beloved, revered, philanthropist and eminent leader whose distinguished name is treasured, R. Yechezkel Trachtenberg,

I inform you of my well being and that of my household, thank God, we are all in life and health. May God thus give and continue to grant that all our household be in life and peace.

I am informing you that I returned home on the above mentioned date, and I received, through Reb P., the letter [from your daughter].

She repeats over and again that she cannot come because of the passports, and also that the border is completely closed. She also states and repeats that I myself should come to Kresilov.

Therefore, I am informing you to return to the first.... What has already happened is nothing, for the time set for the wedding is already past.

As far as the future is concerned, I respectfully request that if you want the bond we have made to be permanent, you must relinquish your highly esteemed honor, and arrange to have the wedding near our community, that is, close to Breslov. It should be arranged no later than the middle of this coming Elul, for I cannot leave my place, even to come a single *parsa*. If this cannot be done, then a high mountain will rise between us[2] (verb sap).

I repeat, please make sure to send your daughter, with her necessities, no later than the date mentioned above, so that the wedding ceremony will take place in the fullness of the moon...[3]

When she comes here, and arrives around 3 or 4 *parsos* from Breslov (25-30 miles), let her send her messenger, and I will write about the exact place where the wedding will take place.

Regarding the passport, see if you can arrange some plan without my passport. Particularly since it is easy to come here without a passport.

Nothing else,[4] just life and peace.[5]

These are the words of the one who closes [saying] may God grant you many good years.

Thus are the words of the one anticipating becoming your son-in-law, and constantly hoping lovingly for your welfare and awaiting your early reply.

Nachman, son of my master Rabbi Simcha.

I send peace and great prosperity to your wife, the modest lady, blessed among women in the tent,[6] the wise and noble ...

1. Cf. Genesis 1:10, 12
2. *Chullin* 7b
3. Cf. *Yoreh Deah* 179:2
4. *Eruvin* 103b
5. Malachi 2:5
6. Judges 5:24

Letter #6

With the help of God, Sunday [week of Torah reading] Emor, 26 to the [Omer] numbering of the Jewish people 5568, Lvov (Lemberg)
Peace and great prosperity to my dear friend, the esteemed Reb Yaakov,

I received your two letters. In the first letter there are the introductions of my friend Rabbi Nathan of Nemirov. And now I have received a second letter from you, containing the note of the printer.

You also write to me that I should send no less than 100 rubles for this. I am very surprised, since you do not indicate through whom it should be sent, to whom, or in whose name. I am also surprised that you did not indicate the size of the edition, whether it will consist of 1000 books or more. You also do not indicate what kind of paper it will be printed on, whether on writing paper (*schreib*) or on *regal* paper. Nor [do you indicate] how much will it cost [if printed] on writing paper, and how much on regal, nor how much you are paying the printer for his work on each signature, and how many signatures will be in the entire book. [I should like] you to write everything clearly, as soon as possible.

Concerning what you wrote that you were having trouble from the Rabbi and that he wants to print some of his own things in the book, I have placed everything in your hands, and you are in control. Therefore, if you understand that you do not need the Rabbi, then leave him alone.[1] Even if you do need him, I warn you not to print even one letter of his. [I want] nothing alien in the book.

Of the two introductions that you sent me, the smaller one seems best in my eyes. Regarding the *haskamos*, I spoke to the Rabbi, not to think this...

Concerning what you mentioned that the brother-in-law of the printer, Rabbi Moshe, did you favors, with God's help I will repay him for every piece [of assistance].

May God give you strength, both materially and spiritually, to complete the printing without any delays.

Regarding my health, let me tell you that in the past few days I have regained some of my strength, but that I still need great mercy [from on High]. Whoever cares for me should pray for mercy for me.

Nachman, son of my master Rabbi Simcha, may God keep him.

Send the letters through the post, each one to its place.

1. paraphrase Job 7:16

Letter #7

Friday, eve of the Sabbath, [Torah reading] Vayishlach (5569) Greetings to my esteemed, beloved son-in-law, the dear, scholarly Rabbi Yitzchok Isaac, and his dear wife, my dear, modest, wise, praiseworthy Sarah,

I received your letter, and my reins rejoiced[1] when I heard of your good welfare. I bless God who has helped us so far, for she has travailed and given birth[2] to her daughter, may she live. I therefore bestow my blessing: May it be for them and for us for good *mazal*, also may children's children be born on your knees[3], and you will be like a watered garden[4] and you will still bring forth fruit in a good old age.[5] Please inform me regularly on your good fortune.

I ask [both] my daughter and son-in-law that they not worry at all, but always be happy.

Peace and life as your desire and the desire of your father who hopes for your good welfare with intense love.

> Nachman, son of my master Rabbi Simcha, may God keep him.

You should also tell me about your studies and how many pages of Talmud you study every day. I very much want you to be diligent in your studies, for this is my entire intention (verb sap).

Peace to your dear wise son, Yisroel, may he live, and peace to your newborn daughter, may she live, and to your father-in-law, the famous esteemed philanthropist, Reb Aryeh Leib, and his modest, esteemed wife and all of their children

1. Proverbs 23:16
2. Isaiah 66:8
3. paraphrase Genesis 50:23
4. Isaiah 58:11
5. paraphrase Psalms 92:15

and household, peace and blessings. And peace to my dear pious brother, Yechiel.

Nachman, son of my master Rabbi Simcha, may God protect him.

Letter #8

With God's help, Tuesday, 12 days in the month of Menachem [Av] (5569)

Peace to my beloved daughter, the modest, wise, Sarah, along with her husband, dear son, and wise daughter,

I received a letter speaking about your modest mother-in-law's health the day after you left here, and I was pleased. May God, continue to do thus, Amen. I should also like to tell you that, thank God, I am feeling healthy and that I miss very much the playfulness and joy of your son, dear Yisroel. Since he left, it is really quiet in the house.

May God always let me hear good news from you, Amen.

I also should like to inform you that I received a letter from your sister, Miriam, from Odessa [saying] that she left on the ship on Thursday, the seventh of Menachem [Av]. She writes that she is happy and joyous and that everyone is kind to her. She sends regards to you all.

I also ask that you listen to me, and not worry too much about the household expenses, but eat meat and drink wine, for your health is more precious to me than my life. You will literally give me life when you can let me know that you are strong and healthy.

Thus are the words of your father, waiting to hear truly good news.

Nachman, son of my master Rabbi Simcha, may God keep him.

Greetings to my dear *mechuten*, the distinguished and scholary Reb Yehuda Leib. I beseech you to take care of the health of my daughter, for my soul is bound to hers.[1] I ask the same of your wife. I also ask you to engage in business, since your doing business involves the needs of things on High,[2] that "nations shall speak of His glory."[3]

Nachman (the aforementioned)

Also send regards to my dear brother and friend, Rabbi Yechiel.

Nachman (the aforementioned) and my wife and daughter.

1. Genesis 44:30
2. *Avodas HaKodesh* §II:1; Cf. *Likutey Moharan* 33:2
3. Psalms 96:3

Letter #9

[Tiberias]

Peace and great prosperity to the one who sits within the chambers of my heart, the renowned Rabbi, holy be said to him,[1] with him is wisdom[2] and understanding of divine knowledge,[3] the honorable and holy Rabbi, Rabbi Nachman may his light shine, of holy roots, grandson of the Baal Shem Tov, of blessed memory, may [his merit] guard us forever, may the light of God shine upon him and grow, and to all his household and his company, much peace, Amen, may it thus be His will.

I am sending you news from the Land,[4] to inform you of the return of our representative of this year in the previous month of Shevat. We rejoiced very much upon hearing of your well-being. You have arrived home safely and we have seen that the thick knot of love[5] has not moved. With all your heart you seek our benefit, and have set out on the path and voyaged yourself to the province of Reissin [Belorussia], may God be with you.

You have certainly already heard by means of our last years representative, the honorable Rabbi Eliezer, of the incident[6] which has passed over us since your words to us and about the compromise which we have reached with the people of Volhynia. We still have not received even once from them and we don't know what will be the end.

And behold we are confused in the Land[7] from great grief and worry, hoping for God's salvation[8] every moment, for we still have not been relieved from any side. Even from the province of Reissin we have no information of what is happening there in this respect, after your voyage there when you met with them and told them about all the difficulties which have found us.[9] We are hoping that you will respectfully inform us in detail of what you did there.

This you must know, that we have remained in debt to the governor [here]. In any case we must pay. It is very difficult to suffer[10] how they demand payments from us constantly with awesome threats.

We are able [to see] that only with wondrous miracles God finds place to provide us with our necessities.

I am hoping to God who hides His face,[11] and am waiting for His salvation, and in Him do I trust that He will again have mercy upon us as the days of our suffering,[12] thus will He make us to rejoice.

(From here on was written in the holy handwriting of the great Rabbi [Avraham Kalisker] himself).

I am steadfast in my love, a constant love, his praises in my mouth with crown and covering,[13] my soul is to God that God shine His face[14] to you from the place of the dwelling of His Shekhinah[15] and shine upon you, shining more and more[16] with His light shining upon your head[17] — the light of the world.[18] And may you be strengthened and fortified with fortitude from God, final act and first in thought.[19] And my soul knows well,[20] and dearly forever, and am seeking your welfare constantly and praying for you. Please do likely and pray for me every moment.

Signed: the small Avraham, son of my master, my father, Rabbi Alexander Katz of blessed memory.

My grandson, the young man, Rabbi Yisroel Eliezer, may he live, seeks your well-being with heart and soul and sends greetings with heart and soul and longs for your prayers.

1. Isaiah 4:3
2. Cf. Proverbs 11:2
3. Proverbs 2:5
4. Cf. Isaiah 32:9
5. Hosea 7:4
6. *Shabbos* 24a
7. Exodus 14:3
8. Cf. Genesis 49:18
9. Numbers 20:4; Nehemiah 9:32
10. Nehemiah 4:4
11. Cf. Psalms 88:15
12. Cf. Psalms 90:15
13. Cf. *Berachos* 51a
14. paraphrase Numbers 6:25
15. *Targum* of Ezekiel 3:12
16. Proverbs 4:18
17. Job 29:3
18. Isaiah 16:19-20
19. *Lecho Dodi*
20. Psalms 139:14

APPENDIX B

TZADDIKIM

"To separate between the light and the darkness" (Genesis 1:4). The Midrash explains: "The light is a reference to the Tzaddikim, the darkness is a reference to the wicked" (Bereshis Rabbah 20).

We have presented here short biographies of the various Tzaddikim mentioned in our text to familiarize the reader with some of our greatest leaders and to let him be aware of our illustrious past. Rabbi Nachman taught: "Mentioning the names of the Tzaddikim is a very great thing" (Sefer HaMidos, Tzaddik II:20), and "Telling stories about them helps purify the mind" (Likutey Moharan I:234).

The Tzaddikim have not been presented in any particular order. Far be it from us to even attempt to gauge who is the greater, who should be first, etc. The pages upon which they appear in the text follow their biographies.

May we merit to walk in their footsteps.

RABBI YISROEL BAAL SHEM TOV — 5458-5520 (1698-1760)

Born in Okup in Podolia, Rabbi Yisroel was orphaned at a young age. He married young but shortly afterwards his wife died. Rabbi Adam Baal Shem, a hidden Tzaddik, directed his son to bring Rabbi Yisroel secret kabbalistic writings through which he developed an extraordinary understanding of the Torah's depths.

Rabbi Yisroel then became engaged to Chana, the daughter of Rabbi Ephraim and sister of Rabbi Gershon Kittover from Brody. His future father-in-law had chosen Rabbi Yisroel upon seeing him demonstrate an outstanding grasp of Talmudic study. Shortly after the *tana'im*, Rabbi Ephraim passed away. At the time of his marriage, he hid himself completely and posed as an ignoramus. During this period of seclusion he reached very high levels of saintliness. The prophets Eliyahu and Achiyah the Shilonite revealed themselves to him and taught him the secrets of the Torah.

At the age of thirty-six he ended his seclusion and began teaching his doctrine of connecting every aspect of life to Torah. It was this doctrine which became known as Chassidism. He attracted some of the greatest scholars in Eastern Europe whom he instructed in his teachings, so that they would be able to spread them further. Even the simplest Jew could now benefit from the spiritual wells of the secrets of the Torah.

At first he settled in Tlust but afterwards moved to Medzeboz. He was Rabbi Nachman's great-grandfather through his daughter Adil.

(pp. 1-4, 8-11, 13, 16, 24, 26, 33, 34, 47, 50, 57f, 59n, 65, 71, 72, 79, 88, 93, 100, 102, 120,121, 123, 127, 144, 152, 161, 163, 178, 182f, 186, 187, 193, 200)

RABBI NACHMAN HORODENKER — 5440-5526 (1680-1766)

The Rebbe's grandfather.

In his youth he undertook difficult devotions such as immersing himself in extremely cold *mikvahs* in order to purify his body and thoughts. He was associated with the pious scholars of the *Kloyz* of Brody.

Around the year 1740 he went with his son R. Shimson to *Eretz Yisroel*, but he left after two years. When Rabbi Elazar Rokeach heard that Rabbi Nachman was in the Land of Israel, he said that if they would both be there together they would be able to bring Mashiach. He rushed to join him, only to find that Rabbi Nachman had already left. Upon hearing in Europe of Rabbi Elazar's voyage, Rabbi Nachman returned to Safed to meet him, but Rabbi Elazar had died in the meantime (on 27 Tishrei) in 1743. Rabbi Nachman returned again to Europe upon the death of his wife.

It was at this point that he became one of the closest followers of the Baal Shem Tov. It was also then that he remarried and Rabbi Simcha, the Rebbe's father, was born.

The Baal Shem Tov once said that Rabbi Nachman (Horodenker) had prayed that he not be able to hear anything which was not necessary for his service of God and his request was granted. He was known for his custom of remarking on every occurence that it was for the best.

He is quoted a number of times in the works of Rabbi Yaakov Yosef of Polonnoye and in *Degel Machaneh Ephraim*.

The Baal Shem Tov restrained Rabbi Nachman from returning to the Land of Israel. However, in 1764, after visiting the Baal Shem Tov's grave, he said that the Baal Shem Tov had appeared to him and given him permission to return.

Rabbi Pinchas of Koretz said that as long as Rabbi Nachman was in what was then Poland, the Cossaks would not be able to enter the country. It was while Rabbi Nachman was on his way to *Eretz Yisroel* that the massacre in Uman took place.

Rabbi Nachman Horodenker is buried in the old cemetery in Tiberias (see Cities, Tiberias).

(pp. 1, ,3, 9, 14f, 28, 34, 41, 41n, 42f, 47 166)

RABBI DOV BER, THE MEZRITCHER MAGID — 5464-5533 (1704-1772)

He was the main leader of the Chassidic movement after the death of the Baal Shem Tov in 1760. Virtually all of the Chassidic masters of that generation were his disciples.

When he first came to the Baal Shem Tov he was already an accomplished scholar, both in Talmudic and Kabbalistic studies, a student of Rabbi Yaakov Yehoshuah Falk author of the *P'nei Yehoshuah*.

He was lame, and the Baal Shem Tov said that if he could have gone to the *mikvah* he would have been able to bring the Mashiach.

When told that a certain Tzaddik said that with every

glance the Magid would see the "Seven Shepherds" (Abraham, Isaac, Jacob, Moses, Aaron, Joseph and David), Rabbi Nachman remarked, "One can believe anything said of the Magid." He is buried in Anipoli.
(pp. 3, 11, 18, 33, 54, 58, 86, 129, 136, 137)

RABBI AVRAHAM "THE MALACH" — 5501-5537 (1741-1776)

Rabbi Avraham was the only son of the Mezritcher Magid.

He was known as a holy man, hardly part of this world, hence the name "Malach" — angel. The Magid assigned him to learn in partnership with Rabbi Shneur Zalman.

After the Magid's death, some of his principle disciples signed a statement of allegiance to the "Malach." But he preferred to seclude himself from the world in the town of Fastov where he died at the age of thirty-six.
(p. 3)

RABBI SHALOM SHACHNEH of PROBISHT — d. 5563 (1803)

Son of the "Malach," he had a different approach to Chassidism than the other leaders of the generation, conducting himself aristocratically. Rabbi Nochum of Tchernoble, his wife's grandfather, said that he sincerely means all that he does for the sake of Heaven. Rabbi Nachman praised him extensively.

He was one of the Chassidic leaders approached by Rabbi Nathan before he met Rabbi Nachman. There is some confusion about the date of his death, various sources citing 13th or 14th Tishrei 1803, or 1804, or 1823, but since he was said not to have lived long, 1823 seems unlikely.
(pp. 3, 20, 22f, 86)

RABBI YAAKOV YOSEF HAKOHEN of POLONNOYE, the "TOLDOS" — 5470-5544 (1710-1784)

Originally a student of the *P'nei Yehoshua*, at a young age he became the Rabbi of Sharograd. When he heard that the Baal Shem Tov was visiting nearby Mohelov, he decided to go there and investigate the Baal Shem Tov's ways. After experiencing a new emotional dimension in prayer, he became irrevocably attached to the Baal Shem Tov. However, his new ways aroused opposition in Sharograd and he was forced to relinquish his position. Subsequently, he became Rabbi of Rashkov, Polonnoye and Nemirov.

His book, *Toldos Yaakov Yosef*, was the first printed work based on Chassidic teachings, and aroused much criticism. The book is filled with quotes from the Baal Shem Tov, as are his other works, *Ben Poras Yosef*, *Tsofnas Pane'ach*, and *K'sones Passim*. These books are the sources of *Keser Shem Tov*, a collection of the teachings of the Baal Shem Tov.

Rabbi Nachman said that even from these great works one cannot appreciate the extent of the holiness of Rabbi Yaakov Yosef.

Rabbi Yaakov Yosef was the father-in-law of Rabbi Avraham Dov Ohrbach of Chmelnik, the Rebbe's *mechuten*, and Rabbi Yoska, the Rebbe's son-in-law was named after him.
(pp. 3, 54, 102)

RABBI PINCHAS SHAPIRO of KORETZ — 5486-5551 (1726-1791)

Born in Shklov, Lithuania, his family moved to Volyhnia. There he met the Baal Shem Tov and became one of his closest disciples.

Although renowned for his scholarship in both Talmudic and Kabbalistic studies, he left no writings. His disciples, however, collected much of what they had heard from him in *Midrash Pinchas* and other works.

Rabbi Yudel, one of Rabbi Nachman's most prominent disciples, was formerly a follower of Rabbi Pinchas. Rabbi Nachman once remarked, "Happy are the eyes which have seen Rabbi Pinchas." He also said that Rabbi Pinchas had been unique in his generation.

When Rabbi Nachman revealed the *Tikkun Haklali* he said, "Many Tzaddikim have searched for this *Tikkun* since Creation; Rabbi Pinchas had attained the knowledge that it involved saying Ten Psalms but had not reached the point of being able to specify which ones."

He settled first in Koretz and later in Ostrog. He died in Shepetevka while on his way to Israel.
(pp. 14, 15, 18)

RABBI ELIYAHU, THE GAON of VILNA — 5480-5558 (1720-1797)

In his childhood he was recognized as an amazing prodigy, demonstrating unusual powers of memory, concentration and understanding. At a young age, he already had an intimate knowledge of all areas of the Torah, including Kabbalah.

He quickly became recognized as leader of the Jewish community in Lithuania, although he held no official position. He was 35 years old when Rabbi Yehonasan Eibschitz requested his intervention to defend him against the attacks of Rabbi Yaakov of Emden.

His joining the groups of scholars opposed to Chassidus was instrumental in limiting the spread of the movement in Lithuania. When Rabbi Menachem Mendel of Vitebsk and Rabbi Shneur Zalman travelled to Vilna to explain their positions, he refused to receive them.

It appears that his opposition to the Chassidic movement was from fear that any popular movement based on the

Kabbalah might lead to the same disastrous results that had been the end of the Shabbatean and the even more recent and closer to home Frankist movements. He felt that Kabbalah should be solely the domain of the most accomplished scholars, and not be divulged to the masses. The Chassidim on the other hand, felt that the thirst the Jewish people had demonstrated for contact with the depths of the Torah during those psuedo-messianic episodes needed to be quenched with genuine Kabbalistic teachings, which would enter into and elevate their lives.
(pp. 3, 23)

RABBI MOSHE CHAIM EPHRAIM of SUDYLKOV — 5500-5560 (1740-1800)
RABBI BARUCH of MEDZEBOZ 5517-5570 — (1757-1810)

The two sons of Adil, the Baal Shem Tov's daughter, they were the Rebbe's uncles, brothers of his mother Feige.

Rabbi Ephraim served as magid in Sudylkov, where he lived in poverty and humility. He never gathered a large group of Chassidim around him; but his *Degel Machaneh Ephraim*, where he often quotes his grandfather the Baal Shem Tov, is regarded as one of the classics of Chassidic literature.

A disciple of Rabbi Pinchas of Koretz, Rabbi Baruch went to be Rabbi of Tulchin in 1780. In 1788 he returned to Medzeboz where he made his home, returning to Tulchin for a month-long visit every summer and winter. His court in Medzeboz was renowned for the splendor with which it was conducted. It included the famous *badchan*, Rabbi Hershele Ostropoler.

Rabbi Baruch was among those present at the assembly of Jewish leaders in Berdichov in 1802 to discuss Russia's projected anti-Jewish measures. When there, he defended Rabbi Nachman from the attacks of the Shpola Zeide. He was often critical of the contemporary leaders, as we find in our text (pp. 159, 179) which records his criticizm of the Rebbe and Rabbi Shneur Zalman.

Rabbi Hershel of Ziditchov described how he hid in Rabbi Baruch's room and heard the awesomeness of his reading of *Shir HaShirim*.

Both brothers are buried in Medzeboz close to their grandfather.

(pp. 2, 4, 6, 22, 43, 45, 54, 57, 64n, 71-73, 92, 99, 100, 116, 127, 129, 140, 152, 159, 177, 178)

RABBI MENACHEM MENDEL of VITEBSK — 5490-5548 (1730-1788)

At the age of nine, his father brought him to the Baal Shem Tov.

The Mezritcher Magid was his childhood teacher and Rabbi Menachem Mendel eventually became his most distinguished disciple. The Magid appointed him leader of the Chassidim of Belorussia. He was made magid of the city of Minsk but met with opposition from the *misnagdim* there.

At the time of the first major wave of opposition to the Chassidic movement in 1772, Rabbi Menachem Mendel visited Vilna twice—the second time with Rabbi Shneur Zalman—in the hope of meeting with Rabbi Eliyahu, the Gaon of Vilna, and making peace between the Chassidim and the *misnagdim*. However, the Gaon refused to see them.

After the *cherem* was made against the Chassidim in 1772, Rabbi Menachem Mendel was one of the leading spokesmen at the meeting in Rovno in the house of Rabbi Dov Ber, where a counter *cherem* was placed. Because of opposition to Chassidism he was forced to leave Minsk and went to Gorodok in the province of Vitebsk where he spread Chassidism in Vitebsk and the environs.

In 1777, Rabbi Menachem Mendel led a group of three hundred followers to settle in *Eretz Yisroel*. They went first to Safed, but the *misnagdim* in Lithuania sent letters to the Sephardic settlers in the town fomenting opposition, and

Rabbi Menachem Mendel and his followers were forced to move to Tiberias, where the first Chassidic synagogue was erected. Rabbi Menachem Mendel sent emissaries to Eastern Europe to raise funds for the support of the settlers.

When Rabbi Nachman set off on his pilgrimage to Israel, Rabbi Mendel appeared to him and revealed the Holy Name which is protective on sea journeys. Rabbi Menachem Mendel is buried in Tiberias.

(pp. 4, 6, 12, 28, 31, 44, 58, 170, 177, 178)

RABBI YAAKOV SHIMSHON of SHEPETEVKA — d. 5561 (1801)

A disciple of the Mezritcher Magid and Rabbi Pinchas of Koretz, he was also close to Rabbi Baruch.

A prominent scholar in Talmud and *halakhah*, he was sent to Rabbi Yechezkel Landau (the *Nodeh BiYehuda*) of Prague to convince him of the righteousness of the Chassidic movement.

After settling in *Eretz Yisroel*, he was sent by the community there to Europe to raise funds. He was also involved in the dispute over the distribution of those funds, as mentioned in our text. He met Rabbi Nachman while in Israel.

(pp. 4, 43, 44n, 62, 65, 157, 187)

RABBI AVRAHAM KATZ of KALISK — d. 5570 (1810)

Rabbi Avraham was originally a disciple of Rabbi Eliyahu, the Gaon of Vilna. Returning to his home town of Kalisk, he spent seven years closed up in his room involved in study and devotion.

He was advised to travel to Rabbi Dov Ber, the Magid of Mezritch, whose disciple he became. When asked by the Vilna Gaon what he had found in Mezritch, Rabbi Avraham replied, " '...and he shall *live* by them' " (Leviticus 18:5). Rabbi Avraham became noted for the fervor with which he prayed and the joy he expressed. His activities evoked the hostility of the misnagdim.

After the death of Rabbi Dov Ber in 1772, Rabbi Avraham became very close to Rabbi Menachem Mendel of Vitebsk and was among the group of three hundred who went to settle in Eretz Yisroel under Rabbi Menachem Mendel's leadership. Upon the latter's death in 1788, Rabbi Avraham succeeded him as leader.

His scholarship and piety also earned him the reverence of the Sephardic settlers. Rabbi Avraham enjoyed a close friendship with Rabbi Shneur Zalman of Liadi, to whom Rabbi Menachem Mendel had given the responsibility of supervising the collection of funds in Eastern Europe for the settlers in the Holy Land. However, Rabbi Avraham was opposed to the approach to Chassidism contained in Rabbi Shneur Zalman's Likutey Amorim. From then on the two became opponents.

During Rabbi Nachman's visit to Israel he visited Rabbi Avraham in Tiberias and a great bond of friendship was forged between them. Rabbi Nachman said of Rabbi Avraham, "I have seen many Tzaddikim but I have seen perfection only in this holy man."

Among his teachings Rabbi Avraham emphasized the importance of the Chassidic group independent of the authority of the Tzaddik, and taught the need for spiritual attachment between friends. Rabbi Avraham's sayings and letters are collected in Chesed LeAvraham and Igros Kodesh.

(pp. 4, 31, 32, 41-43, 45, 46, 53, 55, 56, 63, 71, 92, 111, 177)

RABBI ZVI SEGEL HARKER — 5520-5588 (1760-1827)

Rabbi Zvi came from Gorki (Harki). He was one of the leading followers of Rabbi Menachem Mendel of Vitebsk.

Rabbi Zvi was a great Tzaddik , and rejected all physical enjoyment. According to Rabbi Zev Wolf of Charni-Ostrov, he had clear ruach hakodesh. Rabbi Moshe of Kobrin said that Rabbi Zvi treated every Shabbos as if it were the only one.

He signed his name [Rabbi] Zvi Hirsh, son of Avraham Segel (Segel indicating he was a Levite) Harker.

Rabbi Zvi came to Israel with his first wife, Sashia, (on 24 Cheshvon) in 1784. His second wife was the sister of a *chacham* in Rhodes.

Rabbi Zvi went to Europe as an emissary with his brother Rabbi Moshe in Iyar of 1787. He then returned to Israel at the beginning of 1790.

He was also involved in the dispute between Rabbi Avraham Kalisker and Rabbi Shneur Zalman of Liadi. We find that the Rebbe tried to make peace between them in 1799 (5559) (see text p. 53). However, in the beginning of 1801, this dispute was rekindled. In 1803, Rabbi Avraham Kaliker sent Rabbi Zvi together with Rabbi Chaim Meshares to Rabbi Shneur Zalman and Rabbi Levi Yitzchok of Berdichov, to settle the issue. This did not succeed.

When Rabbi Avraham Kaslisker died in 1810, Rabbi Zvi was one of the leaders of the community in Tiberias. He had a son by the name of Rabbi Shaul, who was also a leader there.

Rabbi Zvi passed away on Wednesday, 12 Tishrei, 5588 (1828).
(pp. 41, 92)

RABBI ZEV WOLF of CHARNI-OSTROV — d. 5583 (1823)

Rabbi Zev Wolf was a leading disciple of the Mezritcher Magid. He visited the Magid at the age of eight.

Rabbi Zev Wolf was a very close friend and *mechuten* of Rabbi Zusia of Anipoli. He was also very close to Rabbi Feivish Zbarez and did not want to leave Europe while Rabbi Feivish was alive.

Rabbi Feivish passed away in 1795, and in 1798, Rabbi Zev Wolf set off for the Holy Land. In Istanbul, he met Rabbi Nachman and they continued their voyage together.

Rabbi Zev Wolf settled in Tiberias where he became a

close friend of Rabbi Avraham Kalisker and one of the leaders of the community. He made one visit to Europe but returned shortly afterwards.

Numerous miracles are told of Rabbi Zev Wolf. His principal disciples were Rabbi Menachem Mendel of Kassov and Rabbi Dovid Shlomo of Soroke.

He is buried in Tiberias.

(pp. 33, 39, 71, 72)

RABBI MORDECHAI SHAPIRO of NESKHIZ — 5502-5560 (1742-1800)

A disciple of Rabbi Yechiel Michel of Zlotchov, he was Rabbi of the communities of Leshnev, Kovel, Ludmir and Neskhiz, where he devoted himself to solving *halakhic* problems. He was also a Kabbalist and a miracle worker, as witnessed by Rabbi Uri the *Seraph* of Strelisk.

Rabbi Nachman visited him at his death bed and discussed with him secrets of the Kabbalah.

(pp. 56, 57, 81, 199)

RABBI MENACHEM NOCHUM of TCHERNOBLE — 5490-5558 (1730-1798)

A great-grandson of Rabbi Adam Baal Shem, Rabbi Nochum visited the Baal Shem Tov twice. He became one of the Mezritcher Magid's principle disciples. Rabbi Pinchas Koretzer wanted Rabbi Nochum to take over the leadership of the Chassidic movement after the Magid's death.

In his position as Magid in Tchernoble, he set out trying to spread the teachings of Chassidism, through his two volume book *Meor Eynayim*, and through personal travel through the Ukraine.

On one of his trips, he met the young Rabbi Nachman, who impressed him immensely. He was very close to Rabbi Nachman's disciple Rabbi Yekusiel, the Magid of Terhovitza.

Rabbi Nochum's son, Rabbi Mordechai, continued the warm relations with Rabbi Nachman and his followers. His

great-grandaughter married Rabbi Nachman's grandson, Reb Yisroel, Sarah's son.
(pp. 11, 16, 23, 58, 70)

RABBI MESHULAM ZUSIA of ANIPOLI — d. 5560 (1800)

Rabbi Zusia was born in the village of Lapachi. In his youth, after his father's death, he wandered from town to town.

While visiting his uncle in Mezritch he became a follower of the Magid. He was known for his humility and saintliness. In 1796 he gave a *haskamah* on the *Tanya* of Rabbi Shneur Zalman. Rabbi Nachman praised him lavishly. Before his death Rabbi Zusia indicated to his disciple, Reb Yitzchok Segel, the son-in-law of the Terhovitzer Magid, that he should become a follower of Rabbi Nachman. Rabbi Nathan had been to him before meeting Rabbi Nachman.
(pp. 22, 56, 68)

RABBI ELIMELECH of LIZHENSK — d. 5547 (1787)

Younger than his brother Rabbi Zusia, it was his brother's influence which brought him to the Mezritcher Magid. For a while he accompanied his brother on his wanderings in exile. Many of the Chassidic leaders of Poland were his disciples. Rabbi Nachman said that his saintliness was much greater than one would assume from his book *Noam Elimelech*.
(p. 8)

RABBI LEVI YITZCHOK of BERDICHOV — 5500-5570 (1740-1809)

Rabbi Levi Yitzchok was born into a distinguished rabbinic family in Husakov (Galicia). In his youth he was known as the *iluy* of Yaroslav (the city where he studied). After his marriage, he settled in Levertov, where he studied together with Rabbi Yosef Teumim, author of the *Pri Megodim*. In nearby Ritchvol, he met, at age seventeen,

Rabbi Shmelka (later of Nikolsberg) who brought him to the Mezritcher Magid.

Rabbi Levi Yitzchok was drawn to Chassidism and studied under Rabbi Dov Ber, the Magid of Mezritch. After he returned from the Magid, where he had studied for a year, he was asked to teach what he had learned during that year. He replied, "I learned that there is a God." "For that you went to the Magid for a whole year?" he was asked. They then called a young girl who was working in the house and asked her, "Is there a God?" She promptly replied, "Of course!" To this, Rabbi Levi Yitzchok answered, "She *says* it! I *know* it!"

In Ritchvol, in 1721, he received his first rabbinical office, taking Rabbi Shmelka's place. He was one of the pioneers in spreading Chassidism to Poland. However, because of the opposition to Chassidism, he was forced to leave his position, as was the case in his subsequent positions in Zelechov and Pinsk. He finally settled in Berdichov in the Ukraine in 1785, where he served as Rabbi of the town and won renown as a Chassidic leader and scholar. His *Kedushas Levi* is regarded as one of the classics of Chassidic literature.

Rabbi Levi Yitzchok's saintliness and deep involvement in the plight of the Jewish people earned him affection from Chassidim and non-Chassidim alike. He convened the meeting of Jewish leaders held in Berdichov in 1802 to consider Russia's projected anti-Jewish moves.

He and Rabbi Nachman shared great mutual respect. Rabbi Nachman called him the pe'er (glory) of the generation. *Likutey Moharan* II, 67 was meant as a eulogy for him.

He was known as the Defender (before God) of the Jewish People.

(pp. 22, 59n, 66, 71, 72, 123, 168, 171-174, 186, 187)

RABBI SHNEUR ZALMAN of LIADI — 5505-5573 (1745-1813)

Founder of the *Chabad* Chassidic movement, Rabbi Shneur Zalman was born in Liozna in Belorussia in 1745. Married in 1760, he devoted himself to intensive Torah study along traditional lines. In 1764, he went to Rabbi Dov Ber, the Magid of Mezritch and he became one of the Magid's closest disciples.

In 1770, the Magid delegated to Rabbi Shneur Zalman the task of composing a *Shulchan Arukh* with the traditional commentaries in the text itself. Only a third of the work was printed — the remainder having been burned — the surviving portion is known as the *Shulchan Arukh HaRav*.

In 1774, he accompanied Rabbi Menachem Mendel of Vitebsk to Vilna to make peace between the Chassidim and the *misnagdim*. When Rabbi Menachem Mendel went to the Holy Land he appointed Rabbi Shneur Zalman as Chassidic leader of Rydzyn in Belorussia, with responsibility for collecting funds for supporting the community in *Eretz Yisroel*.

From Rydzyn, Rabbi Shneur Zalman's influence spread, penetrating even the strongholds of Lithuania. With the publication of his *Likutey Amorim* (known as *Tanya*), it became evident that he had created a distinct type of Chassidism. This evoked opposition from Rabbi Avraham Kalisker and Rabbi Baruch of Medzeboz.

The *misnagdim*, in a final effort to check the spread of Chassidism, informed on Rabbi Shneur Zalman and his followers to the Russian government. In 1798, Rabbi Shneur Zalman was arrested and taken to St. Petersburg for trial on charges of forming a new religious sect (all sectarianism was forbidden in Russia) and helping the Turkish Sultan with the monies he sent to Israel. His self-defense was accepted, and he was released on 19th Kislev (celebrated annually by the *Chabad* movement). Arrested again in 1801 on similar charges, Rabbi Shneur Zalman was later released, and he subsequently settled in the town of Liadi.

During the Franco-Russian war Rabbi Shneur Zalman was among those who saw a victory by the French as potentially disastrous to Judaism, and he therefore brought all his influence to bear in favor of Russia. It was while fleeing with the defeated Russian armies in 1813 that he died.

(pp. 4, 11f, 23, 29, 31, 32, 40, 42-45, 53, 62, 63, 66, 81, 92, 111, 112, 177, 178, 178n)

RABBI ARYEH LEIB of SHPOLA, THE SHPOLA ZEIDE — 5485-5572 (1725-1812)

A disciple of the Chassidic master, Rabbi Pinchas of Koretz, Rabbi Aryeh Leib served as *shamash* in the town of Zlatipolia, and it was there that he became known as a healer and Tzaddik who helped the poor.

Although none of his writings have been preserved, it would appear that he had a simple, popular approach to religion, emphasizing simple faith. There were many stories of his numerous miracles: they were collected in *Tif'eret HaMaharal*.

By Rabbi Nachman's time, Rabbi Aryeh Leib was the oldest surviving Tzaddik of the Chassidic movement, and was accordingly looked up to with respect as one of the leading elders. It was this which added extra weight to the relentless opposition which he showed to Rabbi Nachman, starting in 1800, in spite of the earlier friendship between them.

Rabbi Aryeh Leib was present at the assembly of Jewish leaders held in Berdichov to discuss Russia's projected anti-Jewish measures.

(pp. 14, 52, 60-62, 70-72, 102, 123, 127, 165, 166, 168)

RABBI YAAKOV YITZCHOK HOROVITZ, CHOZEH of LUBLIN — 5505-5575 (1745-1815)

In his youth he visited the Magid of Mezritch, who praised his saintliness. He learned the ways of Chassidism under the tutelage of Rabbi Shmelka of Nikolsberg and Rabbi Levi Yitzchok of Berdichov. Eventually, however, he became the principle disciple of Rabbi Elimelech of Lizhensk.

He first was rabbi of Lantzhut, and later moved to Lublin. He was renowned for his saintliness and *ruach hakodesh*.

One of the few *haskamos* that he ever gave was on Rabbi Nachman's *Likutey Moharan*. Rabbi Nachman told Rabbi Nathan and Rabbi Naftali to send him *kvittelach*.

Most of the Chassidic leaders in Poland and Galicia were his disciples. He was the author of *Zos Zikaron, Zikaron Zos* and *Divrey Emes*.
(pp. 56, 59n, 116, 116n, 154, 168)

RABBI YISROEL HAUPSTEIN, MAGID of KOZNITZ — 5497-5574 (1737-1813)

Rabbi Yisroel was born in Ostrovtza through a blessing the Baal Shem Tov gave to his father, Reb Shabsai.

He was a disciple of the Mezritcher Magid, Rabbi Shmelka, Rabbi Levi Yitzchok and Rabbi Elimelech. He was an accomplished scholar in Talmud and Kabbalah, as witnessed by his many books on all areas of Torah.

Rabbi Chaim of Volozhin, the leading disciple of the Gaon of Vilna, praised his Talmudic scholarship. Nevertheless Rabbi Yisroel was severely attacked by *misnagdim*.

He was physically weak and bedridden for fifteen years. Yet his prayers were said with an unequalled vigor.

According to some accounts he visited Rabbi Nachman at his death bed.
(pp. 154, 199)

RABBI CHAIM of KRASSNOY

A disciple of the Baal Shem Tov and a close friend of Rabbi Pinchas of Koretz.

He attempted to travel to the Land of Israel but when his ship was wrecked he took it as a sign from Above that he must remain in Europe.

He was a frequent visitor to Rabbi Nachman's childhood home in Medzeboz and once brought the young Rabbi Nachman to visit Rabbi Yaakov Yosef of Polonnoye.
(pp. 3, 15, 72)

RABBI ZVI ARYEH (HIRSH LEIB) of ALIK — 5520-5572 (1759-1811)

Born in the last year of the Baal Shem Tov's life, the Baal Shem Tov came to visit the infant and bless him. He was orphaned at a young age.

Shortly after his marriage, while on a trip to Brody, he met Rabbi Yechiel Michel of Zlotchov who introduced him to the ways of Chassidus.

He settled in Alik, close to Rovna. There he was appointed magid and rabbi. He was the author of *Or Chachomim*, a work demonstrating great depth.

Rabbi Nachman visited him and they discussed the secrets of the Torah. Rabbi Nachman said of him, "He did very well in *Yiddishkeit* and was very wise and pious."
(p. 57)

RABBI EPHRAIM ZALMAN MARGOLIES — 5521-5588 (1761-1828)

Famous as author of numerous works, primarily in *halakhah*, Rabbi Ephraim Zalman is best known for his responsa *Beis Ephraim*.

He was a student of his uncle Rabbi Sender Margolies, Rabbi of Satanov, and of the great Kabbalist, Rabbi Yitzchok Isaac HaCohen, author of *Bris Kehunas Olam*. In his youth he was Rabbi of Habenov, but afterwards decided not to use his learning as a source of livelihood and settled in Brody where he engaged in business. His partner directed the business affairs, while he sat in the *Beis Medrash*. From all over Europe the most difficult *halakhic* questions were sent to him.

He demonstated his affection for Chassidus through

numerous *haskamos* to Chassidic works, including Rabbi Nachman's *Likutey Moharan*. He also wrote an introduction to the Chassidic book *Orach LeChayim* and delivered a eulogy on Rabbi Nochum of Tchernoble, which was later printed under the name *Dimas Ephraim*.
(p. 154)

RABBI YISSACHAR DOV, REB BER B'REB BINIM of ZASLOV

A disciple of the Baal Shem Tov, and later of the Mezritcher Magid. He came into contact with Rabbi Pinchas of Koretz while on a mission of redeeming captives. Rabbi Pinchas gave him a blessing that he would have a daughter that year, and she became Rabbi Pinchas' daughter-in-law.

He was one of the first to recognize Rabbi Nachman's potential greatness. He settled in Israel together with Rabbi Yaakov Shimshon of Shepetevka and Rabbi Yissachar Ber of Zlotchov in 1794 and apparently died shortly after. He is buried in Tiberias.
(p. 12f)

RABBI AVRAHAM CHAIM of ZLOTCHOV

Author of *Orach LeChayim*, to which Rabbi Ephraim Zalman Margolies wrote an introduction highly praising the author. Rabbi Avraham Chaim was first the son-in-law of Rabbi Pinchas Horowitz, author of *Haflo'oh* and later son-in-law of Rabbi Yissachar Ber of Zlotchov, whose rabbinical post he accepted when his father-in-law left for the Holy Land in 1794. Rabbi Avraham Chaim gave his *haskama* to Rabbi Nachman's *Likutey Moharan*.
(p. 154)

RABBI MEIR (B'REB TZVI HIRSH) KRISTINOPOLER — d. 5575 (1815)

Rabbi of Brody at the time that Rabbi Nachman visited there, he was an outstanding scholar, author of *Yad Meir* and other unprinted works in all areas of the Torah. He corresponded on *halakhic* issues with the *Nodeh BiYehudah.*

He was at first Rabbi of Kristinopol, whence the name which remained in his family. In 1745 he became Rabbi of Brody. In Chassidus he was a follower of Rabbi Shmelka of Nikolsberg. He gave a *haskamah* to Rabbi Nachman's *Likutey Moharan.*

(p. 154)

RABBI GEDALIA of LINITZ — d. 5564 (1804)

Rabbi Gedalia was the principal disciple of Rabbi Yehudah Leib, the Magid of Polonnoye, and like his mentor, he occupied himself in preaching publicly and spreading the teachings of Chassidism.

He is frequently quoted in *Shevachey HaBaal Shem Tov,* where he is referred to as "the *Rav* of our community." In fact it was Rabbi Gedalia's prediction that miracles would cease, which inspired the compilation of the *Shevachey HaBaal Shem Tov.* He had previously been Rabbi of Ostropol and Miropol.

He wrote the Chassidic book *Teshuos Chen.* Upon seeing the manuscript, Rabbi Levi Yitzchok of Berdichov remarked on its depth.

Lesson 14 in *Likutey Moharan* was meant as a eulogy for Rabbi Gedalia.

Rabbi Gedalia's granddaughter, the daughter of Rabbi Aharon of Tchernoble, married Rabbi Nachman's grandson, Yisroel (Sarah's son).

(pp. 22, 71, 93, 94, 97, 102, 103)

RABBI DOVID SHLOMO EIBSCHITZ — d. 5574 (1814)

Known as Rabbi of Soroke in Bessarabia, he had previously been rabbi of Busnov and Iassi. His teachers were Rabbi Zev Wolf of Charni-Ostrov and Rabbi Meshulam Feivish Keller of Zbarez.

Rabbi Dovid Shlomo authored major works in both *halakhah* and Chassidus. The best known are *Luushey S'rad* on *Shulchan Arukh* and *Arvei Nachal* on the Torah.

Rabbi Avraham Yehoshua Heshel of Apta declared that Eliyahu revealed himself to Rabbi Dovid Shlomo. In 1809, he moved to Safed where he is buried in the same cave as Rabbi Aryeh Leib of Volochisk, the Rebbe's *mechuten*.
(pp. 33, 59)

RABBI ZVI, the BAAL SHEM TOV's SON — d. 5540 (1780)
RABBI AHARON OF TETIEV — d. 5587 (1827)

Rabbi Zvi was the Baal Shem Tov's only son and Rabbi Nachman's great uncle. Rabbi Gershon Kittover was his teacher.

The Baal Shem Tov directed him to be a businessman, and throughout his life the world was unaware of his high level of saintliness. He was physically weak and towards the end of his life lived in poverty.

He is buried in Pinsk.

Rabbi Aharon was the son of Rabbi Zvi, and a grandson of the Baal Shem Tov. Like his father, he did not lead a community of followers. He was, however, recognized by the Tzaddikim of the generation and respected by them. He detached himself from mundane matters.

Rabbi Nachman, his cousin, had personal contact with him as described in our text (p.152).
(pp. 5, 16, 52, 152)

RABBI YECHEZKEL HALEVI LANDAU, THE NODEH BIYEHUDA — 5474-5553 (1714-1793)

Rabbi Yechezkel was born in Apta. His father was Rabbi Yehuda Landau, leader of the *Vaad Arba Aratzot* (see p. 133).

Rabbi Yechezkel was recognized at the early age of 24 as one of the leading authorities in *halakhah* and was appointed head of the rabbinical courts in Brody.

He was later rabbi in Yampoli and subsequently in Prague where he was Chief Rabbi for 38 years until he passed away.

Rabbi Yechezkel is best known for his responsa, the *Nodeh BiYehudah*, a two volume work covering all facets of law. He is also the author of *D'rush LeTzion* and *TZ'LaCH – Tzion L'Nefesh Chayah* — on Talmud.
(p. 76)

RABBI LEIB of TRASTENITZ

Rabbi Leib was born in Trastenitz and lived in severe poverty. The Baal Shem Tov thought very highly of him and used to take Rabbi Leib along when he went to save Jews who were in difficult situations. He also visited Rabbi Baruch of Medzeboz who received him with great respect.

Rabbi Leib was Rabbi Yudel's father-in-law. When Rabbi Yudel was first married, he stayed with Rabbi Leib as was the custom. Due to poverty Rabbi Leib's daily meal consisted of borscht. After a few "meals" Rabbi Leib noticed Rabbi Yudel's lack of appetite. Rabbi Leib then gave Rabbi Yudel to taste from his plate. When Rabbi Yudel tasted Rabbi Leib's portion, he felt a taste of Gan Eden. Rabbi Leib then remarked, "See, my son! It is not the food, it is the eater [of the food]!"

Rabbi Leib passed away on a ship on his way to *Eretz Yisroel*. He had requested that his body be placed on a raft and left alone. The raft made its way to a city where a few years previously a certain Tzaddik passed away. That Tzaddik had made a request that no one be buried next to him except one who's bier has a pillar of fire (see text p. 174). When the raft with Rabbi Leib's body arrived, people saw the pillar of fire and Rabbi Leib was then buried next to that Tzaddik.
(p. 18)

RABBI URI "THE SERAPH" of STRELISK — d. 5586 (1826)

Rabbi Uri was called the "Seraph" (angel), after the

Chozeh of Lublin said that he knew Rabbi Uri had two faces and Rabbi Uri replied that he had four, quoting the verse, "And every one (Seraph) had four faces" (Ezekiel 1:6).

His father was a simple man, first a wagon driver and later a tailor, and his mother an orphan. The Magid of Mezritch promised her that she would have a great son and stood up before her while she was bearing him. Rabbi Uri later said that if his father would have gone to the *mikvah* even once he would have had a much easier time serving God. As it was, everything came with great difficulty.

He went to study Chassidus under many Tzaddikim: Rabbi Elimelech, Rabbi Yaybi, Rabbi Zusia, Rabbi Pinchas of Koretz, and Rabbi Mordechai of Neskhiz, but he eventually became the disciple of Rabbi Shlomo of Karlin.

His center was in Lemberg where he lived for many years. He attracted simple and poor people whose only desire was the service of God. He encouraged study of Talmud and Codes, saying that he had himself reviewed the laws of salting meat and of *Niddah* one thousand times.

He and his followers were known mainly for the great fervor with which they prayed. Each day before going to pray he would bid his family farewell for fear that he might not see them again (because of his great intensity during prayer).

Rabbi Uri is known to have said "With the *Likutey Moharan* in the world how can one say Torah [lessons]?"
(Appendix: Cities, Tzaddikim)

APPENDIX C
THE HOLY LAND

Presented here is a short historical essay on the Holy Land, its cities and inhabitants prior to and at the time of Rabbi Nachman's visit. Its purpose is to help clarify the situation of the communities there at that time.

The Holy Land in Rabbi Nachman's Time

The crushing of the Bar Kochba revolt against Roman rule in the year 135 c.e. put the final seal on the destruction of Jewish autonomy in the Holy Land. Depleted by war and emigration, impoverished and ruthlessly oppressed, the remaining Jews were now a minority — a subject people in the land of their fathers.

In the centuries that followed the Land came under the domination of a succession of different rulers: Byzantine Christians (395-636); Moslem Arabs (636-1099); Christian Crusaders (1099-1291); Moslem Mamelukes (1250-1517), and Moslem Ottoman Turks (1517-1918). Each period brought its own trials and difficulties for the precarious settlements of Jews who remained in the Holy Land throughout the exile.

However, many of the great and outstanding *Tosafists* and codifiers from the period of the *Rishonim* such as Rabbi Moshe ben Nachman (Nachmanides), Rabbi Yechiel of Paris, Rabbi Ovadiyah of Bartenura, Rabbi Mordechai ben Hillel, and Rabbi Yehuda Halevi lived in the Holy Land and were major leaders of the Jewish settlement.

All the persecutions and restrictions which the Jews endured in the lands of their dispersal were visited on those in the Land of Israel with a particular vindictiveness and poignancy. Weak and despised, they were a ready target for the worst vices of greed, jealousy, hatred and cruelty of their rulers. They were excluded from most walks of life and faced with an array of restrictions covering anything from the clothes they wore and the houses they lived in to their very movements from place to place. Burdened with extortionate impositions of taxation, the communities were usually forced to borrow money at extravagant interest rates from gentile money-lenders. When the inevitable happened and the communities became insolvent, their members became the objects of indiscriminate attacks, arrests and torture, and were often saved only by the intervention of Jewish communities abroad.

One story will illustrate both the plight and the greatness of the Jews of the Holy Land, who were held responsible by their rulers even for acts of nature. In 1637, the country was afflicted by drought. An English priest wrote: "The Turks (Moslims) prayed abundantly, and when their prayers were unanswered they threatened to put the Jews of Jerusalem to the sword unless rain fell within three days. The Jews fasted and cried out to Heaven. On the third day they assembled at the tomb of the prophet Zechariah and prayed until noon, whereafter dark clouds gathered; a great downpour came, and all the reservoirs overflowed with water."

When Rabbi Nachman arrived in the Holy Land in 5559 (1798) the country had already been under Turkish rule for more than two hundred years. When the Ottomans first conquered the land in 1517, the Jewish community was small, unstable and impoverished. The community in Jerusalem had been all but ruined by the impositions of a succession of high-handed governors. In the Galilee conditions were a little better, especially in Safed. But in the remainder of the country, the tiny communities which had previously held their own in such places as Ashkelon and Rafa had disappeared. Only the Gaza community remained.

The Turkish conquest led to something of a revival for the Jewish settlement in the Land. The expulsions from Spain (1492) and Portugal (1497) were recent occurrences. Some of the refugees who had gone to Turkey and the Balkan countries now came to live in the Holy Land, as did a steady stream of merchants, artisans and scholars from Sephardic Italy and Ashkenazi Europe. Workshops and factories were set up. In the Galilee, orchards and fields appeared. And scholarship began to return to its rightful place with the opening of a number of yeshivos and centers for the study of Kabbalah.

Although some of the immigrants headed for Jerusalem, most of them made for Safed, which was more prosperous and which began to attract scholars in their hundreds from all over the Diaspora. The late sixteenth century was the golden age of Safed, which boasted such sages as Rabbi Yosef Caro, Rabbi Shlomo HaLevi Alkabetz, Rabbi Moshe Cordovero, Rabbi Moshe Alsheikh and, perhaps most notably, Rabbi Yitzchok Luria, the ARI.

The revival of Tiberias also dates from the middle of the sixteenth century, when Don Yosef Nasi, a wealthy marrano who became a favorite at the court of Sultan Suleiman, was given permission to rebuild the town as a major Jewish center. Despite tremendous opposition from both Christians and Moslems, his grandly-conceived plan was put into operation and some of the ancient glory of Tiberias was restored, until it was devastated by the Druse in the mid-seventeenth century.

Towards the end of the sixteenth century there was a weakening of Turkish authority in the Holy Land. Defiant local governors did as they pleased, and Druse and Bedouin tribes looted and plundered. Safed was badly hit and the Galilee went into a decline. Jerusalem, on the other hand, rose both intellectually and materially, until 1625, when a succession of cruel and corrupt governors brought ruin to the community.

In 1665, Shabbetai Zvi declared himself "Messiah." The scholars of Jerusalem were opposed to him, and eventually he was forced to flee. It was from Gaza that the news of the "coming of the Messiah" was despatched over the entire Jewish world. Shabbetai Zvi's arrest in Constantinople and his subsequent conversion to Islam caused deep splits in the communities in the Holy Land, which became badly demoralized.

The Ottoman defeats in Europe at the end of the seventeenth century further weakened Turkey's grip on Syria and *Eretz Yisroel*. The local sheiks and feudal lords took every opportunity to shake themselves of the yoke of Turkish rule, and they treated the Jews as they pleased.

The community in Jerusalem was particularly badly hit. Most of the Jews there were poor, living off communal funds. There were a number of wealthier Jews with business interests outside the Holy Land. However the burden of taxes imposed upon them was so great that the community was obliged to take loans from the Arab money-lenders, who charged forty percent interest and added the interest to the principal, which thus increased geometrically. It was only when a committee of influential Jews from Constantinople intervened that the community was able to stand on its feet again.

A new era began, with the influx of such scholars as Rabbi Chaim ben Attar (the *Ohr HaChaim HaKadosh*), who founded Midrash Knesset Yisrael, and Rabbi Gedalia Hayun, who founded Yeshiva Bet-El with such lumineries as Rabbi Shalom Shar'abi, Rabbi Chaim Yosef David Azulai (the CHIDA), and Rabbi Avraham Gershon of Kittov, the brother-in-law of the Baal Shem Tov. It was to Rabbi Avraham Gershon that the Ashkenazi community of Jerusalem owed its revival.

In a letter to the Diaspora written in 1741, the scholars of Jerusalem stated that there were ten thousand Jews in the city. However the growth of the community aroused the jealousy of the local rulers, who introduced additional taxation and repression. In 1782, the Moslems wanted to appropriate part of the Jewish cemetery on the Mount of Olives. This was only avoided upon payment of a heavy bribe. Jerusalem was also hit by a succession of natural disasters: an epidemic of smallpox in 1757, an earthquake in 1760, and famine and drought in 1772 and 1787.

Jerusalem remained a religious and scholastic center, as did Hebron nearby. However most of the immigrants preferred to settle in the Galilee, which was the major center of immigration at the end of the eighteenth century. In 1777, the Chassidic leader Rabbi Menachem Mendel of Vitebsk arrived with a party of more than three hundred men, women and children from Lithuania,

Volhynia, Walachei and Podolia. They were not wage-earners, however, and they subsisted off charity from the Jewish communities in Russia. Rabbi Shneur Zalman of Liadi was given the main responsibility for forwarding funds from there, but Rabbi Levi Yitzchok of Berdichov and Rabbi Yaakov Shimshon of Shepetevka also played an important role.

The opposition to Chassidism, which was now at its height in Lithuania, reached *Eretz Yisroel* as well: letters from the *misnagdim* in Vilna were successful in prejudicing the Sephardic residents of Safed against the settlement of Rabbi Menachem Mendel of Vitebsk, who was forced to move to Tiberias in 1781. After his death in 1788, the leadership of the Chassidic settlement in Israel was assumed by Rabbi Abraham Kalisker, who met Rabbi Nachman in Tiberias in 1798.

Rabbi Nachman's itinerary in the Holy Land was restricted to the northern part of the country. He wanted to visit Jerusalem, but this did not work out (see text p. 43).

Acco

During the Crusader era, the Jewish community flourished under the tutelage of such outstanding scholars and Kabbalists as Rabbi Yechiel of Paris, Rabbi Shlomo Petit and Rabbi Yitzchok of Acco, author of *Meiras Eynayim*. Having been the main seaport of the Christian Crusader kingdom, Acco had been a forsaken village for many generations after the destruction of the kingdom in 1291.

Upon the return of the Turks, however, the Jews were treated ruthlessly and the survivors left the city. However, a number of Jewish families remained there. Later on, Rabbi Moshe Chaim Luzzatto, the *RaMChaL*, and Rabbi Gershon Kittover, the Baal Shem Tov's brother-in-law, were there.

Acco was restored in 1750, when Daher el-Omar made it his headquarters. It subsequently became the Turkish capital and seat of the Turkish Pashas. At the time of Rabbi Nachman's visit the Pasha was Ahmad el-Jazzar, who fortified the town and built markets, inns and a water supply. El-Jazzar had a Jewish counsellor and treasurer, Chaim Pharhi, who wielded tremendous influence. There were about a hundred Jewish families in the town.

With the news of Napoleon's advance northwards, Rabbi Nachman hurriedly left Safed and journeyed to Acco in order to leave the Holy Land.

Haifa

The name is derived from *chof*, Hebrew for shore. It is mentioned in Talmud *Shabbos* as the southernmost border of the area where the *chalozon* fish used for the blue die for *tzitzis* was caught. It was here that Rabbi Nachman disembarked on the day before Rosh HaShanah 5559 (September 10th, 1798), and first set foot in the Holy Land.

Haifa had been a town of some importance under Arab domination but it had been destroyed in the course of the Crusader conquest in 1100. It was then superseded in importance by neighboring Acco and was little more than a small, unfortified village until the seventeenth century, when more and more ships started using the port, which was safer than that of Acco. After Haifa's capture by the Turks in 1761 a new port was built and new city walls were erected.

There is a long history of Jewish settlement in Haifa, where Elijah's Cave on Mount Carmel is a point of pilgrimage. However when Rabbi Nachman spent Rosh HaShanah in the town, the community was relatively small and heavily outnumbered by the Moslim and Christian Arabs.

Some accounts say that Rabbi Yechiel of Paris, d. 1268, is buried there.

Meron

The village of Meron, located on a high peak opposite the city of Safed, is noted primarily as the burial site of the *Tanna*, Rabbi Shimon bar Yochai. Rabbi Shimon was author of the *Zohar*, the foundation of modern Kabbalah.

Ruins of ancient synagogues attest to an early Jewish community there. Traditionally, one of the peaks there was Tekoah, where the olive oil used in the *Beis HaMikdash* in

Jerusalem was manufactured. Meron is situated in the area of the tribe of Asher who was blessed with very fine olive groves.

The Talmud (*Bava Metzia* 84b) describes how Rabbi Shimon's son, Rabbi Elazar, came to be buried there, near his father. Other *Tannaim* buried there are Hillel, Shamai, Rabbi Yochanan HaSandler, Rabbi Yosi ben Kisma and many others.

Myriads of Jews from all communities make an annual pilgrimage to the grave of Rabbi Shimon bar Yochai on his *yahrzeit*, Lag Be-Omer (18 Iyar). There, amidst rejoicing and prayer, scholars study the *Zohar* and three year old boys are introduced to the mitzvah of *peyos* at their first haircut. Rabbi Moshe Cordovero, Rabbi Yosef Caro and the ARI were among those accustomed to making the pilgrimage there.

Followers of Rabbi Yisroel Shklover, a disciple of the Gaon of Vilna, spent the Ten Days of Repentance there.

From 1940, many Breslover Chassidim were unable to travel to Uman for Rosh HaShanah. At the suggestion of Rabbi Avraham Sternhartz, they began to gather in Meron for Rosh HaShanah. In recent years there have been over one thousand congregants.

Safed

There is a tradition that it was one of the "cities of refuge" (see Numbers 35; more likely it was one of the cities of the Levites).

The ARI pointed to a pile of stones at the site of the graves of Rabbi Nachum Ish Gamzu and Rabbi Binyamin the Tzaddik as the site of an ancient city. In Safed and its environs are numerous graves from the Tanaitic era and before. Safed's golden age was in the era of the ARI d. 1572, and Rabbi Yosef Caro d. 1575, who are buried in the cemetery there.

Safed had been resettled in 1727, and its ruins rebuilt. However the growth of the Jewish community as a result of immigration led to the imposition of additional demands by the local governors. The city suffered from an outbreak of plague in 1743 and in 1759 there were two severe earthquakes.

Immigration continued nonetheless. When Rabbi Menachem Mendel of Vitebsk and his company arrived there in 1777, they were unable to settle there because of opposition from some of the inhabitants who were followers of Shabbetai Zvi. These inhabitants had also received letters from *misnagdim* in Europe urging them to oppose the Chassidim. The Chassidim then left for Tiberias.

Later on, however, there was a large Ashkenazic community there. The Chassidim were led by Rabbi Leibush of Volochisk — Rabbi Nachman's *mechuten*, Rabbi Avraham Dov of Ovoritch, Rabbi Chaim of Tchernovitz, and Rabbi Dovid Shlomo Eibshitz.

In 1793, six years before Rabbi Nachman's visit, the town was hit by plague and famine. The community became impoverished and oppressed by the burden of taxation and debt.

Tiberias

One of the most ancient cities, perhaps dating back to the time of Joshua's entry in the Holy Land (see *Megillah* 7a), Tiberias is situated on the western shore of Lake Kinneret (Sea of Galilee). After its purification by Rabbi Shimon bar Yochai (see *Shabbos* 34a) it was chosen by the *Sanhedrin* as their residence and remained the Jewish capital of the country until after the Arab conquest in the seventh century. The *Talmud Yerushalmi* (see bibliography) was written mainly in Tiberias.

After the devastation of the town by the Druse in the mid-seventeenth century, Tiberias was in a state of desolation until 1740, when it was revived on the initiative of the Bedouin Sheik Daher el-Omar, ruler of the Galilee. He summoned Rabbi Chaim Abulafia to come and develop Tiberias and he gave him every opportunity to realize his grandiose plans. These plans included the development of trade, crafts and farming, the building of houses and courtyards for the Jews, the erection of a splendid synagogue and bath-house, the construction of roads and rebuilding of the wall around the Jewish quarter.

With the fall of Sheik Daher, however, the city was ruled by a violent and intolerant Turkish governor, and the Jewish community was afflicted with severe debts and other problems. These difficulties are reflected in our text (p. 42) and in the letter sent later to Rabbi Nachman in Russia from Rabbi Avraham Kalisker (see Appendix, Letter #9) who was head of the Chassidic community in Tiberias (also see *Chayay Moharan* #150).

Tiberias contains the tombs of Rabbi Yochanan ben Zakai, Rabbi Akiva, Rabbi Meir Baal HaNess, Rabbi Ami, Rabbi Asi and Rabbi Shimon ben Lakish from the Talmudic era, as well as such later sages as the RaMBaM (Maimonides) and Rabbi Yeshayah Horowitz (the SHeLaH). Rabbi Nachman's grandfather, Rabbi Nachman Horodenker, along with Rabbi Menachem Mendel of Vitebsk, Rabbi Avraham Kalisker and other leaders of the Chassidic community, are also buried there in the old cemetery. The cemetery is located on the main road leading into Tiberias, between the town and the famous hot springs.

Napoleon's Palestine Campaign

When Napoleon's armies entered the Holy Land in 1799, his plan was to pass on through the country to Syria and Asia Minor, sieze Constantinople, gain control of the whole Ottoman Empire and smash British trade in the Mediterranean. At first Napoleon hoped that Ahmad el-Jazzar would join him against the Sultan, but el-Jazzar, who ruled over most of Palestine was not tempted. Napoleon then resolved to conquer *Eretz Yisroel* in order to consolidate his conquest of Egypt. His objective was not Jerusalem but strategic points on the route to Constantinople. On March 6th Napoleon took Jaffa. Stiff resistance from the Turks hampered his advance towards Acco, and his army came to a standstill for several weeks — the last weeks that Rabbi Nachman spent in the Holy Land. Napoleon began his advance on Acco on March 14th, arriving there on March 20th, just two days after Rabbi Nachman left.

The Jews of Acco, led by Chaim Pharhi, sided with the Turks. Napoleon thought that if he could befriend Pharhi he would be able to take Acco and proceed with his plans. It was then that he made his famous call for the Jews of Asia and Africa to rally to his flag for the "restoration of Ancient Jerusalem." He sent emissaries to Pharhi, but Pharhi remained faithful to el-Jazzar, who obtained supplies and arms from a British fleet under Captain Sidney Smith and succeeded in holding Napoleon off.

Had Napoleon succeeded in his plan and gone on to conquer the Ottoman Empire, the entire course of subsequent history would have been very different. Rabbi Nachman's last days in *Eretz Yisroel* thus coincided with one of the most decisive moments in world history.

Napoleon was unable to take Acco and in May 1799, he finally abandoned his efforts. Nothing came of his grandiose program for the restoration of ancient Jerusalem, and if anything, the position of the Jews in the Holy Land deteriorated, because their Turkish rulers continued to suspect them of sympathizing with Napoleon. His declaration of 20th April 1799 had painted a gloomy picture of the situation of the Jews: "Time and circumstances would seem to be least favorable to a restatement of your claims, or even to their expression, and indeed to be compelling their complete abandonment..."

The greatness and holiness of the Land of Israel is a central point in Rabbi Nachman's teachings. When Rabbi Nachman returned to Russia, he would constantly urge his followers to go to the Land of Israel. He would say "Go, go! ... this Israel, with these stones and these houses." And he said, "Wherever I go, I am always going to the Land of Israel."

APPENDIX D

CITIES

This appendix gives the history of some of the cities that figure in the life of Rabbi Nachman. Its purpose is to present a background to the incidents that took place during Rabbi Nachman's association with them.

Berdichov

A town in the historic region of Volhynia (now in Zhitomir oblast). Although there are single references to Jews dating from the end of the sixteenth and beginning of the seventeenth centuries, the first evidence of a community in Berdichov is in 1721. Berdichov was a fair town, and the population increased steadily, especially after 1765, when there were 1,220 Jews out of a total population of 1,541.

Chassidism had a strong hold in the town, and in 1794 Prince Radziwill, the owner of Berdichov, transferred civil jurisdiction from the *kahal*, which was dominated by rabbis with sympathy for the *misnagdim*, to a court elected by a majority Jewish vote. This enabled the Chassidim to secure the election of *dayanim*.

By the end of the eighteenth century, commerce in Berdichov was concentrated in the hands of the Jews, who formed scores of trading companies and banking establishments with agencies in the Russian interior and abroad. Jews also served as agents on the estates of the nobility. By 1847 the Jewish community had grown to 23,160, making it the second largest in Russia.

Haskalah ideas spread early in Berdichov, especially among the wealthier families. However many of these families left in the mid-nineteenth century, and Berdichov entered a period of economic decline, with widespread poverty and illiteracy. At its peak it had had eighty synagogues and *batei medrashim*, and was epitomized in Jewish literature as the typical Jewish town.

In 1919 the community was victim of a pogrom, and in subsequent years the Soviet authorities closed the synagogues. Following the German occupation of Russia, the community was liquidated between July and August 1941. But by 1970 there were 15,000 Jews in Berdichov, with a synagogue, cantor and poultry slaughterer.

The grave of Rabbi Levi Yitzchok of Berdichov is protected with a fence.

Breslov (Braclav)

A small town in Podolia, Ukranian S.S.R., on the right bank of the Bug river, and situated midway between Nemirov to the north and Tulchin to the south. It had been the seat of the Breslov district which covered a large part of Podolia.

Breslov had been a center of Jewish settlement for at least four hundred years before Rabbi Nachman came to the town in 1802. As early as 1506, a Jew is known to have leased the collection of customs dues in Breslov. Thereafter, the Jews there were mainly involved in commerce, including trade with Odessa.

In 1476, Breslov had been invaded by the Tartars, killing six hundred residents, among them four hundred Jews, in a single day. In 1551, it was besieged by the Crimean Khan, Devlet Girei. The garrison fled, and the town was defended by the Jews. In 1569, the Hetmans, Nalivaiko and Kossinsky, attacked Breslov again.

In the early seventeenth century the Jews of Breslov maintained commercial relations with Lvov: in the Council of the Lands, Breslov was attached to the "Land of Russia," of which Lvov was the principle community. In 1635, King Ladislas IV confirmed the rights of the Jews of Breslov.

In 1648, Martin Kalinovski delivered Breslov into the hands of Chmielnicki, who killed the Jews of the community. In 1664, the Russians killed many Jews of Breslov, together with Jews of Kaminetz and Medzeboz.

Those who had fled to Nemirov and Tulchin were murdered in the massacres perpetrated there. There was a further massacre in 1664, when Cossacks from east of the Dnieper invaded the regions west of the river. However, soon afterwards, the community was reconstituted.

By the time of the 1765 census there were 101 Jews registered as living in Breslov itself, with a further 94 in the surrounding villages. By 1790 the numbers had doubled, with 221 in the town and a further 177 in the surrounding villages.

When Rabbi Nachman entered Breslov, the town possessed commercial importance as a market town. However, it did not have a reputation for being a strong center of Jewish life. There had been a following of the Shabbatean and Frankist movements in the town. Perhaps that is why Rabbi Baruch, the Rebbe's uncle, described Breslov contemptuously as "an empty place." Rabbi Nachman himself said that when he first came to the town there were only five "clean" Jewish families.

Breslov then contained one main synagogue and a number of small prayer houses, including one named after the Baal Shem Tov, which shows that Chassidism had already established itself there. It was near this *shul* that Rabbi Nachman was given a house; it overlooked the street leading to the market-place. In due course a synagogue was built in the Rebbe's house itself, and there his followers prayed regularly.

Throughout the Rebbe's stay in Breslov, the entire Jewish community accorded him all due honor and respect, deferring to his wishes in community affairs. Thus it was that Rabbi Nachman brought Rabbi Aaron to Breslov to be the Rav of the town.

On Rosh Chodesh Iyar 5570 (1810) there was a big fire in Breslov, and the Rebbe's house was burned down. It was immediately afterwards that he moved to Uman. Many of his followers were residents of Breslov, and they continued to live there, but because the synagogue in the Rebbe's house had been destroyed in the fire, they were obliged to pray in the main synagogue of the town. There, however, the atmosphere was not conducive to the intense joyousness to which they were accustomed in their prayers.

After the Rebbe's death those in the town who had been influenced by his opponents no longer felt constrained to hide their distaste for his followers. Rabbi Nathan, who was living in Nemirov, began paying regular visits to Breslov in the winter of 1810-11, in order to mobilize the Rebbe's followers to spread his teachings. The only place suitable for his meetings with them was in the main synagogue. However, their opponents instructed the beadle to lock the synagogue immediately after the evening prayers in order to stop the meetings. Rabbi Nathan accordingly started a collection to raise funds for rebuilding the Rebbe's house, and this was accomplished the same winter.

The following summer, there was a big fire in Nemirov and Rabbi Nathan's house was burned down. He then moved to Breslov and lived there until 1835. His activities established Breslov as the main center of the Breslover Chassidim. However, the opposition in the town was also very strong, and later in that year succeeded in persuading the authorities to expel Rabbi Nathan from Breslov. For three years he was confined to Nemirov. In 1839, he was able to move back to Breslov, and he died there in 1844.

The leadership of the Breslov movement then passed to Rabbi Nathan's closest student, Rabbi Nachman of Tulchin. He moved to Breslov in 1848, and stayed there for eighteen years. However in 1866, he moved to Uman, which then became the chief center of the movement. In consequence the community of Breslover Chassidim in Breslov itself went into a decline, even though they continued to maintain a study hall there up to the Second World War.

After Rabbi Aharon the Rav passed away his son, Rabbi Zvi Aryeh, became Rav in Breslov. Rabbi Zvi Aryeh was married to Rabbi Nathan's daughter, who compared him in holiness to an angel.

Rabbi Zvi Aryeh had two sons. The elder was Rabbi Chaim who became Rav after him, and Rabbi Nachman who was to become Rav in Tcherin. Rabbi Avraham b'Reb Nachman of Tulchin, author of *Biur HaLikutim*, *Kochavey Or* and other works (see bibliography), was born there in 1849.

In 1897, there were 3,290 Jews living in Breslov — forty-three percent of the total population.

In the 1919 pogroms about 220 Jews lost their lives and thereafter the Jewish population fell steadily. From July to September 1941 the entire community was annihilated by the Nazis.

Brody

A city in the Lvov district, Brody was one of the largest cities in Galicia, near the Russian border. It's location made it an important center of trade. It was famous for the *Broyder Kloyz* where some of the most outstanding European scholars and Kabbalists gathered. Rabbi Nachman Horodenker and Rabbi Chaim Sanzer were associated with it.

Brody was one of the towns visited by Rabbi Nachman on his mysterious journey of 1807. It had a large Jewish population — in 1779 there were 8,867 Jews in the town — and besides the powerful influence which the community had in trade and commerce, it also was one of the strongest centers of Jewish traditionalism. Thus, in 1756, a rabbinical court, under the auspices of the *Vaad Arba Arotzos* and led by Rabbi Chaim Cohen Rappaport was convened there to investigate the Frankist movement. At the end of the hearing the movement was banned and limitations were introduced regulating the study of Kabbalah.

In 1772, a rabbinical assembly convening in the town excommunicated the followers of the Chassidic movement and burned Chassidic works (see text p. 3). Rabbi Michel of Zlotchov lived there but was forced to leave because of the opposition to Chassidism.

Among the prominent Rabbis there were Rabbi Yechezkel Landau, the *Nodeh BiYehudah*, his son, Rabbi Yakobka and his grandson Rabbi Elazar, author of *Yad HaMelech*. Rabbi Elazar Rokeach, author of *Ma'aseh Rokeach*, Rabbi Hirsh of Gloga, author of *Tiferes Zvi*, and Rabbi Moshe, author of *P'nei Moshe* on the *Talmud Yerushalmi* also resided there. Rabbi Avraham Gershon Kittover, the Baal Shem Tov's brother-in-law, was a *dayan* there.

When Rabbi Nachman visited there in 1807, Rabbi Meir Kristinopoler was Rabbi and Rabbi Ephraim Zalman Margolies author of the *Bais Ephraim* and other major *halakhic* works resided there and both gave their *haskama* to the *Likutey Moharan*.

Brody was the residence of the family of Rabbi Nachman's second wife, the daughter of Reb Yechezkel Trachtenberg.

In Rabbi Nachman's time there were a number of Jews in Brody who were frequent travellers to Germany, and they helped to diffuse the philosophy of the Berlin "enlightenment" in Galicia. Subsequently Brody became a center of *maskilim*: as early as 1815 the community opened a *Realschule* where the teaching was in German.

Later on, Brody became the principal town from which the exodus of Russian Jewry began in 1880. Thereafter over two million Jews left the Pale of Settlement, emigrating to the United States, Britain, Europe, South America and Israel.

Istanbul (Kosta, Constantinople)

As capital of the Byzantine and Ottoman empires and at the crossroads between Europe and Asia, Istanbul was a cosmopolitan community.

The Jewish community in the town had been strong and vibrant ever since 1453, when Istanbul (formerly Constantinople) had been taken from the Byzantine Emperor by the Ottoman Sultan Muhammed II. In his desire to foster the growth of his new capital he brought in large numbers of settlers, often by force, and encouraged the activities of Jewish merchants and craftsmen.

The Jewish community was given extensive internal autonomy. It was made up of a variety of different groups which included: Ashkenazim from Germany, Austria and Hungary; and Sephardim who had been expelled from Spain in 1492 and Portugal in 1497 and from Greece, Syria and Egypt. Also many Jews migrated from there to Eastern Europe, thus some Ashkenazic families can trace their descent to the era of the Spanish inquisition via Turkey.

The friendship of Don Yosef Nasi with Sultan Suleiman the Magnificent and Selim II gave him tremendous influence in state affairs, and this in turn served to strengthen the Jewish community in Istanbul, making it one of the most important Jewish centers in the world in the sixteenth century.

The general decline of the Ottoman Empire thereafter led to a relative decline in the Istanbul Jewish community as well. Nevertheless it continued to play a major role in matters of importance to the international Jewish community. Thus the thousands of Polish Jews who were captured in 1648 by the Cossacks, Tartars and Ukrainians and destined for sale as slaves were in many cases redeemed by the Istanbul community. Istanbul was the site of Shabbetai Zvi's center of activities and later of his conversion to Islam.

Because of its geographical proximity to Israel, Istanbul was one of the most important centers for funds for the settlements in the Holy Land. Not only did the Istanbul community itself make continuous fund-raising efforts for the relief of the communities in the Holy Land, but in addition, the funds destined for *Eretz Yisroel* from Eastern Europe passed through there. It was also there that the letters and recommendations of the emissaries and their missions were verified. The rabbinic leaders in Istanbul maintained especially close relationships with the sages in Israel.

Istanbul had one of the earliest Hebrew printing presses and many of the major *seforim* on *halakha* were published there.

In 1778, twenty years before Rabbi Nachman was there on his way to Israel, there were 120,000 Jews out of a total population of one million. Some of the more prominent Rabbis in Istanbul were: Rabbi Moshe Kapsuli, Rabbi Eliyahu Mizrachi (*R'EM*), Rabbi Yitzchok Caro (uncle of the *Beis Yosef*), Rabbi Yechiel Bassan, Rabbi Yom Tov Ts'halon, Rabbi Avraham Rozanes, and his son-in-law, Rabbi Yehudah Rosanes (*Mishneh L'Melekh*) and Rabbi Yitzhok Becher-David. At the time of Rabbi Nachman's visit there, the chief Rabbi was Rabbi Chaim Yaakov ben Yakar.

Galati, the section of the city Rabbi Nachman first stayed in, had always been a Jewish section.

Kaminetz-Podolsk

A City in Podolia, Ukrainian S.S.R., Kaminetz was the capital of Podolia and seat of the provincial government. It was also an important trade and communications center. Built on a high mountain surrounded on three sides by the Smotrec river, it was a naturally fortified city. The rulers were reluctant to share their security with the Jews. Jews were therefore expelled in 1447, in 1654 and in 1750.

There was a long history of opposition to Jewish settlement in the town. In 1447 Jews had been prohibited from staying for more than three days in Kaminetz, and in 1598 King Sigismund III prohibited them not only from settling in the city and its suburbs but even from engaging in trade there. Nevertheless during the 1648 Chmielnicki massacres large numbers of Jews took refuge in Kaminetz, which withstood the Cossack attacks of that year and in 1652.

Subsequently, King John Casimir II permitted Jews to reside in the town, and they remained there in spite of the unremitting opposition of the Christian inhabitants. Between 1672 and 1699 Kaminetz was under Turkish control. At this time the Jewish residents maintained strong ties with the Jewish community in Istanbul.

In 1737, the city council submitted a request to the Polish state and church authorities to banish the Jews from the city, maintaining that they had no right to settle there and that their competition was impoverishing the Christian inhabitants. In 1750, King Augustus III expelled the Jews from Kaminetz and their houses passed to the city council, which ordered their synagogue to be destroyed. Having been expelled from the city, the Jews settled in the surrounding suburbs and villages, developing extensive trading activities — which led to additional complaints by the Christian citizens.

From the 20th to the 27th of June, 1757, a debate took place between the Frankists on the one side and Rabbinical and lay leaders of the traditional Jewish communities of Podolia on the other. At the end of the disputation the Catholic Bishop

Dembovski ordered all volumes of the Talmud found in Podolia to be burnt. Kaminetz became the scene of public burnings of Jewish books. Within a month, however, Dembovski died and the decree on burning the Talmud was nullified.

With the third partition of Poland in 1795, Kaminetz passed under Russian sovereignty. When Rabbi Nachman paid his mysterious visit there in 5558 (1797), Jews were not permitted to spend the night. Shortly afterwards, in 1797, Czar Paul I confirmed the right of Jews to live in the town, and in the same year 1,367 Jews were registered as inhabitants. Christian opposition to Jewish residence continued, but despite certain restrictions imposed in 1833 and rescinded in 1859, Jewish habitation was never again forbidden.

Kaminetz always had close ties with the Chassidic movement. It was in close proximity to Okup, the birthplace of the Baal Shem Tov. All the synagogues there, except one, followed the Chassidic liturgy.

In 1914 there were 9,510 Jews there out of a general population of 35,300. Kaminetz was the scene of pogroms in 1918-19, and in 1941 the Jewish community was destroyed.

Lemberg (Lvov)

The largest city in Eastern Galicia, Jews had lived there from time immemorial. Evidently the earliest Jewish settlers came from Byzantium, but later migrations of Jews from Bohemia and Germany gave the community its Ashkenazic character.

Lemberg was a transit center for trade between the orient and the west. The Jews of Lemberg played an important role in this, as well as in trade with the interior of the country. They also leased estates, distilleries and breweries, customs and tax collection etc. There were frequent clashes between the Jews and Christians in the town, the latter wishing to restrict Jewish activities. However, the nobility usually supported the Jews.

During the Chmielnicki massacres, heavy losses were inflicted on the Jews in the areas surrounding Lemberg, but those in the town itself were spared on payment of a heavy ransom.

Lemberg was a center of Shabbatean activity, and Jacob Frank visited the town in 1755, although he was subsequently compelled to leave. After the disputation in Kaminetz a second major disputation between the Frankists and the rabbis was held in Lemberg (July-August 1759). Following the disputation, over five hundred Frankists were converted to Christianity amidst great pomp and ceremony.

In 1772, Lemberg was annexed to Austria. The border changes led to an artificial curtailment of the town's role in trading. Nevertheless the Jewish population grew, reaching 18,302 by 1800. About half were engaged in commerce and a quarter in crafts. The Austrian authorities supported the endeavors of the Christians in the town to restrict Jewish activities, and they encouraged the assimilationist tendencies in the community.

The Jewish community there was divided into two *kehillos*, inside the original city boundaries and in the suburbs. Between 1599 and 1680 each *kehilla* had its own Rabbi. Some of the greatest Rabbis of Europe occupied the Rabbinical seats there throughout the centuries.

Lemberg had long been a major center of Torah scholarship. Among the leading scholars who had lived there were Rabbi Yehoshua Follak, author of *Sefer Meiras Eynayim* on *Choshen Mishpat*, and Rabbi Dovid Halevi, author of the *Turei Zohov* on *Shulchan Arukh*. When Rabbi Nachman came there in 1807-1808, during his illness, he commented that he wouldn't mind being buried in the cemetery there among the many great Tzaddikim (see text p. 157, footnote 34).

Rabbi Aharon Moshe Toibes, later Rabbi of Iassi, originally lived there and he may have been the one alluded to in our text (p. 153). At the time of the Rebbe's visit the Rabbi of the two *kehillos* was the renowned Rabbi Yaakov Orenshtein. Rabbi Uri, the *Seraph* of Strelisk, also lived there during the Rebbe's lifetime.

In Rabbi Nachman's time the *haskalah* had begun to make inroads there. When Rabbi Nachman visited the town in 1808 there was already a group of *maskilim* living there. Solomon Judah Leib Rapoport who was to become one of the most influential members of the *haskalah* movement was then a young man of eighteen and already considered a brilliant talmudist of great promise. Under the influence of the notorious Naftali Herz Homberg (1749-1841), whom the Austrian authorities had appointed superintendent of the Jewish schools in Galicia, Lemberg had four boys schools, three girls schools and a teachers' seminary run according to his principles. These included a prohibition against the use of the Hebrew language and the censorship of traditional texts. In 1815, Rabbi Orenshtein declared a ban against the *maskilim*, but was forced to withdraw it under pressure from the local authorities.

Until the end of the eighteenth century the medical schools of Poland and Russia were closed to Jews, and those wishing to study medicine were obliged to travel to Italy. However the Edicts of Tolerance issued by Emperor Joseph II of Austria (January 1782 onwards) threw open Austrian medical schools to Jews, which encouraged Jewish entry into the medical profession. Since Lemberg was now a part of Austria, this must have stimulated the pursuit of medicine among the Jews of the town. In the course of Rabbi Nachman's extended stay in Lemberg he underwent medical treatment.

Lemberg was later to become one of the major battlefields of the assimilationist tendency. In the early and middle nineteenth century the Jewish community in Lemberg became deeply divided on such issues as Jewish dress and the assimilationist proposals to change it. In 1844 a Reform Temple was opened in the town and subsequently a portion of the community embraced Austrian-German or Polish culture.

Nevertheless, the overwhelming majority of the Jewish community in Lemberg were strong traditionalists with Chassidic leanings. Some of the more recent prominent rabbis there were Rabbi Yosef Shaul Nathansohn, author of *Shoel U'Maishiv*, and his brother-in-law, Rabbi Mordechai Zev Ettinger, who together co-authored numerous Talmudic works including *Yam HaTalmud* and *Gilyon HaYerushalmi*. Rabbi Yitzchok Shmelkas, author of *Bais Yitzchok*, also was rabbi there.

Following the First World War, Lemberg came under Polish sovereignty and was Poland's third largest Jewish center, with approximately 150,000 Jews. Most of them were destroyed by the Nazis in a series of brutal deportations, often carried out with the collaboration of local civilians.

Medvedevka, Ossatin and Tcherin (Chigirin)

Three towns in Kremenchug oblast on the Tyasmin river.

Medvedevka, where Rabbi Nachman lived from 1791 until his return from *Eretz Yisroel* in 1799, had once been the home of the Shpoler Zeide. It is in close proximity to Tcherin and Rabbi Nachman regularly visited his Chassidim in the two communities on Shabbos Shirah. We have no further information.

Ossatin, where Rabbi Nachman lived immediately after his marriage, is not to be confused with the well-known Chassidic town Hussiatin on the border between Podolia and Galicia. Our Ossatin was a small village and we have no further information.

Tcherin had been the home of the Cossak leader Chmielnicki.

Rabbi Avraham b'Reb Nachman of Tulchin (see bibliography *Biur HaLikutim*) said that Tcherin was the "country of wealth" referred to in *Rabbi Nachman's Stories* #12.

The Rebbe's disciple, Rabbi Shmuel Yitzchok Rosenfeld, became Rabbi there. His son, Rabbi Simcha married the daughter of Rabbi Aharon, the Rav in Breslov. His descendent, Rabbi Yisroel Abba Rosenfeld (1882-1947), was one of the founders of Breslover Chassidim in America and first president of the Breslov Yeshivah in Jerusalem.

Rabbi Yisroel Abba's son, Rabbi Zvi Aryeh Rosenfeld (1922-1978), was instrumental in the building of the Breslov Yeshivah and synagogue in Jerusalem. A pioneer in working with *ba'alei teshuvah*, he brought Rabbi Nachman's teachings to thousands of people.

Rabbi Nachman Goldstein of Tcherin, author of *Parparaos LeChokhmah* on *Likutey Moharan* and other monumental Chassidic works, was Rabbi there. He was the grandson of Rabbi

Aharon of the Rav of Breslov, and son of Rabbi Zvi Aryeh of Breslov. His grandson, Rabbi Avraham Sternhartz (see bibliography), was born and grew up in Tcherin.

Medzeboz

A town in Chmielnicki oblast, Ukrainian S.S.R., Medzeboz was Rabbi Nachman's birthplace and the scene of his childhood. It was one of the three major Jewish communities in Podolia, together with Kaminetz and Berdichov.

Medzeboz possessed one of the oldest of all the Jewish communities in the Ukraine. Jews are mentioned in records dating from 1518, and subsequently the community grew to be one of the largest in the region.

Rabbi Yoel Sirkes, the *BaCH* (1561-1641), one of the greatest and most famous *halakhic* authorities, was Rav there.

However, heavy losses were sustained during the Chmielnicki massacres of 5408-09 (1648), when some 600 householders were killed there. Massacres recurred in 1651, 1664 and at the start of the eighteenth century.

Medzeboz was famous as the home of Rabbi Yisroel the Baal Shem Tov, founder of the Chassidic movement and Rabbi Nachman's great grandfather, who lived there from 1740 until his death in 1760.

Both the Rabbi and the community leader were sent to Kaminetz in 1757 to debate with the Frankists.

The census of 1765, just seven years before Rabbi Nachman's birth, gives the number of Jews registered in Medzeboz and the surrounding villages as 2,039.

Prominent among the inhabitants of the town was Rabbi Baruch, grandson of the Baal Shem Tov and Rabbi Nachman's uncle. He lived in Medzeboz until 1781, when he left for Tulchin. Rabbi Nachman remained in Medzeboz until his marriage in 1785. Rabbi Baruch returned in 1788, holding court there in a highly luxurious manner. Rabbi Avraham Yehoshua Heshel of Apta also lived in the town for a time.

At the time of Rabbi Nachman, the Rabbi of the town was Rabbi Dov Berish Rappaport, grandson of the renowned Rabbi Chaim Cohen Rappaport. He became involved in a dispute with Rabbi Moshe Chaim Ephraim, the Rebbe's uncle, and the Chassidim then chose their own Rabbi, Rabbi Yissachar Ber Segel Landau. From then on, there were always two Rabbis in Medzeboz.

From 1815-27 a Hebrew printing press published Chassidic and Kabbalistic works. The community was destroyed after the German occupation in 1941.

The Baal Shem Tov, his grandsons the Rebbe's uncles, Rabbi Ephraim of Sudylkov and Rabbi Baruch and Rabbi Avraham Yehoshua of Apta are buried there near each other. Their graves are enclosed by a fence.

The Baal Shem Tov's graveside was the object of frequent visits by his disciples and members of the Chassidic movement. As a boy Rabbi Nachman saw many of the great Chassidic personalities passing through his parents' house.

Nemirov

Town in Vinnitsa oblast, Ukrainian S.S.R. Annexed by Russia in 1793, it was incorporated into the district of Podolia. Under Polish sovereignty Nemirov had been an important fortified city.

Jewish settlement is first mentioned in 1603. In the 1630's, Rabbi Yom Tov Lipmann Heller, author of *Tosafos Yom Tov* on the *Mishnah*, held office in the town.

During the Chmielnicki massacres thousands of Jews fled to Nemirov for safety. Failing to take the city by storm, the Cossacks resorted to a trick: they displayed Polish banners and requested admission to the city. The Jews believed that it was a Polish army that had come to their rescue, and opened the gates. The Cossacks in conjunction with the local Russian inhabitants fell upon the Jews and massacred about six thousand.

The slaughter in Nemirov became a symbol of Jewish suffering in this period. Throughout Poland a fast was observed on the twentieth of Sivan to commemorate the massacre there on that date in 1648. Special *selichos* were composed describing the events and also the murder of the Rabbi, Rabbi Yechiel Halperin, two days later by a gentile cobbler who lived in the town.

Chmielnicki's son later lived in Nemirov and was very cruel to the Jewish population that remained there.

The great synagogue of Nemirov, erected in the early eighteenth century, was notable for its splendor. In 1765, there were 602 Jewish poll-tax payers registered in the town.

Rabbi Nathan was born in Nemirov in 5540 (1780) and spent his childhood there. After returning from his father-in-law's house, he lived there until 1812. In 1835, he was exiled to Nemirov until 1838.

By 1847 the Jewish community had grown to 4,386. The Jews of Nemirov suffered heavily during the atrocities of 1917-21.

Following the German occupation the community was deported in 1941-2.

Ostrog

A city in Volhynia, Ukrainian S.S.R., Ostrog was an important center of trade, particularly in flax.

Jews were there from the end of the 14th century. There are records of Jews dealing in cattle dating to 1532.

It was one of the four leading communities in Volhynia and had a reputation as one of Poland's most important centers of Jewish learning. Among the prominent Jewish leaders there were, Rabbi Shlomo Luria, the *MaHarShal* (c. 1550); Rabbi Shmuel Eideles, the *MaHarSHa* (c. 1580); Rabbi Dovid HaLevi Segel, the *TaZ* (c. 1600); Rabbi Avraham Gombiner, the *Magen Avraham* (c. 1600); Rabbi Yeshayahu Horowitz, the *SHeLaH*; Rabbi Elazar ben Shimon Cohen of Tulchin; Rabbi Yoel Halperin (1690-1710); Rabbi Bezalel Katz (1710-1717) and Rabbi Meir Margolies (d. 1790), author of *Meir Nesivim* and disciple of the Baal Shem Tov.

In the middle of the 17th century, there were 1,500 Jewish households. Following the Cossack massacres (1648-49) only five families remained. The Cossacks destroyed the main synagogue which was afterwards rebuilt by Rabbi Shmelka Zak, father-in-law of Rabbi Naftali Katz of Lublin (a native of Ostrog).

By the end of the 18th century the Jewish population in the town was about 2,000, and several of the disciples of the Baal Shem Tov were active there. The Chassidic community was led by Rabbi Yaakov Yosef (known as *Rabbi Yaybi* after his book) and afterwards by his decendants. Rabbi Pinchas of Koretz also lived there for some time.

In the 18th century the city became divided and so did the Jewish community. On 6-7 Tammuz, 1792 the synagogue was hit repeatedly by cannon-fire (during the Russian-Polish war) but remained standing. Those days were later celebrated as days of thanksgiving by the Jewish community.

There were 8,000 Jews out of a general population of 14,500 in 1905. In 1939, the community was over 10,000 strong. Between July 1941 and October 1942 almost all the Jews were murdered by the Nazis with the collaboration of local forces.

Rhodes

Rudanim mentioned in Chronicles I, 1:7 may refer to Rhodes. According to *Shalsheles HaKabbalah*, Rhodes was built in the time of the Patriarch Jacob by the king of Argolis. Jews lived there at least since 140 b.c.e.

In 656 a Jew from Emesa bought the debris of the Collosus of Rhodes (which had been destroyed by an earthquake in 282 B.C.E.) and brought it to Marmaritza. Rabbi Binyamin of Todela (c. 1000) found 500 Jews there. In 1280, the size of the community was increased by Jews from Paragon, Spain.

Thus, Jews had lived on the Island of Rhodes since at least the end of the Hellenistic period. However, they enjoyed varying fortunes under the rule of the Arabs (653-1309) and the Crusader Order of the Knights of St. John (1309-1522). The Crusaders used thousands of Jewish slaves to build their fortress on the island. These Jews played an important role in helping the Turks to capture the island in 1522, and as a result the Turks showed great favor to the Jewish community. The Rhodes community boasted many well-known scholars as well as numerous merchants and skilled craftsmen.

There were two large synagogues, the Great Synagogue first built in 1440 and the Shalom Synagogue built in 1593. In addition there were two smaller synagogues and some *batei medrashim*.

Prominent Rabbis were Rabbi Chaim ben Menachem Algazi, Rabbi Moshe Yisroel author of *Masas Moshe*, Rabbi Ezra Molcho, Rabbi Moshe ben Eliyahu Yisroel author of *Moshe Y'daber* and Rabbi Yedidyah ben Shmuel Turski.

The Jewish community there, at the time of Rabbi Nachman's visit, was wealthy and was often visited by emissaries from the Holy Land.

Sharograd

Town in Vinnitsa oblast, Ukrainian S.S.R. The Jewish community in the town dates from the seventeenth century. The Jews were victims of continuous Cossack attacks in the course of the eighteenth century.

Jewish merchants played an important role in trade with Turkey. At the end of the seventeenth and beginning of the eighteenth centuries, Sharograd was a center of Shabbateanism. Later on it was the home of the Chassidic personality Rabbi Naftali Herz of Sharograd. Rabbi Yaakov Yosef of Polonnoye, one of the closest disciples of the Baal Shem Tov, held rabbinic office in the town until 1748. In 1805 Rabbi Nachman spent two weeks in Sharograd.

Tulchin

In Vinnitsa oblast, Ukrainian S.S.R., Tulchin was a fortress town.

During the 1648 Chmielnicki massacres, 1,500 Jews, including many who had escaped the slaughter in Nemirov, took refuge in Tulchin and made a joint oath with the Poles in the town that they would not betray one another.

After a long siege the Cossacks promised the Poles that they would leave them at peace if they delivered the Jews into their hands, and the Poles "forgot" their oath. On hearing this a number of Jews wanted to take vengeance on the Poles, but Rabbi Aharon, the Rosh Yeshiva of Tulchin, implored them not to do so. The Cossacks offered the Jews the option of baptism or death, but not a single Jew was prepared to convert. All fifteen hundred Jews were killed.

Following the quelling of the Cossack rebellion Jewish settlement in Tulchin was renewed, but the community suffered from the Haidemack insurrections of 1743 and 1768. In 1781 Rabbi Baruch of Medzeboz became Rabbi of the town, and remained there until 1788. Even afterwards he continued his association with the town, paying periodic visits.

Rabbi Nachman, Rabbi Nathan's leading disciple, was from Tulchin. Also, Rabbi Nathan's son, Rabbi Yitzchok (to whom most of the letters in *Alim LeTerufah* are addressed) lived there. Rabbi Yitzchok was postmaster in Tulchin, as were his sons after him.

The Tulchin community suffered during the 1919 pogroms and was deported by the Nazis in 1941.

Uman

A city in Kiev oblast, Ukrainian S.S.R., Uman was in Poland-Lithuania until the 1793 partition. An important fortified town, Uman was the object of an attack by Haidemacks in 1749. (The Haidemacks were members of a popular movement of fugitive Greek Orthodox peasants, Zaporozhians and Ukrainian Cossacks active in the provinces of Kiev, Volhynia and Podolia from the 1730's onwards and responsible for widespread destruction and bloodshed.) In the 1749 attack large numbers of Jews were killed and part of the town burned. Count Potacki, the landlord of Uman, had the city rebuilt in 1761 and held fairs to encourage its development.

In 1768, following the Haidemack massacres of Jews in Lysyanka and Tetiev in the province of Kiev, tens of thousands of Jews and Poles fled to Uman for refuge. With the advance of the Haidemack forces under the leadership of Maxim Zelieznak, Uman became so crowded that many of the refugees could find no room in the town itself and had to camp in tents outside. The governor of Uman, Mladanovich, had at his disposal a Cossack detachment of the court guard under the command of Ivan Gunta. Gunta had been suspected of sympathizing with the Haidemacks, but Mladanovich nonetheless saw fit to despatch him against Zelieznak. Gunta predictably joined forces with the Haidemacks and on June 18th, 1768, the two armies marched on Uman.

Jews played an active role in the defense of the city, fighting off the besiegers with cannon and rifles. However, Governor Mladanovich conducted peace negotiations with the Haidemacks, and received assurances that they would spare the Poles and attack only the Jews. Prior to Gunta's entry into Uman the saintly Rabbi Dovid Hazan took a number of Jews and hid in a cave. As soon as the Haidemacks entered the town they threw themselves on the Jews in the streets, who were barbarically murdered. Three thousand Jews took refuge in the synagogue, under the leadership of Rabbi Lev Shargorodski and Rabbi Moshe Menaker. Gunta erected a canopy in the courtyard of the synagogue and placed a crucifix beneath it. He announced that all Jews who came out and prostrated themselves would be spared alive. Not a single Jew did so.

When the Haidemacks approached the synagogue, several Jews fought them off with daggers and knives, killing a few men, while the remainder of the community prayed for salvation. The Haidemacks placed a cannon at the entrance of the synagogue and blew open the doors. On entry, they massacred every Jew they could find. The bloodshed in Uman continued for three days, until none of the reamining Jews in the city was left alive. The Haidemacks also slaughtered many Poles, including Mladanovich himself.

When the sounds of the massacre had died down, Rabbi Dovid Hazan and his companions emerged from their hiding place to find the streets flowing with blood and filled with mutilated corpses. In the following days they buried the Jews in two large mounds. Shortly after the massacre in Uman, Polish and Russian troops cooperated in suppressing the Haidemack insurrection. Zelieznak and Gunta were captured by the Russian

General Krechetnikov, and Gunta, having been handed over to the Polish authorities, was sentenced to be flayed alive and quartered.

Estimates put the number of Jews and Poles slaughtered in Uman at no less than 20,000. The anniversay of the commencement of the massacre, 5 Tammuz, was observed as a fast-day, and an account of the events composed by Rabbi Dovid Hazan was read in the synagogues of Uman on that day each year. The massacre in Uman, which took place less than four years before Rabbi Nachman's birth, would have been a vivid memory in the minds of the Jews of the Ukraine in his lifetime.

By the early 1800's Uman had a Jewish population of a few thousand. Among other things, Uman had a reputation as a city of *klezmerim* (Jewish musicians), and the tunes of Uman were widely known.

The town was also one of the first centers of the *haskalah* movement in Russia. Chaikel (Chaim) Hurwitz (1750-1822), his son (or son-in-law) Hirsh Ber Hurwitz, and his son-in-law, Moshe Landau were active in the town, and in their antipathy towards Chassidism had succeeded in preventing Rabbi Levi Yitzchok of Berdichov from taking up the position of Rav in Uman. In 1822, Hirsh Ber Hurwitz set up a school based on the educational principles of Moses Mendelssohn. This was prior to the establishment of the schools in Odessa and Kishinev, but the school was closed after a few years.

Rabbi Nachman's first visit to Uman was in 1799 on his return from the Holy Land. In 1802, on his way from Zlatipolia to Breslov he passed through again, and he returned there in 1810 for the last months of his life.

Rabbi Nachman was buried in the old cemetery in Uman between the mounds containing the victims of the Haidemack massacres. His second wife arranged for the erection of a structure on the site of the grave. On the eve of Rosh Chodesh Shevat 5711 (1811) Rabbi Nathan led a group of the Rebbe's followers in their first pilgrimage to Uman following his death. They subsequently came to Uman each Rosh HaShanah.

Rabbi Nachman's Gravesite c. 1900

On Rosh HaShanah 5590 (1829) so many people were present that it was apparent that the local synagogue was too small. Rabbi Nathan began collecting funds for a new building, and the foundation stone was laid in 1832. The building, which was facing Rabbi Nachman's grave, was completed in 1834.

In 1870, the building was renovated and strengthened on the initiative of Reb Sender of Terhovitza. However it was a timber structure, and in 1902-3 it was taken down and an entirely new building of stone was erected.

Rabbi Nachman of Tulchin, who led the Breslover movement after the death of Rabbi Nathan had moved to Uman in 1866, making it the center of the movement.

The Jewish population of Uman grew steadily. In 1842, there were 4,933 Jews in the town. In 1897, there were 17,945 Jews (59 percent of the total population) and in 1910 their number had grown to 28,267.

During the Bolshevik revolution the community endured great suffering. In the spring and summer of 1919 successive waves of troops passed through the city, perpetrating pogroms. 170 Jews were murdered in the first pogrom and more than 90 in the second. Further atrocities were only narrowly averted through the intervention of the Council for Public Peace, consisting of Jews and Russians. By 1926 the Jewish population had fallen to 22,179.

In 1940, the Soviet authorities closed the synagogue and converted it into a metalwork factory.

Soviet resistance to the Nazi invasion of Russia in June, 1941, led to fierce fighting in the Ukraine, in which most of the older section of Uman was destroyed. In the course of the fighting a hand grenade exploded on the site of Rabbi Nachman's grave, completely destroying the structure over the tomb. The synagogue was untouched, however, and is still used as a factory.

The Nazis deported the entire Jewish community, murdering a total of 17,000. A monument in Uman to their memory bears a Yiddish inscription.

After the war the area comprising the old Jewish cemetery

city synagogue

Chasidei Breslov synagogue

Uman c. 1922 as seen from Rabbi Nachman's grave

Rabbi Nachman's Gravesite 1978

photo: Peretz Rubel

and it surroundings was built over. Today it consists of suburban housing.

The plot of land containing Rabbi Nachman's grave was acquired by a Breslover chassid, R. Zavel Lubarski. The exact position of the grave was no longer readily discernible owing to the destruction of the gravesite during the war. However, R. Zavel was able to find traces of two poles which had stood at the head and foot of the grave to support a rail and shelf for holy books.

Having thus located the exact position of the grave, R. Zavel built a house — 1 Belinsgoko Street (near the corner of Pushkin Street) — designing it in such a way that the exterior wall of the house runs alongside the grave. This is now covered with an unmarked slab and enclosed in the private yard attached to the house.

In 1959 there were 2,200 Jews in Uman — five percent of the total population. The Soviet authorities closed the last synagogue in the late 1950's.

Jews living in the Soviet Union have made regular pilgrimages to Rabbi Nachman's gravesite up to the present day. This was especially true at Rosh HaShanah time.

Access to Jews from outside Russia was barred until 1963, when the late Rabbi Zvi Aryeh Rosenfeld (1922-78; see cities, Medvedevka-Tcherin) organized the first group from the United States to travel to Uman. Since then, the Soviet authorities have shown great co-operation in permitting several groups to visit the tomb.

Zlatipolia

A town in N.W. Kirovograd oblast, Ukrainian S.S.R. Zlatipolia in Russian means gold city.

In 1847, the number of Jews in the town was 2,668 which suggests that by 1800, when Rabbi Nachman moved there, the community could have numbered well over a thousand. This brought him close to Shpola, home of the *Zeide* who became his prime adversary. The *Zeide* had previously lived in Zlatipolia.

Zlatipolia was the first residence of the Brodski family, which established major industrial concerns in the 19th century and played an important role in the Russian economy and in Jewish communal life.

During pogroms by Ukrainian nationalists in 1919, seventy Jews were killed in Zlatopolia. The community perished under the Nazi occupation.

APPENDIX E
RABBI NACHMAN'S WRITINGS

1. Likutey Moharan

ליקוטי מוהר"ן

Anthology of Our Master, Rabbi Nachman — *MoHaRaN* is an abbreviation of *Morenu, HaRav, Rabenu Nachman*.

The book is in two parts and contains 286 lessons in the first part and 125 in the second. Some of the lessons were recorded by Rabbi Nachman himself, marked *leshon Rabenu*, but most of them were written down by Rabbi Nathan. After hearing a lesson Rabbi Nathan would write it down from memory, and usually reviewed it with Rabbi Nachman later on. A few of the lessons were written down by Reb Avraham Peterberger, who recorded the Rebbe's teachings in the period before Rabbi Nathan became his follower. The lessons written by Reb Avraham are marked *leshon chaverim*.

The majority of lessons date from 5562-5571 (1801-10) but some of them date from as early as 5550 (1789-90).

The first edition was printed in 1808 in Ostrog and contained what is now part one of *Likutey Moharan*. It had a short introduction. In 1811, Rabbi Nathan had the second part printed in Moghilev (Mohelov).

In 1821, Rabbi Nathan re-edited the book, adding sources. It was then printed in Rabbi Nathan's own house in Breslov, without a permit from the censor. (There was a prohibition on printing Chassidic books in Russia at that time.) The title page bears the words "Moghilev Press," but this was written intentionally in order that Rabbi Nathan's press should not be discovered. This edition contains an extensive introduction (as printed in present-day editions) and, in addition, approbations from Rabbi Avraham Chaim,

Rabbi of Zlotchov; Rabbi Meir, Rabbi of Brody; and Rabbi Ephraim Zalman Margolies.

In the fifth edition, printed (1876) in Lemberg by the Tcheriner Rav, additional citations of sources were given in footnotes, and the approbations of the Chozeh of Lublin and the Magid of Koznitz were included.

In the tenth edition, published in 1938 in Warsaw by Reb Israel Fried, the text was printed in block letters (previously it had always been printed in Rashi script). It has been printed more than forty times to date.

An English translation is currently being prepared by the Breslov Research Institute.

2. *Sippurey Ma'asios* סיפורי מעשיות

Rabbi Nachman's Stories.

The book contains thirteen mystical stories told by Rabbi Nachman. He began telling his stories in the year 5566 (1806) and continued until the middle of 5570 (1810).

The *Sippurey Ma'asios* was written by Rabbi Nathan in Yiddish, mostly verbatim. Having heard the Rebbe say that it was his intention to have the book printed with the stories in Hebrew at the top of the page and in Yiddish at the bottom, Rabbi Nathan translated the stories into Hebrew.

It was first printed in 1815-16 in Ostrog with one introduction. At the end of the work were printed Rabbi Nachman's "Conversations" (included in *Rabbi Nachman's Wisdom*) as well as corrections and addenda to the 1808 edition of *Likutey Moharan*.

A second introduction was printed in the 1850 edition (no location given). From the wording it appears that Rabbi Nathan wrote it as an introduction to a second edition which he never got a chance to print.

In the sixth edition printed in 1902 in Lemberg by Reb Tzvi Weislov and Rabbi Israel Halperin, extracts from Rabbi

Nathan's *Likutey Halachos* relevant to the stories were included, together with *Rimzey HaMa'asios* by the Tcheriner Rav, and a second work of the same name by Rabbi Avraham the son of Rabbi Nachman of Tulchin.

The first English translation of the stories by Breslover Chassidim was prepared by Esther Koenig and edited by Mordechai Kramer. It was published in 1978 in Jerusalem.

A new English translation by Rabbi Aryeh Kaplan with extensive notes on the stories based on Breslover works, was published by the Breslov Research Institute in Jerusalem in 1983.

3. *Sefer HaMidos*   ספר המדות

The Book of Attributes. Also known as the *Aleph-Beis* Book, and *Sefer Hanhagos Yesharos*.

Sefer HaMidos is a collection of aphorisms about the various character traits, good and bad, as well as other aspects of the spiritual life of the Jew. It is arranged by subjects in alphabetical order. The work is divided into two parts.

The first part was written by Rabbi Nachman in his youth in order to direct and encourage himself in his struggle to attain holiness. The second part is similar to the first in form and structure, and the aphorisms are, for the most part, on the same subjects as in the first part. However, it was written later on in his life and Rabbi Nachman said that it was based on deeper understanding of the sources than the first part.

Rabbi Nachman kept the existence of *Sefer HaMidos* a guarded secret until after his arrival in Breslov in 5562 (1802). Thereafter he began dictating the first part of the book to Rabbi Nathan. After long intervals, the bulk of part of the work was finished before Chanukah 5566 (1805). Although Rabbi Nachman's own manuscript contained references to the sources relating to the aphorisms, he did not dictate them to Rabbi Nathan.

As for the second part of the book, Rabbi Nachman gave the material to his followers and asked them to arrange the aphorisms in alphabetical order according to subject. Later on, he gave additional material to Rabbi Nathan who arranged the entire work in order. The aphorisms in the second part were evidently not accompanied by references.

Rabbi Nachman did not reveal more than a portion of *Sefer HaMidos* as it was written in his own private manuscript. This contained much additional material including as many as two hundred paragraphs on the subject of Healing.

Rabbi Nathan arranged the two parts of the book in such a way that the subjects were to be printed in alphabetical order with the relevant aphorisms from the first part printed first, followed by the aphorisms on the same subject from the second part. However when Rabbi Nathan had the book printed in 1810-11 in Moghilev, he was not present to supervise the printing and the printers printed the two parts separately. The first edition already contained two introductions by Rabbi Nathan as printed today.

In 1820-21 Rabbi Nathan rearranged the material as he had first intended it to be printed. He printed it on his own press, but in order to conceal its existence "Moghilev" was put on the title page. This second edition incorporated some corrections and contained a number of source references added by Rabbi Nathan.

Later on, the Tcheriner Rav prepared full references to the sources, and they were printed together with the references prepared by Rabbi Nathan in all subsequent editions.

In 1907-8 a new edition of the book was published containing further sources by Rabbi Tzadok HaCohen of Lublin.

A Hebrew version with expanded references is now being published by the Breslov Research Institute and an English translation is under way.

4. Tikkun HaKlali   תיקון הכללי

Rabbi Nachman's Tikkun. "The Comprehensive Remedy."

In the year 5565 (1805) Rabbi Nachman revealed that the ten types of song as listed in the Talmud (*Pesachim* 117a) are a comprehensive remedy for nocturnal pollution caused by impure thought or deed. In the winter of 5569 (1808-9) or possibly 5570 (1809-10), Rabbi Nachman revealed the Ten Psalms which constitute the remedy. Viz. Psalms: 16, 32, 41, 42, 59, 77, 90, 105, 137 and 150.

The first time the *Tikkun HaKlali* was printed as a separate book was in 1820-21. The book was printed in Rabbi Nathan's house on the initiative of his son Rabbi Shachneh. The Ten Psalms were accompanied by an introduction, a related lesson from *Likutey Moharan* I:205, and the prayer composed by Rabbi Nathan to be recited after the psalms themselves.

Subsequent editions of the *Tikkun HaKlali* have been printed with additional material from *Likutey Moharan* II:92, and *Sichos HaRan* #141 (the account of how the *Tikkun HaKlali* came to be revealed), and in some cases with commentaries on and translations of the Ten Psalms, and additional prayers, etc.

An English translation of the Ten Psalms together with an English transliteration of the psalms, translations of the introductory material, and a new English introduction, was published by the Breslov Research Institute in Jerusalem, in 1984, under the title, *Rabbi Nachman's Tikkun*.

5. Shevachey HaRan   שבחי הר"ן

The Praises of Rabbi Nachman and *Seder Nesiaso LeEretz Yisroel*, — *Masa'os HaYam*, Sea Voyages — The Account of Rabbi Nachman's Pilgrimage to the Land of Israel.

Shevachey HaRan is an account of Rabbi Nachman's spiritual attainments. *Masa'os HaYam* is an account of his pilgrimage to the Holy Land in 5558-59 (1798-99). The works were written by Rabbi Nathan and first printed in 1815-16 at the end of the Stories.

An authoritative English translation of *Shevachey HaRan* and *Masa'os HaYam* by Rabbi Aryeh Kaplan and edited by Rabbi Zvi Aryeh Rosenfeld, is included in "Rabbi Nachman's Wisdom." The book was published on the initiative of Rabbi Rosenfeld in 1973, and reprinted by the Breslov Research Institute in 1984.

6. *Sichos HaRan*   שיחות הר"ן

Conversations of Rabbi Nachman. A collection of conversations and teachings ranging from simple, everyday advice to the most esoteric Kabbalistic mysteries.

In the 1815-16 edition of the Stories published by Rabbi Nathan, the conversations (Nos. 1-111 of later editions) were printed at the end of the book.

Subsequent editions included the remainder of the conversations as printed in present-day editions. On occasion the work was published under the titles *Ma'aglei Tzedek* (Paths of Righteousness) or *Magid Sichos* (Teller of Conversations).

An authoritative English translation of *Sichos HaRan* with full references and some explanatory notes by Rabbi Aryeh Kaplan, edited by Rabbi Zvi Aryeh Rosenfeld, was published in 1973 under the title "Rabbi Nachman's Wisdom," and reprinted by the Breslov Research Institute in 1984.

7. *Chayay Moharan*   חיי מוהר"ן

The Life of Rabbi Nachman; with *Shevachey Moharan*, The Praises of Our Master, Rabbi Nachman.

The book is divided into two parts. The first part, *Chayay Moharan*, includes: accounts of the way in which many of Rabbi Nachman's lessons came to be revealed together with the events associated with them; dates of many of the lessons, and other relevant material; accounts of some of Rabbi Nachman's dreams and visions and other mystical experiences; and an account of his life including details about many of the major events and incidents at that time.

The second part, *Shevachey Moharan*, describes Rabbi Nachman's spiritual attainments and contains additional conversations and teachings on a variety of subjects.

The book was written by Rabbi Nathan in order to convey a sense of the unique vitality of Rabbi Nachman — a man who, as Rabbi Nathan put it, was truly *alive* — and in order to preserve as many of Rabbi Nachman's conversations as possible.

It was evidently written after 1824 but remained unpublished, circulating privately among Rabbi Nathan's pupils.

The book was first printed in 1873-74 by Rabbi Nachman of Tcherin together with additional notes on a number of topics. An English translation is complete and will be published, God willing, in 1985.

8. *Megilas Sesarim*   מגילת סתרים

Scroll of Hidden Secrets — Unpublished Manuscript.

Megilas Sesarim was never printed, nor were its contents revealed outside Rabbi Nachman's innermost circle.

Rabbi Nathan writes in *Yemey Moharnat*: "In 5566 (1806) on Sunday, 5 Menachem Av, we heard from his lips a full account of how Mashiach would come.... Rabbi Nachman left on a journey through the Ukraine and we accompanied him. When he left Ladizin we sat in his carriage, and on the way he revealed to us this secret."

The material was written down allusively with the use of abbreviations and initials, etc. Rabbi Nachman warned that the manuscript was not to be copied and certainly not to be printed. Much of the original conversation was forgotten and not incorporated in the manuscript.

A note in *Yemey Moharnat* suggests that after the death of Rabbi Nathan the manuscript of *Megilas Sesarim* was lost. However, it was known in Breslov circles that Rabbi Avraham the son of Rabbi Nachman of Tulchin knew the contents of *Megilas Sesarim*, and it is possible that Rabbi Nachman of Tulchin had discovered the manuscript and handed it down to his son.

Rabbi Alter of Teplik, the son-in-law of Rabbi Nachman of Tulchin and the brother-in-law of Rabbi Avraham, also had a copy of *Megilas Sesarim*, and copied it in a volume which included material deleted from the printed version of *Chayay Moharan* and other works. Rabbi Alter's copy of *Megilas Sesarim* included explanations of many of the abbreviations etc.

There are copies of this manuscript today in the hands of some Breslover Chassidim.

9. *Sefer HaNisraf* ספר הנשרף

The Burned Book.

The work consisted of four parts and was written down by Rabbi Nathan at Rabbi Nachman's dictation in the winter of 5566 (1805-6).

Rabbi Nathan said that he understood nothing of the book but was overwhelmed by its greatness. Rabbi Nachman said that no one could understand a word of the book except one who was a great Tzaddik, unique in his generation, and proficient in the seven branches of wisdom.

When Rabbi Nachman was in Lemberg (5568—1807-8) he knew that he would either have to die or destroy the work. After consulting Rabbi Shimon he gave orders for him to return to Breslov and burn the book.

10. *Sefer HaGanuz*   ספר הגנוז

The Hidden Book.

Rabbi Nachman said that the holiness of *Sefer HaGanuz* was greater than that of *Sefer HaNisraf*. It was written in 5566 (1805-6). No one ever saw the work.

11. Manuscripts of Rabbi Nachman

Rabbi Nachman composed a number of works whose nature and contents were never revealed. Prior to his death he gave the key of his bureau to Rabbi Shimon and Rabbi Naftali with instructions that after his death they should take the manuscripts it contained and burn them. Immediately after Rabbi Nachman's passing, Rabbi Shimon went to the bureau, removed several books and assorted papers and burned them.

12. Parables, Stories, Anecdotes

A variety of material was handed down by oral tradition among Rabbi Nachman's disciples and their followers. Many of these traditions have been recorded in diverse works, including *Kochavey Or, Aveneha Barzel, Tovos Zichronos* and *Sippurim Niflaim*.

Translations of the parables were included in "Rabbi Nachman's Stories" published by the Breslov Research Institute in 1983.

APPENDIX F
RABBI NACHMAN'S FOLLOWERS

Moses received the Torah from Sinai and gave it to Joshua; Joshua gave it to the Elders; the Elders...   (Avos 1:1)

"The Tzaddik himself is impossible to grasp, for he is beyond understanding. Only through his followers is it possible to understand the greatness of the Tzaddik: one sees how they are men of achievement – God-fearing men, who have perfected themselves..."
(Likutey Moharan I:140)

This appendix presents biographical sketches of some of the followers of Rabbi Nachman. They were compiled from the various books mentioned in our text. Additional stories and information are oral traditions from Rabbi Eliyahu Chaim Rosen *zal*, Rabbi Levi Yitzchok Bender and Rabbi Nachman Burstyn.

If we are able to appreciate the greatness of the followers, we may merit to grasp the greatness of the master.

Rabbi Nachman remarked, "I would like my own candelabra" — a reference to the seven-stemmed candelabra in the Temple. His six closest students were: Rabbi Nathan, Rabbi Naftali, Rabbi Shimon, Rabbi Aharon, Rabbi Yudel and Rabbi Shmuel Isaac. Together with Rabbi Nachman they were to light the world.

Rabbi Shimon was attracted to Rabbi Nachman when the latter was only thirteen years old. The story is told of how on his wedding day in Medvedevka, after covering the face of the bride and before the wedding ceremony, the young Rabbi Nachman entered into conversations with the local youth, subtley feeling out their true attitudes towards wealth, pleasure and other worldly vanities. Only Rabbi Shimon remained steadfast in his declarations that his only aim was to achieve spiritual purity.

Rabbi Nachman then revealed himself a little and spoke so inspiringly that Rabbi Shimon immediately attached himself to him. As he put it later on, "I abandoned all the renowned leaders and followed this young boy."

Rabbi Shimon was physically strong and had great presence of mind (as we see from the story when he once saved the Rebbe's life by jumping from the carriage and preventing an accident; see text p. 9). He may have been Rabbi Nachman's attendant on the Rebbe's pilgrimage to Israel.

He later spent several years in "exile" east of the Don river. While there a non-Jewish woman tried to seduce him and in desperation he tore his lips until the bood ran, frightening her away.

After his return Rabbi Shimon remained one of Rabbi Nachman's closest disciples, attending him on many occasions and entrusted with important missions (such as the burning of the Sefer HaNisraf, etc.). He requested that he should be Rabbi Nachman's attendant in the World to Come as well, and eventually Rabbi Nachman agreed.

Rabbi Shimon once asked the Rebbe to use his special abilities to pray on behalf of his child, who was seriously ill. Rabbi Nachman did not respond. That night, Rabbi Shimon's wife sat next to the child's cradle and prayed with simplicity for her son.

The following morning, when the Rebbe saw Rabbi Shimon he said, "Do you see how great the power of prayer is. The decree that the child would die had already been sealed; yet she, with her prayers, not only won him life but long life at that!"

Rabbi Shimon's son recovered and lived for close to one hundred years.

Despite his business activities, Rabbi Shimon devoted much of his time to his devotions, especially hisbodedus. He lived at the edge of the town close to the forest in order to be able to go out to pray and meditate there day and night. Once Rabbi Shimon had gone out into the countryside for hisbodedus. Suddenly he saw a bear which was about to attack him. He immediately pulled off his coat, put a knife in this hand and wrapped the coat around his arm. When the bear attacked and bit his arm, the coat protected him while he was able to use the knife to kill it.

He is also known to have written his own Torah chidushim. Rabbi Nathan found them and remarked on their brilliance. He kept them with the thought of printing them. Rabbi Shimon waited until Rabbi Nathan's attention was diverted from them and burned them.

After Rabbi Nachman's death Rabbi Shimon settled in Israel, where he lived in Safed, again on the outskirts of the town. It happened several times that in the course of his devotions alone in the hills he was set upon by Arabs, and it was as a result of wounds thus sustained that he died (date unknown).

He is buried in the old cemetery in Safed at the side of the path leading down from the grave of the ARI to that of Rabbi Yosef Caro.

Rabbi Yudel, the leader of the Dashev group, had been a disciple of Rabbi Pinchas Koretzer. By the time Rabbi Yudel met Rabbi Nachman, he already had a knowledge of Kabbalah (which he had studied with his father-in-law Rabbi Leib Trastenitz). Rabbi Nachman directed him to pray according to the siddur of the ARI.

It was through Reb Dov (see below) that Rabbi Yudel initially journeyed to meet the Rebbe. When he came to the Rebbe for the first time, Rabbi Yudel started to speak in the manner of prominent Chassidim. "Let the Rebbe show us the path of serving the Creator," he said. To this Rabbi Nachman replied, "On the earth [you want] to know the way?" (Psalms 67:3) implying that Rabbi Yudel could not achieve this as long as he was insufficiently detached from his worldliness.

Rabbi Nachman then exposed him to a profound fear of Heaven and Rabbi Yudel was unable to withstand the intensity of the experience. Confused, he retreated to the door of the room. He remained there, afraid of moving any closer to the Rebbe. Rabbi Nachman then began smiling at Rabbi Yudel, thereby easing his fear a bit. "Why are you afraid of me?" he said. "I am human just like you, only I am smarter than you." He calmed him with these words and Rabbi Yudel again moved closer to the Rebbe.

Then once more Rabbi Nachman exposed Rabbi Yudel to this profound fear and again he retreated in bewilderment. The same procedure was repeated a number of times, after which Rabbi Nachman directed Rabbi Yudel to confess before him.

A strong bond was formed between them. Thus, in spite of his age and standing, Rabbi Yudel surrendered his position of leadership over the Dashev circle and became a lifelong follower of Rabbi Nachman. He quickly moved to the Medvedevka area in order to be close to his master.

In his later years, whenever Rabbi Yudel would travel through Breslov, he would visit with Rabbi Zvi Aryeh, the Rav of the town. Each time, Rabbi Yudel would relate the story of how he first came to be one of Rabbi Nachman's followers. He would conclude his story saying, "Perhaps you see the story as an old one. But for me, it is brand new!"

At the height of the controversy against Rabbi Nathan after the Rebbe's death, Rabbi Nathan said, "What is there for us to be afraid of, if we have people at our table like Rabbi Yudel who hear the heavenly voice call out, 'Shuvu resho'im She'olah' ('Wicked people, return to Hell') on motzoai Shabbos?" (referring to those who are released from Gehenom for the Sabbath).

After the Rebbe's death, Rabbi Yudel continued to devote himself to Torah and prayer day and night. Rabbi Yudel was looked to as one of the leading figures after the Rebbe's death.

When the Rebbe, prior to his death, allocated specific roles to each of his principle followers, Rabbi Yudel was given the power of redemptions (interceding for the sick and childless etc.).

There was once a young married man whose wife had been in labor for more than twenty-four hours unable to give birth. When he told this to Rabbi Yudel, the Rebbe's disciple handed the young man a snuff box and instructed him to open it.

Seeing that he was not able to open the box, Rabbi Yudel called him a schlemiel saying, "I will open it!" "Go home," Rabbi Yudel then told him. "On your way you will be given a Mazel Tov." On his way back the young man was greeted with the news that his wife had already given birth.

Rabbi Nathan was also one of the many who sent pidyonos to Rabbi Yudel. Rabbi Yudel was once passing through Breslov on his way to the Rebbe's grave in Uman. Rabbi Nathan's wife was seriously ill at the time and their prayers for her speedy recovery had as yet not been answered.

Hearing of Rabbi Yudel's arrival in the town, Rabbi Nathan's wife quickly ran to see him, despite her weak condition. She cried to Rabbi Yudel and begged him to intercede on her behalf. Rabbi Yudel listened carefully to her pleas, but answered nothing.

When she departed, he turned to one of those standing nearby and said, "What can I do, Rabbi Nathan is destined to have another two children." A short while later, Rabbi Nathan's wife died. Rabbi Nathan remarried and indeed two more sons, R. Nachman and R. Yosef Yonah, were born.

Rabbi Yudel died in 5598 (1838).

Rabbi Shmuel Isaac, another member of the Dashev group, was Rabbi Yudel's close friend and he became a follower of the Rebbe when Rabbi Nachman lived in Medvedevka. Rabbi Shmuel Isaac lived in abject poverty.

Rabbi Shmuel Isaac was physically strong. Rabbi Nachman told him to speak in turn to each of his limbs about the purpose of earthly existence. He was to do so until they were totally subdued. Later on, when someone would speak to him about physical desires, Rabbi Shmuel Isaac would faint.

After Rabbi Nachman's move to Zlatipolia (in 1800), Rabbi Shmuel Isaac dreamed that he was in an immense forest and met a man with a double-edged sword. The man took him to a house and told him he would only be able to take a sword of his own if he had reached the point of being cleansed from all worldly blemishes. The man then thrust him out of the house. Rabbi

Shmuel Isaac immediately journeyed to Zlatipolia. On reaching Rabbi Nachman's house, he knocked on the door, but Rabbi Nachman refused to open it for him until he started weeping. Then Rabbi Nachman admitted him, and before he even told him about his dream, Rabbi Nachman spoke to him in the same images as those he had dreamed.

Rabbi Shmuel Isaac subsequently devoted himself primarily to prayer. He said, "If I were to say *Shema Yisroel* today as I did yesterday, I would lie on the threshhold for my head to be cut off." Rabbi Nathan commented, "The Rebbe led him on the blade of a sword."

In the winter of 1811, Rabbi Nathan organized a trip to Rabbi Nachman's graveside in Uman for the first time since the Rebbe's death. He went from village to village collecting Rabbi Nachman's followers. When they arrived in Dashev, they went to Rabbi Shmuel Isaac's cottage. Rabbi Shmuel Isaac would adorn *talis* and *tefillin* and begin his morning prayers at dawn, continuing his devotions without interruption until the afternoon. Thus, when Rabbi Nathan arrived, the family told him that Rabbi Shmuel Isaac was still praying and they were afraid to disturb him. Rabbi Nathan decided to proceed with his party to Uman, leaving one of their number — the young Rabbi Zvi Aryeh, son of Rabbi Aharon, the Rav of Breslov — behind to travel to Uman with Rabbi Shmuel Isaac the next day. He instructed Rabbi Zvi Aryeh to hire a coach and provided him with the necessary funds, for he knew well that Rabbi Shmuel Isaac was extremely poor and would not be able to afford such a journey.

When Rabbi Zvi Aryeh was finally allowed in to see Rabbi Shmuel Isaac, the latter was most disappointed that he had not been informed of the arrival of Rabbi Nathan "in whose face radiated the Rebbe's countenance."

The only place for Rabbi Zvi Aryeh to sleep that night was in the room where Rabbi Shmuel Isaac practiced his devotions, the only other room in the house being used for the family and as a kitchen. For *Maariv*, Rabbi Shmuel Isaac instructed his guest to go to one of the local synagogues. Rabbi Zvi Aryeh remained there even after the prayers had ended, as he knew that Rabbi Shmuel Isaac would still be deeply immersed in the evening service. He waited until the synagogue was closed for the night and only then returned to Rabbi Shmuel Isaac's house.

When he approached the cottage, he was taken aback by the magnificent and awesome sounds of Rabbi Shmuel Isaac's voice, as his host had still not completed the prayers. Afraid that his entry would disturb Rabbi Shmuel Isaac, Rabbi Zvi Aryeh remained outside in the icy snow of what was then the heart of the Russian winter. Once he estimated that Rabbi Shmuel Isaac had already begun the silent prayer, he quietly entered the room. Cramping himself into a corner, he laid down upon a chest which stood against the back of a heating oven. Rabbi Shmuel Isaac stood at the other side of the oven, immersed in prayer.

Though he would have wanted to rest from his day's journey and the strain of standing in the freezing cold, Rabbi Zvi Aryeh could not help being aroused by the heartbreaking sighs and groans which accompanied Rabbi Shmuel Isaac's prayers. Once more he felt obliged to depart from the room and wait outside until Rabbi Shmuel Isaac had finished. But the winter's frost was again too much to bear and he returned to huddle on the chest as before.

Rabbi Zvi Aryeh did not sleep at all that night. The midnight prayers as well as the other awesome devotions of Rabbi Shmuel Isaac that he witnessed, were to leave a lasting impression on Rabbi Zvi Aryeh and they deeply influenced his own practices in the years which followed. (For more on Rabbi Zvi Aryeh see Appendix: Cities, Breslov.)

The Rebbe allocated to Rabbi Shmuel Isaac the power of *tikkun neshamos*, the rectification of souls.

Rabbi Shmuel Isaac lived in Dashev. His followers from the town of Kiblitch journeyed to him one Friday afternoon. When they left their town, one of their group was on his deathbed and they wanted Rabbi Shmuel Isaac to pray on his behalf. They arrived to find that Rabbi Shmuel Isaac had already begun the Friday afternoon prayer, which normally took him four hours to complete. To their amazement, they noticed that their friend's name already appeared on Rabbi Shmuel Isaac's list of those he was to mention in the blessing of "reviving the dead."

Rabbi Shmuel Isaac withstood great hardships in carrying out his missions of "rectifying souls." One stormy motzoai Shabbos, he appeared at the door of Rabbi Mordechai, the dayan of Teplik. Before Rabbi Mordechai could question him on the purpose of his unexpected visit, or for that matter on how he had physically managed an impossible journey from his home in Dashev during such a blizzard, Rabbi Shmuel Isaac instructed Rabbi Mordechai to put on his winter coat and come along. Without asking for an explanation, Rabbi Mordechai accompanied him out into the freezing cold and followed Rabbi Shmuel Isaac, not knowing where or why.

They walked together in silence until they had arrived at Rabbi Shmuel Isaac's destination — the local cemetery. Rabbi Mordechai trembled as he watched Rabbi Shmuel Isaac remove a bottle of wine and a cup from his pocket. Immediately, Rabbi Shmuel Isaac began reciting the havdalah prayer in a loud voice. After each of the four blessings in the prayer, Rabbi Mordechai heard an awesome terrifying voice call out from one of the graves — Amen. Once he had finished his mission, Rabbi Shmuel Isaac turned and departed from the cemetery, with Rabbi Mordechai following close behind.

Whenever Rabbi Shmuel Isaac traveled to see Rabbi Nachman, his excitement was so great that after his wagon would reach the town he would jump off and run on foot to the Rebbe's house. Once, Rabbi Shmuel Isaac arrived so exhausted that he stumbled into the room and collapsed at the Rebbe's feet. At the time he entered, Rabbi Nachman had been discussing the political issue of the day with some of his followers. Paul, the Russian Czar, had been murdered and there was a divergence of opinion within the Jewish leadership as to which of his two sons, Alexander, the religious zealot, or Nikolai, the heretic, would be a preferable choice to inherit the empire (see text pp. 64-65). While

Rabbi Shmuel Isaac was still lying on the floor, Rabbi Nachman said, "Leave him be, in Heaven they are asking his opinion on who should be the next Czar." It was only after twenty-five years had gone by, during which time the Rebbe himself had died, that the meaning of his words came to be understood.

Rabbi Shmuel Isaac outlived the Rebbe by more than fifteen years. The end of his life coincided with a change in rulership within Russia. Alexander, who had followed his father as Czar, died and his anti-religious brother replaced him. Nikolai immediately went to work on enforcing policies harmful to the Jewish community, thereby proving that those Tzaddikim, including Rabbi Nachman and Rabbi Shmuel Isaac, had been correct in preferring his brother. With Nikolai now the new Czar, Rabbi Shmuel Isaac no longer had any desire to remain alive in a world faced with growing heretical secularism.

During Rosh HaShanah, 5587 (1826), Rabbi Shmuel Isaac was overheard saying again and again, "Either him or me! Either him or me!" Later on that year, Rabbi Shmuel Isaac died.

Rabbi Aharon, the son of Rabbi Moshe of Kherson, was a prodigious young scholar who came from a long line of distinguished rabbis. His outstanding ability in the field of *halakhic* decision was acknowledged in Kherson even during his father's lifetime, when he was often asked to give decisions.

It happened that Rabbi Aharon was once asked to travel to Medvedevka to mediate in a business dispute. Upon his arrival in town, Rabbi Nachman, who was then living in Medvedevka, sent his attendant to ask him to come see him. Unable to refuse, Rabbi Aharon stayed with Rabbi Nachman from late afternoon until dawn the next morning. He later said that if he had come into the world only for that night — a night in which he hardly knew if he was in the physical world at all — it would have been enough for him.

Rabbi Nachman showed Rabbi Aharon that the foundation of *halakhic* decision-making must lie in faith of the highest order. He blessed him with the ability to clarify the *halakhah* free of the distortions of the imagination.

Rabbi Aharon was also noted for the beauty of his voice. He was the *chazan* in the main synagogue on Rosh HaShanah in Breslov.

When Rabbi Nachman moved to Breslov he summoned Rabbi Aharon to be Rav in the town. Shortly after Rabbi Nathan became a follower of Rabbi Nachman, the Rebbe sent him to Rabbi Aharon's house. When he arrived, he found Rabbi Aharon sitting with tears running from his eyes. Returning to the Rebbe, Rabbi Nathan told him what he had seen. Rabbi Nachman applied to Rabbi Aharon: "*As one seated in secrecy to appeal to the face of the King, so was the appearance of the priest*" (*Mussaf* Liturgy Yom Kippur; describing the appearance of the High Priest when he emerged from the Holy of Holies). This was the level of Rabbi Aharon's *hisbodedus*.

After the death of the Rebbe, Rabbi Aharon continued to serve as Rav in Breslov. He and Rabbi Nathan became very close friends, and they made a pact to remain together even after death. They bought plots next to each other in the middle of the cemetery. When, after Rabbi Nathan passed away, someone placed Rabbi Nathan's grave at the entrance of the cemetery, Rabbi Aharon became very upset over losing his close friend as a neighbor (see below, Rabbi Nathan).

The Rebbe told him that he would die in the month of Av. One year he fell ill during Av. When Rosh Chodesh Elul arrived he made a feast for all his family, telling them that he knew he would be alive for at least another year. Each year on Rosh Chodesh Elul he would make a similar feast.

When he finally became seriously ill, and he realized that he would soon die, he called all his children and grandchildren to his bedside and said to them: "The world says that I am wise and a scholar. If this is so, then it stands to reason that what I chose was good. I say to you that I chose the Rebbe." He then added, "And I am giving you this as an inheritance."

He died on Rosh Chodesh Av, 5546 (1846).

Rabbi Nathan. Foremost among Rabbi Nachman's followers was Rabbi Nathan, 5540-5605 (1780-1844). It was immediately after Rabbi Nachman's entry to Breslov in 1802 that Rabbi Nathan became one of his followers. Although the Rebbe was already surrounded by all these outstanding figures mentioned above, he was to reveal himself to Rabbi Nathan more than to all the others.

Rabbi Nathan had been raised by wealthy parents in Nemirov. He married the daughter of the renowned *halakhic* authority Rabbi Dovid Zvi Ohrbach, Rabbi of Mohelov, Sharograd and Kremenitz. Rabbi Nathan, who was already an outstanding Talmudist and *halakhic* authority, was also completely knowledgeable in the seven types of wisdom (topography, mathematics, music etc.). With one glance at a building he could give its dimensions.

His father-in-law was opposed to Chassidism and would lecture the family against it. Rabbi Dovid Zvi did not look kindly upon Rabbi Nathan's accepting Rabbi Nachman's leadership and wanted him to take over one of his rabbinical posts.

His father-in-law, however, recognized Rabbi Nathan's greatness. Once, on a Friday night, when an important guest was visiting, Rabbi Nathan came home from *shul* and went into a small room to sing the customary *Sholom Aleichem, Eishes Chayil* etc. The guest was very angry that Rabbi Dovid Zvi, a world renowned scholar, should wait for the young Rabbi Nathan. Rabbi Dovid Zvi said, "Leave him be! He does everything with complete sincerity."

The Rebbe himself said that Rabbi Nathan understood more about him than any of his other followers. Rabbi Nathan was a talented writer and was given the task of putting Rabbi Nachman's teachings into writing. Rabbi Nachman said that if it were not for Rabbi Nathan, not a single page of his teachings would have survived.

Rabbi Nathan also collected the Rebbe's practical guidance in the *Kitzur Likutey Moharan* and *Likutey Etzos*, and upon Rabbi Nachman's suggestion composed *Likutey Tefilos* and *Likutey Halachos*, both based on the Rebbe's teachings.

Rabbi Nathan often travelled to the Rebbe's grave in Uman for the eve of Rosh Chodesh. He made it a practice of securing a covered coach so that he would be able to pray and study Torah along the way. On one such occasion he took along Rabbi Moshe Breslover.

They set out in the middle of the night from an inn where they had stopped to sleep. At daybreak, Rabbi Nathan adorned *talis* and *tefillin*. He began reciting the *Shacharis* prayer in a low voice and with a broken heart. This not only surprised Rabbi Moshe, who was accustomed to hearing Rabbi Nathan pray in a loud and joyous manner, but the sad tones so affected him that Rabbi Moshe began to cry.

When Rabbi Nathan reached the words, "Sing to the Lord, His righteous ones," (Psalms 30:5) he stopped. A few moments passed, after which Rabbi Nathan began singing the Rebbe's tune for *Eishes Chayil*. This lasted for about twenty minutes, and the awesome spiritual emotion with which Rabbi Nathan sang brought a tremendous awe upon Rabbi Moshe.

Then suddenly, Rabbi Nathan clapped his hands a number of times and began joyously and energetically shouting, "Sing to the Lord, His righteous ones; give praise to the remembrance of His holiness." Rabbi Nathan then continued the morning prayer in splendid *devekus*, clapping his hands and joyfully reciting the words of the prayer. His voice was so inspiring, and his prayer so sweet, that the people of the town he was passing through came out to follow the wagon.

Afterwards, Rabbi Nathan offered Rabbi Moshe an explanation of his actions. "Before I began praying," said Rabbi Nathan, "I started thinking about the purpose of my journey. When Rabbi Nachman was alive, I would always talk to him about all the things which were happening in my life. He always asked about any fresh developements stemming from our discussions about serving God. But today, while traveling to his grave, I could not find in myself any new growth of this kind. This broke my heart. When I began praying, I felt despondent and embarrassed that I would be coming to the Rebbe like this.

"Then I remembered," continued Rabbi Nathan, "what the Rebbe once told me, 'When you have nothing else to revive yourself with, revive yourself with a song.' In thinking about this, I recalled the tremendous spiritual uplifting I felt the first time I was with the Rebbe on Shabbos and heard him sing *Eishes Chayil*. This thought revived me, and I started singing the tune with the same feelings I had when I first merited to hear it. [This tune is available on cassette from the Breslov Research Institute.] When I realized that in the prayers I reached the words, 'Sing to the Lord, His righteous ones,' I thanked God that I am included in His righteous ones — that I am a Chasid of Rabbi Nachman, and I am now traveling to his gravesite. This brought me to very great happiness and gave me the strength to pray the way I did."

Rabbi Moshe Breslover later said that, from that time onward, his heart had been opened to partially understand how one can revive one's spirit through prayer — inspired by the Rebbe.

An outline of the life of Rabbi Nathan has already been published as an appendix to *Advice* (1983). Fuller details are to be found in *Yemey Moharnat*, Rabbi Nathan's autobiography, and in *Tovos Zichronos, Kochavey Or, Sippurim Niflaim, Sichos VeSippurim* and *Aveneha Barzel*, etc.

Rabbi Nathan's unique position was accepted by Rabbi Nachman's other followers. After the Rebbe's death, Rabbi Aharon recalled how, on his last Shabbos Chanukah, Rabbi Nachman quoted the verse, "And Joshua the son of Nun was filled with the spirit of wisdom, for Moses had rested his hands upon him" (Deuteronomy 34:9), and how all those present had understood that the Rebbe was referring to Rabbi Nathan.

Rabbi Shimon once returned from *Eretz Yisroel* to visit in the

Ukraine. When he saw Rabbi Nathan giving a lesson, he remarked, "I thought he was a student of the Rebbe. Now I see that he is [the embodiment of] the Rebbe himself!"

Rabbi Nachman assigned him the most difficult of roles: to work with people constantly, drawing them close to God, and to spread Rabbi Nachman's teachings in the world.

Rabbi Nathan had said, "Whoever will even pass by my grave, I will help him." Rabbi Nathan passed away just before Shabbos began, and his burial (in the plot that Rabbi Nathan had bought in the middle of the cemetery), was delayed until Saturday night. Rabbi Nathan ben Reb Laibel Reuven (author of *Kuntres HaTzerufin*) wanted as many people as possible to pass by Rabbi Nathan's grave so that Rabbi Nathan would intercede on their behalf. As soon as Shabbos was over, he went to the cemetery and dug the grave for Rabbi Nathan by himself — at the entrance to the cemetery.

It was Rabbi Nathan who, more than anyone else, was responsible for the continuation of Breslover Chassidus even to the present day.

Rabbi Naftali had been Rabbi Nathan's friend in Nemirov and the two of them came together to meet Rabbi Nachman in Breslov.

The Rebbe once said, "Nobody understands me except Nathan, and Naftali a little." Only the two of them heard the Rebbe's *Megilas Sesarim*.

When Rabbi Naftali first became attached to the Rebbe, he was involved in business. When he told Rabbi Nachman that he spent the entire day in his store, the Rebbe replied, "*All* day?" Rabbi Naftali understood him to mean that he should spend more time in study and devotion, and reduced the number of hours he spent in his store.

When he told Rabbi Nachman that he now worked only part of every day, the Rebbe replied, "*Every* day?" Rabbi Naftali subsequently restricted his activities to market-days. When he told this to Rabbi Nachman, he replied, "Do you mean that whenever there's a market-day you have to be there?" Rabbi Naftali understood that he was to devote himself entirely to Torah and prayer and did so.

Rabbi Nachman advised him that though the letters of NaFTaLI are the same as TeFILliN, he should pay special attention to the mitzvah of tzitzis. Once Rabbi Naftali had climbed up a ladder to attend to some repairs when his tzitzis tore. He would not move until a new garment with valid tzitzis was brought to him, and subsequently he always carried a spare tzitzis with him.

The Rebbe once said, "I saw in the upper world that there was someone praying a wonderful prayer. I uncovered his face and I saw it was my Naftali." He also had a very nice singing voice.

When the Russian authorities introduced compulsory military service for Jews in 5585 (1825), press-gangs would often come round asking to inspect Jewish boys' exemption certificates. Upon receiving them, they would tear them up and press the boys into service.

Once one of these gangs came to Rabbi Naftali's house where a young boy had lodgings. The boy's father was afraid they would take his son. He made a big commotion bringing as many people as possible to the house to be witness if there was any attempt to destroy the boy's exemption certificate. Rabbi Naftali was praying at the time.

Afterwards the boy's father apologized to him for disturbing his prayers. Rabbi Naftali said he heard nothing and knew nothing about the whole affair. When he prayed he was completely separated from the physical world.

Rabbi Naftali was the closest follower of the Rebbe after Rabbi Nathan. He sent his son, Rabbi Efraim, to study with Rabbi Nathan. Rabbi Efraim later composed Likutey Even and Tefilos Haboker.

Rabbi Naftali moved to Uman in his later years and lived in a small room above the Breslover kloyz.

Rabbi Naftali said that he had realized from Rabbi Nathan's dancing on the previous Rosh HaShanah that "he was already separated from us." Rabbi Nathan passed away on a Friday afternoon in Breslov. Rabbi Naftali was in Uman, but yet, that Shabbos he said that Rabbi Nathan had already died. When asked how he knew, he replied, "I had a dream in which I saw Rabbi Nathan running. I asked him where he was running to and Rabbi Nathan replied, 'Me? straight to the Rebbe!' "

Once, in Uman, there was a *sholom zochor* in the house of one of their friends. It was winter time, however, and there was an exceptionally strong snow blizzard which made it impossible for them to go. Rabbi Naftali said they should recite *Shemos HaTzaddikim* (see *Rabbi Nachman's Tikkun*, 1984), and the blizzard cleared up. One of the group said they now knew what to do in such cases. Rabbi Naftali said, "I have to tell you!"

Rabbi Nachman told Rabbi Naftali that "After my death, you should give a Torah lesson during the third meal of Shabbos — in a closed room." "But who will hear it?" asked Rabbi Naftali. "If I tell you to do so, you need not worry," the Rebbe replied. His friends later heard Rabbi Naftali carrying out the Rebbe's instructions faithfully.

He was the last of the Rebbe's followers to survive. Rabbi Naftali died on 19th Av 5520 (1860).

Rabbi Yekusiel, the Magid of Terhovitz, who was one of Rabbi Nachman's most devoted followers, was himself one of the most prominent Chassidic leaders of his time. A disciple of the Magid of Mezritch, he had authority over a region of no less than eighty-four towns and villages.

He was among those asked to give their approbation to the Chassidic *siddur* edited by Rabbi Shneur Zalman of Liadi, founder of the *ChaBaD* movement. He was a lifelong friend of Rabbi Nochum of Tchernoble — it is said that every year on Shavuos the two of them used to dance together for the whole night, even when they were old.

The date of birth of the Magid of Terhovitz is unknown, but he was already advanced in years by the time Rabbi Nachman was first becoming more widely known. It is possible that the Magid visited Rabbi Nachman while he was still in Ossatin: Medvedevka and its environs was in the "territory" of the Magid. It was he who later brought his friend Rabbi Nochum of Tchernoble to see Rabbi Nachman.

Rabbi Yekusiel submitted himself to Rabbi Nachman's leadership more completely than any of the other leading Chassidic leaders of the time. The Magid influenced many of his own followers to submit themselves to Rabbi Nachman, notably his own son-in-law, Rabbi Yitzchok, who was a notable scholar in his own right.

With the growing opposition to Rabbi Nachman after his entry to Zlatipolia, there were attempts to persuade the Magid to lessen his attachment. "They are shooting arrows at my heart because of my closeness to you," he told Rabbi Nachman. "But I will not turn back from the truth. You have succeeded in hiding yourself from everybody else. Do not hide yourself from me. This is my place."

The other Tzaddikim called Rabbi Yekusiel the "Guardian of the border." Terhovitza (Targowice) stood at the border between the provinces of Kiev and Kherson and the Magid prevented the non-Jewish culture in the Kherson province from reaching the Jewish community in the Ukraine. (Before the second partition of Poland, in 1793, this was the border separating Poland from Russia. The Confederation defining the terms of the partition was signed in Targowice; see text p. 15.)

Rabbi Nachman once let it be known that he knew of a particular scribe who wrote *tefillin* with exceptional holiness. Though he would not reveal the name of this *sofer*, fearing that such publicity would be detrimental, the Rebbe said that it would be very desirable were his followers to obtain the scrolls written by this man.

When Rabbi Yekusiel heard of this, he questioned Rabbi

Nachman further as to the identity of this scribe. The Rebbe provided the Magid with additional details including the name of the city in which this man lived, Bravenitz. Rabbi Yekusiel traveled there in search of this holy scribe. In speaking with the townspeople, Rabbi Yekusiel learned of his whereabouts, though the town's inhabitants were quick to add that there were many other scribes whom they considered far more capable than this *sofer*.

Undaunted in his desire to follow Rabbi Nachman's advice, Rabbi Yekusiel went to see the man whom the Rebbe had so highly praised. When he entered the house he was surprised by the dire poverty in which the scribe lived. The Magid approached the man, who had not even turned his face from the wall to see who it was that entered, and asked to purchase *tefillin* scrolls. The scribe tried to decline and then asked for an extremely high price, hoping that this would dissuade the Magid. Without hesitating, Rabbi Yekusiel produced the sum and agreed to return in three day's time to receive his scrolls.

When the Magid came back, he found the scribe in the same position as he had been when Rabbi Yekusiel first visited — his face turned to the wall. Without so much as glancing at the Magid, the *sofer* handed him the scrolls he had written. When Rabbi Yekusiel returned to Rabbi Nachman, treasure in hand, the Rebbe rejoiced and praised the *tefillin* which the Magid had succeeded in acquiring. Because of their great value, he advised Rabbi Yekusiel to cherish them and to wear them only on Rosh Chodesh.

Rabbi Yekusiel was renowned as a wonderful singer. The *nusach* (score) of the High Holyday prayers which Breslover Chassidim use today is by and large drawn from the tunes which the Magid introduced.

The exact date of the Magid's death is unknown, but it was certainly after Rabbi Nachman's. The Magid was once at the Rebbe's graveside and was heard singing each of the Ten Psalms of the *Tikkun HaKlali* with a different melody — the Ten Kinds of Song (see Rabbi Nachman's Tikkun).

Rabbi Gershon, the Magid's grandson, joined the following during the same period as had his grandfather, when the Rebbe lived in Medvedevka. Rabbi Gershon lived in dire poverty and Rabbi Nachman wanted to better his disciple's lot. But Rabbi Gershon had no desire for wealth and refused the Rebbe's offer. He preferred a life of poverty, feeling that it was the preferable choice for serving God.

Once, the Rebbe asked Rabbi Gershon why he did not want riches, and said, "Why, because of a candle worth no more than a penny, it is possible to ruin an *Amidah* prayer." Rabbi Gershon, however, had no idea of what Rabbi Nachman meant by this.

Years passed and Rabbi Gershon's financial plight only grew worse. It once happened that Rabbi Gershon did not even have enough money to buy a candle. His house was very dark and this only exacerbated the family's desperate situation. Distraught and pained, Rabbi Gershon tried to pray, but was unable to collect his thoughts. It was then that he realized the meaning of Rabbi Nachman's words.

Rabbi Yitzchok Isaac, one of the Terhovitzer Magid's followers, was a money-changer by trade. When he came to Rabbi Nachman, the Rebbe directed him in very stringent devotions suitable to the root of his soul. The most difficult of these prescriptions was the Rebbe's advice that he go an entire year without speaking to anyone (other than the Terhovitza Magid).

Rabbi Yitzchok Isaac entirely divorced himself from his worldy preoccupations and devoted day and night to Torah study and prayer. He did this despite the fierce harrassment and accusations of insanity his silence earned him from the members of his family, particularly from his wife and father-in-law. When Rabbi Nachman became aware through his *ruach hakodesh* of the anguish that their attacks were causing his disciple, he hurriedly set off for Terhovitza.

He arrived there at night and went straight to the house where Rabbi Yitzchok Isaac lived with his father-in-law. Rabbi

Yitzchok Isaac had already begun saying the bedtime prayers in another room and was not present to hear the Rebbe admonish the father-in-law for persecuting his son-in-law. "Were a gentile who had no concept of *tefillin* to stand in front of you one morning while you — refusing to speak — wound the straps of animal hide around your arm, would he not accuse you of having gone mad?" With this and similar arguments, Rabbi Nachman was able to convince Rabbi Yitzchok Isaac's father-in-law to discontinue his harrassment of his son-in-law for his devoted efforts in serving God.

Once Rabbi Yitzchok Isaac had finished his prayers, the Rebbe entered his room. His spirit was renewed by the great joy he took in seeing Rabbi Nachman and he was no longer disturbed while practicing his devotions.

He died young, in 5564, about a year after Rabbi Nathan came to the Rebbe. Once, after serving him soup on his sickbed, Rabbi Nachman said, "Today I have served a true Torah scholar."

Reb Dov of Tcherin was originally from Medvedevka. He had been living in Dashev in the house of his father-in-law, who had agreed to support him for a time while he studied, in accordance with the custom of the period. Reb Dov was a member of a group of intensely devoted Chassidim under the leadership of Rabbi Yudel.

When the time came for Reb Dov to return to Medvedevka, his companions urged him to continue in the path laid down by Rabbi Yudel and asked him not to visit Rabbi Nachman, so as not to be distracted by a new influence.

Back in Medvedevka, however, Reb Dov found himself unable to achieve his spiritual goals, and in desperation went to Rabbi Nachman, who showed him that perfection is not achieved all at once but slowly, stage by stage. Thus Reb Dov found his mentor.

Soon afterwards, he went to visit his family and friends in Dashev. He told his comrades about Rabbi Nachman. Far from recriminating him for disloyalty, Rabbi Yudel and his group immediately hired carriages — in spite of the financial straits in which they lived — and traveled to Rabbi Nachman in Medvedevka.

After he became a follower, he asked Rabbi Nachman to pray that he have children. The Rebbe told him to give to charity. When he replied that he had none to give, the Rebbe said, "Have faith. *Emunah* (faith), has the same numerical value of *banim* (children)."

Rabbi Nachman said of him that he fears God as much as one fears physical torture from the Russians.

Reb Dov became a businessman. He was scrupulous in distributing one-fifth of his profits to the poor, as the Rebbe had directed him. His daughter married the Rebbe's grandson, Rabbi Avraham Dov (son of Adil).

Rabbi Nathan had a disciple in Tcherin, called Rabbi Moshe Breslover. Rabbi Moshe and Rabbi Avraham Dov used to get together every day and speak to each other about the Rebbe. One day, Rabbi Avraham Dov was not there. Reb Dov asked Rabbi Moshe to talk to him instead. Rabbi Moshe Breslover said, "You have seen the Rebbe himself. I only knew Rabbi Nathan." Reb Dov answered, "You know more about the Rebbe from Rabbi Nathan, than I know from the Rebbe himself."

Rabbi Chaikel was an excellent cantor and the Rebbe wanted to make him his permanent cantor in Breslov, but he was not prepared to accept what was then considered a lowly position.

Rabbi Chaikel was once travelling in a coach with the Rebbe. Rabbi Nachman was sitting in awesome *devekus*. Rabbi Chaikel did not realize this and presumed that the Rebbe was dozing. When the coach passed by the house of a distant relative of Rabbi Chaikel, he ordered the driver to stop there. Rabbi Nachman, whose way it was never to be obstinate, acted as though he knew nothing and also alighted from the coach.

When they entered the house, the man, who was somewhat of a follower of the Rebbe, greeted them warmly. Rabbi Chaikel asked his relative if he had any drink or sweets with which to honor his revered guest. The man answered that he had nothing — his house was completely empty. The host then took his wife's Shabbos candlesticks, went to a nearby inn, and purchased a small amount of drink and delicacies. As a cup was being poured for the Rebbe, the man's children walked by. They were barefoot and had on torn and tattered clothing.

Rabbi Chaikel motioned to the Rebbe to take notice of this and to provide the man with some sort of a blessing. The Rebbe answered, "I have no blessing for him. If you want, provide the blessing yourself." Rabbi Chaikel was afraid of angering the Rebbe, until Rabbi Nachman gave him pemission three times.

Rabbi Chaikel then took a pitcher of water and poured it out in the center of the house. Then he divided the water saying, "Abundance to the east, abundance to the west, abundance to the south, abundance to the north." After doing this, they left.

Shortly afterwards, a group of merchants stopped at this man's house. They asked for food and drink and the man replied that he had none. They lent him money to buy some drink and delicacies for when they returned from selling their wares. From then on these merchants began to lodge at his house and eventually commissioned him to sell their goods for them. He prospered and became very wealthy, and very preoccupied with business.

It happened that there was once a fair in Breslov and this man was there, busily running through the market buying and selling goods. Rabbi Nachman, whose windows faced the marketplace, noticed the man and called him. Having no choice, he entered the Rebbe's house. "Have you looked at the sky today?" the Rebbe asked. "No," he replied.

Calling him to the window, Rabbi Nachman said, "Tell me, what do you see?" "I see carriages and horses and people scurrying about," replied the man. The Rebbe then said, "Fifty years from now there will be another fair. There will be other horses, other carriages and different people. I won't be here and neither will you, like we are here today. I ask you, why are you so preoccupied that you don't even have the time to look at the sky?"

Turning to Rabbi Chaikel who was nearby, the Rebbe said, "Look Chaikel, see what you achieved with your blessing! He does not even have time to look at the sky!"

Rabbi Nachman was once speaking with Rabbi Chaikel, who was explaining to the Rebbe how with proper knowledge one could hold a snake by its head without being harmed. Hearing this, Rabbi Nachman threw his handkerchief to the floor where it turned into a snake. He then instructed Rabbi Chaikel to take hold of it, which he did. "Don't hold it in your hand because I've told you to, but because of your knowledge," said the Rebbe. Rabbi Chaikel was not prepared to do so.

He had been a close confidant of Rabbi Nachman in his early days, but had occasion to regret the advice he gave the Rebbe (see text p. 64).

Rabbi Shmuel Yitzhok was a scholar. He accompanied Rabbi Nachman on his trips of Novoritch and Lemberg. On the course of these trips he was witness to a number of miraculous incidents and revelations.

Rabbi Mordechai of Teplik was an outstanding Torah scholar. While accompanying Rabbi Nachman on his travels he was made Rabbi of Teplik.

Rabbi Avraham Peterberger was wealthy and highly intelligent. He had an extensive knowledge of the business world, besides being an accomplished linguist and an able writer.

The Rebbe, however, wanted him to devote himself to Torah learning. When Rabbi Avraham asked the usual question, "What will we eat?" the Rebbe told him he would have to take from people. Rabbi Avraham was very upset and stopped going to the Rebbe for a period of two years. During this period he lost all his money. Only then did he go back to the Rebbe, who said to him, "If you listen to me now you'll be able to take from people with dignity. If you don't, you'll be pathetic."

Rabbi Avraham still did not want to listen to the Rebbe and live a life of Torah and simplicity. Later on, however, he came round to the Rebbe's view, and he himself told others the story of what had happened.

Rabbi Nachman said that he would like to have "sixty warriors" (60 disciples) as [great as] the Baal Shem Tov had.

In the anecdotes which have come down concerning the Rebbe's relations with his followers, there is a great variety of incidents in which the Rebbe was involved. Generally speaking he spent most of the day closed up and inaccessible. Only late in the day were people admitted to speak to him.

In Breslov the Rebbe instituted regular occasions for his followers to gather. First and foremost was Rosh HaShanah, when Rabbi Nachman insisted that all his followers should come. In addition they came to Breslov for Shabbos Chanukah and Shavuos. Then on Shabbos Shirah, Shabbos Nachamu and one other Shabbos during the winter, the Rebbe himself traveled to centers which those of his followers who lived further away could more easily reach.

On Rabbi Nachman's last Rosh HaShanah, in Uman, several hundreds of his followers traveled to be with him. The following year, when Rabbi Nathan organized the first Rosh HaShanah by the Rebbe's graveside, only about sixty of his followers were present. But the very fact that they came at a time when the opponents of Breslover Chassidus were saying that the episode was now closed is testimony to the degree of their attachment to Rabbi Nachman. For Rabbi Nachman had once told Rabbi Nathan: "I have three kinds of followers: those who come to eat my leftovers; those who come to hear my Torah; and those on whose very heart I am inscribed."

APPENDIX G
RABBI NACHMAN'S FAMILY

Adil, Rabbi Nachman's grandmother, was the only daughter of Rabbi Yisroel, the Baal Shem Tov, and his wife, Chana Chabad Lea Rochel. Her father said that he took the name ADiL from the verse in the Torah which concludes with the words, "*Aish Das Lamo*" (Deuteronomy 33:2).

Adil was known for her righteousness and was blessed with *ruach hakodesh*. The Baal Shem Tov thought very highly of his daughter and treated her as one of his holy disciples. Adil accompanied her father on his attempted pilgrimage to the Holy Land.

Adil was married to Rabbi Yechiel Ashkenazi, who was known as the *Daitchel* — coming from Germany. Together they had three famous children: Rabbi Moshe Chaim Ephraim of Sudylkov, author of the *Degel Machane Ephraim*; Rabbi Baruch of Medzeboz, author of *Butzina DeNehora*; and Feiga, Rabbi Nachman's mother.

The Rebbe was once asked to describe his grandmother's unique quality. "My grandmother, Adil, always yearned for God. She constantly looked for ways to please her Creator," he responded.

The date of Adil's death is not known, but from our text it can be seen that she was no longer alive in 5547 (1787), when the Rebbe named his first daughter after her. In *Hatamim* there is a letter from her dated Monday, Breishis, 5547, which is at the beginning of the year.

Rabbi Simcha, Rabbi Nachman's father, was born around 5510 (1750). His father, Rabbi Nachman Horodenker, was one of the leading and closest disciples of the Baal Shem Tov. Rabbi

Simcha's mother was the sister of Rabbi Yitzchok Drovitcher.

When Rabbi Nachman Horodenker disappeared right after their wedding, his wife asked the Baal Shem Tov to help her find her husband. When Rabbi Nachman reappeared, he explained to his mentor that he had seen that his wife would die in childbirth and had therefore gone away. Despite this forbidding omen, she was prepared to bear Rabbi Nachman's child, and Rabbi Simcha was born. In answer to her prayers that she be given some time with her newborn son, Rabbi Simcha's mother lived for another month. Rabbi Nachman Horodenker later said that had his wife requested for long life, this too would have been granted.

After his mother died, Rabbi Simcha was taken into the Baal Shem Tov's home. His father, Rabbi Nachman Horodenker, was often away fulfilling the spiritual errands which his mentor would send him on, and Rabbi Simcha was cared for by the Baal Shem Tov's daughter, Adil. Under the watchful eye of the founder of Chassidus, Rabbi Simcha was trained in a lifestyle devoted to God. He would spend long hours away from home, in the fields or in some distant village, privately serving his Creator. He was about ten years old when the Baal Shem Tov died in 5520 (1760).

Some three years later, after his bar mitzvah, Rabbi Simcha was married to Adil's daughter, Feiga. The couple were given the house of the Baal Shem Tov as their wedding present. There they often played host to the numerous Tzaddikim of the generation, who would journey to Medzeboz to be at the gravesite of the Baal Shem Tov. Rabbi Simcha and Feiga had four children, three sons, including the Rebbe, and a daughter.

Very little else has been recorded about Rabbi Simcha, who from childhood on preferred to keep the details of his life and his devotions to God well hidden. It is known that he accompanied the Rebbe to Berdichov in the summer of 5562 (1802), when the famous meeting (see text p. 71) and the wedding of the Volchisker's son, Rabbi Sh., took place.

Despite living in Medzeboz, famous for having been the center of the Chassidic movement, the date of Rabbi Simcha's passing — whether during Rabbi Nachman's lifetime or after — and the place of his burial are not known for certain.

Feiga, Rabbi Nachman's mother, was born in Medzeboz to her parents, Rabbi Yechiel Ashkenazi and Adil, the Baal Shem Tov's daughter. She married the Rebbe's father, Rabbi Simcha, in 5523 (1763). This match had been agreed upon by the Baal Shem Tov and Rabbi Nachman Horodenker, Rabbi Simcha's father, before either Feiga or her husband had been born. It was the "fee" Rabbi Nachman Horodenker was willing to pay the Baal Shem Tov for his arranging Rabbi Nachman's own marriage to the sister of Rabbi Yitzchok Drovitcher.

Feiga was known for her *ruach hakodesh* and righteousness. She was called "Feigaleh the prophetess" by her renowned brothers Rabbi Ephraim of Sudylkov and Rabbi Baruch of Medzeboz, who were aware of her ability to see into the future and speak of events before they actually came to be.

Nearly thirty years after Rabbi Nachman was born, and his fame had become widely known, his mother Feiga overheard the Rebbe's followers discussing her son's greatness. "I shall tell you," interjected Feiga, "what a Rebbe you have. From this you will realize his holiness and the holiness of his soul!" She then related events leading up to Rabbi Nachman's birth.

Rabbi Simcha, Feiga's husband, often left home for long periods of *hisbodedus*. On one such occasion, Rabbi Simcha, who had told his wife to expect him for Shabbos, had been away for nearly two weeks. It was Friday morning and Feiga was planning to go to the *mikvah* that night, providing her husband would return. When she performed the mitzvah of taking a tithe from the dough she was preparing for the Shabbos *challahs*, Feiga made use of special unifications of the Holy Names in the hope of determining her husband's whereabouts. To her great dismay, she was shown nothing. Later that day, when she lit the Shabbos candles, she again attempted to attain the required Divine inspiration for learning of Rabbi Simcha's location. Once again she was not shown.

Laying down to rest, Feiga fell asleep and her mother, Adil, appeared to her. Accompanying Adil were the Matriarchs, Sarah, Rivkah, Rachel and Leah. "Don't worry," they told her, "your husband will be home for Shabbos." They then took Feiga and guided her to the "chamber of souls." Taking note of a soul which shone brightly, she was informed that this was the soul of her grandfather, the Baal Shem Tov. Walking on, she spotted yet another luminous soul whose brightness was even greater than the first. "Whose soul is that?" she asked. "This soul is to be given to you," came the reply.

She awoke to find that her husband had already returned home. What had caused his delay? Rabbi Simcha, in describing his journey, told Feiga that he had gotten lost, only to find himself near Medzeboz before Shabbos had come.

Feiga went to the *mikvah* and later that night conceived a child. This child was given the soul which Feiga had seen in her vision. "And this is your Rebbe," she concluded.

According to a second source, Feiga, failing to learn the whereabouts of Rabbi Simcha, through her use of the Sacred Names, decided to go to the grave of the Baal Shem Tov. As it was her custom to light the Shabbos candles a full two hours before nightfall, there was still sufficient time for her to go to her grandfather, to ask that her prayers be answered in his merit. This time, her tears and supplications were not denied, and the Baal Shem Tov came to her with the answer she sought. "He is coming, he is already within close proximity," Feiga's grandfather told her. When she returned home after going to the *mikvah*, Feiga found that Rabbi Simcha had already returned.

After the Rebbe was married, he lived in Ossatin, more than two hundred miles from Medzeboz, his birthplace. Each year, he would travel this distance to visit his parents and be by the grave of the Baal Shem Tov. In 5558 (1798), when Rabbi Nachman set out on his mysterious journey which eventually took him to Kaminetz, he stopped off in Medzeboz. "My son," asked Feiga, "When are you going to go to your great-grandfather?" "Let the Baal Shem Tov come here," replied the Rebbe. One night, while the Rebbe was still with his parents, Rabbi Nachman had a dream in which he was visited by the Baal Shem Tov. He said nothing about this the next morning as he prepared to depart for Kaminetz. Before he left, Feiga again questioned her son, "When will you go to your great-grandfather's grave, now that he has already been to see you."

Feiga's name appears time and again throughout the early history of Breslov Chassidus. Yet, perhaps the greatest tribute to her valor came from the Rebbe himself. Rabbi Nachman cautioned that any one wishing to have a request of Heaven answered in his merit should refer to him as Rabbi Nachman, son of Feiga, (unlike others who after their passing are recalled by their father's name).

Feiga died in Medzeboz on the 19th of Adar 5561 (1801).

Rabbi Yisroel, one of Rabbi Nachman's two brothers, was either the first or second son born to Rabbi Simcha and Feiga (see text p. 2). He was a very weak child, and when he was still young, Rabbi Yisroel became seriously ill. Feiga went to the grave of the Baal Shem Tov, where she cried bitterly for her grandfather to intercede on her son's behalf. Rabbi Yisroel recovered. The Baal Shem Tov later appeared to Feiga to inform her that in his rush to answer her bitter prayers, he had not been particular in chosing the soul which he had given to the child. This explained why afterwards Rabbi Yisroel had the appearance and gait of a dead man. He was known as Rabbi Yisroel Mes, and did not live very long.

According to some sources, Feiga waited a long time before being blessed with a child. During her first pregnancy, the Baal Shem Tov appeared to her in a dream and told her that she would have a son whom she was to name Yisroel. This surprised her, as she knew that her grandfather had asked that no one name their child after him. Feiga would not have paid attention to the dream had it not repeated itself another two times.

When her son was born she named him Yisroel. When he was two years old, Yisroel became ill and died. Feiga took her child to her grandfather's grave. "Is this the child you promised me?" she said, leaving her dead son on the Baal Shem Tov's grave. Later that day, a number of people who had gone to pray at the grave, found the baby alive and well. They returned him to the city where his mother came to get him.

Afterwards, the Baal Shem Tov appeared to Feiga, saying, "Why did you do this? You could have just come yourself to my grave. You caused me great difficulty. The child's soul had already been mixed with millions of others and it was very difficult looking for this soul to return it to the body."

Rabbi Yechiel Zvi, the Rebbe's brother, was also one of Rabbi Nachman's earliest and closest followers. He was most probably named after his mother's father, Rabbi Yechiel, and possibly after Rabbi Zvi, the Baal Shem Tov's son. The Rebbe regarded his brother highly and referred to him as the "completely wise one." He made his home in Kremenchug.

Before Rabbi Yechiel became one of the Rebbe's followers, he came to visit Rabbi Nachman in Medvedevka. At the Shabbos table on Friday night, Rabbi Yechiel was very impressed by his brother's devotions. The next morning, however, Rabbi Yechiel was displeased by what he considered to be unbefitting behavior at the Sabbath meal. He did not appreciate Rabbi Nachman's practice of listening to what seemed to be the mundane conversations of his followers.

That night, Rabbi Yechiel went to see the Rebbe and express his disappointment. "Do you remember what stories were discussed at the the table?" asked Rabbi Nachman. Rabbi Yechiel could not recall even one of the matters spoken of by the followers. "I remember them all!" said the Rebbe. Rabbi Nachman then revealed to his brother how all these stories were in fact rooted in the deep mysteries of the Torah. Their conversation lasted throughout the night, and only ended when the Rebbe realized that the time had come for the morning prayers.

Rabbi Yechiel was astounded by the experience and he could

not eat or sleep on the days which followed. The arousal for God which the Rebbe had motivated by merely explaining these matters so inspired his brother that, from that point on, Rabbi Yechiel subjugated himself entirely to Rabbi Nachman's leadership. He became one of the Rebbe's closest and most devoted followers.

Afterwards, Rabbi Yechiel himself made it a practice of speaking to people about the need for coming closer to God, particularly according to the prescriptions of the Rebbe. Rabbi Nachman supported his brother's efforts and assured him that the conversations he engaged in for this purpose would be elevated by the holy words of Torah spoken at other times. When, in 5567 (1807), Rabbi Yechiel encountered bitter criticism and controversy, the Rebbe wrote him a very encouraging letter in support of his activities and devotion to the Rebbe's ways (see Appendix, Letter #3).

In 5569 (1809), Rabbi Nachman asked his brother to journey to Medzeboz. The Rebbe was seriously ill from the tuberculosis which eventually took his life, and he wanted Rabbi Yechiel to pray for his recovery at the grave of the Baal Shem Tov. Upon occasion, Rabbi Nathan also found it rewarding to turn to Rabbi Yechiel for encouragement, as he did in Uman right before the Rebbe's death.

Rabbi Yechiel did not live for very long. He died not long after the Rebbe, leaving one known child, a daughter, Feiga.

Perel, the Rebbe's sister, was the only daughter of Rabbi Simcha and Feiga. Her uncle, Rabbi Baruch of Medzeboz, would often ask her about the Rebbe's health and well-being. Perel was highly regarded by Rabbi Baruch and Rabbi Ephraim and she was the one who tried to restore peace when a dispute developed between Rabbi Nachman and her uncle from Medzeboz.

Perel's first marriage ended in divorce. The Rebbe advised his sister to leave her husband, who was not a well man. She later married Rabbi Pinchas Meir.

Perel lived in Chmelnick before moving to *Eretz Yisroel*. When Rabbi Nathan visited Safed in 5582 (1822), he met the Rebbe's sister who had recently been widowed from her second husband.

Sashia, Rabbi Nachman's first wife, was the daughter of Rabbi Ephraim of Ossatin. She was married to the Rebbe in 5545 (1785) and was mother to all his children.

When her son, Shlomo Ephraim, died in 5566 (1806), Sashia was greatly grieved by his loss. It was her lament to Rabbi Nathan and Rabbi Naftali that the Rebbe did not take care of himself, that he traveled too much and that he did not intercede to prevent the child's death, which moved Rabbi Nachman to speak of what a true loss Shlomo Ephraim's death had been for the world.

When Rabbi Nachman was in Ostrog in 5567 (1807), he sent his attendant to bring Sashia from Breslov. The Rebbe's wife had been suffering from consumption and he wanted her to be treated by the well known and righteous Dr. Gordon. Sashia joined the Rebbe in Ostrog but she preferred to be treated by physicians in Zaslov, where she had family.

Sashia died in Zaslov on the eve of Shavuos. Many of the Rebbe's followers, who had come to Zaslov to be with Rabbi Nachman for the holiday, were there. The Rebbe was at Sashia's side when she died. He later told Rabbi Nathan that despite his grief and confusion at the time of her passing, he nevertheless had succeeded in providing his wife's soul with what it required. He also later said that had he realized the greatness of one's first marriage, he would have made sure that she lived.

Rabbi Nachman's second wife, whose name is not known, was the daughter of Rabbi Yechezkel Trachtenberg of Brody. The Rebbe carried on with his mysterious journey of 5567 (1807) even after his first wife's death and he came to Brody during Tammuz. Disguising himself, he visited the houses of many rich people. When he entered the house of Reb Yechezkel, he found Reb Yechezkel's wife and widowed daughter discussing possible marriage partners. "I want such a man," said the daughter when she saw Rabbi Nachman.

The Rebbe then spoke with Reb Yechezkel and told him he was willing to offer a large dowry — three hundred rendels — to marry his daughter. The *tana'im* were arranged soon afterwards in nearby Radvil. On his way back to Breslov after the engagement, Rabbi Nachman contracted tuberculosis. He nevertheless married Reb Yechezkel's daughter, who accepted the Rebbe's condition that they not live together as man and wife.

The wedding took place some two months later (Elul, 5567) in Vatchak near Breslov. And though she was later to say of the Rebbe, "I imagine you, I call you, but I never knew you" (*Shir HaKavod*), Rabbi Nachman's second wife was the one who arranged for a special building to be built around his grave.

> Rabbi Nachman once said, "What will happen with me I do not know, but this I have achieved from God – Mashiach will be one of my descendants." The Rebbe and his wife Sashia had eight children, six daughters and two sons. The Rebbe charged us to respect and honor his children, calling them very precious trees which will produce very wondrous fruits. He added, "I have taken my offspring from the world of Atzilus.

Adil, Rabbi Nachman's first child, was born in Ossatin in 5547 (1787). She was named after the Rebbe's grandmother, the Baal Shem Tov's daughter.

On Rosh Chodesh Elul, 5560 (1800), Adil was married to Rabbi Yoske, the son of Rabbi Avraham Dov, the Rav of Chmelnick. Among those who came to Chmelnick for the celebration were many of the Baal Shem Tov's descendants and members of the Rebbe's own family, including Rabbi Nachman's mother Feiga and her two renowned brothers, Rabbi Baruch and Rabbi Ephraim. Feiga, whom her brothers called a prophetess, said that she had also seen the Baal Shem Tov at the wedding.

Rabbi Nachman valued Adil's opinions and personally discussed many issues with her. After the Rebbe's death, Rabbi Nathan was known to place credence in Adil's dreams, though he was loathe to pay attention to dreams in general.

Adil gave birth to a number of children during the early years of marriage, but each one died in infancy. Rabbi Nachman once visited his daughter and Rabbi Yoske while they were still sitting *shivah* for one of these children. Noticing their grief, the Rebbe offered them consolation, "Believe me, everyone will yet envy you for your children." To his son-in-law he said, "You will live to see children..." Then turning to Adil, he added, "And children's children!"

It was Rabbi Nachman's custom to spend the last day of Pesach in Adil's home. She would honor her father each year by serving him two *kneidelech*. Once, when Adil brought the *kneidelech* the Rebbe smiled and said, "In reward for these two *kneidelech* you will have two children who will be the envy of the world." Adil did indeed have two outstanding children, R. Avraham Dov and Rivkah Miriam, though for the rest of her days she regretted having served only two *kneidelech* and no more.

Rabbi Yoske, as the Rebbe predicted, lived to see children. However, he died very young and never knew his grandchildren. Adil, on the other hand, lived for sixty-seven years, during which time she merited seeing her children's children — just as the Rebbe had indicated.

Some time after Rabbi Yoske died, Adil's sister Sarah also passed away and she married Rabbi Yitzchok Isaac, Sarah's widower. Adil's daughter Rivkah Miriam and Rabbi Yitzchok Isaac's son, Reb Simcha Baruch, were also husband and wife.

Though she was the oldest of Rabbi Nachman's children, Adil lived longer than any of her sisters. She died in 5624 (1864), and was buried in the Breslov cemetery. Before she died, Adil was overheard saying, "Welcome, father."

Rabbi Avraham Dov, son of Adil and Rabbi Yoske, was born as a result of the honor his mother had shown the Rebbe. He married the daughter of Moshe Chenkes, known as Reb Moshe beHaRav, one of Rabbi Nachman's wealthy partners. When his father-in-law joined those who persecuted Rabbi Nathan during the years 5595-99 (1835-39), Rabbi Avraham Dov divorced Moshe Chenkes' daughter. In 5596 (1836) he remarried, taking the daughter of Rabbi Dov of Tcherin, a disciple of the Rebbe, as his wife.

Rabbi Avraham Dov, known as Reb Avraham Ber'nyu, was very wealthy and contributed generously to help Rabbi Nathan publish the Rebbe's teachings. Undistracted by his riches, the Rebbe's grandson was known for his righteousness and fear of Heaven.

When Rabbi Avraham Sternhartz (see Bibliography) was a young boy, he was sent to join Rabbi Avraham Dov for a meal. The young boy watched his host carefully, while the table was set with a meal befitting a king. As soon as Rabbi Avraham Dov put the first spoonful in his mouth, he turned his eyes Heavenward and sat in awesome *devekus* and longing for God. He repeated this procedure with each additional spoonful, using his physical wealth as a means for spiritual devotion.

Rabbi Nachman, the Rav of Tcherin, once said: "People make a big mistake. They think that the thirty-six hidden Tzaddikim in each generation have to be poor and live in abstract poverty. Not so! They might even be like our Reb Avraham Ber'nyu."

Rabbi Avraham Dov died in 5640 (1880). Of his children, a son and two daughters died during their childhood. He was survived by his son, Reb Yosef.

Sarah, Rabbi Nachman's second daughter, was born in 5550 (1790), after the Rebbe had taken up residence in Medvedevka. Sorke, as she was known, was the first of the Rebbe's daughters to become engaged. This took place before Rabbi Nachman's pilgrimage to the Holy Land in 5558 (1798) at the behest of her future father-in-law, Rabbi Leib Dubravner, who was willing to pay the high price exacted by the Rebbe for his daughter's hand in marriage.

On Rosh Chodesh Nissan 5563 (1803), Sarah was married to Rabbi Leib's son, Rabbi Yitzchok Isaac, in Medvedevka, amidst great celebration and splendor. At the wedding, which was held in the house of the wealthy Reb Meir and his wife Feiga, the Rebbe sang a melody with which he summoned the Patriarchs. Rabbi Nathan, who had made a special effort to attend, later described how Rabbi Nachman had danced for the bride and what a spiritually uplifting experience it had been for those there to witness it.

Each of Rabbi Nachman's daughters excelled in the virtues particular to the outstanding Jewish women of the ages. "My daughters have been blessed with a divine spirit nearing prophecy," he said, "and I am not even talking [about the qualities] of my daughter Sarah."

A few of the letters (see Appendix, Letters #7, 8) sent by the Rebbe to his daughter and son-in-law indicate just how highly he regarded Sarah. In one such correspondence he writes that he hopes to visit soon, looking forward to spending time with her and enjoying her wise and pious conversation; comparing Sarah to a myrtle branch growing in the wilderness. For her part, Sarah was exceedingly humble and did not take her father's praise at face value. "You see," she cried when reading his letter, "My father must see how lowly I am. Why else would he make such an effort to give me encouragement through his praises."

Rabbi Nachman spent much time discussing the subject of hospitality with Sarah. He very much wanted to impress upon her the importance of this mitzvah. Once she had come to appreciate its great value, however, Sarah grew concerned, fearing that it was not possible to ever completely fulfill one's obligation in this regard. Rabbi Nachman assured her, saying that all that was required was "another piece of roll and a part of the tablecloth."

Sarah was often ill during her life. Her anguish pained the Rebbe, and he often spoke of her suffering. Once, when she was greatly distressed by a toothache, Rabbi Nachman advised her to be happy and this would bring about her cure. "How can I be happy?" she wondered, feeling that her pain was too much to overcome. "Even if it is hard to be happy," replied the Rebbe, "you must force the happiness to come." Rabbi Nachman explained to his daughter that from the imagined joy which she felt despite her pain, she would eventually come to such a real experience of joy that she would begin to dance. Through this she would be cured. Sarah took her father's advice to heart. Closing the shutters of her house, she began to dance and before long her pain had disappeared.

Another time, when Sarah was ill, Rabbi Nachman suggested that she picture herself as being better off now than before she had been beset by her pains. This too seemed an impossibility for Sarah, whose anguish gave her no peace. But the Rebbe did not give up, and asked her to follow his instructions. The power of one's thoughts are very great, he explained. By thinking positively about what is yours, you can actually turn your situation to the good.

On yet one other occasion, the Rebbe visited his daughter, only to find her bedridden and in great agony. Rabbi Nachman was grieved by her suffering and intently listened to the details of her illness. A short while later, the Rebbe fell asleep and the Baal Shem Tov appeared to him in his dream. Rabbi Nachman's great-grandfather advised him that he need not worry and quoted the verse, "Great deliverance He gives to His king; and shows steadfast love for His annointed, to David and his seed, evermore" (Psalms 18:51). The Rebbe took this to mean that Sarah's healing could be secured by telling her a story about the deliverance which God performed for a Tzaddik. Upon awakening, the Rebbe took a seat at Sarah's bedside and related an awesome story about the MaHaRShA (Rabbi Shmuel Eliezer Eidels c. 1580). As soon as he finished the story, Sarah rose from her bed, completely recovered. She subsequently told over this story to other sick people and they too returned to health.

After her marriage, Sarah made her home in Kremenchug

where her father-in-law lived. Nearly four years later (5567, 1807) she was pregnant with her first child. Rabbi Nachman, who customarily traveled from Breslov to Medvedevka to be with his followers for Shabbos Shirah, made an unexpected stopover in Kremenchug on his return trip in order to be with his daughter when she gave birth. He waited there for several weeks, during which time he was very distressed. Sarah finally gave birth to her first son, Yisroel. After the *bris milah*, Sarah again took ill and his tremendous grief devitalized the Rebbe's spirit. He quickly left Kremenchug and returned home.

Two other sons, Simcha Baruch and Ephraim, and a daughter, Feiga Sashia, were born to Sarah and her husband, Rabbi Yitzchok Isaac. Of all his grandchildren, Rabbi Nachman reserved the highest praise for Sarah's children. He even indicated that the Mashiach would be one of her descendants.

Rabbi Yisroel, as mentioned earlier, was born in the winter of 5567 (1807). When he was close to four years old, he was with the Rebbe for Rosh HaShanah in Uman. Rabbi Nachman asked his grandson to pray on his behalf and then used the child's simple prayer as an example for his followers to follow (see text p. 196).

Rabbi Yisroel was married ten years later to the granddaughter of Rabbi Mordechai of Tchernoble. At the wedding, Rabbi Mordechai referred to Rabbi Nachman's followers, many of whom had come to join in the celebration, as Tzaddikim in their own right.

Sarah's second son, Rabbi Simcha Baruch, was married in Kremenchug to his cousin, Rivkah Miriam, Adil's daughter, on Rosh Chodesh Kislev, 5593 (1833). This took place not long after Sarah's widower, Rabbi Yitzchok Isaac, had himself been married to her sister Adil, whose husband had died some time earlier.

Feiga Sashia, Sarah's only daughter, was married to Reb Ephraim, a grandson of the Rebbe's uncle, Rabbi Baruch of Medzeboz.

Sarah's third son, Rabbi Ephraim, was born on Chanukah, 5592 (1832). He was well known for his knowledge of Torah, fear of Heaven and righteousness. Rabbi Ephraim had two children, Reb Nachman and Feiga (see Family Tree). But Sarah did not live to see the bris milah of her son, as she died the day after he was born, on erev Shabbos Chanukah (27 Kislev) 5592.

Miriam, the Rebbe's third daughter, was born in 5552 (1792) in Medvedevka. She was about seven years old when Rabbi Nachman arranged a marriage agreement for her. This happened during his visit to Tiberias while on a pilgrimage to the Holy Land. When he agreed to Miriam's betrothal to the grandson of Rabbi Menachem Mendel of Vitebsk, the Rebbe said, "It must be God's will that my daughter come to Eretz Yisroel. The truth of his words were only evidenced a full decade later when Miriam settled in the Holy Land. She never did marry the Vitebsker's grandson, who died soon after Rabbi Nachman left for Europe.

During Elul of 5560 (1800), right after her sister Adil's wedding, Miriam was engaged to Rabbi Pinchas. He was the son of Rabbi Leibush Segel, the Rabbi of Volochisk and disciple of the Mezritcher Magid. They were married during the first week of Cheshvon 5565 (1805), in Volochisk.

On the Shabbos preceding the wedding, Rabbi Nachman was very happy and joined in the dancing. When the song which is customarily used to request the presence of close friends and relatives to the celebration was sung, the Rebbe sang along and invited the souls of the Baal Shem Tov, Rabbi Nachman Horodenker and his mother Feiga. At the wedding, Miriam honored Rabbi Leibush's objection and refused to dance the traditional mitzvah tantz with the Rebbe. This disrespect for her father's custom was later taken to be the reason for her not having left any surviving children. It was also understood to have prompted Rabbi Nachman's hinting to Miriam's eventually having to undergo yibum (the leviratic marriage). The Rebbe alluded to this when he taught Likutey Moharan I, 21, which speaks about the Biblical Miriam being punished with the "aspect" of *yibum* for having shown disrespect for Moses.

That summer, Miriam's father-in-law, Rabbi Leibush, decided to settle in *Eretz Yisroel*. He was taking his teenage son Rabbi Pinchas with him and wanted his daughter-in-law to come along. However, Miriam was not willing to leave her home. Rabbi Nachman also objected to her going, saying that one of his reasons was his fear they would encounter highwaymen, who were prevalent at the time. At one point, Miriam's divorce from her husband of six months seemed imminent.

Four years later, in 5569 (1809), one of Rabbi Pinchas' brothers came to the Rebbe. He and a number of his brothers, who had remained in Europe, were on their way to join their father and Rabbi Pinchas in the Holy Land. This brother was willing to take responsibility for Miriam's safety. For her part, Miriam was ready to go. Rabbi Nachman consented, saying, "I will give her — to you!" This comment was later understood when Rabbi Pinchas died childless and Miriam wed this brother-in-law in the leviratic marriage. She had a son with this second husband, but the child died very young.

Miriam left for the Holy Land during the period of the "Three Weeks." Rabbi Nachman accompanied her for a long distance out of the city. He refused to travel by coach adding that, "One must be willing to go on foot to *Eretz Yisroel*."

Miriam's sister, Sarah, came to Breslov to see her off. Soon after Miriam left, she sent a letter to her father from Odessa telling him that all was well and that she was happy. Rabbi Nathan was left as overseer of her property and he sent large sums yearly to Miriam and her husband for as long as they lived.

Miriam was seventeen when she left Breslov and she lived in Israel for nearly thirteen years. She died in the spring of 5582 (1822). The Rebbe's daughter is buried in a cave together with her father-in-law, her husband and young child in what is today the famous cemetery of Safed, not far from Rabbi Shimon's grave (see Appendix, Followers).

A fourth daughter was born during the early part of 5558 (1798), while Rabbi Nachman was on the way back from his mysterious journey to Kaminetz. She died right after the Rebbe returned home, even before she had been given a name.

The Rebbe said that others like her would also be taken from him because of the spiritual *tikkunim* he had undertaken to achieve.

Chaya, Rabbi Nachman's fifth child and fifth daughter, was born in 5561 (1801), while the Rebbe was living in Zlatipolia. After her birth, a number of days went by and Rabbi Nachman inexplicably had not given her name. Rabbi Chaikel, one of Rabbi Nachman's close followers, spoke to him about this and expressed his fear that it would only bring further talk against the Rebbe and his followers. Rabbi Nachman, whose way it was never to be obstinate, replied, "Then let her be called Chaya." Later that same day, word arrived from Medzeboz that the Rebbe's mother, Feiga, had died (on Adar 19). Everyone, and particularly Rabbi Chaikel, realized the reason for Rabbi Nachman's behavior. The Rebbe knew of his mother's passing through *ruach hakodesh* and had obviously intended to name his newborn daughter Feiga after her.

Chaya was ten years old when her father died. Before his death, the Rebbe had attempted to find a marriage partner for her. Of the numerous willing suitors, only one match — with the son of Rabbi Yaakov Yosef Lubarski of Zlatipolia, one of the Rebbe's long time and respected followers — found favor in Rabbi Nachman's eyes. But the arrangements for this match could not be concluded during the Rebbe's lifetime. In his will, Rabbi Nachman asked that three hundred rubels be given to Chaya, to provide what would be needed for her marriage.

After the Rebbe died, Rabbi Nathan took it upon himself to find a match for Chaya. Rabbi Yaakov Yosef sent a letter to Rabbi Nathan saying that he was still very much interested in his son marrying the Rebbe's daughter. However, the problem, as it had been during Rabbi Nachman's lifetime, was that he did not have the financial means for undertaking such a prestigious match. Rabbi Nathan knew that the Rebbe wanted this marriage, and had even indicated that it would one day take place. Before Purim 5572 (1812), nearly a year and a half later, the arrangements for this match were finally concluded.

Chaya was married to Rabbi Zalman Lubarski on the second of Elul, 5574 (1814), in Medvedevka. Their only child was born sometime between 5575 and 5579 (1815 and 1819). Chaya named the baby after her father and he came to be known as Rabbi Nachman Chayalas.

Rabbi Zalman did not live very long after that. Chaya's second husband was Rabbi Aharon Zaslavski, the Rav of Kremenchug. Rabbi Aharon was the grandson of Rabbi Shneur Zalman, and a son of the *Baal HaTanya's* daughter Freida. They had no children by this marriage.

It is not known how long Chaya lived.

Rabbi Nachman Chayalas lived in Tulchin. He is mentioned often in Rabbi Nathan's letters to his son Rabbi Yitzchok, who also lived there. Rabbi Nathan encouraged their friendship and suggested they build a relationship based upon Torah study and devotion. The Rebbe's grandson was married to the daughter of Rabbi Dov, the son of Rabbi Shlomo of Karlin. At the end of his life he moved to Uman, where he died in 5649 (1889).

Feiga, Rabbi Nachman's sixth child was born in 5563 (1803). He named his daughter after his mother, who had died some two years earlier. For reasons unknown, Feiga was sent to Ladizin where she was cared for by a nurse. When she fell ill, the family turned to a gentile to try and cure her.

Feiga died the following summer. Rabbi Nachman had been away from Breslov on his customary Shabbos Nachamu visit to the Tcherin-Medvedevka vicinity to be with his followers. On the return journey, the Rebbe indicated that he was aware of her passing through *ruach hakodesh*. However, when he returned home the family kept her death from him and because of this he did not sit *shivah* at the time. This took place at the close of 5564 (1804). A little more than a month later, on the Shabbos immediately following Rosh HaShanah, 5565 (1805), the Rebbe insisted that his oldest daughter tell him the truth about Feiga's passing. After nightfall, he sat an hour's time mourning her death.

Later that same night, Rabbi Nachman revealed to his disciples that Feiga had come to him complaining that the gentile hired to cure her had been a sorcerer. The witchcraft he used had blemished her soul. The Rebbe's insistence that he be told of her death was intended as a *tikkun* for this.

Shlomo Ephraim, Rabbi Nachman's first son, was born around Rosh Chodesh Nissan, 5565 (1805). At the *bris*, the Rebbe himself served as *sandek* and *mohel*, while Rabbi Nathan was given the mitzvah of *periah*.

Sometime during the first year of his life, Shlomo Ephraim contacted tuberculosis. When Rabbi Nachman handed over his manuscript of the "Burned Book" to Rabbi Nathan in early summer of 5566 (1806), the Rebbe entreated him to pray for the child. Rabbi Nachman knew that Shlomo Ephraim's illness was directly related to the secrets revealed in this book. The Rebbe himself traveled to the Baal Shem Tov's grave in Medzeboz to pray for his son. He stayed there for some time, but departed realizing that he had not succeeded on his son's behalf.

Shlomo Ephraim died that Sivan, while the Rebbe was still on his way back from Medzeboz. Rabbi Nachman later spoke of the greatness that the child could have one day achieved. He likened the reason for Shlomo Ephraim's death to that of the ARI's son, who died because of the secret his father had revealed.

A few weeks later, on the yahrzeit of the ARI z'l, the Rebbe set out on his usual summer visit to Medvedevka and Tcherin. On the way, he spoke about the Mashiach and revealed his *Megilas Sesarim*. Rabbi Nachman told his followers that the Mashiach's coming had been readied and that he knew the exact year, month and day when this was to have taken place. But now this was not going to happen in the near future — the loss of Shlomo Ephraim had caused the delay.

Yaakov, the Rebbe's eighth and last child, was born about half a year after his brother, Shlomo Ephraim, had died. His *bris milah* took place on a Shabbos right before Chanukah 5567 (1807). He died not long afterwards.

Rabbi Nachman's Yarmulka

photo: Joel Fishman

BIBLIOGRAPHY

GLOSSARY

INDEX

Adas Tzaddikim. A collection of stories about the Baal Shem Tov and his followers by Rabbi Michael Levi Frumkin. First published in 1865. Not known where published.

Alim LeTerufah. Collection of letters by Rabbi Nathan (ben Naftali Hertz) Sternhartz of Nemirov (1780-1845), first published in Berdichov, 1896, and in Jerusalem, 1911. A more complete edition was published by Rabbi Aaron Leib Tziegelman in Jerusalem, 1930. [We have used the Jerusalem, 1968 edition.] Rabbi Nathan was the foremost disciple of Rabbi Nachman, and publisher of many of his works.

Asifas Zekenim. An anthology of commentaries on Tractate *Rosh HaShanah*. The author, Rabbi Nathan Zvi, Rabbi of Monkbib and Vengrab, included Chassidic stories in his introduction. First printed in Vengrab, 1928.

Aveneha Barzel. Stories and teachings of Rabbi Nachman and his disciples, collected by Rabbi Shmuel Horowitz (1903-1973), first printed in Jerusalem, 1935. [We have used the Jerusalem, 1972, edition, printed together with *Kochavey Or* (q.v.).] The author was an important Breslover leader in Jerusalem.

Avos. See Talmud.

Ayeh. An English translation on lesson #12 in *Likutey Moharan* II and other Breslover literature related to that lesson. It sets forth the principle of finding the Divine in even the most profane places and situations. Published by the Breslov Research Institute in Jerusalem, 1984.

Aylimah Rabasi. The deepest of Rabbi Moshe Cordovero's Kabbalistic writings and the only one which touches upon the complex subject of the *partzufim*. It also explains many philosophical questions according to the Kabbalah. First printed part in Brody and part in Lvov in 1881.

Azamra. An English translation on lesson #282 in *Likutey Moharan* I and other Breslover literature related to that lesson. It sets forth the principle of finding the good points in others and in oneself. Published by the Breslov Research Institute, Jerusalem, 1984.

Bais Rebbe. A biography of Rabbi Shneur Zalman of Liadi and his descendents. Written by Rabbi Chaim Meir Heilman. First published in Berdichov, 1900.

Bechinas Olam. A philosophical and ethical discourse in verse by Rabbi Yedayah Hapnini ben Rabbi Avraham Badarshi who was the major apologist for the scholars of Provence when they were condemned by the RaSHBA for the study of philosophy. First published in Mantua in 1478.

Bender, Rabbi Levi Yitzchok. A prominent elder of Breslover Chassidim today, Rabbi Levi Yitzchok was a student of Rabbi Avraham (Chazan HaLevi) ben Reb Nachman of Tulchin (q.v.), author of *Biur HaLikutim, Kochavey Or, Yemey HaTalaos* etc. A resident of Uman and its environs for over twenty five years, Rabbi Bender arrived in Israel in 1949 and now resides in Jerusalem.

Berachos. See Talmud.

Bikurim. See Talmud.

Biur HaLikutim. Commentary on *Likutey Moharan* (q.v.) by Rabbi Avraham (Chazan HaLevi) ben Reb Nachman of Tulchin, (1849-1917) printed in part in Jerusalem, 1908, and in greater part, B'nei B'rak, 1967.

Bromberg. The series *Migedoley HaTorah VehaChassidus* single volume biographies of the great Torah leaders of Europe. The first volume on Rabbis Chaim and Yechezkel Shraga Halbershtam was published in Jerusalem, in 1949. Our text usually refers to the volume on Rabbi Levi Yitzchok of Berdichov.

Burstyn, Rabbi Nachman. Oral teachings, by a leading figure in Breslov in Jerusalem.

Butzina Denehora HaShalem. Combining *Butzina Denehora*, a collection of the teachings of Rabbi Baruch of Mezeboz together with *Makor Baruch*, Rabbi Reuven Margolies' biography of Rabbi Baruch. *Butzina Denehora* was first published in Lvov, 1880, and *Makor Baruch* in 1938.

Chachmey Yisroel. A collection of short biographies of leading Rabbis of the sixth millenia (since Creation) by Rabbi Dovid Hachakhmi (Veissbrod). First addition published 1958, second edition 1980. Published by Tiferes HaSefer, B'nei B'rak.

Chagigah. See Talmud.

Chayay Moharan. Important biographical work on Rabbi Nachman, by his chief disciple, Rabbi Nathan of Nemirov (see *Alim LeTerufah*), printed with notes by Rabbi Nachman of Tcherin, Lemberg, 1874. [We have used the Jerusalem, 1962, edition and the newly released Jerusalem, 1983, edition with vowels.]

Chayay Moharan HaShmotos. A section printed in the end of *Chayay Moharan* including omissions from previous sections of text.

Degel Machaneh Ephraim. A major Chassidic work arranged according to the weekly Torah readings and quoting prolifically the teachings of the Baal Shem Tov. Written by Rabbi Nachman's uncle, Rabbi Moshe Chaim Ephraim of Sudylkov. First printed in 1808.

Eser Oros (part of *Eser Kedushos* or *Zchus Yisroel*). A collection of descriptions of Chassidic leaders related to the author, Rabbi Yisroel Berger, the Rabbi of Bucharest. It includes teachings, sayings, customs and stories of each Rabbi. First printed in sections between 1906-28.

Etz Chaim. The major classic of Kabbalah, based on the teachings of the ARI (Rabbi Yitzchok Luria, 1534-1572), and written by Rabbi Chaim Vital (1542-1620), and first published in

Koretz, 1782. Both the ARI, and his disciple Rabbi Chaim Vital, were the leaders of the Safed school of Kabbalah. Many consider the ARI to be the greatest of all Kabbalists.

HaShmotos Chayay Moharan. Unpublished manuscript including material deleted from the printed text of *Chayay Moharan*. Recorded by Rabbi Alter Tepliker, in 1898, author of *Meshivas Nefesh* (q.v.).

HaTamim. A periodical published by Chasidei Chabad in Warsaw from 1935-1938 and reprinted several times in a single volume. It includes much historical and biographical information about early Chassidim.

Hillulah Rabbah DeTzaddikaya. A list of the Tzaddikim with their *yahrzeits*. Also includes various prayers to say at their gravesides. Published by R. Yehoshua Heshel Drucker in Lemberg 1863.

Igros Hakodesh. A collection of letters from the leaders of the Chassidic movement in Israel primarily Rabbi Menachem Mendel of Vitebsk and Rabbi Avraham Kalisker. Publication date and place unknown.

Igros Kodesh. A collection of letters of Rabbi Shneur Zalman of Liadi including many hitherto unpublished manuscripts. Published by Kehoth (Chabad) 1983.

Ir Vilna. An authoratative collection of biographies of Rabbis and Roshei Yeshivos in the city of Vilna, including numerous tomb-stone inscriptions. By Rabbi Hillel Noach Magid. Printed in Vilna 1900.

Kahal Chassidim. Stories of the Baal Shem Tov and his disciples. Collected by Rabbi Aaron Valden, author of *Shem HaGedolim HeChadash* (q.v.). Printed in Warsaw, publication date omitted.

Keser Shem Tov. An anthology of the teachings of the Baal Shem Tov, collected from the works of Rabbi Yaakov Yosef of Polonnoye, and edited by Rabbi Aharon b'reb Zvi HaCohen of

Apta. It was first printed in two volumes in 1794 in Zolkova.

Kesubos. See Talmud.

Kiddushin. See Talmud.

Kochavey Or. Stories and teachings of Rabbi Nachman and his disciples, by Rabbi Avraham ben Reb Nachman of Tulchin, (see *Biur HaLikutim*) first printed in Jerusalem, 1896. [We have used the Jerusalem, 1972, edition.]

Koenig, Rabbi Gedaliah Aharon (ben Eliezer Mordechai) 1921-1980. A leading disciple of Rabbi Avraham Sternhartz. Rabbi Koenig transcribed *Tovos Zichronos* (q.v.) and was the author of *Chayay Nefesh* and other unpublished manuscripts on Breslover Chassidus.

Kuntres HaHisbodedus. An anthology of sources outside of Breslov Chassidism endorsing the practice of *hisbodedus* (private prayer and meditation). Written by Rabbi Aryeh Kaplan (1935-1983), the author of our present text, as an appendix to *Hishtap'khuth HaNefesh*, published in Jerusalem by the Breslov Research Institute in 1980.

Likutey Amorim: Tanya. The major work of Rabbi Shneur Zalman of Liadi. A guide to divine devotion and battling the evil inclination for the *beinonim* (middle category) and basis of Chabad Chassidism. First published in Slevita 1798.

Likutey Amorim, by Rabbi Menachem Mendel of Vitebsk. One of several works by Rabbi Menachem Mendel on Chassidic teachings in great depth. First published in two volumes in Lvov in 1911.

Likutey Halachos. Monumental work on Breslover thought and Kabbalah, following the order of the *Shulchan Arukh* (q.v.), by Rabbi Nathan of Nemirov, Rabbi Nachman's foremost disciple. First part printed in Iassi (Jasse), 1843, with subsequent sections published through 1861. [We have used the eight volume, Jerusalem, 1970, edition.]

Likutey Moharan. Primary work of Rabbi Nachman of Breslov, first printed in Ostrog, 1808, and in more than 40 subsequent editions. See Appendix, Rabbi Nachman's Writings.

Likutey Moharan Tinyana. The second part of *Likutey Moharan*, first printed in Moghilov, 1811. The two sections of *Likutey Moharan* were printed together in Breslov, 1821, and in all subsequent editions.

Ma'aseh MiBitachon. Story #29 translated in *Rabbi Nachman's Stories* by Rabbi Aryeh Kaplan, on page 485. First published by Rabbi Tzvi Dov ben Avraham of Berdichov, Jerusalem, 1905. (See below Rabbi Nachman's Stories).

Ma'asios U'Mashalim. Stories by Rabbi Nachman, preserved by his disciple, Rabbi Naftali of Nemirov (d. 1809), printed as part of *Sippurim Niflaim* (q.v.), 1849, p. 14 ff.

Maaver Yabok. A collection of laws concerning visiting the ill and customs pertaining to death and mourning by Rabbi Aharon Brechiya (ben Moshe) of Modina, d. 1639. The author was a disciple of Rabbi Menachen Azarya of Panu, the leading Kabbalist of Italy, and was said to have been taught Torah by a Magid (angel). Rabbi Aharon Brechiya wrote a commentary to *Tikkuney HaZohar*. The *Maaver Yabok* was first published in Mantua in 1625.

Magen Avraham. Major commentary on *Shulchan Arukh, Orach Chaim* qv. Written by Rabbi Avraham Gombiner of Ostrog. First published in 1692, in Direnport.

Manuscript. An unpublished collection of stories about Rabbi Nachman, Rabbi Nathan and their followers. Compiled from oral traditions as told by Rabbi Levi Yitzchok Bender (q.v.).

Mazkeres Shem HaGedolim. A collection of biographies and teachings of 18 disciples of the Baal Shem Tov. Published in Pieterkov 1908.

Megillah. See Talmud.

Meiras Eynayim. Stories, descriptions and praises of the Baal Shem Tov, collected from various Chassidic works. Collected by Rabbi Nathan Nata HaCohen of Kalbiel, and edited by Rabbi Shimon Menachem Mendel Vidnik of Givarchav. Originally printed as an appendix to *Sefer HaBaal Shem Tov* in Lodz, 1938, and reprinted in 1921 as an appendix to *Shevachey HaBaal Shem Tov*.

Meor Enayim. A major work in Chassidic literature arranged according to the weekly Torah portions and the holidays by Rabbi Menachem Nochum Twerski, Magid of Tchernoble, a major Chassidic leader in the Ukraine and a close friend of Rabbi Nachman. Many excerpts from this book are included in Rabbi Nachman of Tcherin's (q.v.) anthology *Derekh Chassidim*. *Meor Eynayim* was first published in Slovita 1798.

Meoros HaGedolim. Chassidic stories published in Bilgorey 1911.

Meshivas Nefesh. Excerpts from Rabbi Nachman's and Rabbi Nathan's writings concerning strengthening oneself against despair, as the Rebbe said, "Despair does not exist at all." Collected by Rabbi Alter (Moshe Yehoshua) Bezhilianski of Teplik. First published in Lemberg in 1902 by Rabbi Zvi Veissleib and Rabbi Yisrael Halpern (Karduner). Translated into English by Avraham Greenbaum, under the title "Restore My Soul," and published by the Breslov Research Institute in Jerusalem, 1980.

Mesillas Yesharim. The best known work of the great Italian Kaballist, Rabbi Moshe Chaim Luzzatto, 1707-1746. It is a guide to self perfection based on the teaching of Rabbi Pinchas Ben Yair (*Avodah Zarah* 20b). First printing was in Amsterdam 1740.

Michtevey Baal Ha-Tanya U-Vnei Doro (sometimes referred to in our text as *Igros Baal HaTanya*). A collection of correspondence between Rabbi Shneur Zalman of Liadi and his contemporaries, accompanied by explanatory footnotes by the editor, Rabbi Dovid Zvi Heilman. Published in Jerusalem in 1953.

MiGedoley HaChassidus. Biographies of Rabbi Levi Yitzchok of Berdichov, Rabbi Pinchas of Koretz, Rabbi Menachem Nochum of Tchernoble, Rabbi Mordechai of Tchernoble, Rabbi Menachem Mendel of Riminov and Rabbi Shalom Rokeach of Belz. Written by Rabbi Mattisya Yechiel Gutman and published in Bilgorey between 1930-35.

Mishnas Yoel. Biography of Rabbi Shneur Zalman of Liadi by Rabbi Yoel Diskind, accompanied by a collection of *takanos* (directives) and letters. Edited by Rabbi Yitzchok Orenstein. Published in Jerusalem 1941.

Nachal Novea. An introduction to Breslover Chassidism including stories, sayings and samplings from Breslover literature. Published in Jerusalem by R. Yitzchok Isaac Zilberman in 1961.

Nedarim. See Talmud.

Nevey Tzaddikim. Historical bibliography of all Breslover works, by Rabbi Nathan Tzvi Koenig, published in B'nei B'rak, 1969.

Niddah. See Talmud.

Nodeh BiYehuda. Responsa of the renowned Rabbi Yechezkel Segel Landau, chief Rabbi of Prague. First published in Prague from 1776-1811. See Appendix: Tzaddikim.

Ohel Rochel, by Rabbi Chaim Lieberman. A collection of articles that were previously printed in periodicals, including a section on the relationship between Chassidic leaders and the early *maskilim*. Published in New York 1981.

Or HaGalil. A collection of biographies of the Chassidic leaders who settled in Safed and Tiberias, particularly in the major Chassidic *aliya* of 5537 (1777). Edited by Rabbi Bezalel Friedman and published by Rabbi Yaakov Shalom Gefner in Jerusalem 1976.

Orach Chaim. First section of the *Shulchan Arukh* (q.v.) dealing with prayers and holy days.

Outpouring of the Soul. An English translation of *Hishtap'khuth HaNefesh*, an anthology of Breslover teachings concerning *hisbodedus* (personal prayer and meditation) assembled by Rabbi Alter (Moshe Yehoshua) Bezhilianski of Teplik, and translated by Rabbi Aryeh Kaplan. Published by the Breslov Research Institute in New York in 1980.

Parparaos LeChokhmah. Major commentary on *Likutey Moharan* (q.v.) by Rabbi Nachman of Tcherin, first published in Lemberg, 1876.

Pri Etz. A Chassidic commentary on the Torah by Rabbi Menachem Mendel of Vitebsk, a principal disciple of the Mezritcher Magid and leader of the Chassidic pilgrimage of 5537 (1777). Included in the volume is a copy of *Ashkavta DeRebbi*, a letter from the Chassidim of Tiberias informing their colleagues in Europe of Rabbi Mendel's death. First printed in Zhitomir in 1874.

Pri Megodim. An important *halakhic* work explaining the commentaries on the *Shulchan Arukh*, by Rabbi Yosef (ben Rabbi Meir) Teumim. First published in Frankfort on Oder between 1785-87.

Rabbi Nachman's Stories. A new annotated English translation of Rabbi Nachman's famous stories and parables by Rabbi Aryeh Kaplan, and published by the Breslov Research Institute in Jerusalem 1983.

Rabbi Nachman's Tikkun. *Tikkun HaKlali* (q.v.) with an English translation and transliteration. First edition published by the Breslov Research Institute in 1980. Second revised edition 1982.

Rabbi Nachman's Wisdom. Translation of *Shevachey HaRan* and *Sichos HaRan* (q.v.) by Rabbi Aryeh Kaplan, published in New York, 1973.

Rabbi Shneur Zalman of Liadi. A detailed biography of Rabbi Shneur Zalman of Liadi by Rabbi Avraham Chanoch Glitzenstein. The first volume of *Sefer HaTolados* collected from various Chabad sources. Published by Kehoth 1967.

Rashi. Acronym of Rabbi Shlomo (ben Yitzchok) Yarchi (see *Shem HaGedolim*) or Yitzchaki (1040-1105), author of the most important commentaries on the Bible and Talmud, printed in almost all major editions. His commentary on the Torah was the first known Hebrew book to be published (Rome, c. 1470). He headed yeshivos in Troyes and Worms, France. His commentaries are renowned for being extremely terse, immediately bringing forth the main idea of the text.

Rimzey Ma'asios. Commentaries on the Stories, by Rabbi Nachman of Tcherin. First printed in Lemberg, 1902, and with all subsequent editions of the Stories.

Rimzey Ma'asios, Hashmotos. Additional commentaries on the Stories by Rabbi Abraham ben Nachman of Tulchin, printed in the Lemberg, 1902, edition of *Sippurey Maasios*.

Rosen, Rabbi Eliyahu Chaim (1899-1983). Founder and dean of the Breslov Yeshivah in Jerusalem. Rabbi Rosen arrived in Uman in 1914 and was a student of Rabbi Avraham (Chazan Halevi) ben Reb Nachman of Tulchin (q.v.). A resident of Uman for twenty-two years, he was instumental in the survival of many Uman residents during the famine of 1933 in the Ukraine by establishing contact with the Joint Distribution and other Jews in Europe. He was arrested for his activities and imprisoned. Rabbi Rosen arrived in Jerusalem in 1936, where he established the Breslov Yeshivah in the old city of Jerusalem in 1937.

Rosh HaShanah. See Talmud.

Sanhedrin. See Talmud.

Sefer Baal Shem Tov. Anthology of writings of the Baal Shem Tov (1698-1760), founder of the Chasidic movement, by Rabbi

Shimon Mendel Vidnik of Givarchav, first published in Lodz, 1938.

Sefer HaMidos. Alphabetical listing of concise practical aphorisms, by Rabbi Nachman of Breslov, first published in Moghilov, 1811.

Shaar HaKollel. An explanation of the sources of all the changes in the liturgy included in Rabbi Shneur Zalman's *Siddur*, which are not found in the writings of the ARI. Written by Rabbi Avraham Dovid Lavut of Nikolayev. First printed in Vilna in 1906.

Shaarey Kedusha. A short ethical composition of Rabbi Chaim Vital as transcribed by Rabbi Avraham Eiden Asher concerning reward and punishment and including a guide to acquiring *ruach hakodesh*. First published in Amsterdam, 1814.

Shaarey Tzion. A collection of prayers and *tikkunim* based upon the writings of the ARI. Compiled by Rabbi Nosson Nota (ben Reb Moshe) Hanover, d. 1683. First published in Prague 1662. The author was a leading Kabbalist.

Shabbos. See Talmud.

Shach. Abbreviation for Sifsey Cohen, an important commentary on *Yoreh Deah* and *Choshen Mishpat* sections of the *Shulchan Arukh*, by Rabbi Shabsai (ben Rabbi Meir) HaCohen (Rappaport), a leading disciple of Rabbi Herschel of Cracow. A major leader of European Jewry, he was instrumental in reorganizing the Jewish communities immediately after the Chmielnicki massacres of 5408-09 (1648-49). First published in Cracow 1606-07 and later with most standard editions of the *Shulchan Arukh* (q.v.).

Shem HaGedolim HeChadash. Short biographies and bibliographies of latter Rabbis and Rabbinic literature following the style of the *Shem HaGedolim* of the CHIDA. Written by Rabbi Aharon Valdem.

Shemos HaTzaddikim. A list of the names of all known

Tzaddikim from Adam to the present day to comply with Rabbi Nachman's advice in *Sefer HaMidos*, "Whoever the Holy One, Blessed-Be-He, is important in his eyes will write in a book all the names of the Tzaddikim and the *Tanaim* and the righteous for a rememberence." First compiled by Rabbi Nathan and printed in 1821 as an appendix to the *Sefer HaMidos*. Subsequent editions included additional names.

Shevachey HaARI. Stories about the birth and life of the ARI and his disciples, taken from the introduction of the Kabbalistic work *Emek HaMelech* by Rabbi Shlomo Shimmel (beReb Chayim Meinstril). First published separately in Spalov, 1795.

Shevachey HaBaal Shem Tov. A collection of stories of the Baal Shem Tov and some of his closest followers, whose accuracy Rabbi Nachman confirmed. Assembled by Reb Dov Ber (beReb Shmuel) Shubb of Linetz, the son-in-law of the Baal Shem Tov's scribe. During Rabbi Nachman's life the book was distributed in manuscript form. It was first printed in Berdichov in 1815.

Shevachey HaRan. Highlights of Rabbi Nachman's life, including his pilgrimage to the Holy Land, by Rabbi Nathan of Nemirov, first published in Ostrog, 1816. Translated into English as part of *Rabbi Nachman's Wisdom* (q.v.). Parts are included in the *Gems of Rabbi Nachman*, by Rabbi Aryeh Kaplan, New York, 1980.

Shevachey Moharan. Anecdotes and teachings of Rabbi Nachman, compiled by Rabbi Nathan of Nemirov, printed together with *Chayay Moharan* (q.v.).

Shluchey Eretz Yisroel. A historical study on the emissaries for the community in the Holy Land from the time of the destruction of the Second Temple until the 19th century. Compiled by Avraham Ya'ari and published by Mosad HaRav Kook, Jerusalem, 1977.

Shulchan Arukh. The standard code of Jewish Law, by Rabbi

Yosef (ben Ephraim) Caro (1488-1575), first published in Venice, 1564. Divided into four parts, *Orach Chaim, Yoreh Deah, Evven HaEzer,* and *Choshen Mishpat.* Born in Spain, the author migrated to Turkey after the expulsion in 1492, and then to Safed, where he served as Chief Rabbi. With the addition of the *Hagah,* the *Shulchan Arukh* became the standard work on Jewish Law for all Jewry.

Sichos HaRan. Short teachings and sayings of Rabbi Nachman of Breslov, collected by Rabbi Nathan of Nemirov, first published together with *Sippurey Maasios,* Ostrog, 1816. An expanded edition, including much new material, was published in Zolkiev, 1850. Translated into English as part of *Rabbi Nachman's Wisdom* (q.v.). Selections are included in *Gems of Rabbi Nachman* by Rabbi Aryeh Kaplan, New York, 1980.

Sichos VeSippurim. Exposition of Rabbi Nachman's teachings by Rabbi Avraham ben Nachman of Tulchin, published in Jerusalem, 1913. Reprinted as part of *Kochavey Or* (q.v.).

Sippurey Chassidim. Stories about Chassidic leaders and Tzaddikim arranged according to the weekly Torah readings (originally published as a series in periodicals). Collected and revised and when necessary translated into the Hebrew by Rabbi Shlomo Yosef Zevin. Published in Jerusalem 1955. Present copyright by Hillel Press.

Sippurey Ma'asios. The Stories of Rabbi Nachman. First published in Ostrog, 1816, and with a new introduction, in Lemberg, 1850. See Rabbi Nachman's Stories (q.v.).

Sippurim Niflaim. Anecdotes and teachings involving Rabbi Nachman of Breslov, as well as previously unpublished stories, collected by Rabbi Shmuel Horowitz (1903-1973). First published in Jerusalem in 1935.

Smichas Chachomim. The major work of Rabbi Naftali ben Rabbi Yitzchok Katz, the Rebbe's ancestor whose grave he visited in Istanbul. The work consists of an explanation for the order (*smichos*) of the various tractates of the Talmud. Rabbi Naftali Katz, descendant of the MaHaRal of Prague, was chief Rabbi of Posen and was regarded as one of the greatest Tzaddikim of his generation 1649-1719. Wondrous stories are recorded concerning his death in Istanbul while attempting a pilgrimage to Israel. First published in Frankfort, Adar 1705.

Sotah. See Talmud.

Succah. See Talmud.

Ta'anis. See Talmud.

Taharos HaKodesh. A major commentary on Talmud, *Seder Kodshim*, by Rabbi Yitzchok (beHaRav Tzvi) Ashkenazi. The first volume on tractate *Zevochim* was published in Lvov in 1792.

Talmud. The embodiment of the Oral Torah, as taught by the great masters from approximately 50 b.c.e. until around 500 c.e. The first part to be codified was the Mishnah, set in its present form by Rabbi Yehudah the Prince, around 188 c.e. Subsequent discussions were redacted as the *Gemora* by Rav Ashi and Ravina in Babylonia around 505 c.e., and it is therefore often referred to as the *Babylonian Talmud*. Next to the Bible itself, it is the most important work on Jewish law and theology. Individual volumes of the Talmud were printed in Soncino, Italy, as early as 1482, but the entire Talmud was first printed by David Bomberg in Venice, 1523, along with the commentaries of Rashi and Tosafos (q.v.). A second compilation of the Talmud, thought to have been redacted around 240 c.e. by Rabbi Yochanan (182-279 c.e.) and his disciples in Tiberias with the concurence of the sages of Jerusalem is the *Talmud Yerushalmi*. It is a work of major importance, although considered secondary to the Babylonian Talmud. It was first printed in Venice, 1523.

Avodah Zarah: Tractate dealing with idolatry.

Avos: Tractate dealing with moral matters.

Berachos: Tractate dealing with prayers and blessings.

Bikurim: Tractate dealing with first fruit offerings.

Chagigah: Tractate dealing with the festival sacrifice.

Kesubos: Tractate dealing with marriage contracts and obligations.

Kiddushin: Tractate dealing with the laws of engagements and marriage.

Megillah: Tractate dealing with the laws of Purim.

Nedarim: Tractate dealing with the laws of vows.

Niddah: Tractate dealing with family purity and menstrual laws.

Rosh HaShanah: Tractate dealing with the laws of Rosh HaShanah and shofar.

Sanhedrin: Tractate dealing with laws of courts and judges.

Shabbos: Tractate dealing with the laws of Shabbos.

Sotah: Tractate dealing with adultery and immorality.

Succah: Tractate dealing with the laws of the holiday of Succos.

Ta'anis: Tractate dealing with the laws of public fasts and Tisha B'Av.

Yoma: Tractate dealing with the laws of Yom Kippur.

Zevachim: Tractate dealing with the laws of sacrifices.

Teshuos Chen. A book of Chassidic interpretations arranged according to the weekly Torah readings by the renowned Rabbi Gedalia of Linitz, a prominent Chassidic leader of Rabbi Nachman's generation. First published in Berdichov in 1816.

Tevor HaAretz. A description and history of the holy city of Tiberias. Written by her Chief Rabbi, Rabbi Moshe Kliers. Published 1906.

Tikkun HaKlali. The Ten Psalms prescribed by Rabbi Nachman as a "General Rectification" for sexual and other sins, first published by Rabbi Nathan of Nemirov, Breslov, 1821. Available in English as *Rabbi Nachman's Tikkun* published by the Breslov Research Institute, Jerusalem, 1982.

Tikkuney Zohar. Part of the Zoharic literature, consisting of seventy chapters on the first word of the Torah, by the school of

Rabbi Shimon bar Yochai (circa 120 c.e.), first printed in Mantua, 1558. However, a second edition, Orto Koy, 1719, provided the basis for all subsequent editions. The work contains some of the most important discussions in Kabbalah, and is essential for understanding the system of the *Zohar* (q.v.).

Toldos Chachmey Yerushalayim. A history of the early Ashkenazic *yishuv* in Jersalem by Rabbi Aryeh Leib Frumkin. First published 1928-30 and reprinted with footnotes and additions by Rabbi Eliezer Rivlin in 1969 in Tel-Aviv.

Toldos Yaakov Yosef. The first Chassidic work, by Rabbi Yaakov Yosef of Polonnoye (died 1782), first published in Koretz, 1780. The author was the senior disciple of the Baal Shem Tov, founder of Chassidism.

Torah Lishmah. An anonymous collection of responsa in both *Halakhah* and Kabbalah. Assumed to have been authored by the *Ben Ish Chai*, Rabbi Yosef Chaim of Bagdad, one of the greatest luminaries of Sephardic Jewry of recent times.

Tosafos. Collection of commentaries, using Talmudic methodology on the Talmud itself. The work was a product of the *yeshivah* academies of France and Germany between around 1100 and 1300, begun by the students of Rashi (q.v.) and his grandsons, most notably, Rabbi Yaakov Tam (circa 1100-1171). It is printed in virtually all editions of the Talmud.

Tovos Zichronos. Breslover traditions, by Rabbi Avraham (ben R. Naftali Hertz) Sternhartz (Kokhav Lev) (1862-1955). It was transcribed by Rabbi Gedaliah Aharon Koenig (q.v.) and published in Jerusalem, 1951. Rabbi Avraham was Rabbi Nathan's great-grandson and grandson of Rabbi Nachman of Tcherin (q.v.) and a leading Breslover authority in Kremenchug and Uman. He was *chazan* in the Uman *kloyz* for nearly fifty years on Rosh HaShanah. Rabbi Avraham came to Israel in 1936 and was received and recognized as an outstanding Breslover elder of his generation. Among his disciples were a number of the major Breslover leaders of the past two decades including: Rabbis Moshe and Nachman Burstyn, Rabbi Michel Dorfman, Rabbi Gedaliah Aharon Koenig, Rabbi Zvi Aryeh Lippel, Rabbi Zvi Aryeh Rosenfeld, Rabbi Shmuel Shapiro and Rabbis Dovid and Yaakov Meir Shechter.

Turei Zohov *TaZ*. One of the principal commentaries on the *Shulchan Arukh*. Written by Rabbi Dovid beReb Shmuel HaLevi, a leading disciple of Rabbi Herschel of Cracow. First published in Lublin 1646.

Tzavo'as Rivash. A collection of directives and methods of conduct taken from the teachings of the Baal Shem Tov and his followers. Assembled by Rabbi Yeshaya of Yanov (whose grave Rabbi Nachman visited in his youth). First published in Zolkova, date omitted. Second printing was in 1793.

Yad. Short for *Yad Chazakah*, otherwise known as *Mishneh Torah*, the monumental Code of Jewish Law by Rabbi Moshe ben Maimon (Maimonides) 1135-1204, better known as the RaMBaM. The work was so named because of its fourteen divisions, the numerical value of *Yad*. It was the first systematic codification of Jewish law, and the only one that encompasses every aspect of the laws of Torah. Considered one of the great classics of Torah literature, it was first printed in Rome, 1475. It has been printed in many editions, and is the subject of dozens of commentaries.

Yemey HaTalaos. A history of the difficulties of Rabbi Nathan and his followers during the years 1835-39, and including some of the deleted sections of *Chayay Moharan* and *Yemey Moharnat*. Written by Rabbi Avraham beReb Nachman of Tulchin. First published as the fifth section of *Kochavey Or* in 1933, and subsequently in limited editions as a separate pamphlet.

Yemey Moharnat. Autobiography of Rabbi Nathan of Nemirov. The first section was printed in Lemberg, 1876, and the second part, dealing with Rabbi Nathan's pilgrimage to the Land of Israel, was printed in Jerusalem, 1904.

Yerushalmi. See Talmud.

Yoma. See Talmud.

Yoreh Deah. Second section of the *Shulchan Arukh* (q.v.), dealing with dietary laws and other areas requiring rabbinical decision.

Zevachim. See Talmud.

Zohar. The primary classic of Kabbalah, from the school of Rabbi Shimon bar Yochai (circa 120 c.e.), compiled by his disciple, Rabbi Abba. After being restricted to a small, closed circle of Kabbalists and hidden for centuries, it was finally published around 1290 by Rabbi Moshe (ben Shem Tov) de Leon (1239-1305). After considerable controversy, Rabbi Yitzchok Yehoshua (ben Yaakov Bonet) de Lattes (1498-1571) issued an opinion that it was permitted to print the *Zohar,* and it was published in Mantua, 1558-1560. It has been reprinted in over sixty subsequent editions, and is the subject of dozens of commentaries.

GLOSSARY

Aleph-Bais: first two letters of the Hebrew alphabet, used here to refer to all 22 letters of the alphabet

Adar I, II: last month of the Jewish calendar, which in leap years is repeated, hence I and II

aliya: literally, to go up; refers to going "up," to settle in the Holy Land

Amalek: historical foe and nemesis of the Jewish people

Amida: literally, the standing prayer; refers to the Eighteen Benedictions recited thrice daily

Anochi: opening word of the fourth lesson in *Likutey Moharan* from the verse, "I am God your Lord, who brought you out of Egypt..." (Exodus 20:2)

ARI: an acronym for Ashkenazi Rabbi Yitzchok (Isaac) the name of Rabbi Y. Luria (1534-1572), leader of the Safed school of Kabbalah

Arikh Anpin: a Kabbalistic term for the Upper Divine Emanations

Atah: one of the Holy Names of God which provides protection when travelling on the sea

Atah Niglesa: opening words of one of the liturgical hymns for the Shavuos holiday

Av: fifth month of the Jewish calendar

avon mash: free of sin

Azamer BiShevachin: title of a Sabbath song composed by the ARI

baal habayis: master of the house; landlord

badchan: comedien; a jester

bar mitzvah: a Jewish boy of thirteen, at which age he assumes religious obligations

Beis HaMedrash (Medrash): House of Study; studyhall

Bereshis: both the opening portion and the title for the first of the Five Books of Moses; Genesis

Birkas HaMazon: blessing recited after eating a meal containing bread

bris milah: the ceremonious act of circumcision.

chacham: a wise man; the Sephardic term equivilent to rabbi

Chanukah: the holiday celebrated in commemoration of the Maccabean victory over the Greeks and the kindling of the Temple *menorah* with the "miracle" oil found by the priests

chazan: a cantor

cheref: to insult, abuse

cherem: ban, excommunication

Cheshvon: eighth month of the Jewish calendar

chevra kadisha: burial society

chidushim: innovative commentary on all branches of Torah

chokhmah i'la'ah: higher wisdom; the wisdom of the teacher as opposed to the lower wisdom of the disciple

Chol HaMoed: the intermediary days of the festival (*Pesach* and *Succos*)

chometz: leaven, which is forbidden during Passover

Choni HaMaagel: the Talmud (*Ta'anis* 23b) relates that this man fell asleep and slept for seventy years. When he awoke, the world around him had changed and he was no longer recognized

choref: winter

Chozeh: literally, a seer; the title given to Rabbi Yaakov Yitzchok of Lublin because of his visionary abilities

chupah: wedding canopy.

daven: Yiddish for to pray

dayan: rabbinical judge (pl. *dayanim*)

Devarim: both the opening portion and the title for the fifth of the Five Books of Moses; Deuteronomy

devekus: level of self-negation when cleaving to God

dreidel: the spinning top traditionally played with on Chanukah

Elul: sixth month of the Jewish calendar; a period of repentance before Rosh HaShanah

Eretz Yisroel: the Holy Land, Israel

erev: the eve of

esrog: a citron; one of the "four species" special to the Succos holiday (pl. *esrogim*)

Fast of Gedaliah: 3rd day of Tishrei, the anniversary of the death of Gedaliah the son of Achikam (Jeremiah 41:2)

forshpiel: Yiddish title for the customary celebration in honor of a groom, held on the Sabbath preceding the wedding

gedolim: great men; leaders

Gehenom: hell

Gemora: the Talmud

gilgul: reincarnation (pl. *gilgulim*)

guter Yid: Yiddish for a good Jew (referring to a Tzaddik)

hachnosas orchim: hospitality

haftorah: weekly portion from the Prophets read in the synagogue after the regular Torah reading

Hallel: selected psalms added to the prayers on holidays and other special days of the Jewish year

hambar: Yiddish for summer house

HaMotzi: blessing recited over bread

Hashiva Shoftenu: literally, return our judges; refers to the eleventh of the Eighteen Benedictions (see *Amidah*)

haskalah: enlightenment; movement founded by Moses Mendelssohn

haskamah: approbation (pl. *haskamos*)

havdalah: ceremony at the end of the Sabbath which separates it from the six days of the week

hisbodedus: private prayer and meditation; a major principle of Rabbi Nachman's teachings

Hodu: Psalm 107 which speaks of praising God for having saved one from his troubles, recited by Chassidim as part of the afternoon prayer on the eve of the Sabbath

Hoshana Rabbah: literally, the Great Willow Branch; refers to the last of the intermediate days of Succos on which small willow branches are bound together and held by the congregants as they circle around the Torah scroll during the morning prayers

hust: Yiddish for cough or tuberculosis

Idra Rabbah: see bibliography

iluy: a genius

Iyar: second month of the Jewish calendar

Kabbalah: esoteric teachings of the Torah of which the *Zohar* and the teachings of the ARI are the major classics

Kaddish: mourner's prayer

kahal: congregation; title given to the principle agencies of Jewish self-government (*kehilos*)

kesubah: wedding contract

Kiddush: blessing recited over wine to inaugurate and sanctify the Sabbath or holiday

Kiddush Levanah: blessing of the moon recited monthly

Kislev: ninth month of the Jewish calendar

klipah: husks; forces of repression against that which is holy

Kol Nidrei: ancient prayer recited at the onset of Yom Kippur for the dispensation of vows

korban todah: a thanks offering
kvittel: piece of paper with one's name and request which is given to the Tzaddik for his prayers (pl. *kvittelach*)

Lag Be-Omer: 33rd day of the *Omer* counting, (see *Omer*) which is a day of joyous celebration, commemorating the passing of Rabbi Shimon bar Yochai
lamdan: a scholar
lashon hara: slander
leshon chaverim: literally, the language of friends; used here in reference to those of Rabbi Nachman's Torah lessons recorded by Rabbi Avraham Peterberger
Lev Basar: literally, a heart of flesh; contains the same Hebrew letters as the name Breslov
lulav: a palm branch; one of the "four species" special to Succos
Luley HaShem: from the opening verse of Psalm 124, "Were it not for God..."

Maariv: evening prayer
Magid: a preacher
Maginey Eretz: literally, protectors of the earth
maskilim: intellectual; contemporaries and disciples of Moses Mendelssohn
matzah: unleavened bread eaten on Passover
mazal: literally, fortune; used here to refer to a person's soul, which is more capable of detecting spirituality than one's regular perception
mazal tov: congratulations
mechutan: a relative by marriage (pl. *mechutonim*)
Megillah: the Book of Esther read on Purim; also a tractate of the Talmud
melamed: a tutor
menorah: candelabra
mezuzah: parchment scroll containing Deuteronomy 6:4-9 and 11:13-21 fixed to doorpost, as prescribed by the Torah
Miketz: from the opening verse of the Torah portion by the same name, "...came to pass at the end of two years..." (Genesis 41:1)
mikvah: pool for ritual immersion
Minchah: afternoon prayer
minyan: quorum of ten adult males required for communal prayers
Mishnah: collection of oral laws collected by Rabbi Yehudah HaNasi, which forms the basis of the Talmud (pl. *Mishnayos*)

Misnagdim: those opposed to the Chassidic movement

mitzvah: commandment (pl. *mitzvos*)

mohel: circumciser

Motzoai Shabbos: the evening after the Sabbath

Mussaf: additional prayer added to morning service on Sabbath and holidays

Mussar: moralistic teachings

Nachamu, Nachamu: opening words of the *haftorah* read after the Torah portion of Deuteronomy from the verse, "Comfort ye, comfort ye, My people..." (Isaiah 40:1)

nadan: dowry

Neilah: the Closing Prayer of Yom Kippur

netilas yadayim: washing hands

Nissan: first month in the Jewish lunar calendar (the years are counted from Tishrei, the months from Nissan); the historical month of redemption

Omer: counting of the 49 days between the second day of Passover and Shavuous

parsa: unit of distance equal to ten *verst* (Russian) and 6.629 miles (10.67 km.)

parsha: a portion, section

Parshas HaChodesh: (Exodus 12:1-20) last of the "four portions" each of which is read during *Adar* in addition to the regular Torah reading on one of the Sabbaths which precedes (though not consecutively) the holiday of Passover. These "four portions" also include *Parshas Shekalim* (Exodus 30:1-16), *Parshas Zachor* (Deuteronomy 25:11-19) and *Parshas Parah* (Numbers 19:1-22)

Parshas Parah: see *Parshas HaChodesh*

partzufim: a Kabbalistic term for the Upper Divine Emanations (*see Arikh Anpin*)

pe'er: glory

periah: uncovering the corona in circumcision by splitting and pulling down the membrane

Pesach: the holiday of Passover

peyos: sidecurls

pheter: Yiddish for uncle

pidyon: money or something of monetary value given as a redemption (pl. *pidyonos*)

piyut: liturgical hymn (pl. *piyutim*)

prostock: Yiddish for simple and devoid of knowledge
prutah: a coin small in value
Purim: festival celebrating the rescue of the Jews in Persia as recorded in the Book of Esther

Rabbenu: our Rabbi
Rashi: acronym for Rabbi Shlomo (ben Yitzchok) Yarchi (1040-1105), author of the most important commentaries on the Bible and Talmud
Rav: rabbinical authority
Red Heifer: the sacrifice of the unblemished, completely red cow whose ashes were used for the sprinkling water, as a means of purification (Numbers 19)
rendel: Russian monetary unit
Rosh Chodesh: the New Moon
Rosh HaShanah: two day holiday at the beginning of Tishrei, celebrating the start of the new year
ruach hakodesh: divine inspiration
ruble: Russian coin subdivided into 100 kopecks

safek: doubt
sandek: person on whose lap the baby is placed during circumcision
Seder: ceremonious meal performed on Pesach night, the 15th of Nissan, commemorating Jewish redemption from bondage in Egypt
sefer: a holy book (pl. *sifrei* or *sforim*)
sefer Torah: a Torah scroll containing the five Books of Moses
Selichos: special liturgy requesting forgiveness, recited prior to Rosh HaShanah and Yom Kippur and on other selected days of the year
Shaarey Tzion: important collection of Kabbalistic prayers, by Rabbi Nathan Nata (ben Moshe) Hanover (died 1683)
Shabbos Bereshis: the first Sabbath after Succos, when the first portion of the Torah, Bereshis, is read in the synagogue
Shabbos Chanukah: the Sabbath which coincides with one of the eight days of Chanukah
Shabbos Chazon: the Sabbath which immediately precedes the fast on the ninth of Av, on which the portion read from the Prophets begins, "Chazon Yeshayahu — the vision of Isaiah" (Isaiah 1:1)
Shabbos HaChodesh: the Sabbath which immediately precedes the New Moon of Nissan, on which the portion, "*HaChodesh ha'zeh* — this month" is read (see also *Parshas HaChodesh*)
Shabbos HaGadol: the Sabbath which immediately precedes Passover
Shabbos Nachamu: the Sabbath immediately following the 9th of Av,

on which the portion read from the Prophets begins, "*Nachamu, Nachamu* — Comfort ye, comfort ye" (Isaiah 40:1)

Shabbos Parah: the Sabbath which precedes Shabbos HaChodesh, on which the portion of the *Parah Adumah*, the Red Heifer is read (see also *Parshas HaChodesh*)

Shabbos Shekalim: the Sabbath which immediately precedes the New Moon of Adar, on which the portion "When you take a census... give a half *shekel*" is read (see also *Parshas HaChodesh*)

Shabbos Shirah: the Sabbath on which the *Shirah*, the Song of Moses (Exodus 15:1-19), is read in the synagogue

Shabbos Shuvah: the Sabbath which falls between Rosh HaShanah and Yom Kippur, which is a time of *teShuvah*, repentance

Shabbos Zachor: the Sabbath which immediately precedes the festival of Purim, on which the portion, "*Zachor* — remember what Amalek did to you" is read (see also *Parshas HaChodesh*)

Shacharis: morning prayer

shamesh: caretaker

Shavuos: the holiday of Pentecost celebrated on the 6th of Sivan, in commemoration of the giving of the Torah at Sinai

shechitah: ritual slaughtering

Shemini Atzeret: the eighth and final day of Succos

Shemoneh Esray: literally, eighteen; a reference to the Eighteen Benedictions (see *Amidah*)

Shevat: the eleventh month of the Jewish calendar

shidduch: perspective marriage partner (pl. *shidduchim*)

Shir HaKavod: popularly known as *Anim Ze'miros*, this alphabetical poem is attributed to Rabbi Yehudah HaChasid of Regensburg (1148-1217)

shirayim: left overs, from the food eaten by the Tzaddik which is distributed amongst his followers

shivah: the seven days of mourning for close relatives

shochet: a ritual slaughterer

shofar: ram's horn sounded 100 times on Rosh HaShanah

shoin, shoin: Yiddish, for "already, already"

sholom zochor: celebration held on the Friday night preceding the circumcision to welcome the birth of a baby boy

sholosh se'udos: the third meal of Sabbath, a time when Chassidic masters would give a Torah discourse

Shovavim: period of repentance lasting through the weeks when the first six (and in a leap-year eight) Torah portions from the book of Exodus are read in the synagogue

shtreimel: fur hat traditionally worn by Chassidim on the Sabbath and holidays

Shushan Purim: the second day of Purim, on the 15th of Adar; this is the main day of celebration in Jerusalem and cities which were walled in the time of Joshua

Sichah: conversation; used here to refer to teachings that were not given as part of a regular Torah lesson

Siddur: prayer book

Simchas Torah: Rejoicing of the Law, holiday celebrated on eighth day of Succos in Israel, and on the next day in the diaspora, on which the last portion and the opening of the first portion of the Torah is read

Sivan: the third month of the Jewish calendar

sofer: scribe

srefah: a fire

succah: booth erected to replace one's home during the holiday of Succos, commemorating the "miracle clouds" which accompanied the Jewish people through the desert on their way to the Holy Land

taharah: ritual purification performed on a corpse before burial

tallis: prayer shawl

Tammuz: fourth month of the Jewish calendar

tana'im: engagement contract

Tanna: a rabbi of the Mishnaic era (pl. *Tannaim*)

Tashlich: prayer recited on the first day of Rosh HaShanah after *Minchah*, preferably near a body of water, symbolically casting off one's sins "into the depths of the sea" (Michah 7:19)

tefillin: phylactery

Teruah: literally, a joyful note; one of the sounds blown from a *shofar* on Rosh HaShanah

Teves: tenth month of the Jewish calendar

thaler: a silver coin

Three Weeks: three mourning weeks beggining with the fast of the 17th of Tammuz and concluding with the fast on the 9th of Av

tikkun: spiritual rectification

Tikkun Chatzos: the midnight lament in memory of the destruction of the Temple

tikkun habris: rectification of sexual sins

Tikkun HaKlali: Ten Psalms prescribed by Rabbi Nachman as a "General Rectification" for sexual and other sins

Tikkun lail Shavuous: set order of learning for Shavuous night

Tishrei: seventh month of the Jewish calendar, in which the world was created

Torah: body of wisdom and law contained in Jewish scripture, sacred literature and oral tradition; also used here to refer to an original discourse given by a Rebbe to his followers

Tzaddik: righteous and saintly individual; Chassidic Rabbi (pl. *Tzaddikim*)

tzava'ah: will

tzedakah: charity

tzetel: a note (pl. *tzetlach*)

ukase: Russian, for statute

Unesaneh Tokef: prayer-poem authored by Rabbi Amnon just before he died from wounds inflicted by the rulers of Mayence, France when he refused to denounce his faith; it is recited during the *Mussaf* service on Rosh HaShanah and Yom Kippur

ushpizin: the seven visitors (the Seven Shepherds) who come to the *succah*

vach nacht: Yiddish for the "night of watch"; the night preceding circumcision during which Torah is studied to protect the baby from evil forces

verst: Russian unit of distance equal to 0.06629 mile (1.067 km)

viduy: confession for sins

Viduynikers: name given to those who practice confession

Yaaleh: alphabetical acrostic in reverse order recited at the close of the *Kol Nidrei* prayers of the evening service for Yom Kippur

yahrzeit: anniversary of one's passing

yibum: levirate marriage (see Deuteronomy 25:5)

yishuv: referring to the Jewish communities in the Holy Land

Yom Kippur: the Day of Atonement on the 10th of Tishrei

Index of Lessons

Geographical Index

General Index

Index of Names